JOURNAL FOR THE STUDY OF THE NEW TESTAMENT SUPPLEMENT SERIES
85

Executive Editor
Stanley E. Porter

JSOT Press
Sheffield

Returning Home

New Covenant and Second Exodus as the Context for 2 Corinthians 6.14–7.1

William J. Webb

Journal for the Study of the New Testament
Supplement Series 85

Copyright © 1993 Sheffield Academic Press

Published by JSOT Press
JSOT Press is an imprint of
Sheffield Academic Press Ltd
The University of Sheffield
343 Fulwood Road
Sheffield S10 3BP
England

Typeset by Sheffield Academic Press
and
Printed on acid-free paper in Great Britain
by Biddles Ltd
Guildford

British Library Cataloguing in Publication Data

Webb, W.J.
    Returning Home: New Covenant and Second
    Exodus as the Context for 2 Corinthians
    6.14–7.1. —(JSNT Supplement
    Series, ISSN 0143-5108; No. 85)
    I. Title II. Series
    227

ISBN 1-85075-418-7

CONTENTS

ABBREVIATIONS

AB	Anchor Bible
AGJU	Arbeiten zur Geschichte des antiken Judentums und des Urchristentums
AnBib	Analecta Biblica
ATANT	Abhandlungen zur Theologie des Alten und Neuen Testaments
AusBR	*Australian Biblical Review*
BAGD	W. Bauer, W.F. Arndt, F.W. Gingrich and F.W. Danker, *A Greek-English Lexicon of the New Testament and Other Early Christians Literature*
BDF	F. Blass, A. Debrunner and R.W. Funk, *A Greek Grammar of the New Testament and Other Early Christians Literature*
BETL	Bibliotheca ephemeridum theologicarum lovaniensium
BEvT	Beiträge zur evangelischen Theologie
BFCT	Beiträge zur Förderung christlicher Theologie
BGBE	Beiträge zur Geschichte der biblischen Exegese
BHT	Beiträge zur Historischen Theologie
Bib	*Biblica*
BSac	*Bibliotheca Sacra*
BTB	*Biblical Theology Bulletin*
BTH	Bibliothèque de Théologie Historique
CBC	Cambridge Bible Commentary
CBQ	*Catholic Biblical Quarterly*
CGT	Cambridge Greek Testament
CNieT	Commentaar op het Nieuwe Testament
CNT	Commentaire du Nouveau Testament
CR	*Classical Review*
CurTM	*Currents in Theology and Mission*
EB	Expositors Bible
EBib	Études Bibliques
EchBib	Echter-Bibel
ENT	Erläuterungen zum Neuen Testament
ETL	*Ephemerides theologicae lovaniensis*
EvQ	*Evangelical Quarterly*
ExpTim	*Expository Times*
GCS	Geneva Series Commentaries
GNS	Good News Studies
GTB	Van Gorcum's Theologische Bibliotheek

GTW	Grundriss der Theologischen Wissenschaften
HAR	*Hebrew Annual Review*
HKNT	Handkommentar zum Neuen Testament
HNT	Handbuch zum Neuen Testament
HNTC	Harper's NT Commentaries
HSNT	Die heilge Schrift Neuen Testaments
ICC	International Critical Commentary
Int	*Interpretation*
JAARSup	*Journal of the American Academy of Religion Supplements*
JBL	*Journal of Biblical Literature*
JSNT	*Journal for the Study of the New Testament*
JSNTSup	Journal for the Study of the New Testament Supplement Series
JSOT	*Journal for the Study of the Old Testament*
JSOTSup	Journal for the Study of the Old Testament Supplement Series
JTS	*Journal of Theological Studies*
KAT	Kommentar zum Alten Testament
KKHSNT	Kurzgesaszter Kommentar zu den heiligen Schriften Neuen Testament
KNT	Kommentar zum Neuen Testament
LCRL	Limited Classical Reprint Library
LNT	Literature of the New Testament
LTP	*Laval Théologique et Philosophique*
MeyerK	H.A.W. Meyer, Kritisch-exegetischer Kommentar über das Neue Testament
MNTC	Moffat NT Commentary
NCB	New Century Bible
NEBNT	Neue Echter Bibel Neues Testament
NFTL	New Foundations Theological Library
NICNT	New International Commentary on the New Testament
NovT	*Novum Testamentum*
NovTSup	*Novum Testamentum* Supplements
NTD	Das Neue Testament Deutsch
NTG	Neue Theologische Grundrisse
NTS	*New Testament Studies*
OTL	Old Testament Library
OTM	Oxford Theological Monographs
OTWSA	*Die Ou-Testamentiese Werkgemeenskap in Suid-Africa*
RB	*Revue Biblique*
SANT	Studien zum Alten und Neuen Testament
SBLDS	SBL Dissertation Series
SCath	*Studia Catholica*
SJLA	Studies in Judaism in Late Antiquity
SMB	Serie Monografica di Benedictina
SNTSMS	Society of New Testament Studies Monograph Series
StBibTh	*Studia Biblica et Theologica*

STR	Studia Travaux de Recherche
SUNT	Studien zur Umwelt des Neuen Testaments
TC	Theological Collections
TD	Theologischen Dissertationen
TNTC	Tyndale New Testament Commentaries
TS	*Theological Studies*
TSK	*Theologische Studien und Kritiken*
TynBul	*Tyndale Bulletin*
TOTC	Tyndale Old Testament Commentaries
USQR	*Union Seminary Quarterly Review*
VEv	*Vox Evangelica*
VSpir	*Vie Spirituelle*
WBC	Word Biblical Commentary
WC	Westminster Commentaries
WUNT	Wissenschaftliche Untersuchungen zum Neuen Testament
ZNW	*Zeitschrift für die neutestamentliche Wissenschaft*

All secondary sources are cited in the footnotes by the author's last name and a convenient short title. Full titles and other bibliographic information are provided in the Bibliography.

PREFACE

This work has been enhanced through the assistance of many individuals. It was originally submitted as a ThD dissertation at Dallas Theological Seminary in 1990. I am grateful to my supervisors, David Lowery, Darrell Bock and Robert Chisholm, who gave thorough and gracious guidance throughout each stage of the research and writing process. I must give special credit to Darrell Bock, for it was his lectures on the use of the Old Testament in Luke–Acts that sparked the idea of investigating the traditions in the fragment and its present context. At that juncture, I abandoned the initial direction of my research and pursued what developed into a traditions study.

In its current form as a monograph, it is a work reborn. David Hill interacted with my thesis in its original state, causing me to rework my arguments at a number of crucial points. My own brother, Robert Webb, patiently and meticulously assisted in two revisions beyond the original work. I owe a great deal to both these men for strengthening this book, and I would like to thank them for expanding my horizons. Likewise, Andrew Kirk has been of great assistance in seeing the editorial stage of this work to a successful completion.

In the revision process, my colleagues Jerry Colwell and David Barker read and critically commented on extensive portions of the drafts. They have not only helped shape the content of this book, but added immeasurably to its clarity and style. I thank them along with the rest of the faculty, staff, administration, and board of Heritage Theological Seminary who have provided a warm and caring atmosphere for our family. Their Christian fellowship and encouragement in the writing of this book has meant a great deal to Marilyn and myself.

To my family I owe the greatest debt of gratitude. My parents, Dr Bud Webb and Mrs Doreen Webb, and my wife's parents, Major Barry McFadyen and Mrs June McFadyen, have continually offered us strength and encouragement in the task. Of more profound significance, they instilled in us a love for the Scriptures. My wife, Marilyn, and our three children, Jonathan, Christine and Joel, are my constant joy. This book is dedicated to the four of them, most especially to Marilyn, who holds my deepest affection and has become my dearest friend. Without her support and love, this work could never have been completed.

William J. Webb
London, Ontario, Canada
May 12, 1993

Chapter 1

INTRODUCTION

This initial Chapter provides a brief and uncomplicated orientation to the book. Without getting bogged down in too many details, I wish to introduce the problem which this book seeks to address, its corresponding hypothesis, and the contribution each Chapter makes towards that hypothesis. This introductory 'roadmap' should make the journey through the rest of the book a more enjoyable experience.

1. *The Problem*

The text of 2 Cor. 6.14–7.1, commonly called 'the fragment', has been the focus of much debate. Due in particular to its contextual problem, 2 Cor. 6.14–7.1 has been referred to as 'the enigmatic paragraph',[1] 'the notoriously difficult text',[2] or 'an enigma within 2 Corinthians, neither its origin nor its place in the context being entirely clear'.[3] The words of W.G. Kümmel are indicative of many New Testament scholars: '2 Cor. 6.14–7.1 forms a difficulty probably not to be solved, for this section is without thematic connection to its context and interrupts the good connection between 6.13 and 7.2.'[4]

1. Barrett, 'Things Sacrificed to Idols', p. 140.
2. Hafemann, *Suffering and the Spirit*, p. 85.
3. Furnish, *II Corinthians*, p. 383.
4. Kümmel, *Introduction to the New Testament*, p. 214. Cf. Young and Ford (*2 Corinthians*, p. 32) who comment on the fragment: 'It is generally agreed that a satisfactory explanation of their position here [6.147.1] in 2 Corinthians has not been so far advanced. They are usually treated as an insertion.' Likewise, Collange (*Énigmes*, p. 319) writes, 'Au chapitre 6, enfin, la difficulté réside dans l'explication de la présence à cet endroit précis de l'épître du fragment 6.14–7.1'. Moffat (*Introduction*, p. 225) refers to 6.14–7.1 as 'an erratic boulder' standing out of place from its context. Fee ('Food Offered to Idols', p. 142) similarly states, 'What strikes one as he reads the vast array of literature on this passage is the general unwillingness . . . to deal with the contextual question.' A list of similar comments

Even the casual reader of 2 Corinthians would acknowledge that the removal 6.14–7.1 smooths the contextual flow, while its presence adds a certain abruptness and its subject matter is not easily explainable within the context.

2. *Statement of the Hypothesis*

It is the problem of contextual integration, then, which this book seeks to address. My hypothesis is that *the fragment is related to its present context through the use of new covenant and exilic return traditions,* particularly in light of Paul's identification with the *'ebed Yahweh* (an identification which allows him to formulate his proclamation-message in second exodus language, 'Come out. . . '). The book's short-form title, *Returning Home*, represents a convenient reduction of the longer title, *Coming Out of Babylon and Returning Home.* Along with the return motif, this reflects the imperative: 'Come out of Babylon!' I have chosen this title in view of its crucial role in the contextual theory, echoing the cry for a new exodus. Its wording derives from a piece of the fragment's tradition ('Come out from among them') which has been heavily redacted in order to reiterate the opening exhortation in 6.14a. In this respect, the book's title epitomizes the call of the fragment from a traditions perspective: 'Come out of Babylon and return home'.

3. *Contribution of Chapters towards the Hypothesis*

Each Chapter contributes towards the hypothesis. Chapter 2 traces the history of the interpretation of 2 Cor. 6.14–7.1 from the Reformation to the present day. This historical survey not only provides the 'broader picture' of how larger trends in New Testament studies have influenced different interpretations of the passage, but grants the interpreter the all-too-rare opportunity of seeing one's own position in light of the ebb and flow of these historical trends. In the process, this Chapter introduces the reader to the legacy of scholarship upon which my own book builds and articulates how this study represents a new direction in research on the fragment.

on the fragment's lack of contextual continuity could be reproduced to fill several pages. These should be a sufficient sample.

The third, fourth and fifth Chapters develop the core of my proposed traditions hypothesis. Chapter 3 examines the fragment itself as an isolated unit apart from its present context in an attempt to understand its traditions—their sources, redactional modifications, and theological contributions. Chapters 4 and 5 study the fragment's remote (2.14–5.10) and immediate (5.11–7.4) context for traces of Old Testament traditions similar to those found in the fragment. A detailed correlation between the fragment and its context is then proposed on the basis of this investigation.

The sixth Chapter offers a critique of alternative contextual theories both on their own merits and in light of the traditions investigation just completed. A critical evaluation is made of alternative attempts to explain the relationship between the fragment and its present context. The seventh Chapter concludes with a brief summary of the book's contextual hypothesis and a review of areas where this study contributes to existing research on the fragment.

The two essays in Appendixes A and B apply the contextual findings to the crux interpretive issue in 6.14a. Beyond offering a solution to the contextual problem, the traditions hypothesis contributes towards the understanding of who the 'unbelievers' are and what the 'unequal yoke' refers to.

Chapter 2

THE HISTORY OF INTERPRETATION:
FROM REFORMATION TO THE TWENTIETH CENTURY

1. *Introduction*

The purpose of this second chapter is to trace the history of the interpretation of 2 Cor. 6.14–7.1 from the Reformation era to the present day. Admittedly, such a task cannot be entirely objective; it should perhaps be viewed as an *interpretive* analysis of the history of the interpretation of 2 Cor. 6.14–7.1. It is written at one point within that history and from the perspective of one individual. As an interpretive analysis there are a number of stages through which the interpretation of 2 Cor. 6.14–7.1 has progressed.[1] It seems more than coincidence that these stages relate to broader trends within New Testament studies.

The historical investigation will be limited to scholars from the Reformation period on. Early in church history the text provided the *locus classicus* for all kinds of separation. However, when going back earlier than the Reformation era to quotations and allusions in the Fathers (Ante-Nicene, Nicene, and Post-Nicene) it is difficult to determine whether they are actually interpreting the text or simply applying it. Much of their discussion seems to revolve around the latter. Consequently, this historical sketch will begin with commentators from the Reformation era.

Within the last 500 years the interpretation of 2 Cor. 6.14–7.1 may be divided into five periods: (1) the influence of Reformation

1. For other (condensed) accounts of the history of interpretation see: Allo, *Seconde Épître aux Corinthiens*, pp. 190-91; Windisch, *Der zweite Korintherbrief*, pp. 18-19; Braun, *Qumran und Das Neue Testament*, pp. 201-204; Zahn, *Introduction to the New Testament*, pp. 349-50; Moffatt, *An Introduction to the New Testament*, pp. 125-26; Heinrici, *Der zweite Brief an die Korinthier*, pp. 236-39.

exegesis—*Calvin to Emmerling* (1546–1823); (2) the rise of the historical-critical method and interpolation theories—*Emmerling to Fitzmyer* (1823-mid 1900s); (3) the period of Qumran discoveries—*Fitzmyer to Dahl* (1950s-early 1960s); (4) post-Qumran perspectives—*Dahl to Furnish* (late 1960s-early 1980s), and (5) current status—*Furnish and beyond* (1980s-present).

2. *The Influence of Reformation Exegesis—Calvin to Emmerling (1546–1823)*

The Reformation introduced an era of almost three hundred years during which the interpretation of 2 Cor. 6.14–7.1 remained fairly constant. Although this period had its influential and independent thinkers,[1] their impact was not felt significantly upon this passage. Reflecting the tenor of the times in general, the authenticity and integrity of the text of 2 Cor. 6.14–7.1 went unchallenged. As a result, during this period there was little or no discussion concerning how the fragment fitted within its context.

Two individuals may be selected as representative examples of the period from the 1500s to the early 1800s: John Calvin (1546)[2] and Cornelius À. Lapide (1635).[3] During this early stage in the history of interpretation, debate centered around the ἑτεροζυγοῦντες referent(s)—to what does the 'unequal yoke' refer? Calvin, for example, interpreted ἑτεροζυγοῦντες narrowly, while Lapide included in it almost every pagan-Christian situation mentioned in 1 Corinthians and elsewhere. Most later commentators follow one of these two approaches.

During this period the ἄπιστοι referent was seldom discussed (almost all commentators assumed the ἄπιστοι to be non-Christian pagans). However, Leonhard Usteri (1821)[4] and later Hermann Olshausen (1855)[5] designated the ἄπιστοι referent as Paul's opponents. Their respective studies of the opponents within 2 Corinthians led them to view 2 Cor. 6.14–7.1 as part of Paul's direct attack against these false teachers.

1. Cf. Bruce, 'The History of New Testament Study', pp. 34-38.
2. Calvin, *Epistles of Paul to the Corinthians*, pp. 253-62.
3. Lapide, *Commentary of Cornelius à Lapide*, pp. 93-97.
4. Usteri, *Entwickelung der Paulinischen Lehrbegriffes*, pp. 174-76.
5. Olshausen, *Second Epistle to the Corinthians*, pp. 329-32.

This first period represents the least complex stage in the history of interpretation. The focus was primarily on the ἑτεροζυγοῦντες referent issue, since at this point ἄπιστοι had only two options (either pagans or the false apostles and the latter was seldom considered).

3. *The Rise of the Historical-Critical Method and Interpolation Theories—Emerling to Fitzmyer (1823–mid 1900s)*

The next historical phase in the interpretation of 2 Cor. 6.14–7.1 coincides with the dramatic impact of enlightenment thinking and the historical-critical method upon New Testament studies.[1] The key figure to change the course of scholarship on 2 Corinthians was Johann Salomo Semler (1725–1791). In his commentary, *Paraphrasis II: Epistolae ad Corinthios* (1776), Semler was the first to postulate that 2 Corinthians was composed of several distinct fragments. Although Semler never labeled 2 Cor. 6.14–7.1 as a separate fragment, it was his influence which opened the floodgates to the many subsequent partitioning theories and elaborate reconstructions of Corinthian correspondence.[2] Semler's challenge to orthodox understanding of the canon was of tremendous methodological significance, especially the prevailing theory of 'the final perfection of Scripture', *perfectio finalis scripturae*.[3] Early Christianity neither knew of, nor was bound to, the canon which came into existence much later. This marked change in perspective loosened the material within 2 Corinthians as a whole and allowed for a critical rethinking of its historical origins.

This new investigative era not only detected the fragment's contextual problem, it spawned five distinctly different solutions. Almost fifty years after Semler's commentary, C.A.G. Emmerling (1823) was the first to note the severe contextual difficulty with 2 Cor. 6.14–7.1.[4] Emmerling argued that Paul (upon reading the letter again) inserted the section by his own hand. After Emmerling had awakened New

---

1. On individuals who shaped the course of the enlightenment period for NT studies, see Hasel, *New Testament Theology*, pp. 18-28.

2. For a recent historical survey of partitioning theories, see Betz, *2 Corinthians*, pp. 3-27.

3. Betz, *2 Corinthians*, p. 3. Cf. Semler, *Abhandlung von freier Untersuchung des Canon*.

4. Emmerling, *Epistola Pauli ad Corinthios*, pp. 73-79.

Testament scholars to the problem, the next one hundred years saw the development of five approaches to the passage: (1) a non-Pauline interpolation; (2) an interpolation from Paul's previous letter; (3) an interpolation from a dislocated portion of 1 Corinthians; (4) a dislocated part of 2 Corinthians; (5) a paragraph written by Paul for its present context (with the emergence of contextual integration theories in infantile form). Each of these perspectives are developed below.

In 1835, twelve years after Emmerling identified the glaring contextual problem, Karl Schrader was the first to declare the paragraph non-Pauline.[1] For Schrader, the contextual disruption and non-Pauline spirit of the passage were sufficient to merit such a conclusion. Those who followed Schrader would emphasize these and other non-Pauline features.[2] For example, Ewald (1857) pointed out that defilement and cleansing of the flesh were impossible for Paul; Straatman (1863) reaffirmed the narrow spirit of the passage; Baljon (1884) emphasized the works-sanctification in ἐπιτελοῦντες ἁγιωσύνην. The standard explanation was that the fragment represented some kind of later, Catholic-like theology, such as that found in Barnabas or 1 Clement.

A moderating response to Schrader's proposal soon followed. It became popular to see the paragraph as part of Paul's strict and misunderstood pre-canonical letter (1 Cor. 5.9). This conjecture was first made by Adolf Hilgenfeld (1875).[3] For him, an interpolation from the pre-canonical letter accounted for the contextual break, explained the non-Pauline spirit of separation, and yet retained Pauline authorship. Consequently, the pre-canonical letter theory provided a reasonable alternative to viewing the fragment as a non-Pauline insertion. Although Hilgenfeld first proposed the connection with the pre-canonical letter, it was August Herman von Franke

---

1. Schrader, *Der Apostel Paulus*, IV, pp. 300-306.
2. E.g., Ewald, *Die Sendschreiben des Apostels Paulus*, pp. 231, 281-83; Straatman, *Kritische Studiën*, I, pp. 138-40; Holsten, *Zum Evangelium des Paulus und Petrus*, (1868) pp. 386-90; Renan, *Saint Paul*, (original French work, 1869) pp. lxii-lxiii, 241; Rovers, *Nieuw-Testamentlische letterkunde*, (1876) I, pp. 37-38, 138; Baljon, *De tekst der brieven van Paulus aan de Corinthiërs*, pp. 147-50; Krenkel, *Briefe des Apostels Paulus*, (1890) p. 332; Halmel, *Zweite Korintherbrief des Apostels Paulus*, (1904), pp. 115-21; Völter, *Paulus und seine Briefe*, (1905) p. 90; Scott, *Pauline Epistles*, (1909), pp. 236-37.
3. Hilgenfeld, *Historisch-kritische Einleitung in das Neue Testament*, p. 287.

(1884) and others who undertook to develop the theory.[1] The most convincing piece of evidence was the similar wording of the advice in 1 Cor. 5.9-10 and the fragment (ἐξελθεῖν in 1 Cor. 5.10; ἐξέλθατε in 2 Cor. 6.17).

A third approach developed during this era was to take the fragment as originally part of 1 Corinthians (or connected in some way through partition theories with material from 1 Corinthians). Although proponents of the non-Pauline and pre-canonical letter theories had suggested this possibility earlier,[2] Adolf Hausrath (1879) was the first to endorse the idea as a part of his partitioning scheme and to place the fragment behind 1 Cor. 10.22.[3] Similarly, Johannes Weiss (1910) places the fragment into his letter 'A' in addition to 1 Cor. 10.1-23; 6.12-20; 11.2-34.[4] Even Philipp Bachmann (1922), who originally argued against the removal of 6.14–7.1, later suggests that the paragraph is probably a scattered piece of Pauline literature (although he does not identify the source).[5]

A more restrained approach, formulated by Hans Windisch (1924), relocated the fragment within 2 Corinthians (by only a few verses) in order to smooth the contextual connection. Accordingly, Windisch proposed that the fragment originally followed 2 Cor. 6.1-2.[6]

---

1. E.g., Franke, '2 Kor. 6,14–7,1 und 1 Kor. 5, 9-13', pp. 544-83; Whitelaw, 'A Fragment of the Lost Epistle to the Corinthians', (1890) pp. 12, 248, 317; Sabatier, *The Apostle Paul. A Sketch of the Development of His Doctrine*, (1896), pp. 177-78; Lisco, *Entstehung des zweiten Korintherbriefes*, (1896), pp. 14-19; McGiffert, *History of Christianity in the Apostolic Age*, (1897), p. 332; Bacon, *Introduction to the New Testament*, (1900) p. 95; Moffatt, *Historical New Testament*, (1901) pp. 628-29; Pfleiderer, *Das Urchristentum, seine Schrifen und Lehren*, (1902) I, p. 134; Dobschütz, *Die Urchristlichen Gemeinden*, (1902), pp. 29, 45; Clemen, *Paulus: sein Leben und Wirken*, (1904) I, p. 77; II, p. 202; Barth, *Einleitung in das Neue Testament*, (1914) p. 44; Clayton, 'Epistle to the Corinthians', (1915) p. 254; Smith, *Life and Letters of St. Paul*, (1919), pp. 236, 654.

2. E.g., Ewald (*Die Sendschreiben des Apostels Paulus*, p. 283) gave the alternate *possibility* of an insertion after 1 Cor. 6.1. Cf. Pfleiderer, *Das Urchristentum, seine Schrifen und Lehren*, I, p. 134.

3. Hausrath, *Neutestamentliche Zeitgeschichte*, III, p. 302; IV, pp. 55-57. Cf. Blass, 'Textkritisches zu den Korintherbriefen', (1906), pp. 51-63.

4. Weiss, *Der erste Korintherbrief*, p. xli; cf. idem, *Das Urchristentum*, p. 271.

5. Bachmann, *Zweite Brief an die Korinther*, pp. 287-94. Cf. Koch, *Fortolkning til Paulus' andet brev til Korinthierne*, (1917), pp. 55-56.

6. Windisch, *Der Zweite Korintherbrief*, pp. 19, 212.

Convinced that the paragraph stood in the wrong place, Windisch suggested that it had been inserted after 6.13 as opposed to after 6.2 because of wrongly ordered manuscript leaves.

A final alternative, although not new in substance, was an attempt to strengthen the traditional position of contextual integrity. Commentators such as Meyer (1870),[1] Klöpper (1874),[2] Godet (1914),[3] and Plummer (1915)[4] were now forced, not only to respond to these theories, but also to pursue positive theories of their own in support of contextual integration.[5]

4. *The Period of Qumran Discoveries—Fitzmyer to Dahl (1950s–early 1960s)*

The next major turn in the interpretive road may be described as 'the period of Qumran (DSS) discoveries'. The discovery of the Dead Sea Scrolls in 1947 and their publication later (gradually being made available in the 1950s) generated considerable interest in the 'Qumran-like elements' of 2 Cor. 6.14–7.1. Herbert Braun's work (1966) captures the excitement of New Testament scholars as they pursued an understanding of the relationship between Qumran literature and the fragment during those early years.[6] Many scholars pointed out features in the fragment's vocabulary and theology that were reminiscent of the Qumran material. However, the most influential writers during this period, later to be labeled the 'Qumranists' (indicating their perspective),[7] were Joseph A. Fitzmyer and Joachim Gnilka.

The article by Fitzmyer in 1961 made a heavy impact upon subsequent thinking about the origin and interpretation of the fragment.[8] Fitzmyer observed significant contact points with Qumran literature in the fragment's intense dualism, opposition to idols, the testimonia-like concatenation of Old Testament texts, cleansing of the flesh, Beliar,

---

1. Meyer, *Epistles to the Corinthians*, pp. 554-57.
2. Klöpper, *Zweite Sendschreiben an die Gemeinde zu Korinth*, pp. 334-53.
3. Godet, *La seconde Épître aux Corinthiens*, pp. 208-20.
4. Plummer, *Second Epistle to the Corinthians*, pp. 202-13.
5. A fuller development of these contextual integration theories will be provided in Chapter 5.
6. Braun, *Qumran und Das Neue Testament*, I, pp. 201-204.
7. Rensberger, '2 Corinthians 6.14–7.1', p. 27.
8. Fitzmyer, 'Interpolated Paragraph', pp. 271-80.

strict separation ideas, etc. Given these strong ties with Qumran and the numerous non-Pauline elements in the fragment, Fitzmyer concluded that the passage originally was a 'Christian reworking of an Essene paragraph which has been introduced into the Pauline letter'.[1]

About one year later (April 13, 1962), Gnilka delivered a lecture at the Oriental Institute in Vienna.[2] His research led to conclusions quite similar to those of Fitzmyer: that the fragment reflects Qumran thought in addition to ideas from the Testaments of the Twelve Patriarchs. Likewise, Gnilka held that the non-Pauline vocabulary and rupture with the context precludes Paul as author and inserter. However, Gnilka differed with Fitzmyer in the handling of the 'Christian elements' of the fragment (i.e., the mention of Christ and the believer-unbeliever contrast). Rather than seeing the document as originally from Qumran (and then modified), he suggested that the author was some unknown Christian who was influenced by Essene tradition as he composed the fragment.

Whether an Essene document modified by a Christian or a Christian composer influenced by Essene thought, both Fitzmyer and Gnilka point to the source of the fragment as being closely linked to Qumran literature. Their efforts led to a growing recognition of the Qumran-like nature of the paragraph. In several ways they turned the course of interpretive history. First, the standard source explanation by non-Pauline interpolation theories had in the past tied the fragment to second century Catholic writings; with Fitzmyer and Gnilka this view virtually died overnight. Second, the new interest in Qumran parallels, combined with a waning interest in elaborate partitioning theories, resulted in a dramatic decrease in scholars who endorsed Pauline interpolation theories (e.g., the pre-canonical letter theory). Third, the work of Fitzmyer and Gnilka initiated an entirely new generation of scholarship on the fragment.

---

1. Fitzmyer, 'Interpolated Paragraph', pp. 279-80.
2. The lecture was published in 1963: Gnilka, '2 Kor 6,14–7,1 im Lichte der Qumranschriften und der Zwölf-Patriarchen-Testamente', pp. 86-99. Later, in 1968 it was published in English.

5. *Post-Qumran Perspectives—Dahl to Furnish*
(late 1960s–early 1980s)

The interpolation theories by the 'Qumranists' (Fitzmyer and Gnilka) have had a profound influence upon almost all subsequent exegesis of 2 Cor. 6.14–7.1. In terms of those who have fully embraced their theories, the numbers remain quite small. However, their *indirect* influence has been immense. On the one hand, the Qumranists have accentuated the weaknesses in the traditional interpretation of the passage: (1) its lack of contextual framework (an old problem revisited); (2) its theological tension in calling for 'strict' separation (something that runs against the grain of Pauline theology, yet sounds very much like the DSS). On the other hand, they established for many the influence of Qumran upon the passage (subsequent theories would take other routes to explain this influence). By raising these weaknesses and by arguing for a link with Qumran, Fitzmyer and Gnilka inadvertently sparked at least six or seven alternative theories—each of which would account for the data differently.

One such response to the Qumranists (and to weaknesses in the traditional position) was to interpret ἄπιστοι as a reference not to pagans outside the church, but to the false apostles who were opposing Paul's ministry. In 1969, at the Annual Meeting of the Society of Biblical Literature in Toronto, Nils Alstrup Dahl articulated this view.[1] Such a solution was indeed timely. His proposal immediately solved both the contextual abruptness and the theological tension. Also, it allowed for the final redactor (who could well have been Paul himself) to have modified and inserted an Essene piece of material. Dahl's 'false apostles' hypothesis was later used by Collange (1972)[2] and developed more extensively by Rensberger (1978).[3]

Although some have thought that the false-apostles view was first proposed by Dahl,[4] it can be traced back to Olshausen (1855),[5] Usteri

---

1. The SBL paper was later published in 1977: Dahl, 'A Fragment and Its Context', pp. 62-69.
2. Collange, *Énigmes*, pp. 302-17.
3. Rensberger, '2 Corinthians 6.14–7.1', pp. 25-49.
4. Rensberger ('2 Corinthians 6.14–7.1', pp. 41-42) states, 'the identity of the *apistoi* in 2 Cor. 6.14 was first proposed by Dahl (in 1969)'. Apparently, Rensberger at the time of writing his article was unaware of Usteri, Olshausen, and

(1821),[1] and possibly even Anselm (1491).[2] However, it has only been in this post-Qumran period that the view has made a significant impact. Nonetheless, Dahl and his followers added a new twist to the false-apostles theory by introducing a modification of Qumran material in the source equation. Their view has become particularly attractive because it answers the pressing need for contextual integration, coherence in Pauline theology, and contact with Qumran.

Another response carried Fitzmyer's proposal of non-Pauline origins to its 'ingenious, logical end'.[3] In 1973, Hans Dieter Betz proposed that the fragment's obvious Jewishness (aligning here with Fitzmyer and Gnilka) actually reflects the theology of Paul's opponents.[4] Betz takes ἑτεροζυγοῦντες to refer to the 'yoke of the Torah' and the ἄπιστοι as Gentile believers who refuse to keep the Torah. Thus the interpolated fragment is anti-Pauline, since it encourages Jewish believers not to associate with Gentiles who do not submit to the Law. The self-contained paraenesis, then, urges the Corinthian community *not* to follow Paul. In order to explain its presence in 2 Corinthians, Betz argues that 'it must be assumed that the redactor of the Pauline corpus, for reasons unknown to us, has transmitted a document among Paul's letters which in fact goes back to the movement to which Paul's opponents in Galatia belonged'.[5]

In 1978, J. Duncan M. Derrett introduced a third post-Qumran perspective which attempted to answer the fragment's contextual disruption and theological incompatibility.[6] His view breaks away from the traditional understanding of ἄπιστοι—stating that the term refers not to pagan unbelievers, but to 'untrustworthy' or 'unfaithful'

Anselm. Similarly, Dahl and Collange make no attempt to pursue the historical roots of their position.

5. Olshausen, *Commentary on Paul's First and Second Epistles to the Corinthians*, pp. 329-32.

1. Usteri, *Entwickelung des Paulinischen Lehrbegriffes*, p. 236.

2. The works of Saint Anselm, Archbishop of Canterbury (1033-1109), were not published until 1491. According to Lapide (*Commentary of Cornelius À Lapide*, p. 93), Anselm held that by ἄπιστοι Paul was referring to the Judaizing false apostles, who were attempting to undermine faith in Christ by making the ceremonies of the law of Moses binding on Christians.

3. As pointed out by Fee, 'Food Offered to Idols', p. 141.

4. Betz, 'Anti-Pauline Fragment', pp. 88-108.

5. Betz, 'Anti-Pauline Fragment', p. 108.

6. Derrett, '2 Cor. 6,14ff. a Midrash on Dt. 22,10', pp. 231-50.

individuals in general (in contrast to Paul as 'trustworthy'). Paul's *actual point* is that he is πιστός and the Corinthians should be joined with him. Acknowledging the Jewish nature of the fragment (reminiscent of Qumran), Derrett takes the rest of the fragment to be a midrash on Deut. 22.10, a 'purple passage'[1] which Paul derived from some sermon material (perhaps his own). In other words, the fragment is a midrashic digression simply to underscore the (implied) point that the Corinthians should join together with the apostle.

During this time of post-Qumran perspectives, several attempts were made to bolster the sagging traditional view (that of Pauline authorship and the ἄπιστοι as pagans). In turn, these became contextual integration theories in themselves. For example, in a paper delivered at Aberdeen in August 1975, Margaret E. Thrall set out her own integration theory.[2] Thrall argues that the passage is Pauline and that a contextual framework can be found. Taking up Windisch's suggestion that 6.14–7.1 is a logical continuation of 6.1-2, she postulates a Pauline digression in 6.3-13.[3] Furthermore, Thrall suggests a closer contextual link to 'idols' in 6.16 through ἡ καρδία ἡμῶν πεπλάτυνται in 6.11 (which recalled Deut. 11.16 for Paul and the situation of following false gods). She reduces the theological tension by suggesting that Paul has (indiscriminately) used a pre-existing Old Testament catena.

A further attempt to counter the Qumranists and subsequent post-Qumran solutions was made in 1977 by Gordon D. Fee.[4] After arguing that the content of the fragment is Pauline, Fee proposed that Paul's prohibition in 1 Corinthians 8–10 against joining unbelievers at pagan temple feasts was rejected by some of the Corinthians and that part of their argument was *ad hominem*. Thus in 6.14–7.1 Paul is

---

1. Other than the initial exhortation, the fragment contributes little, if anything, in a direct way to its present context in 2 Corinthians.

2. Thrall initially presented the paper at a seminar on 2 Cor. led by Ernest Best, which met before the SNTS meeting in Aberdeen (August, 1975). An expanded and slightly altered version was later published in 1977: Thrall, 'The Problem of II Cor. VI. 14 - VII', pp. 132-48.

3. Thrall ('The Problem of II Cor. VI. 14 - VII. 1', p. 144) points out that 'He [Paul] momentarily returns yet again to the subject of the apostolic office with which he has been concerned in chapters iii–v. At vi. 14 he resumes where he had left off in vv. 1-2 and supplies the exhortation which logically should have followed immediately.'

4. Fee, 'Food Offered to Idols', pp. 140-61.

responding to their *ad hominem* argument, while at the same time reinforcing his position against eating at pagan temples. The apostle underscores the exhortation of 6.1-2 by saying that in everything he has not become a stumbling block (6.3-10; like they also should not become in this matter of eating at pagan temples) and by arguing that their own affections, not his actions, have restricted their freedom (6.11-13; as they were charging him). Thus, Fee removes the theological tension by limiting Paul's exhortation in 6.14a to the situation of eating at pagan feasts.

Finally, in 1978 Jan Lambrecht wrote an article defending the Pauline origins and integrity of the fragment.[1] Once again, the article responds to the Qumranists, Collange, Betz, etc. and their arguments against the authenticity of the fragment. Lambrecht offers little new in the discussion but his article is significant for our historical survey, since it represents a broader turning of the tide among New Testament scholars away from Qumran interpolation theories.

6. *Current Status—Furnish and Beyond (1980s–present)*

The final stage in our historical sketch might perhaps be subsumed under post-Qumran perspectives, for the impact of Qumran remains quite evident. However, since the dust stirred up by the initial Qumran finds has settled, more sober thinking prevails on the contact between 2 Cor. 6.14–7.1 and Qumran, and a trend has emerged which strikes a balance between the Qumranists and the Paulinists (that is, the rise of Pauline modification theories). Aside from this trend, there is really no monolithic approach to the passage in the 1980s to the present. The following observations will highlight some of the more important developments of this final period.

The trend towards a position between the Qumranists[2] and the Paulinists[3] is represented in the recent commentaries by Victor

---

1. Lambrecht, 'The Fragment 2 Cor. VI 14–VII 1', pp. 143-61. Cf. other studies by Lambrecht on 2 Cor.: '"Om samen te sterven en samen te leven". Uitleg van 2 Kor. 7,3', pp. 234-51; 'La Vie Engloutit ce qui est Mortel: Commentaire de 2 Cor. 5.4c', pp. 237-48; 'Transformation in 2 Cor. 3.18', pp. 243-54; 'Structure and Line of Thought in 2 Cor. 2.14--4.6', pp. 344-80; 'Philological and Exegetical Notes on 2 Cor 13,4', pp. 261-69; 'The Nekrosis of Jesus Ministry and Suffering in 2 Cor 4, 7-15', pp. 120-43.

2. E.g. Fitzmyer and Gnilka.

3. E.g. Thrall, Fee, and Lambrecht.

P. Furnish (1984),[1] Ralph P. Martin (1986)[2] and Friedrich Lang (1986).[3] These commentators seek to maintain some degree of Pauline involvement in the composition and placement of the passage. Acknowledging the influence of Fitzmyer and Gnilka, they suggest that *Paul has modified* a pre-existing fragment—either an actual Essene document or a piece written by a Jewish Christian who had been heavily influenced by Qumran thought.

Despite the mediating trend, the influence of the former Qumranists continues to be strong. The clearest example of this is seen in the commentary by Hans-Josef Klauck (1985)[4] who takes the fragment as a non-Pauline interpolation from what was originally part of the baptismal liturgy of a Judaeo-Christian group in contact with Qumran writings. The fragment was then inserted by the editor who compiled the whole of 2 Corinthians.

On the other hand, a number of current writers follow in the path of former Paulinists and are unimpressed by the Qumran parallels. One of these is Jerome Murphy-O'Connor (1987–88), who has published two articles on the fragment.[5] In the first, Murphy-O'Connor refines Thrall's contextual hypothesis (which itself was a modification of Windisch's theory) by postulating that 6.3-13 is not simply a digression; rather, the central thrust of the chapter is contained in 6.1-2, 11, and 14. In the second article, he rejects previous attempts to align the passage with Qumran, since significant parallels are also found in Philo. The passage is Pauline, but it reflects Philonic overtones as part of Paul's response to the 'pneumatikoi' at Corinth—a group accustomed to articulating its religious experience in Philonic categories.

Finally, a new line of research has emerged which addresses the problem of contextual disruption. Investigating the Old Testament traditions within the fragment and its surrounding context, two recent studies have argued for contextual integration based on this criterion. G.K. Beale (1989) published an article proposing that Old Testament restoration themes lay in the background of Paul's view of

1. Furnish, *II Corinthians*, pp. 359-83.
2. Martin, *2 Corinthians*, pp. 189-212.
3. Lang, *Die Briefe an die Korinther*, pp. 308-311.
4. Klauck, *2 Korintherbrief*, pp. 60-73.
5. Murphy-O'Connor, 'Relating 2 Corinthians 6.14–7.1 to Its Context', pp. 272-75; 'Philo and 2 Cor 6.14–7.1', pp. 55-69.

'reconciliation' (καταλλάσσω), and that these themes unite the material in the fragment with its context.[1] In 1989 I was involved in dissertation studies on 2 Cor. 6.14–7.1 (completed late 1989; defended early 1990)[2] and explored a contextual integration theory which utilized a similar traditions approach. Ironically, we had struck on the same methodology (independent of one another) to arrive at a contextual solution.

However, while sharing a similar methodology to that of Beale, my own work takes a slightly different route.[3] First, I view the conceptual threads which tie together the Old Testament traditions (both outside and inside the fragment) under the broader rubric of 'new covenant and second exodus/return theology'. This perspective strengthens the contextual continuum by adding the crucial dimension of 'new covenant' to the contextual-continuity package (along with certain negative implications from second/new exodus). Second, I seek to establish a series of verbal links which unite the Old Testament traditions, beyond the conceptual links (discussed by Beale). Third, my approach includes a broader analysis of the context (2.14–7.4) and attempts to avoid Beale's localization of the Old Testament theology into one particular Pauline word, καταλλάσσω. Lastly, I propose that the Old Testament traditions-bridge which ties the fragment into its context does so in view of the close *personal identification* of the apostle Paul (himself a suffering servant) with the message and mission of the *'ebed Yahweh*.

7. Summary and Conclusion

The history of the interpretation of 2 Cor. 6.14–7.1 over the past five hundred years has moved through at least five phases. First, from *Calvin to Emmerling* (1546–1823) the traditional interpretation and authenticity of the passage was maintained with little variance. The only significant debate was over the ἑτεροζυγοῦντες referent (with almost universal consensus that ἄπιστοι referred to pagans).

As part of the second phase, *Emmerling to Fitzmyer* (1823–mid 1900s), came the rise of the historical-critical method and interpolation theories. With canon no longer a sacred and perfected entity,

1. Beale, 'Old Testament Background', pp. 550-81.
2. Webb, 'Contextual Framework', pp. 1-310.
3. For a more extensive review of differences see Chapter 7, § 3.

New Testament scholars partitioned 2 Corinthians, and eventually 6.14–7.1 was viewed as a separate fragment. Emmerling was the first to notice the contextual disruption. His observation sparked a host of alternatives: non-Pauline interpolation theories, Pauline interpolation theories (the fragment originally being part of the pre-canonical letter 1 Corinthians, or relocated in 2 Corinthians), and fledgling theories to explain the fragment's contextual integration.

During the third phase, from *Fitzmyer to Dahl* (1950s–early 1960s), the Qumran discoveries produced a new breed of interpolation theories in which 'the Qumranists' tied the origin of the fragment in various ways back to the Essene documents. This position led to the instant modification of earlier non-Pauline theories (which viewed the source of the fragment as second century theology) and to the decreasing popularity of Pauline interpolation theories.

The fourth era, from *Dahl to Furnish* (late 1960s–early 1980s) produced a number of post-Qumran perspectives in response to the Qumranists. Some took their conclusions to the logical end (Betz's anti-Pauline interpolation theory for example). Others countered with contextual theories which altered the traditional understanding of ἄπιστοι to refer to the false apostles (Dahl, *et al.*) or to refer indirectly to Paul as πιστός (Derrett). Still others, labeled as 'the Paulinists', maintained not only Pauline composition of the fragment, but also the ἄπιστοι reference to pagans. They argued for the authenticity of the fragment (Lambrecht) as well as for contextual integration theories relating the fragment back to 6.1-2 (Thrall's modification of Windisch's old theory) or to a reworking of an earlier discussion about meat offered to idols (Fee).

Finally, the current status of investigation, *Furnish and beyond* (1980s–present), lacks any monolithic patterns. Some New Testament scholars have chosen to follow in the path of earlier Qumranists (Klauck), while others have pursued contextual theories along the lines of former Paulinists (Murphy-O'Connor's refinement of Thrall's theory). However, the predominant trend in recent years (Furnish, *et al.*) moderates between the Qumranists and the Paulinists by postulating Paul's modification of either an Essene document or a Christian document influenced by Essene thought.

It is at this multidirectional juncture in the history of interpretation, then, that I wish to forge a new approach to the contextual problem. This line of research (represented by myself and Beale) proposes that a suitable framework for contextual integration may be found through an investigation of the Old Testament traditions both within the fragment and in the surrounding context. The next three Chapters will pursue such a traditions approach—first within the fragment itself, then within the context of 2.14–7.4. After completing the traditions journey, a critique of competing theories will be offered.

Chapter 3

THE CONTENT OF THE FRAGMENT: NEW COVENANT AND SECOND EXODUS TRADITIONS IN 2 CORINTHIANS 6.14–7.1

1. *Introduction*

Setting aside the authenticity debate (which appears to have ended in a stalemate[1]) my objective here is to examine the fragment *in isolation* from its present literary context for the presence of traditional material. It immediately becomes apparent that the traditions in this text are located around two foci: new covenant and second exodus. I use the expression 'second exodus' here for the broader category of 'exilic return' traditions in order to draw attention to the distinctive 'exodus' feature within the return traditions. Methodologically, the investigation begins with, and places its primary emphasis on, the Old Testament quotations (having the advantage of at least two contexts and definite sources to evaluate). Such an approach represents a significant departure from most recent studies, which start with the material outside the catena and then appeal to a 'pre-existing catena' at points where their hypotheses do not fit with the traditions.[2]

Next, an analysis is made of the 'outer shell' of the fragment, that is, the five rhetorical contrasts (6.14b-16b) and the closing admonition (7.1). Here again, the same traditions investigation is pursued. Direct discussion of the opening appeal (6.14a), the more traditional starting point of study, is deferred until Appendixes A and B.

Finally, the relationship between the Old Testament catena and its outer shell is given some attention. After summarizing the redactional influences and various points of correlation between the catena and its

1. From our historical survey (Chapter 2) the trend towards a mediating position reveals that many recent writers do not find the evidence conclusive either for or against Pauline authorship.

2. This methodological departure and its comparative value over current studies of the OT catena will be given more attention below.

shell, I discuss implications from these findings for setting the direction of my work (in contrast to other New Testament studies).

2. The Catena of Old Testament Quotations (2 Corinthians 6.16d-18)

The catena draws together a mosaic of Old Testament quotations: (1) Ezek. 37.27 cited with influence from Lev. 26.11-12; (2) Isa. 52.11; (3) Ezek. 20.34, *et al.*; (4) 2 Sam. 7.14 with influence from Isa. 43.6. After looking at the literary structure, each quotation will be examined in detail through a two-step process. First, an analysis will be made to determine source, form, and redactional changes to the Old Testament texts. Second, the theology of each quotation will be probed in order to determine its contribution to a traditions hypothesis.

Literary Structure of the Old Testament Catena

The composer of the catena has woven together the four Old Testament quotations with a striking degree of skill and design. In fact, the catena's literary structure seems to override the exact boundaries of the quotations (that is, source structure), making the movement between quotations is hardly noticeable. A literary-compositional analysis of the catena reveals a chiastic structure:

καθὼς εἶπεν ὁ θεὸς ὅτι...

A　　Promise of　$\begin{cases} \text{presence (6.16d2)} \\ \\ \text{relationship—covenant formula (6.16d3)} \end{cases}$

　　B　　Imperative of separation (6.17a-b)
　　　　　　... λέγει κύριος

　　B′　　Imperative of separation (6.17c)

A′　　Promise of　$\begin{cases} \text{presence (6.17d)} \\ \\ \text{relationship—covenant formula (6.18)} \end{cases}$
　　　　　　　　... λέγει κύριος παντοκράτωρ

It would appear that this Old Testament catena was designed to emphasize its literary structure rather than its source structure. A number of factors suggest this. First, only a literary structure adequately explains why the λέγει κύριος formula interrupts the Isa.

52.11 quotation. Why did the composer not finish the quotation, then introduce the formula? Seemingly his purpose was to impart a bi-fold structure to the whole through the repeated λέγει κύριος. The final λέγει κύριος 'refrain' adds the appellation παντοκράτωρ to provide a climax and heightened intensity.

Second, the literary structure depicts the balanced framing of the quotations: A (promise), B (imperative), B′ (imperative), A′ (promise). On the one hand, the first promise-imperative cycle (6.16d-17b), through διό, bases the call for separation upon the promises. On the other hand, the second cycle, through its juxtaposition of imperative-promise, implies that the promises are contingent upon the reader's fulfillment of the imperative.

Third, the catena's structure appears to have been created in order to fit it within the larger fragment, its outer shell. The catena may have been molded in view of the appeals in 6.14a and 7.1, since 6.14a aligns with the imperatives in the Old Testament catena, while 7.1 picks up the promises. Also, bracketing the Old Testament imperatives with promises anticipates the move to a hortatory (polite/softer) subjunctive in 7.1. Of course, a pre-existing catena could have been expanded to include the outer shell. However, this structural harmony with the larger fragment seem to favor a unified composition theory.

Quotation 1: Ezekiel 37.27 Cited; with
Influence from Leviticus 26.11-12

MT: וְהָיָה מִשְׁכָּנִי עֲלֵיהֶם   (Ezek. 37.27; cf. 37.23)
       וְהָיִיתִי לָהֶם לֵאלֹהִים וְהֵמָּה יִהְיוּ־לִי לְעָם:

       וְנָתַתִּי מִשְׁכָּנִי בְּתוֹכְכֶם וְלֹא־תִגְעַל נַפְשִׁי אֶתְכֶם: (Lev. 26.11-12)
       וְהִתְהַלַּכְתִּי בְּתוֹכְכֶם
       וְהָיִיתִי לָכֶם לֵאלֹהִים וְאַתֶּם תִּהְיוּ־לִי לְעָם:

       וְעָשׂוּ לִי מִקְדָּשׁ וְשָׁכַנְתִּי בְּתוֹכָם: (Exod. 25.8)

       וְהָיוּ לִי לְעָם וַאֲנִי אֶהְיֶה לָהֶם לֵאלֹהִים: (Jer. 32.38)

LXX: καὶ ἔσται ἡ κατασκήνωσίς μου ἐν   (Ezek. 37.27)
       αὐτοῖς,
       καὶ ἔσομαι αὐτοῖς θεός, καὶ αὐτοί
       μου ἔσονται λαός.

       καὶ θήσω τὴν διαθήκην μου ἐν ὑμῖν,   (Lev. 26.11-12)
       καὶ οὐ βδελύξεται ἡ ψυχή μου ὑμᾶς·
       καὶ ἐμπεριπατήσω ἐν ὑμῖν

καὶ ἔσομαι ὑμῶν θεός, καὶ ὑμεῖς
ἔσεσθέ μου λαός.

καὶ ποιήσεις μοι ἁγίασμα,   (Exod. 25.8)
καὶ ὀφθήσομαι ἐν ὑμῖν

καὶ ἔσονταί μοι εἰς λαόν, καὶ ἐγὼ   (Jer. 39[32].38;
ἔσομαι αὐτοῖς εἰς θεόν.   cf.38[31].1)

NT: ἐνοικήσω ἐν αὐτοῖς καὶ   (2 Cor. 6.16d)
      ἐμπεριπατήσω,
      καὶ ἔσομαι αὐτῶν θεός, καὶ αὐτοὶ
      ἔσονται μου λαός.

Source, form and redaction analysis. The origin of the first Old
Testament quotation in 2 Cor. 6.16d, 'I will dwell among them. . . '
is debated.[1] At least six views exist: (1) only Lev. 26.11-12 is cited;[2]
(2) Lev. 26.11-12 is cited with influence from Ezek. 37.27;[3] (3) both
Lev. 26.11-12 and Ezek. 37.27 are equally in view;[4] (4) Ezek. 37.27
is cited with influence from Lev. 26.11-12;[5] (5) Lev. 26.12; Ezek.
37.27 along with MT Exod. 25.8 for ἐνοικήσω ἐν αὐτοῖς,[6] and (6)

1. Beale ('Old Testament Background', p. 570) incorrectly suggests that there is
'unanimous agreement' on the source issue of the first quotation.
2. Gnilka, '2 Cor. 6.14–7.1', p. 51; Lambrecht, 'The Fragment 2 Cor. VI 14–
VII 1', p. 154; seemingly also, Schlatter, *Paulus Der Bote Jesu*, p. 578; Heinrici,
Der zweite Brief an die Korinther, p. 243; Meyer, *Epistles to the Corinthians*,
p. 556.
3. Betz, 'An Anti-Pauline Fragment', p. 93; Martin, *2 Corinthians*, p. 204; Fee,
'Food Offered to Idols', p. 159; Ellis, *Paul's Use of the Old Testament*, p. 152;
Furnish, *II Corinthians*, p. 364. Windisch (*Der Zweite Korintherbrief*, p. 216)
concludes that the eschatological-mystical understanding of the temple and the
changed wording of Lev. 26.12 has come from Ezek. 37.27. Cf. Cornely, *Epistolae
ad Corinthios*, pp. 190-91.
4. Hughes, *Second Epistle to the Corinthians*, pp. 253-54; Barrett, *Second
Epistle to the Corinthians*, p. 200; Bachmann, *Der zweite Brief des Paulus an die
Korinther*, p. 290; Bruce, *1 and 2 Corinthians*, p. 215; Carrez, *La Deuxième Épître
aux Corinthiens*, p. 167; Godet, *Seconde Épître aux Corinthiens*, p. 215;
Lietzmann, *Korinther I & II*, p. 129; Bonsirven, *Exégèse rabbinique et Exégèse
paulinienne*, p. 333; Fitzmyer, 'Interpolated Paragraph', p. 278; N.J. Hommes,
Het Testimoniaboek, pp. 304-305; Lang, *Die Briefe an die Korinther*, p. 310.
5. Rensberger, '2 Corinthians 6.14–7.1', pp. 38, 48 n. 65; Klinzing, *Die
Umdeutung des Kultus*, p. 178; seemingly also, Héring, *Second Epistle to the
Corinthians*, p. 50.
6. A few commentators suggest the possibility of the MT Exod. 25.8, וְשָׁכַנְתִּי בְּתוֹכָם

Lev. 26.12; Ezek. 37.27 along with Jer. 32.38.[1] The fifth[2] and sixth[3] options are so unlikely, they will not be considered in the discussion below. A careful examination of the quotation's form and context is needed in order to determine which source (Lev. 26.11-12 or Ezek. 37.27) is being cited.

Considering the quotation's form, the first part, ἐνοικήσω ἐν αὐτοῖς, finds no exact parallel in either Lev. 26.11-12 or Ezek. 37.27. Neither passage has the verb ἐνοικέω in the LXX—Ezek. 37.27 has ἡ κατασκήνωσις μου; whereas Lev. 26.11 has τὴν διαθήκην μου. Clearly, however, the LXX Ezek. 37.27, 'my dwelling place' (ἡ κατασκήνωσις μου) is conceptually much closer to ἐνοικέω than the LXX Lev. 26.11, 'my covenant' (τὴν διαθήκην μου). Only if one were to argue that the quotation has come strictly from the MT (which has מִשְׁכָּנִי in both cases), could Lev. 26.11 be the source of this portion.[4] And, if Paul was the one who composed or modified the

---

accounting for ἐνοικήσω ἐν αὐτοῖς. E.g., Grosheide, *De tweede Brief ann de Kerk te Korinthe*, p. 191; cf. Bruce (*1 and 2 Corinthians*, p. 215) who lists Exod. 25.8 but without comment.

1. K. Aland *et al.* (eds.), *The Greek New Testament*, UBS, 3rd edn, p. 632 n. 16.

2. That the LXX Exod. 25.8, ὀφθήσομαι ἐν ὑμῖν, did not supply ἐνοικήσω ἐν αὐτοῖς for the NT is obvious. However, the MT Exod. 25.8, וְשָׁכַנְתִּי בְּתוֹכָם, likewise adds little that is not already found in either MT Lev. 26.11-12 (מִשְׁכָּנִי בְּתוֹכְכֶם) or MT Ezek. 37.27 (מִשְׁכָּנִי עֲלֵיהֶם), except for the verbal form. Also, MT Exod. 25.8 omits much of the material needed for the NT citation, and cannot account for the third person plural ἐν αὐτοῖς. Grosheide (*De tweede Brief ann de Kerk te Korinthe*, p. 191) argues that Paul, 'heeft naar aanleiding van het verband de pronomina van den tweeden persoon in den derden overgebracht'. However, he fails to assess the context accurately. In fact, a switch from the third person to the second would have been expected in view of the context, both from the catena's other two promises and the statement immediately preceding the catena (with second person pronouns). The third person makes the flow conspicuously rough. The only way Grosheide's suggestion could have any validity is if Ezek. 37.27 (not Lev. 26.12) is being cited (see discussion below). Yet, even if Ezek. 37.27 is cited, the above mentioned problems still make Exod. 25.8 quite improbable for verbal dependence.

3. That Jer. 32.38 (cf. 31.1) had indirect conceptual influence upon the composer of the catena is possible. However, its actual citation here is improbable since it contains no material which would account for ἐνοικήσω ἐν αὐτοῖς καὶ ἐμπεριπατήσω, and the 'their God-my people' formula is in a reverse order to that found in 2 Cor. 6.16d.

4. That the MT was used exclusively to compose the first quotation is unlikely. If

catena, then the redactional shift can be explained in terms of his lexical preference and theology.[1] Also, the conspicuous third person pronouns throughout the first quotation supports the use of the Ezekiel passage rather than Leviticus.[2] Here, ἐν αὐτοῖς corresponds precisely with the third person ἐν αὐτοῖς in Ezek. 37.27 (cf. MT עֲלֵיהֶם), in contrast to the second person ἐν ὑμῖν in Lev. 26.11 (cf. MT בְּתוֹכְכֶם).

The second part, καὶ ἐμπεριπατήσω, aligns with LXX Lev. 26.11, and is not found in Ezek. 37.27. It is almost certain that ἐμπεριπατήσω is due to Lev. 26.11.[3] Yet the New Testament catena *omits* the preceding οὐ βδελύξεται ἡ ψυχή μου ὑμᾶς and the following ἐν ὑμῖν which border καὶ ἐμπεριπατήσω in Lev. 26.11. Thus, it seems more plausible that καὶ ἐμπεριπατήσω has been inserted into Ezek. 37.27 (from Lev. 26.11), rather than Lev. 26.11 being the passage directly cited.

The third element, καὶ ἔσομαι αὐτῶν θεός καὶ αὐτοὶ ἔσονται μου λαός, resembles Ezek. 37.27 more closely than Lev. 26.12. The 'their God–my people' formula follows Ezek. 37.27 closely except for a slight change from αὐτοῖς to αὐτῶν in the first half, and a rear-

the translation practices throughout the LXX can be used as a hypothetical measure, the derivation of ἐνοικήσω from the MT מִשְׁכָּנִי is improbable. Of its 44 occurrences in the LXX, only once is ἐνοικέω used to translate מִשְׁכָּן; usually, it translates יָשַׁב. On the other hand, ἡ κατασκήνωσις and its verbal form (out of 62 occurrences) are used to translate some form of שָׁכֵן 55 times. Also, see the argument below regarding the change to third person in the Leviticus hypothesis.

1. The verb ἐνοικέω occurs 5 times in the NT (only in material attributed to Paul); whereas ἡ κατασκήνωσις is distinctly non-Pauline (occurring 6 times in the NT in verb and noun forms, *never* in Paul's writings). Also, Paul tends to use the term ἐνοικέω theologically to describe the indwelling of the Spirit (e.g., Rom. 8.11), an emphasis which would be contextually quite appropriate. By way of contrast, ἐνοικέω (usually translating יָשַׁב) is never used by the LXX in reference to God.

2. The Leviticus view has to propose that the composer (for some reason?) has changed the text from the second to the third person. However, all the evidence suggests that this is an extremely unlikely hypothesis. The NT context appears to require a 'you' rather than a 'them'. The second person was used of the reader in the preceding material (6.14a, although cf. 16b ἡμεῖς), in the two promises to follow (ὑμᾶς, ὑμῖν, and ὑμεῖς), in the conclusion (7.1), and even in the non-promise quotation (6.17). *The change to third person makes the flow conspicuously rough.* Conversely, the second person of Leviticus would have been a much more natural fit. Why would the composer have altered the Leviticus passage to make it *less* conducive to the catena and the rest of the fragment?

3. This is especially the case since ἐμπεριπατεῖν occurs only 9 times in the LXX.

rangement of the word order in the second half (μου follows, rather than precedes, the verb). On the other hand, this third element diverges to a much greater extent from Lev. 26.12 with the change from ὑμῶν to the third person pronoun αὐτῶν in the first half, and from ὑμεῖς ἔσεσθέ to αὐτοὶ ἔσονται in the second half.[1]

A consideration of each of the Old Testament contexts also favors Ezek. 37.27 as the primary citation. Both contexts of Lev. 26.11-12 and Ezek. 37.27 involve God's covenant promises to Israel, but in Leviticus 26 the promise has a *present* focus, related to Israel obeying God's commandments (cf. Lev. 26.3, 14, 15); whereas in Ezekiel 37 the context is predominantly *eschatological*, depicting a (new) ever-lasting covenant of peace that God will establish with his people. Ezekiel 37 looks to a future time when Judah and Israel will be joined together as one nation, under one Davidic king. Thus, within the catena (and its eschatological promises),[2] the eschatological context of Ezekiel is preferred over the Torah context of Leviticus. As Hughes points out, *the contextual emphasis on the new temple (2 Cor. 6.16) almost certainly requires Ezek. 37.27 to be the source.*[3]

In sum, both form and context favor Ezek. 37.27 as the source for the first citation. The change from second person to third in the Leviticus hypothesis cannot be adequately explained. However, it would seem that ἐμπεριπατήσω has been inserted from Lev. 26.11 (perhaps from memory). Furthermore, the eschatological new temple context of the Ezekiel passage fits better with the import of the other quotations in the catena and the rest of 6.14–7.1.

New covenant and second exodus/return theology. For the purposes of my argument, it is significant that the first quotation expresses *new covenant* promises. The first half, emphasizing Yahweh's temple presence, ἐνοικήσω ἐν αὐτοῖς καὶ ἐμπεριπατήσω,[4] is essential to

1. These same changes would be required if the MT were used for either Ezek. 37.27 or Lev. 26.12 (except that μου would more naturally follow the verb, as in the NT).

2. Note, for example, the διό conjunction which inferentially links the first quotation to the second from Isa. 52.11 (a passage itself related to the second exodus and establishment of the new covenant). See the discussion below concerning the second quotation.

3. Hughes, *Second Corinthians*, pp. 253-54.

4. This 'dwelling' imagery directly develops the earlier affirmation, ἡμεῖς γὰρ

the new covenant. In Ezek. 37.26, the verse immediately preceding the material quoted, Yahweh promises, 'I will make a covenant of peace with them; it will be an everlasting covenant (בְּרִית עוֹלָם) with them' (Ezek. 37.26). The seal[1] or realization[2] of this new covenant with Yahweh's people comes through the corresponding promise, 'I will set my sanctuary in their midst forever (לְעוֹלָם)' (v. 26b; cf. v. 28).[3] Thus, this new temple-dwelling promise is an ultimate realization of Yahweh's new covenant with his people.[4]

Again, the second half of the New Testament quotation, ἔσομαι αὐτῶν θεός, καὶ αὐτοὶ ἔσονται μου λαός, lies at the heart of new covenant theology. Most Old Testament scholars refer to the statement in Ezek. 37.27b, וְהָיִיתִי לָהֶם לֵאלֹהִים וְהֵמָּה יִהְיוּ־לִי לְעָם (cf. 37.23), as 'the covenant formula'.[5] The words express an exclusive covenant bond between Israel and its God.[6] Jeremiah, for example, employs the formula to recall God's expectation of the past exodus/Sinai event[7] and to express his own expectations of a future covenant between God and his people.[8] Ezekiel, on the other hand, uses it only as an expression

ναὸς θεοῦ ἐσμεν ζῶντος (2 Cor. 6.16b).

1. Eichrodt, *Ezekiel*, p. 515.

2. Zimmerli, *Ezekiel 2*, p. 277.

3. עוֹלָם is a key term in the passage, linking the promises together (עַד־עוֹלָם v. 25; לְעוֹלָם vv. 25, 26, 28; בְּרִית עוֹלָם v. 26). The motif of a permanent בְּרִית is a feature of new covenant expectations (e.g., Ezek. 16.60; 37.26; Isa. 55.3; 61.8).

4. Cf. discussion below on ναὸς θεοῦ.

5. Eichrodt, *Ezekiel*, p. 515; Zimmerli, *Ezekiel 2*, p. 277; Greenberg, *Ezekiel, 1-20*, p. 254; Brownlee, *Ezekiel 1-19*, pp. 164, 204; Holladay, *Jeremiah 1*, p. 262. Compare Köhler's statement (*Theologie des Alten Testaments*, p. 73) regarding Exod. 6.7, 'Der ganze Bund war beschlossen in dem Wort: "Ich nehme euch mir zum Volk und werde für euch Gott seins"'. Similarly, Baltzer (*The Covenant Formulary*, p. 102) comments, 'the relationship between Yahweh and Israel. . . can be reduced to the formula, "I will be your God, and you shall be my people"'.

6. The formula is probably derived from the legal terminology used in marriage and adoption (Weinfeld, *Deuteronomy and the Deuteronomic School*, p. 80-81). Similarly, Wolff (*Hosea*, p. 21) notes that the negative terminology of Hos. 1.9, 'For you are not my people and I am not your God', is a formula of divorce. If so, then, marriage phraseology may well stand behind the formula here in Ezekiel (cf. Ruth 1.16; 1 Kings 22.4).

7. Jer. 7.23; 11.4; 13.11. These passages in Jeremiah echo the frequent use of the covenant formula in relation to leaving Egypt and establishing a covenant at Sinai (e.g., Exod. 6.7; Lev. 26.12-13; Deut. 4.20).

8. Jer. 24.7; 30.22; 31.1; 32.38. That the expression represents the core of new

of the future new covenant, which will restore the ideal covenant bond.[1]

Before leaving Ezekiel 37, it is worth noting that the eschatological return theme is also present. To begin with, Ezek. 37.15-28 functions as a unit.[2] After the sign of two sticks becoming one (37.15-18), the repeated prophetic instruction 'say to them' (vv. 19, 21) divides the section into two parts—a brief explanation of the sign (37.19-20), and then a more extensive one (37.21-28). In the expanded discussion (37.21-28) Yahweh portrays the gathering out from among the nations, restoration to the land, formation of one kingdom under one king, and establishment of Yahweh's renewed temple presence among his people. In this section, then, the temple-dwelling and 'their God—my people' promise (vv. 26-28) *presupposes* a regathering—a return of the exilic community to the land (v. 21).[3]

Furthermore, one finds at least traces of the exodus pattern reappearing. The covenant formula, 'I will be their God, and they will be my people', expresses an (unfulfilled) expectation of the first journey out of Egypt.[4] However, as a pattern of God's acts in history, the

covenant promise can hardly be debated, for in Jeremiah one finds it related to the promise of a new heart (24.7) and introducing the explicit discussion on the new covenant (31.1). Cf. 32.38 which also groups the covenant formula together with the promise of one, undivided heart (32.39a), a fear of Yahweh in their hearts (32.39b-40), and an everlasting covenant (32.40).

1. Besides Ezek. 37.23, 27 the covenant formula is repeated several other times within the book, always of the expected new covenant age (11.20; 14.11; 34.24, 30; 36.28). On these occasions 'my people-their God' is closely related to other distinctly new covenant features—e.g., a new heart and spirit (11.19; 36.26), the covenant of peace (34.25), and God's Spirit placed within his people (36.27).

2. The introductory statement, 'The word of the Lord came again to me. . . ' (Ezek. 37.16) marks this vision off from the previous dry bones vision (37.1-15). However, the two are related. The first portrays Israel's restoration from exile as a miracle of resurrection from death; the second goes one step further and describes this restoration as a reunion of the two kingdoms which had split under Solomon's sons (Eichrodt, *Ezekiel*, p. 512).

3. The concept of a return is clearly pictured in v. 21: 'Behold, I [Yahweh] will take the sons of Israel from among the nations where they have gone, and I will gather them from every side and bring them into their own land'. See discussion below on the third quotation for the link in promise between return and the new covenant.

4. Many OT references place the covenant formula as an expectation of the exodus. E.g., Jer. 11.4, 'I commanded your forefathers in the day that I brought

covenant formula is to be eventually realized through a second, greater exodus intended to establish a new covenant.[1]

Quotation 2: Isaiah 52.11

MT: (Isa. 52.11) סוּרוּ סוּרוּ צְאוּ מִשָּׁם טָמֵא אַל־תִּגָּעוּ
צְאוּ מִתּוֹכָהּ הִבָּרוּ נֹשְׂאֵי כְּלֵי יְהוָה׃

(Jer. 51.45) צְאוּ מִתּוֹכָהּ עַמִּי
וּמַלְּטוּ אִישׁ אֶת־נַפְשׁוֹ מֵחֲרוֹן אַף־יְהוָה׃

LXX: ἀπόστητε ἀπόστητε ἐξέλθατε ἐκεῖθεν (Isa. 52.11)
καὶ ἀκαθάρτου μὴ ἅπτεσθε,
ἐξέλθατε ἐκ μέσου αὐτῆς ἀφορίσθητε,
οἱ φέροντες τὰ σκεύη κυρίου.

[no parallel text of MT Jer. 51.45 in the LXX] (Jer. 51.45)

NT: διὸ ἐξέλθατε ἐκ μέσου αὐτῶν (2 Cor. 6.17a-c)
καὶ ἀφορίσθητε, λέγει κύριος,
καὶ ἀκαθάρτου μὴ ἅπτεσθε·

Source, form and redaction analysis. While a similar imperative (צְאוּ) is found in Jer. 51.45 (and at times Jer. 51.45 is listed for comparison),[2] it is quite evident that the 2 Cor. 6.17a-c quotation is from Isa. 52.11 with little or no influence from Jer. 51.45.[3]

A comparison of 2 Cor. 6.17a-c with Isa. 52.11 (either in the MT or

them out of the land of Egypt. . . saying, 'Listen to my voice, and do all that I have commanded you; so that you shall be My people, and I will be your God'. Cf. Jer. 7.22-26; 13.11; Exod. 6.7; Deut. 4.20.

1. Inasmuch as the covenant formula functions as an expectation of the future return (e.g., Jer. 24.7; 30.22; 31.1; 32.38; Ezek. 11.20; 36.28), it echoes the unfulfilled expectation of the first exodus (Exod. 6.6-7; Jer. 7.22-26; 11.4; 13.11). Thus there is an implicit pattern of a second exodus.

2. E.g., Hughes, *Second Epistle to the Corinthians*, p. 254; Barrett, *Second Epistle to the Corinthians*, p. 200; Bonsirven, *Exégèse rabbinique et Exégèse paulinienne*, p. 316; Allo, *Seconde Épître aux Corinthiens*, p. 186. One might also compare Zech. 2.7 (cf. 2.10-11).

3. The MT Jer. 51.45 (no LXX equivalent exists) does not account for the NT ἀφορίσθητε and ἀκαθάρτου μὴ ἅπτεσθε (elements which *are* found in Isa. 52.11). The NT quotation omits 'my people' (עַמִּי) which Jer. 51.45 has as distinct from Isa. 52.11.

the LXX)[1] reveals that a number of changes have been made to the text. (1) The conjunction διό is added in order to relate the text inferentially with the previous temple-dwelling promise. (2) The catena's exhortation ἐξέλθατε ἐκ μέσου αὐτῶν inverts the order, placing it before καὶ ἀκαθάρτου μὴ ἅπτεσθε (cf. MT), and changes the LXX αὐτῆς (cf. MT, מִתּוֹכָהּ) to αὐτῶν. The inversion emphasizes this particular imperative (putting it first in the series) and can be explained as an attempt to give it a parallel force and meaning with the exhortation of 6.14a. Similarly, the change from feminine singular to masculine plural—'come out of *her* midst' to 'come out of *their* midst'—reflects a deliberate modification of the Old Testament text in order to correspond to the previous ἄπιστοι referent (6.14a). Furthermore, in this reordered quotation the redactor appears to have intentionally placed ἀκαθάρτου μὴ ἅπτεσθε in the third position (of the imperatival series) to link it with the shell's closing admonition, καθαρίσωμεν (7.1). (3) A καί is added before ἀφορίσθητε, probably for symmetrical purposes.[2] (4) Also, λέγει κύριος is added to the text, in order to balance out the closing λέγει κύριος παντοκράτωρ. (5) The catena omits οἱ φέροντες τὰ σκεύη κυρίου (cf. MT, נֹשְׂאֵי כְּלֵי יְהוָה) and the MT הִבָּרוּ. Though omitted, these contextual elements serve as important hermeneutical clues when understanding how the passage fits conceptually within 6.14–7.1. First, the reference to 'those who carry the vessels of the Lord (i.e., the Levites)' continues the temple theme in 2 Cor. 6.16b and in the first quotation (6.16d). Second, the MT הִבָּרוּ, 'purify yourselves' (as well as the quoted portion, ἀκαθάρτου μὴ ἅπτεσθε) probably accounts for the closing admonition, καθαρίσωμεν ἑαυτούς, 'let us cleanse ourselves' (2 Cor. 7.1).[3] The closing thought, then, simply extends the ritual cleansing imagery begun in the catena.

---

1. The LXX follows the MT closely in Isa. 52.11, but it omits הִבָּרוּ (which is likewise omitted by the NT).

2. Each of the verbs in the catena have a καί preceding it.

3. בָּרַר and its derivatives frequently portray cultic and ethical purification as in Isa. 52.11 (e.g., 2 Sam. 22.27; Ps. 18.26; cf. 2 Sam. 22.21, 25; Job 9.30; 22.30; Isa. 1.25). Also, the reflexive niphal הִבָּרוּ, corresponds well with the reflexive idea expressed in καθαρίσωμεν ἑαυτούς. When this contextual feature is examined (along with the verbal link in the quoted portion of Isa. 52.11, ἀκαθάρτου μὴ ἅπτεσθε), then the influence upon καθαρίσωμεν ἑαυτούς in 2 Cor. 7.1 seems undeniable.

Isa. 52.11-12 and second exodus/return theology. In language reminiscent of the exodus from Egypt, Isa. 52.11-12 pictures the return of Israel (and especially the Levites) from the defiled city of Babylon.[1] Touching nothing unclean,[2] (not) leaving in haste,[3] and Yahweh's going before and after his people[4] recall patterns from the first exodus. The prophetic call is to 'come out' (אֵצ/ἐξέλθατε, v. 11), to depart from Babylon; but unlike the first exodus, the exiles will not come out in haste (אֵצֵם/ἐξελεύσεσθε, v. 12). This new exodus, with Yahweh as leader and protector, will be a journey made in peace and security. The objective, presumably, is to travel in a holy procession to the newly cleansed Jerusalem (Isa. 52.1-2), and once there, to worship Yahweh.[5]

1. For an extended discussion of the second exodus theme in Isaiah, see Anderson, 'Exodus Typology', pp. 177-95. Anderson lists several passages in Second Isaiah where the theme of the new exodus is prominent: 40.3-5; 41.17-20; 42.14-16; 43.1-3, 14-21; 48.20-21; 49.8-12; 51.9-10; 52.11-12; 55.12-13. In these passages the new exodus occurs in at least four stages: the promise itself, deliverance from Egypt, journey through the wilderness, and re-entry into the promised land. Cf. Foulkes, *The Acts of God. A Study of the Basis of Typology in the Old Testament*, pp. 21-22; Anderson, 'Exodus and Covenant in Second Isaiah', pp. 339-60; Daube, *Exodus Pattern in the Bible*; Zimmerli, 'Le nouvel "exode" dans le message des deux grands prophètes de l'exil', pp. 216-27; Blenkinsopp, 'Scope and Depth of Exodus Tradition in Deutero-Isaiah 40–55', pp. 41-50; Patrick, 'Epiphany Imagery in Second Isaiah's Portrayal of a New Exodus', pp. 125-42.

2. Pieper (*Isaiah II*, p. 428) notes on Isa. 52.11 that the exhortation to 'touch no unclean thing' stands in contrast to the command given to the Israelites when they departed from Egypt to borrow from their neighbors vessels of gold and silver (Exod. 11.2).

3. Isa. 52.11-12; cf. Exod. 12.11; Deut. 16.3. Bernard ('Exodus Typology in Second Isaiah', p. 183) and Westermann (*Isaiah 40–66*, p. 253) both point to this parallel.

4. Again, the imagery recalls events of the former exodus, when Yahweh was the 'rear guard' and 'went before' his people in a pillar of cloud (Exod. 13.21-22; 14.19-20; cf. Deut. 1.30-33). Similarly, Ziegler (*Isaias*, p. 155), with the added parallel of consecration notes, 'Die Heiligung ist deshalb gefordert, weil man die heiligen Tempelgeräte mitträgt, die einst Nebukadnezar geraubt hatte (vgl Esr 1.7-11; 6.5), und weil Jahwe selbst diese Prozession führt und sie schleisst wie einst beim Auszug aus Ägypten vgl Ex 13.21f; 14.19'.

5. The objective of the journey (to establish a new temple and worship Yahweh) is hinted at by the designation, נֹשְׂאֵי כְּלֵי יְהוָה. The carrying of the holy vessels by the returning exiles may have been literal, since in the process of captivity certain vessels

While Isa. 52.11-12 refers to a literal departure from Babylon,[1] the catena clearly does not. As noted above, the fragment has altered the Old Testament text by changing the referent from 'her' (Babylon) to 'them' (i.e., the ἄπιστοι of 6.14a). A non-literal exodus is suggested by the kind of temple constructed at the end of the journey. The new temple is no longer a physical edifice located in Jerusalem, but the community itself: ἡμεῖς ναὸς θεοῦ ἐσμεν ζῶντος (6.16b). This shift from a literal to a symbolic/moral meaning may have found its impetus in the Old Testament text itself, since contextually the emphasis of the cry, ἐξέλθατε ἐκ μέσου αὐτῆς, is on the ethical purity of God's people (of which the cultic purity serves as a ritual reflection). Within Isaiah, the commands, צֵאוּ אַל־תִּגָּעוּ טָמֵא and הִבָּרוּ, (although envisioning a literal separation) are equally directed towards a spiritual separation from idolatry and a return to the God.[2] It seems to be this non-geographical kind of 'second exodus' which the fragment has in view.[3]

Quotation 3: Ezekiel 20.34, et al.

MT:

וְהוֹצֵאתִי אֶתְכֶם מִן־הָעַמִּים   (Ezek. 20.34; cf. 20.41)
וְקִבַּצְתִּי אֶתְכֶם מִן־הָאֲרָצוֹת

וְקִבַּצְתִּי אֶתְכֶם מִן־הָעַמִּים   (Ezek. 11.17)
וְאָסַפְתִּי אֶתְכֶם מִן־הָאֲרָצוֹת

בָּעֵת הַהִיא אָבִיא אֶתְכֶם וּבָעֵת קַבְּצִי אֶתְכֶם   (Zeph. 3.20)

אֲנִי אֶהְיֶה־לּוֹ לְאָב וְהוּא יִהְיֶה־לִּי לְבֵן   (2 Sam. 7.14)

were taken to Babylon (2 Chron. 36.7, 10, 18).

1. Even though the historical referent is the literal departure from Babylon, one should be careful not to attribute a *literal* nature to the reused tradition itself (it is unlikely that Yahweh literally went before and after his people). For, as Westermann (*Isaiah 40–66*, p. 252) points out, 'its diction is shot through with suggestions of old traditions'.

2. Furthermore, such a shift is consistent with the second exodus theology of Isaiah, which broadens the return motif (a pattern of the first exodus, and again the Cyrus exilic return) to speak of an eschatological return of those from many nations to Yahweh. As Anderson ('Exodus Typology', p. 194) notes, 'Second Isaiah's eschatological hope is shaped by images drawn from Israel's *Heilsgeschichte*, particularly the crucial event of the Exodus, from which flow consequences reaching into the present and on into the future'. The initial exodus, then, forms a pattern for the new exodus with deeper soteriological meaning and world-wide implications.

3. This is especially the case if the (new) temple is equated with the community itself (2 Cor. 6.16).

וּמְאַסֵּפְכֶם אֱלֹהֵי יִשְׂרָאֵל (Isa. 52.12b)

LXX: καὶ ἐξάξω ὑμᾶς ἐκ τῶν λαῶν   (Ezek. 20.34; cf. 20.41)
καὶ εἰσδέξομαι ὑμᾶς ἐκ τῶν χωρῶν

καὶ εἰσδέξομαι αὐτοὺς ἐκ τῶν ἐθνῶν   (Ezek. 11.17)
καὶ συνάξω αὐτοὺς ἐκ τῶν χωρῶν

ἐν τῷ καιρῷ ἐκείνῳ ὅταν καλῶς ὑμῖν   (Zeph. 3.20)
ποιήσω,
καὶ ἐν τῷ καιρῷ ὅταν εἰσδέξωμαι
ὑμᾶς·

ἐγὼ ἔσομαι αὐτῷ εἰς πατέρα,   (2 Sam. 7.14)
καὶ αὐτὸς ἔσται μοι εἰς υἱόν·

καὶ ὁ ἐπισυνάγων ὑμᾶς κύριος ὁ θεὸς   (Isa. 52.12b)
Ἰσραήλ

NT: κἀγὼ εἰσδέξομαι ὑμᾶς   (2 Cor. 6.17d)

Source, form and redaction analysis. The brevity and general nature of the third quotation, κἀγὼ εἰσδέξομαι ὑμᾶς, raises uncertainty as to what Old Testament text is being cited. Six possibilities have been proposed: (1) Ezek. 20.34;[1] (2) Ezek. 11.17;[2] (3) Zeph. 3.20 as a likely alternative;[3] (4) general use of Old Testament return language;[4]

1. Most commentators view the third quotation as coming from Ezek. 20.34. See Gnilka, '2 Cor. 6.14–7.1', pp. 52, 59-60; Héring, *Second Epistle to the Corinthians*, p. 50; Windisch, *Der Zweite Korintherbrief*, p. 217; Klöpper, *Das zweite Sendschreiben an die Gemeinde zu Korinth*, p. 347; Plummer, *II Corinthians*, p. 209; Barrett, *Second Epistle to the Corinthians*, p. 201; Belser, *Der zweite Brief des Apostels Paulus an die Korinther*, p. 212; Godet, *Seconde Épître aux Corinthiens*, p. 215; Heinrici, *Der zweite Brief an die Korinther*, p. 243; Lietzmann, *Korinther I & II*, p. 129; Schlatter, *Paulus Der Bote Jesu*, p. 578; with less certainty, Furnish, *II Corinthians*, p. 364.
2. Grosheide (*De tweede Brief ann de Kerk te Korinthe*, p. 191) places Ezek. 11.17 first out of several options. Cf. Martin (*2 Corinthians*, p. 206) who lists Ezek. 11.17 along with 20.34, as does Plummer (*II Corinthians*, p. 209).
3. Some commentators suggest Zeph. 3.20 as a possible alternative to Ezek. 20.34 (although they would concur that Ezek. 20.34 is the more likely source). E.g., see Gnilka, '2 Cor. 6.14–7.1', p. 52; Windisch, *Der Zweite Korintherbrief*, p. 217.
4. Rensberger ('2 Corinthians 6.14–7.1', p. 37) comes fairly close to Betz's position, but suggests that εἰσδέξομαι is possibly due to general OT (presumably 'return') language.

(5) an interpretation of 2 Sam. 7.14,[1] or (6) a re-working of Isa. 52.12b.[2] Of these options, the sixth[3] may be dismissed as improbable.

The fifth option, proposed by Hans D. Betz, requires close scrutiny. Betz argues that κἀγὼ εἰσδέξομαι ὑμᾶς should be considered, 'an interpretation of the quotation from 2 Sam. 7.14 which follows'.[4] His view is not without merit. First, although not mentioned by Betz, a 2 Samuel source offers one way to account for the ἐγώ of κἀγὼ εἰσδέξομαι ὑμᾶς (cf. 2 Sam. 7.14a, ἐγὼ ἔσομαι αὐτῷ εἰς πατέρα) which is not specified in Ezek. 20.34 or any other passage. Second, there is admittedly a close correlation between κἀγὼ εἰσδέξομαι ὑμᾶς and the following quotation. Betz is correct in pointing out that to 'receive' those who are pure is a promise of reception as sons and daughters—that is, the two promises are fused together. Third, the lexical idea of εἰσδέξομαι in the LXX (as a frequent translation of קבץ) does connote (although probably not denote) the idea of regathering God's people from among the nations. And thus in 2 Cor. 6.16, εἰσδέξομαι retains, to a certain extent, the idea of Yahweh's 'regathering'.[5]

Nonetheless, Betz's position is not convincing for several reasons. First, the ἐγώ could have been supplied through the fusion of quotations three and four without *necessarily* requiring κἀγὼ εἰσδέξομαι ὑμᾶς to be an expansion or 'interpretation' of the fourth quotation. Splicing or injecting one Old Testament text into another is not uncommon (note the first quotation from Ezek. 37.27 and Lev. 26.11 above). Second, the conceptual relationship between the third and fourth quotation (reception as sons and daughters) need not diminish

---

1. Betz, 'An Anti-Pauline Fragment', pp. 96-97.

2. A few older commentators, such as Osiander (*Zweiten Brief Pauli an die Korinthier*, pp. 260-61), saw κἀγὼ εἰσδέξομαι ὑμᾶς as a reproduction of the sense of LXX Isa. 52.12b, καὶ ὁ ἐπισυνάγων ὑμᾶς κύριος ὁ θεὸς Ἰσραήλ.

3. Isa. 52.12b is not a likely source for κἀγὼ εἰσδέξομαι ὑμᾶς since it does not account for the verbal composition of the quotation. However, the observation of 'sense' similarity is correct (see discussion below).

4. Betz, 'Anti-Pauline Fragment', p. 97; cf. Lambrecht ('The Fragment 2 Cor. VI 14–VII 1', p. 155) who assumes Betz's position.

5. However, Betz would no doubt maintain that κἀγὼ εἰσδέξομαι ὑμᾶς, if from an LXX return text, *must* be translated, 'and I shall gather you together', instead of the more contextually appropriate translation (for the fragment), 'and I will receive you'.

the distinctiveness of the third quotation. In fact, it is only when κἀγὼ εἰσδέξομαι ὑμᾶς is viewed in terms of the eschatological regathering and return tradition that the motivation for the redactional changes to 2 Sam. 7.14 can be adequately explained.[1] Third, Betz's lexical argument is faulty. Not only does he fail to distinguish between sense and referent (i.e., the defining sense of εἰσδέξομαι can still be 'receive', while the referential event is the eschatological 'regathering' of God's people), but his reasoning would require εἰσδέξομαι to have exactly the same meaning as that which it translates (קָבַץ). Such a tight correspondence is rare in translations. It is the broader meaning of 'receive' (different, but not changing the sense of קָבַץ) which accounts for the Ezekiel 20 interplay between εἰσδέξομαι ὑμᾶς and its similar cognate promise, προσδέξομαι ὑμᾶς (see the discussion of Ezek. 20 below).[2] Fourth, Betz overlooks the strong conceptual relationship between quotations two and three. Quotation two, with its call to 'come out of Babylon' (Isa. 52.11), is tied to the regathering of Israel by Yahweh—they are corollaries of the same event, ἐξέλθατε... εἰσδέξομαι.[3] By virtue of its conceptual relationship to quotation two alone, the third quotation is colored with return imagery. Finally, even if one agreed with Betz that a קָבַץ source required εἰσδέξομαι to be translated 'regather' in 2 Cor. 6.17d, it would not be so serious a shift of context (in light of the preceding quotation) if one sought Betz's alternate proposal.

The remaining four options, with their overlapping focus, may now be examined together. From the standpoint of form, option one (Ezek. 20.34) offers an exact quotation.[4] Furthermore, the Ezekiel 20 source is attractive because of the threefold repetition of the same promise only a few verses later, through the close parallel, καὶ εἰσδέχεσθαι ὑμᾶς (Ezek. 20.41b),[5] and through the cognate expressions of the

1. See discussion on καὶ θυγατέρας below.

2. This fluidity in the promise also allows εἰσδέξομαι to be contextually pertinent. Cf. Chapter 5 (§4) in which δέξασθαι, δεκτῷ, and εὐπρόσδεκτος in 2 Cor. 6.1-2 is discussed.

3. So Heinrici, *Der zweite Brief an die Korinther*, p. 243; Windisch, *Der zweite Korintherbrief*, p. 217.

4. The crasis of ἐγώ and καί into κἀγὼ is probably due to its fusion (Ezek. 20.34, καὶ εἰσδέξομαι ὑμᾶς) with the following fourth quotation (2 Sam. 7.14, ἐγώ ἔσομαι αὐτῷ. . .).

5. Note the use of εἰσδέχεσθαι in Ezek. 20.40b instead of the εἰσδέξομαι in

promise, καὶ ἐκεῖ προσδέξομαι (Ezek. 20.40) and προσδέξομαι ὑμᾶς (Ezek. 20.41b). Option two (Ezek. 11.17) in the LXX is not as close with its change from ὑμᾶς το αὐτούς; however, the MT does provide an exact parallel, וְקִבַּצְתִּי אֶתְכֶם, like Ezek. 20.34. Option three (Zeph. 3.20) likewise differs from the catena's form with its LXX addition of ἐν τῷ καιρῷ ὅταν and MT additions of וּבָעֵה and infinitive, קַבְּצִי. Option four includes the above-mentioned passages along with other less similar passages which use some form of εἰσδέχομαι (see below).[1] On the basis of form and its repeated use Ezek. 20.34 is the most likely candidate (with Ezek. 11.17 as a second possibility).

The criteria of context is not so helpful in determining source, since *similar* theological undercurrents appear in each of the competing options—Ezek. 20.34; 11.17; Zeph. 3.20; and the other more general references. Perhaps this factor, along with the brevity of the quotation, should caution against designating *with certainty* any one Old Testament text as the source. Therefore, we will proceed with an understanding of Ezek. 20.34 (cf. Ezek. 11.17) as the most likely candidate for the third quotation, but acknowledge its much broader usage within general Old Testament return language.

Referent changes. In Ezek. 20.34 (cf. 11.17) and the other passages, Yahweh's promise to receive/regather his people refers to their acceptance as they return to *Jerusalem*. However, the place in which God receives his people in 2 Cor. 6.17d is not entirely obvious. Few commentators even mention the issue. Of those who do, several suggestions have been made: (1) heaven;[2] (2) the community temple/

Ezek. 20.34 and 2 Cor. 6.17d.

1. On the basis of promise formula, and identifying who is referred to as subject and object, the survey below narrows the passages to Mic. 4.6; Zeph. 3.19, 20; Jer. 23.3; Ezek. 11.17; 20.34, 41; Zech. 10.8, 10.

2. Heinrici (*Der zweite Brief an die Korinther*, p. 243) writes, '... κἀγὼ εἰσδέξ. ὑμ. [bezieht sich] auf die Aufnahme zur Kindschaft, s. V. 18. Es ist dem ἐξέλθατε correlat; die Ausgezogenen will Gott aufnehmen in sein Vaterhaus. . . '. Similarly, Betz ('Anti-Pauline Fragment', p. 97) argues that the community (though God's temple and people on earth) will only be his sons and daughters in heaven. However, such a perspective is hardly consistent with return theology (see discussion below on the fourth quotation and Isa. 43.6; 49.22; and 60.4). Another who takes the heavenly reception view is Windisch, *Der zweite Korintherbrief*, p. 217.

The only substantial evidence in favor of the eternal perspective is the mention

church,[1] or (3) salvation[2] (that is, an entirely metaphysical-soteriological reception, but in the present). The heavenly reception view may be rejected, since the context focuses on a present, not a future, reception.[3] Choosing between the other two views, however, is more difficult; both find some support. There is clear emphasis on the communal temple (6.16b); yet the formation of the covenant bond (6.16c)[4] and the series of strong contrasts[5] (and if read within the present context)[6] places the reception on a soteriological level. Perhaps the best solution is to see the reception as taking place in communal worship, but with strong salvific implications.

New covenant and second exodus/return theology. The LXX uses εἰσδέχομαι 19 times, always in translating קבץ. Of those, the expression occurs 14 times in the prophets, 9 of which are specifically in a *promise formula* with Yahweh as the subject and remnant Israel as the object—that is, in a form which would correspond to 2 Cor. 6.17d. These nine may be listed as follows:

> Mic. 4.6, 'In that day . . . *I will gather* the outcasts [the remnant of v. 7] . . . '
>
> Zeph. 3.19, '*I will receive* her who was rejected [MT: those who grieve about the appointed feasts] . . . '

of μερίς (6.15b), which has eschatological inheritance overtones. As Windisch (*Der zweite Korintherbrief*, p. 214) notes, 'der Anteil [μερίς], die Gemeinschaft bezieht sich entweder aus das Zusammenleben in diesem Äon 1 Kor 5,9-13, order aus das eschatologische Geschick Kol 1,12 Lk 12,46'. However, the present aspect of the 'temple of God' assertion brings these passages into the present.

1. Appealing to the present tense in 6.16b and 7.1, Klöpper (*Das zweite Sendschreiben an die Gemeinde zu Korinth*, p. 349) notes the realized nature of these promises: 'keine lediglich in die Zukunft weisenden mehr, sondern bereits principiell realisirte'. Unfortunately, he does not differentiate further.

2. Meyer, *Epistles to the Corinthians*, pp. 554, 556; cf. Harris ('2 Corinthians', p. 360) who appears to take this view.

3. E.g., the communal temple is a present reality: ἡμεῖς ναὸς θεοῦ ἐσμεν [νῦν] ζῶντος (v. 16). Also, ἐξέλθατε ἐκ μέσου αὐτῶν (6.17a; cf. 6.14a) is calling for present action.

4. The covenant-formula (6.16c) is inferentially related to the leaving Babylon quotation (6.18a-c), which may imply that the establishment of the bond is in view. Also, if quotations 3 and 4 are fused (as argued below), the idea of being received as sons and daughters sounds highly soteriological.

5. Cf. especially the contrast of believer vs. unbeliever (6.15b).

6. Cf. 6.1-2.

Zeph. 3.20, 'at that time when *I will receive you* . . . '

Jer. 23.3, 'then *I Myself will gather the remnant of My people* [MT: My flock] out of all of the countries. . . '

Ezek. 11.17, '*I will receive them* [MT: you] from among the heathen. . . '

Ezek. 20.34, 'I will bring you out from the peoples, and *I will gather you* from the lands where you were scattered. . . '

Ezek. 20.41, 'I will accept you with/as a soothing aroma, when I bring you out from the nations, and *I will gather/receive you* out of the lands where you were dispersed;. . . '

Zech. 10.8, 'I will make a sign to them, and *I will gather them* in; for I will redeem them, and they will be multiplied according to their number before. . . '

Zech. 10.10, 'And I will bring them again from the land of Egypt, and *I will gather them* in from among the Assyrians; and I will bring them into the land of Gilead and to Lebanon; and there shall not even one of them be left behind.'

From these passages, it is evident that the use of the same term in the catena's third quotation explicitly conveys return theology, for Yahweh promises to receive his people upon their pilgrimage to Jerusalem. And, in the passages cited, Yahweh's reception/gathering of his people is clearly rooted in the pattern of return from Babylon—a pattern of second/new exodus.[1]

To reinforce this point, several additional features common to the background of the 'I will gather/receive you' passages may be brought forward. At least three predominant themes provide the setting for this promise from Yahweh: (1) an eschatological/promise perspective; (2) a cultic or worship regathering of the remnant, and (3) a new covenant framework. Although all three elements are not present in every context, the chart below demonstrates that they are frequently woven together.

---

1. The pattern of a new exodus is reinforced through reminiscent terminology or events: shame turned into renown and praise (Zeph. 3.20; cf. Deut. 26.18-19) and judgment on the nations immediately before regathering (Jer. 23.2; cf. Exod. 32.34; Ezek. 20.28, 36) recalls the first exodus (making the historical parallels explicit).

Text	Eschatological	Cultic Regathering	New Covenant
Mic. 4.6	'the last days' (4.1) 'in that day'(4.6)	'house of the Lord' (4.1) 'Come let us go up to. . . to the house of God (4.2)	'the Lord will reign. . . in Mount Zion' (4.7)[1] 'the former dominion will come. . . (4.8)[2]
Zeph. 3.19	'in that day' (3.16)[3]	'my worshipers . . .will bring My offerings' (3.10)[4]	'the King of Israel . . . is in your midst' (3.15; cf. 3.17)[5]
Zeph. 3.20	'at that time' (3.20)		
Jer. 23.3	'days are coming' (23.5)		'I shall raise up for David a righteous branch' (23.5) 'He will be called "the Lord our righteous−ness"' (23.6)[6]
Ezek. 11.17	'I *will* gather you'(11.17)[7]		'I will give them one heart, and will put a new spirit within you. And I shall take the heart of stone out of their flesh. . . ' (11.19)[8]

1. Cf. Jer. 33.20-26 which relates this as one of the elements of the new covenant.

2. Cf. Zech. 9.10 in which one of the elements related to the '(new?) covenant' (9.11) is the reign of 'the king' (9.9) whose 'dominion will be from sea to sea'.

3. Cf. 'the day when I rise up to the prey' (Zeph. 3.8).

4. Cf. 'all of them may call on the name of the Lord to serve Him' (Zech. 3.9).

5. One dimension of the 'covenant of peace' and 'everlasting covenant' described in Ezek. 37.24-28 is that Israel would be united under one Davidic King and Yahweh would place his sanctuary 'in their midst forever' (37.26; cf. 37.28).

6. Jeremiah brings both the 'branch of David' and name 'the Lord our righteousness' into new covenant (Jer. 33.14-22; cf. Isa. 9.7).

7. The eschatological context of Ezek. 11.14-21 is seen in the response to the question raised in 11.13, 'Alas, Lord God! Will you bring the remnant to a complete

Ezek. 20.34	'I *will* gather you' (20.34)	'on My holy mountain. . . I will accept them, and there I will seek your. . . gifts'(20.40)	'I will bring you into the bond of the covenant' (20.37)[1]
Ezek. 20.41	'When I. . . gather you from the land where you were scattered' (20.41)	'soothing aroma' (20.41)[2]	
Zech. 10.8	'The people wander like sheep (10.2). . . I *will* gather them together' (10.8)		'And they will be as numerous as they were before' (10.8)[3]
Zech. 10.10	'I *will* gather them. . . until no [room] can be found for them' (10.10)[4]		'And I will bring them into the land of Gilead' (10.10)[5]

end?' In response to that question of complete future elimination, Ezekiel receives the word of the Lord promising a future assembling of the scattered people, only this time with a new heart and spirit.

8.   The new heart and spirit is one of the more central aspects of the new covenant which Ezekiel later develops in 36.26-27 (cf. Jer. 32.39).

1.   In Ezek. 20.37 Yahweh is sifting the people, after which he will impose covenant obligations on those who 'pass under the rod'; this is the *future* counterpart of the past laws imparted at Sinai (cf. Greenberg, *Ezekiel, 1-20*, p. 373).

2.   In contrast to the vexatious offerings of v. 28, the eschatological gathering will approach Yahweh by means of sacrificial offerings properly made. Thus a central purpose of the future gathering is for worship.

3.   This parallel promise of making the people as numerous as they were before contains a definite allusion to new covenant promises of Jer. 33.22, 'so I will multiply the descendants of David my servant', and Ezek. 36.11, 'and I will multiply on you man and beast;. . . and I will cause you to be inhabited as you were formerly', extending previous promises.

4.   Zechariah's bringing the lost sheep of Israel back to pasture in the hill country of Gilead is a metaphor which Jeremiah had used at an earlier date in a context of Israel coming to join themselves to God in an 'everlasting covenant' (Jer. 50.5, 19).

5.   The LXX has καὶ οὐ μὴ ὑπολειφῇ ἐξ αὐτῶν οὐδὲ εἷς, 'and not even one of

These three composite motifs sustain our traditions hypothesis as well as demonstrating the close correspondence between the catena and its shell. The Old Testament worship/cultic setting of the reception and its eschatological-promise formula (2 Cor. 6.17d) merges well with new temple (2 Cor. 6.16b) and promise focus (2 Cor. 7.1) of the outer shell.

Quotation 4: 2 Samuel 7.14 Cited; with Influence from Isaiah 43.6 (cf. 49.22; 60.4)

MT:

(2 Sam. 7.14) אֲנִי אֶהְיֶה־לּוֹ לְאָב וְהוּא יִהְיֶה־לִּי לְבֵן

(Isa. 43.6) הָבִיאִי בָנַי מֵרָחוֹק וּבְנוֹתַי מִקְצֵה הָאָרֶץ

(Isa. 49.22) וְהֵבִיאוּ בָנַיִךְ בְּחֹצֶן וּבְנֹתַיִךְ עַל־כָּתֵף תִּנָּשֶׂאנָה

(Isa. 60.4) בָּנַיִךְ מֵרָחוֹק יָבֹאוּ וּבְנֹתַיִךְ עַל־צַד תֵּאָמַנָה

(Jer. 31.9) כִּי־הָיִיתִי לְיִשְׂרָאֵל לְאָב וְאֶפְרַיִם בְּכֹרִי הוּא

(Hos. 2.1 [ET 1.10]) וְהָיָה בִּמְקוֹם אֲשֶׁר־יֵאָמֵר לָהֶם לֹא־עַמִּי אַתֶּם יֵאָמֵר לָהֶם בְּנֵי אֵל־הָי

LXX:

ἐγὼ ἔσομαι αὐτῷ εἰς πατέρα, καὶ αὐτὸς ἔσται μοι εἰς υἱόν·	(2 Sam. 7.14)
ἄγε τοὺς υἱοῦς μου ἀπὸ γῆς πόρρωθεν καὶ τὰς θυγατέρας μου ἀπ᾽ ἄκρων τῆς γῆς	(Isa. 43.6)
καὶ ἄξουσιν τοὺς υἱούς σου ἐν κόλπῳ, τὰς δὲ θυγατέρας σου ἐπ᾽ ὤμων ἀροῦσιν	(Isa. 49.22)
ἰδοὺ ἥκασιν πάντες οἱ υἱοὶ σου μακρόθεν, καὶ αἱ θυγατέρες σου ἐπ᾽ ὤμων ἀρθήσονται	(Isa. 60.4)
ὅτι ἐγενόμην τῷ Ισραηλ εἰς πατέρα, καὶ Εφραιμ πρωτότοκός μού ἐστιν	(Jer. 38[31].9)
καὶ ἔσται ἐν τῷ τόπῳ οὗ ἐρρέθη αὐτοῖς, οὐ λαός μου ὑμεῖς, ἐκεῖ κληθήσονται υἱοὶ θεοῦ ζῶντος	(Hos. 1.10)

them will be left behind' (Zech. 10.10d), indicating a future gathering back to the land which will not leave any of the scattered people behind in the foreign countries (cf. Isa. 49.19-20).

NT: καὶ ἔσομαι ὑμῖν εἰς πατέρα, (2 Cor. 6.18)
καὶ ὑμεῖς ἔσεσθέ μοι εἰς υἱοὺς καὶ
θυγατέρας

Source, form and redaction analysis. Most scholars view the fourth quotation as coming *primarily* from 2 Sam. 7.14, and with this I agree.[1] However, there are four major changes to the Old Testament text:[2] (1) the New Testament has added the conjunction καί; (2) ἐγώ from the LXX has been omitted; (3) the third person singular, αὐτὸς ἔσται μοι εἰς υἱόν (cf. MT), has been changed to second person plural, ὑμεῖς ἔσεσθέ μοι εἰς υἱούς, and (4) the New Testament has added καὶ θυγατέρας.

Alterations (1) and (2) can be explained as formal or stylistic changes in order to fit the quotation into the sequence. From this perspective, the added καί serves as the common connective which has been used before each verbal statement in the catena. And, the omission of the ἐγώ (or, more probably, its relocation)[3] is due to κἀγώ beginning the third quotation.

The third redactional change (3) is likely to have happened for grammatical and theological reasons. The change from singular to plural is needed in order to maintain the catena's address to a community, not an individual.[4] Yet a more pressing question is what hermeneutical and theological axioms would explain the change as a legitimate alteration? Donald Juel identifies this kind of alteration as a 'democratization' of messianic promises—that which applied to the Israelite king and, ultimately, to the Messiah in the Davidic covenant

1. That the composer had in mind 2 Sam. 7.14 (despite major alterations) is favored by the closing formula, λέγει κύριος παντοκράτωρ, which parallels exactly LXX 2 Sam. 7.8.
2. The LXX 2 Sam. 7.14 follows the MT exactly.
3. See discussion above on the third quotation.
4. Martin (2 *Corinthians*, p. 206) likewise points out that the change is needed 'to keep consistency with respect to the subject of the community of believers as a whole and to enforce the paraenetic call to his readers'. Each of the earlier three quotations are addressed to the community. However, as a motivation, this alone is weak, for the composer was reluctant to make contextual 'smoothings' to the third person of the first quotation, and it still does not explain the radical theological implications in the change.

is broadened to include the entire community.[1] Juel's observation hints at a solution in the direction of ἐν Χριστῷ. If a Christian setting for the fragment is appropriate, it may be argued that the believing community now resides ἐν Χριστῷ and thus the community becomes the recipient of the promises about the Messiah.[2]

Or, to put it another way, the democratization of 2 Sam. 7.14 represents a re-reading of the Davidic covenant *in light of the community-oriented new covenant*.[3] The prophets' close interfacing of the two covenants has already laid the groundwork for viewing 2 Sam. 7.14 through the new covenant in a nationalized sense (as the most interesting predecessor see esp., Isa. 55.3-5;[4] cf. Jer. 30.9; Ezek.

1. Juel, *Messianic Exegesis*, p. 108. For another example, Juel cites 1 Pet. 4.13-14 as a democratization of the messianic promise of Isa. 11.2, 'And the Spirit of the Lord shall rest upon him'.

2. Certainly this is a well-known construct within Pauline thought. Cf. ἐν Χριστῷ in 2 Cor. 5.17, 19, 21 (and especially the wordplay in 1.21 between εἰς Χριστόν and χρίσας which at least expands messianic identity to the apostolic community, if not also to the readers). Barrett (*Second Epistle to the Corinthians*, p. 201) likewise appeals to the theological premise that 'the promise of 2 Sam. 7.14 was originally addressed to the king; the king is Jesus, and *in him* men and women participate in his status before God' (my emphasis). Similarly, Windisch (*Der Zweite Korintherbrief*, p. 217) acknowledges a possible Christological perspective, 'V. 18 ist in seinen zwei ersten Zeilen dem bekannten Spruch über den Davidssohn entnommen. . . doch von diesem [2 Sam. 7.14] aus die Christen insgesamt (οἱ τοῦ Χριστοῦ) übertragen: der Sohn hat die Erlösten zu Miterben und Söhnen Gottes gemacht Röm 8,17 Gal 4,7 Hebr 2, 10'; however, later he suggests possible OT influences. Cf. Derrett ('2 Cor. 6,14ff. a Midrash', p. 246) who suggests, 'Co-heirs with Jesus are precisely co-heirs to the promises'.

3. Similarly, Ellis (*Paul's Use of the Old Testament*, pp. 135-39) views the pluralization of 2 Sam. 7.14 here under the category of new covenant exegesis and the related presupposition of solidarity.

4. Isa. 55.3-5 is a much debated passage. Most OT scholars understand the text to be saying that the promises made to David have been *completely transferred* to the nation as a whole (as though replacing the king as the recipient of Nathan's prophecy). For example, von Rad (*Old Testament Theology*, II, p. 240), who sees no messianic hope in second Isaiah, understands the prophet to be boldly reinterpreting (democratizing) the promises to David, so that now the nation Israel, instead of a new David, becomes the sovereign ruler (נגיד) of the peoples. Similarly, Eissfeldt ('The Promises of Grace to David in Isaiah 55.1-5', pp. 196-207) argues that second Isaiah has radically altered the (shared) traditions of Psalm 89—Israel, not the Davidic dynasty, fulfills the promise of rule and mission in the world. Along

3. *The Content of the Fragment*

34.23-24; 37.24-28). Also, in the two passages cited most frequently for comparison with 2 Sam. 7.14 (Jer. 31.9[1] and Hos. 1.10[2.1][2]), similar father-son sentiments are expressed in a nationalized form (but without any clear recall of 2 Sam. 7.14, and without royal connotations). Later intertestamental[3] and other New Testament[4] writers con-

---

the same lines, Volz (*Jesaia II,* p. 139) notes, 'Das Bemerkenswerte unserer Stelle ist vielmehr, dass die Davidsverweissagung auf das Volk Israel übertragen wird'. Cf. Anderson, 'Exodus and Covenant in Second Isaiah', pp. 339-60; Whybray, *Isaiah 40–66,* p. 192; Sanders, 'Isaiah 55.1-9', p. 293; Westermann, *Isaiah 40–66,* p. 283; Conrad, 'The Community as King in Second Isaiah', pp. 99-111).

However, that the nation has *replaced* the king as a recipient of Davidic promises goes somewhat beyond the text of Isa. 55.3-5. Here, the promises made to David, and David himself, become the model (or recurring pattern) for what Yahweh will also accomplish through the nation. The (new) בְּרִית עוֹלָם with the nation is fashioned in such a way to effect the fulfillment of the Davidic promises. The king and nation are already closely linked (e.g., 1 Kgs 9.6-7; Ps. 144), rule by the nation was needed in order to fulfill the aspect of universal rule in the Davidic covenant anyway (Pss. 2.8-9; 72.8-11; 89.25), and the leadership of restored Israel under a new David is a pervasive tradition (e.g., Jer. 30.9; Hos. 3.5). Therefore, it seems quite plausible that the prophetic text has an integration, rather than a replacement formula in view.

Nonetheless, it would be fair to assert that formulation of the new covenant has raised the implied national elements of the Davidic covenant to *a new explicit level.* What is significant for our hypothesis is exactly this point. Already in Isaiah the Davidic promises are becoming re-understood (i.e., more explicitly understood relative to the people without a king) through the nationalizing perspective of the new covenant. Thus the terms 'democratization' and 'nationalization' of the Davidic promise will be used in a *limited* sense in this work—implying not replacement of the Davidic king, but an expansion of clearly Davidic promises to a national level (through new covenant theology). The new covenant brought about a realization of the national import of the older Davidic traditions. For further discussion of Isa. 55.3-5 see comments on Rev. 21.7 below (where, possibly, it is the perspective of Isa. 55.1-5 which spurs another democratization of 2 Sam. 7.14).

1. See Lategan, 'Moenie met Ongelowiges', p. 22.

2. A number of commentators add Hos. 1.10(2.1) for comparison with 2 Sam. 7.14. See Héring, *Second Epistle to the Corinthians,* p. 51; Hughes, *Second Epistle to the Corinthians,* p. 256.

3. E.g., *Jub.* 1.22-25; Tob. 13.3-5; cf. *T. Jud.* 24.1-6 (?). For the only clear example of intertestamental democratization of 2 Sam. 7.14, see *Jub.* 1.24-25 where Yahweh promises: 'And I shall be a father to them, and they will be sons to me; and they will all be called "sons of the living God"'. At least on a formal level, one may speculate on the midrashic *Stichwort* influence of Hos. 1.10-11 in the

tinued to democratize 2 Sam. 7.14, usually in a context of eschatological promise (although the precise motivation is not always clear).

The fourth alteration (4) has been explained in at least two different ways. One explanation, held by a number of scholars,[1] suggests that καὶ θυγατέρας was added by Paul in order to raise women to a place of equality with men. Although such a solution is feasible within the framework of Pauline thought, for two reasons it fails to serve as an adequate motivation. First, it incorrectly implies that here, as in Pauline usage, υἱούς alone would not have been understood in a generic sense.[2] Second, there is no contextual support for the status of women being an issue either within the larger fragment, 6.14–7.1, or within its present literary setting of 2 Cor. 2.14–7.4. A convincing

democratization process. However, as with Tob. 13.3-5 (where the complete father-son formula does not appear) the theological presuppositions for the nationalization of the Davidic promise are not clear.

At Qumran, *4QFlor* 1.11 likewise contains the father-son formula, but with a traditional messianic interpretation (and in a non-democratized form). Similarly, the Targumim on 1 Chron. 17.13 retains an individual perspective, although with a more familial sense, 'I will love him as a father loves a son, and he will love me as a son loves his father'. For further discussion of the Targumim on 2 Sam. 7 and 1 Chron. 17 see Juel, *Messiah and Temple*, pp. 182-92.

4. In Rev. 21.7 the author of the apocalypse also alludes to 2 Sam. 7.14: καὶ ἔσομαι αὐτῷ θεὸς καὶ αὐτὸς ἔσται μοι υἱός. His text follows the order of the LXX, but differs in wording with the omission of ἐγώ, and the substitutions of predicate nominatives for εἰς plus the accusative, and θεός for πατέρα. Although its form is not plural, ὁ νικῶν κληρονομήσει (21.7) indicates a democratized understanding of the Davidic promise (cf. Charles, *The Revelation of St. John*, II, p. 215). It seems possible (as suggested above for the catena's fourth quotation, 2 Cor. 6.18) that the democratization process in Rev. 21.7 was due, at least in part, to an ideological influence of Isa. 55.1-5. An allusion to Isa. 55.1 comes directly before the democratizated quotation (Rev. 21.6).

1. E.g., Plummer, *II Corinthians*, p. 210; Barrett, *Second Epistle to the Corinthians*, p. 201; Héring, *Second Epistle of Saint Paul to the Corinthians*, p. 51; Martin, *2 Corinthians*, p. 207; Lambrecht, 'The Fragment 2 Cor. VI 14–VII 1', p. 155 n. 29; Rensberger, '2 Corinthians 6.14–7.1', p. 38.

2. Barrett (*Second Epistle to the Corinthians*, p. 201) explicitly states, 'in Christ *men* became sons of God (Gal. 3.16; cf. 4.6; Rom. 8.15)' (my emphasis) in contrast to the inclusion of women here with καὶ θυγατέρας. But this approach classifies υἱούς in a gender-oriented, non-generic category. That this is not the case can be demonstrated contextually, since in the passages quoted (Gal. 3.16; cf. 4.6; Rom. 8.15) υἱούς refers to the entire believing community (both men and women).

hypothesis along these lines should find some basis for the redaction within the immediate 'fragment' context.

A more feasible explanation is that καὶ θυγατέρας has been added from Isa. 43.6 (cf. Isa. 56.5; 60.4).[1] Most commentators explain this redaction simply from the use of υἱούς and θυγατέρας in these Isaiah passages. However, there is a much stronger conceptual-contextual argument. The editorial καὶ θυγατέρας demonstrates the influence of the previous two quotations on the fourth. Such a closer-to-home motivation is apparent from several pieces of evidence. First, influence from the previous quotations is already hinted at by the formal fusion of quotations three and four (i.e., κἀγώ). Second, by virtue of its relationship to quotations two and three alone (even without the added καὶ θυγατέρας),[2] quotation four is 'colored' by return theology. The promise(s) of being received as sons and daughters is contingent upon the readers' obedience to Isa. 52.11, 'ἐξέλθατε... '. Third (and most importantly), the Old Testament texts themselves which contain the receiving-sons-and-daughters traditions (Isa. 43.6; 49.22; 60.4) tie in conceptually with the previous two quotations.[3] For example, in Isa. 43.6 Yahweh promises that in the upcoming return his 'sons' and 'daughters' will be brought back to Zion from the ends of the earth—aligning precisely with the return theology of Isa. 52.11 and Ezek. 20.34, 41 *et al.*[4] Therefore, there

---

1. Those who hold to the direct influence of Isa. 43.6 are: Schlatter, *Paulus Der Bote Jesu*, p. 579; Hughes, *Second Epistle to the Corinthians*, p. 256; Héring, *Second Epistle of Saint Paul to the Corinthians*, p. 51; Bonsirven, *Exégèse rabbinique et Exégèse paulinienne*, p. 333; Allo, *Seconde Épître aux Corinthiens*, p. 186; Lietzmann, *Korinther I & II*, p. 129; Belser, *Der zweite Brief des Apostels Paulus an die Korinther*, p. 212; Bruce, *1 and 2 Corinthians*, p. 215; Cornely, *Epistolae ad Corinthios*, p. 190; Godet, *Seconde Épître aux Corinthiens*, p. 215; Furnish, *II Corinthians*, p. 364. Klauck (2 *Korintherbrief*, p. 62) likewise notes the influence of return theology: the fourth quotation blends the prophecy of Nathan with 'der prophetischen Vision der Heimholung Israels'.

2. The relationship to quotation two is shaped through a couple of factors: first, fusion with quotation three, and second, quotation four's function within the catena as a promise contingent upon 'coming out'.

3. In addition to conceptual affinities, note also the promise-formula in Isa. 43.5-6, ' [Yahweh] will bring your offspring from the east, and gather you from the west; I will say to the north, "Give them up!" and to the south, "Do not hold them back; bring my sons from far away, and my daughters from the ends of the earth. . . " '

4. Similarly, in Isa. 49.22 Yahweh signals the nations who respond by carrying

exists good contextual motivation (on a conceptual level) for the addition of καὶ θυγατέρας.

In sum, the fourth quotation extends the new exodus and reception idea (from quotations 2 and 3) to form a composite picture: not only of leaving Babylon (quotation 2) and being received by Yahweh (quotation 3), but a jubilant reception of being embraced as his children, sons and daughters of Zion (quotation 4).[1] In essence, the fourth quotation completes the image. Furthermore, the democratized form of the fourth quotation evidences the use of new covenant ideology in the re-understanding (though not replacement) of older Davidic traditions—a move already begun in the prophets.

New covenant and second exodus/return theology. Much of the theology of quotation 4 has been surfaced through the redactional study above. The objective here is not to argue that the final quotation is a new covenant promise. Obviously, it is not. However, from the discussion of the editorial changes made to 2 Sam. 7.14 (the fusion with quotation three, democratization of the promise, and addition of καὶ θυγατέρας), it seems certain that this Davidic promise has been reinterpreted through the grid of new covenant and return theology.

---

his people, sons and daughters of Zion, back to their homeland. Again, in Isa. 60.4 those in Jerusalem are told to 'lift their eyes' and see the train of people, her sons and daughters, as they return to Zion (cf. 56.5)—they will be carried from afar. Cf. in personified form, Zechariah's call to escape from the daughter of Babylon and join the daughter of Zion (2.7, 10; note the temple-dwelling promise in v. 10). One should also note the heavy emphasis on return motifs in other OT father-son passages (e.g., Isa. 63.8, 16; Jer. 3.19; 31.7-9; Hos. 1.10-11; 11.10-11), although in these passages there is no mention of daughters and no explicit democratization of the 2 Sam. 7.14 text. Cf. Bar. 4.14-16. Interestingly, the democratized forms of 2 Sam. 7.14 in Tob. 13.3-5 and *Jub.* 1.22-25 (cf. 1.12) display a strong correlation with the return. For instance, in Tob. 13.3-5 Yahweh, as a chastening father, scattered Israel, but in his mercy he will regather them.

1. To fill in the rest of the picture with the first two quotations, the new temple dwelling of Yahweh amongst his people and maintenance of the covenant relationship (quotation 1) require a holy people (quotation 2). Grosheide (*De tweede Brief ann de Kerk te Korinthe*, p. 192) captures the transition between quotations 1 and 2 rather well: 'De inwoning Gods is de heerlijkheid van het volk, maar vraagt ook heiligheid van het volk'.

3. *The Outer Shell of the Fragment (2 Corinthians 6.14-16b; 7.1)*

My next task is to investigate the 'outer shell' of the fragment—the five rhetorical contrasts (6.14-16b) and closing exhortation (7.1)—in order to determine their relationship to new covenant and exilic return traditions. Anyone examining these verses should acknowledge at the outset the less objective nature of the investigation (by comparison with the Old Testament quotations), due to their lack of explicit Old Testament material, terse rhetorical style and lexical ambiguity. With this in mind, the following analysis of the rhetorical contrasts moves from the most decisive data to the least.

The (New) Temple versus Idols
The final contrast provides the strongest support for my thesis.[1] Whether or not one views the referent to εἴδωλον here as literal, metonymical, or metaphorical,[2] it cannot be disputed that departure from the idols of Babylon and a return to Yahweh's new temple lay at the core the prophets' new covenant/return message (e.g., Ezek. 36.16-28; 37.21-28).[3] The promises of regathering,[4] a new heart,[5] and a covenant bond (your God-my people)[6] are all directly associated with forsaking idolatry. Egypt[7] and Babylon[8] become paradigms for

---

1. And, if the fragment is moving towards clarification with the successive rhetorical questions, the last one may well depict most clearly the direction of thought.

2. These options will be addressed in Appendix B.

3. For a thorough discussion of the new eschatological temple see McKelvey, *The New Temple*, pp. 9-24. McKelvey notes that after God's judgment a remnant would grow (Isa. 4.2-4; Jer. 23.5-8), the outcasts of Israel would be gathered home (Isa. 11.11-16; 27.13; Jer. 31.6-22; Ezek. 20.40-44; 34.11-16) and the temple would be restored and become the center not only of Israel but of the nations (Isa. 2.2-4; Mic. 4.1-3; Jer. 3.17-18). In both Isaiah and Ezekiel the new temple extends to include Gentiles. Cf. Isa. 60.4-5, 7; 56.6-8; and 66.18-21 where creation of the new temple is related to the new heavens and new earth. For a treatment of the Christian community as the [new] temple not made with hands in Marcan material and its relationship to Judaism, see Juel, *Messiah and Temple*, esp. pp. 159-209.

4. E.g., Ezek. 36.18, 25.

5. E.g., Ezek. 18.30-31 (cf. 18.6, 12, 15); 36.25-26.

6. E.g., Ezek. 36.25-28; 37.23.

7. E.g., Ezek. 30.13 (cf. 23.7, 30, 37); Isa. 19.1-25.

8. E.g., Ezek. 21.21; Jer. 50.2, 38; 51.47, 52.

idol worship, so that those who journey back to Jerusalem must leave their idols behind.[1] Ultimately, the point of the pilgrimage back to Jerusalem was to worship Yahweh in the new eschatological temple.[2]

Covenant Vocabulary—μετοχή, κοινωνία, συμφώνησις, μερίς, *and* συγκατάθεσις

A lexical study of the five linking words in the rhetorical chain by no means identifies them as 'technical' covenant terms.[3] However, within their semantic fields, each at times is used to depict the close, covenantal relationship between God and his people or between two people—κοινωνία,[4] συμφώνησις,[5] συγκατάθεσις,[6] μετοχή,[7] and

1. The new exodus return to Jerusalem leaves the idols behind (Isa. 42.17). Similarly, the casting away of idols is connected with the old exodus from Egypt (Ezek. 20.7, 30, 37). In the litigation speeches of Isaiah the prediction of Yahweh's new thing is designed to silence the idols (Isa. 44.10; 45.20-25; 48.3-5).

2. The eschatological temple is the center of worship to which both Israel and the nations stream in holy pilgrimage (Isa. 2.2-4; 56.6-8; 60.4-5, 7; 66.18-21; Mic. 4.1-3; Jer. 3.17-18). For a detailed development of new temple expectations see McKelvey, *The New Temple*, pp. 1-23. On pilgrimage and procession as two forgotten themes of the return, see Merrill, 'Pilgrimage and Procession: Motifs of Israel's Return', pp. 261-72.

3. That is, 'technical' in the sense that their semantic fields are very narrow and *only* applied to covenant ideas.

4. κοινωνία, for example, is a favorite expression for the marital bond as the most intimate relationship between human beings (e.g., 2 Macc. 14.25; *3 Macc.* 4.6; Josephus, *Ant.* 1.304; cf. BAGD, p. 438). In this vein, LXX Mal. 3.14 correlates treachery in marriage covenants (... καὶ αὕτη κοινωνός σου, καὶ γυνὴ διαθήκης σου) with treacherous treatment by the people in their covenantal relationship with Yahweh (cf. Mal. 2.10, 15; cf. 3.1). Also, κοινωνός and κοινωνέω are used for entering into fellowship with the gods of the high places (LXX 4 Kgdms 17.11), and of business alliances between two kings (LXX 2 Chron. 20.35). Cf. Currie ('Koinonia in Christian Literature to 200 AD', pp. 1-58, 239-40) who concludes that Paul uses κοινωνία as part of his new covenant vocabulary, expressing an 'in Christ' alliance (though Currie does not comment on 2 Cor. 6.14–7.1, since he holds the fragment to be non-Pauline).

5. συμφώνησις is used to denote '[mutual] agreement', usually between two persons (BAGD, p. 781; Louw and Nida, *Lexicon*, I, p. 368). At times, the musical connotation predominates (e.g., σύμφωνια in Lk. 15.25). The term is often used, however, of some kind of written contract or verbal agreement. E.g., in the papyri, συμφώνησις and σύμφωνος are often used of settling accounts or of written business agreements, συμφώνου γράμματος (Moulton and Milligan, *Vocabulary*

less directly μερίς.[1] One might also note that several of the words or

of the Greek Testament, p. 599). Similarly, in Mt. 20.2, 13 the landowner makes a verbal agreement with the laborers for a denarius a day. Compare the well defined agreements between husband and wife for conjugal abstinence (1 Cor. 7.5) or for withholding property (Acts 5.9), and, with theological overtones, the agreements between believers which are bound/loosed in heaven (Mt. 18.18-19). Again, in the LXX συμφώνησις and its various forms are used of military alliances (Gen. 14.3; cf. Isa. 7.2, συνεφώνησαν Ἀρὰμ πρὸς τὸν Ἐφραΐμ) and of the one who keeps Torah (*4 Macc.* 7.7, σύμφωνε νόμου stands opposed to ἐκοινώνησις μειροφαγίᾳ).

6. συγκατάθεσις conveys the idea of 'agreement' or 'union with consent' (BAGD, p. 773; Louw and Nida, *Lexicon*, I, p. 368). It is often used of entering into a 'pact' or 'agreement' with a group, of joining/uniting for a common cause— e.g., Lk. 23.51 says that Joseph had not joined in the agreement with the council to bring harm to Jesus (οὗτος οὐκ ἦν συγκατατεθειμένος τῇ βουλῇ καὶ τῇ πράξει αὐτῶν). Similarly, LXX Exod. 23.1 condemns joining together with others to give false witness (οὐ συγκαταθήσῃ μετὰ τοῦ ἀδίκου γενέσθαι μάρτυς ἄδικος).

Yet the agreement can be on a more formal (covenant) level. Significantly, in LXX Exod. 23.33 συγκατατίθημι is used in a prohibition against *joining in covenant* with other inhabitants (e.g., Philistines, Canaanites, etc.) and their foreign gods: οὐ συγκαταθήσῃ αὐτοῖς καὶ τοῖς θεοῖς αὐτῶν διαθήκην. Cf. the use of συντίθημι in forming a peace treaty between opposing Kings (e.g., LXX 3 Kgdms 16.28; 1 Macc. 9.70), in making military alliances with the added custom of giving of a daughter (e.g., 1 Macc. 11.9), and in confirming a previously made covenant with the accompaniment of gifts (e.g., between Antiochus and Simon in 1 Macc. 15.27; cf. *4 Macc.* 4.16).

7. μετοχή here has the idea of 'partnership'—a relationship involving shared purposes and activities (Louw and Nida, *Lexicon*, I, p. 447). Usually μετοχή is with other human beings; yet in some cases the human relations have a direct bearing on one's relationship with God. μετοχή is used in LXX Ps. 121(122).3 to describe the fellowship in Jerusalem during the pilgrim feasts. By way of contrast, Ephraim violates her covenant with Yahweh by joining herself to the Canaanite idols (μέτοχος εἰδώλων) and committing adultery in the high places (LXX Hos. 4.17).

1. While μερίς means 'part [of a whole]', it often denotes a 'share' or 'portion' with the idea of inheritance (BAGD, p. 505). Frequently μερίς and its other forms are used this way (of earthly inheritance in Lk. 12.13; of present spiritual allotments in 1 Cor. 7.17; Heb. 2.4; and of eschatological inheritance, i.e., reward/judgment in Mt. 24.51; Lk. 12.46; Rev. 20.6; 21.8; 22.19). The lot of those who serve idols is often contrasted with the lot of those who serve Yahweh (e.g., LXX Isa. 17.14; 57.6, Jer. 10.16; 13.25; 28(51).18-19). The clearest Pauline use of μερίς for theological inheritance is found in Col. 1.12, εἰς τὴν μερίδα τοῦ κλήρου τῶν ἁγίων ἐν τῷ φωτί (notice the similar light/darkness imagery; cf. *1QS* 11.7). μερίς, then, does not

their cognates are used in this manner within the Pauline corpus.[1] Therefore, when understood in the context of the fragment which clearly articulates the new covenant bond, ἔσομαι αὐτῶν θεός... , and which recalls the (democratized) Davidic covenant formula, ἔσομαι ὑμῖν εἰς πατέρα... , it appears quite certain that these five rhetorical contrasts, whatever the activity to which they refer,[2] portray some kind of *serious violation of the covenant bond between God and his people*. This rhetorical[3] series of questions *implies* that God has already established a partnership, a fellowship, an agreement, a union, and inheritance expectations with the readers of the fragment.

At this point Beale's traditions work encounters some difficulty. He suggests that the five linking words (2 Cor. 6.14b-16a) can be incorporated into an 'Old Testament restoration' grid by characterizing the peaceful conditions and lack of hostility which would exist between God and his people upon their return from an estranged land.[4] While a peaceful/restored relationship would no doubt exist, a 'return' orientation to the the linking terminology appears forced. A more feasible approach would be to explain the linking words as having a *direct* affinity with Old Testament covenant traditions (especially with the covenant formulas in the catena) and then develop the close proximity between new covenant and restoration/return traditions. Without new covenant as a prominent category, the Old Testament traditions bridge weakens considerably.

---

describe a covenant relationship directly. Rather, it depicts the result of, or the blessings derived through, the covenant.

1. For example, using words like κοινωνός, μετοχή, and μετέχω Paul aligns eating at pagan temple (1 Cor. 10.14-22), with eating and drinking in the Lord's covenant meal (1 Cor. 10.16; 11.25). The fact that the 'fellowship/sharing' (in either the pagan meal or the Lord's supper) is done on a physical level should not alter what the ritual represents: a spiritual sharing and fellowship in the (new) covenant relationship with God. Cf. Levine, *In the Presence of the Lord*, pp. 27-35; and on the anthropological approach to ritual, see Wenham, *Numbers*, pp. 25-39.

2. Cf. the focus of Appendix B.

3. Words in rhetorical texts, as Black (*Linguistics*, p. 132) points out, 'are frequently charged with rhetorical connotations that sometimes say more than their lexical denotations' (cf. the excellent treatment of rhetorical language by Nida, *Style and Discourse*, pp. 1-55, 165-75).

4. Beale, 'Old Testament Background', p. 556.

Light versus Darkness

Light and darkness are broadly used metaphors. Nevertheless, φῶς and σκότος are well suited to new covenant and return theology, especially as a feature of the *'ebed Yahweh's* new creation, light-in-darkness ministry.[1] Along these lines, Morna Hooker and C.J.A. Hickling have suggested a natural development of Isa. 9.2 and 42.6-7.[2] A similar proposal was made much earlier by A. Klöpper, although appealing to different servant passages, 'der "Knecht Jehovas" war bestimmt εἰς φῶς ἔθνων (Jes. 49,4 LXX vg. 51,4).'[3] These are hardly whimsical options in view of the new covenant/return motifs found in the Old Testament quotations. Yet such precise alignment goes beyond the data. At the very least, however, the φῶς-σκότος contrast finds a comfortable home within the theology of the catena's Old Testament material.

Righteousness versus Lawlessness

δικαιοσύνη and ἀνομία likewise are widely used terms, so an exact identification of the traditions involved is nearly impossible. It can be demonstrated, however, that δικαιοσύνη is firmly imbedded in Old Testament return theology, depicting an ethical dimension of the exiles' physical and spiritual return to God.[4] Likewise, δικαιοσύνη

1. For a detailed referencing of these OT traditions see Chapter 4, §4.

2. This suggestion was made in a seminar on 2 Corinthians in Aberdeen, August, 1975 (as reported by Thrall, 'The Problem of II Cor. VI. 14–VII. 1', p. 137 n. 5). Thrall's rationale for such a traditions link comes primarily from the fragment's verbal connection with 2 Cor. 4.1-6 (the use of Isa. 9.2 in that material). Unfortunately, such an approach is methodologically problematic, making a direct appeal to the 2 Corinthians context without analyzing the strength of the material's tradition history within the fragment itself as an isolated unit.

3. Klöpper, *Das zweite Sendschreiben an die Gemeinde zu Korinth*, p. 344.

4. Recalling the first exodus procession, this new exodus will have δικαιοσύνη at the front and Yahweh in the rear (Isa. 58.8). The people involved in the (physical and spiritual) 'return' are themselves to return in righteousness (Isa. 26.2, 9, 10; 45.13; 61.3), as is their leader (Isa. 42.6; 59.17), for the new Jerusalem towards which they are headed is a city of righteousness (Isa. 1.21, 26; 62.1-2; Jer. 4.2; cf. 32.16, 17; 61.11). This approaching day of σωτηρία is often found in poetic parallel with the δικαιοσύνη of that day (Isa. 51.5, 6, 8; 54.14; 56.1).

voices new covenant expectations.[1] Yet these observations can only be used to argue for contextual compatibility.

Believer versus Unbeliever

The ἄπιστοι-πιστοί contrast appears not to make any direct contribution to our traditions search. The primary reason for this is that ἄπιστοι is rarely used within the LXX and has not developed the Christian usage of 'unbeliever' versus 'believer'. Therefore, these expressions do not predominate the primary source material relating to return traditions. However, when New Testament writers utilize return traditions, they bring the believer/unbeliever category into focus. For example, in 2 Cor. 4.3-6 the ἄπιστοι have had their minds blinded to the glory-light gospel, a passage that draws upon new exodus/return ideas.[2] Similarly, in Rev. 21.8 it is the ἄπιστοι who do not receive the promises of a new temple and covenant fellowship with God (Rev. 21.1-7); their character is more conducive to old Babylon than to the new Jerusalem.[3]

Christ versus Beliar

Again, Χριστός and Βελιάρ are such broadly used terms it would be dangerous to build any theory upon their presence. Nonetheless, in the intertestamental literature Beliar's mission is often related to return theology—he leads people into captivity;[4] he puts stumbling blocks in the path of those who would return to God;[5] he diverts 'returning exiles' off the Isaianic highway of holiness.[6] Ultimately the return

---

1. For several examples where δικαιοσύνη expresses new covenant expectations see LXX Isa. 42.6; 54.10, 14; 56.1, 4; 59.21 (cf. 59.9, 14, 17); 61.8 (cf. 61.3, 11); Jer. 31.23. Cf. δικαίωμα in Ezek. 11.20; 36.27.

2. See Chapter 4, §4.

3. Cf. Caird (*Revelation*, p. 268), 'By their own choice Babylon and not the new Jerusalem is their eternal home'.

4. *T. Iss.* 6.1; *T. Zeb.* 9.8; cf. *T. Ben.* 7.1-2.

5. In *4QFlor* Belial is the one who puts stumbling blocks in the way of God's people, to lead astray those who follow the path of light. Cf. *1QS* 3.24; *1QH* 17.7-8, 23-24; *T. Rub.* 4.7 (see also Mt. 16.23).

6. For example, the text of *1QH* 6.20-21 alludes to Isa. 35.8; 52.1 (cf. 52.11) and the moral/spiritual return highway to God:

> You have given them commandments, O God,
> that they might have profit in their lives
> by walking in Your way of ho[liness],

from exile is accomplished through a war with Beliar in which God will free Beliar's captives and lead them back to the land.[1] Again, Χριστός has much too broad a usage to develop a traditions base. If related to the fourth quotation (2 Sam. 7.14), Χριστός *may* recall the new David. But it is at best pale, in view of its highly redacted form.

Closing Exhortation (2 Corinthians 7.1)

The final verse (7.1) concludes the entire fragment, but in a special sense it draws together the four Old Testament quotations. The mention of τὰς ἐπαγγελίας refers back to quotations 1, 3, and 4 (each with promise-formulas: 'I [Yahweh] will. . . ');[2] καθαρίσωμεν recalls ἀ-κάθαρτου from quotation 2;[3] and ἐπιτελοῦντες ἁγιωσύνην likewise draws from the imagery of quotation 2. So, naturally (without going beyond the fragment), aspects of return theology surface—those who would leave Babylon and return to the new temple should prepare themselves for the trek with cleansing and holiness. The appeal in 7.1 echoes similar ideas to those found in Isaiah's description of the roadway back to Jerusalem: 'There shall be a way of purity (ὁδὸς καθαρά), and it will be called a "highway of holiness" (ὁδὸς ἁγία); and the unclean (ἀκάθαρτος) will not travel on it, neither shall there be an unclean way (οὐδέ... ὁδὸς ἀκάθαρτος)' (LXX Isa. 35.8).[4] The prophets were concerned that

whereon the uncircumcised, the unclean, and the profane do not pass.
But they veered from the way of Your heart
and ensnared themselves in their lusts.
Belial has been counseling their hearts
[and in accord]ance with the scheme of ungodliness
they defile themselves with transgression.

1. *T. Dan.* 5.7-11.

2. As developed above, the promises referred to in quotations 1 and 3 are *new covenant* promises. Furthermore, the Davidic promise in quotation 4 has been modified through *new covenant and return ideas.*

3. Perhaps it also reflects the instruction from the MT text for the returning community to cleanse themselves (הִבָּרוּ), though the same idea could be derived conceptually from the LXX (especially with its verbal tie to ἀκαθάρτου).

4. Cf. καθαρίζω in other passages where those who returned on God's highway were to be cleansed (e.g., LXX Isa. 57.14 where they were to cleanse/purge away the stumbling blocks [of idolatry] in order to return on this highway; cf. Isa. 1.16; contrast Isa. 66.17; Jer. 13.27; Ezek. 24.13). Cf. Rev. 17.4 for a description of Babylon as ἀκαθάρτης.

those making the pilgrimage back to the new Jerusalem did so in holiness (particularly in light of Yahweh's promise to dwell in the midst of his people).[1] Again, this concern for cleansing,[2] holiness,[3] and the fear of the Lord (within the heart)[4] develops those things which the new covenant was intended to produce.

In conclusion, investigation of the fragment's outer shell reveals a number of elements that strengthen the new covenant and return framework, while others simply fit comfortably within that setting. The (new) temple versus idols, covenant terminology, and 7.1 form the main contribution. The remaining features at least fall within the boundaries of my traditions search, although their usage is too broad to pinpoint any one source. Only the believer/unbeliever contrast is not part of the original exilic traditions; however, these terms have been integrated into later Christian reworking of the return traditions.

4. *The Relationship between the Old Testament Catena and its Outer Shell*

The last area which requires some attention is the relationship between the 'Old Testament catena' (6.16d-18) and the 'outer shell' (6.14-16b; 7.1). Having examined them separately, it is important to ask how they impact each other. After summarizing this relationship, I will draw some implications for the direction of this study.

A Summary of the Catena-Shell Relationship

Observations on the catena-shell interplay have been interspersed throughout the preceding two sections; what follows is a summary of the findings thus far. The first quotation (Ezek. 37.27; with influence from Lev. 26.11-12) emphasizes Yahweh's temple presence—a feature which clearly aligns with the shell's new temple focus (6.16).

1. Ezek. 20.40; 28.25; Isa. 48.2; 62.12; cf. Isa. 23.18; (LXX Isa. 30.19, 29; Ezek. 20.40). The regathering and related new covenant promises vindicate Yahweh's holiness before other nations (Ezek. 20.39, 41; 36.23; 39.25, 27; Isa. 29.23). The people come to worship Yahweh at the 'holy mountain' (Isa. 4.3; 27.13; 56.7; 57.13; 65.11, 25; 66.20; cf. 64.11) and in the 'holy city' of Jerusalem (Isa. 52.1).
2. Jer. 33.8; Ezek. 36.25, 29, 33; 37.23; Mal. 3.3.
3. Ezek. 20.39; 36.20-36; 37.28; cf. Jer. 31.23.
4. Isa. 59.19, 21; Jer. 32.39-40; 33.9.

Also, the direct quotation of the (new) covenant formula corresponds closely with the covenant language in the shell's rhetorical contrasts (6.14b-16a).

The second quotation (Isa. 52.11) has undergone the heaviest redactional modification to fit it within the outer shell. Both the inverted order (giving ἐξέλθατε ἐκ μέσου αὐτῶν prominence) and its change to the masculine plural (αὐτῆς to αὐτῶν) reflect a deliberate alteration of the Old Testament text so that it corresponds with the ἄπιστοι (6.14a) in the shell. Furthermore, the redactor appears to have intentionally placed ἀκαθάρτου μὴ ἅπτεσθε in the third position (of the imperatival series) in order to verbally link it with the shell's closing admonition, καθαρίσωμεν (7.1). In both cases, the inverted order makes the second quotation more suitable to its shell. Other features in the second quotation, however, simply align well with the shell (where the direction of redactional flow is more difficult to determine). For example, the contextual elements of the Isaiah quotation—LXX, οἱ φέροντες τὰ σκεύη κυρίου (cf. MT, נֹשְׂאֵי כְּלֵי יְהוָה and MT, הִבָּרוּ—respectively extend the shell's new temple theme (6.16) and its closing admonition to cultic purity (7.1). Also, the διό between quotations 1 and 2 reflects the same kind of promise-imperative inference found in the closing verse of the shell (7.1).

The third quotation (Ezek. 20.34, *et al.*) has been integrated into the outer shell rather well. Its promise-formula, 'I [Yahweh] will. . . ' (along with the promises from quotations 1 and 4), corresponds with the shell's τὰς ἐπαγγελίας (7.1). In addition, the new temple worship setting of the 'I will receive you' promise (found in various Old Testament passages) merges with the new temple imagery of the outer shell (2 Cor. 6.16b).

The fourth quotation (a democratized 2 Sam. 7.14; with influence from Isa. 43.6) constitutes one of the 'promises' referred to by the shell (7.1). Also, the covenant bond depicted in the fourth quotation, like that of quotation 1, aligns with the linking vocabulary of the rhetorical contrasts (6.14b-16a). The redacted return imagery of the 'sons and daughters' coming back to Zion (when joined with the return traditions of quotations 2 and 3) also serves to reinforce the 'imperatives' in the shell (6.14a; 7.1), extending the return 'imperatives' of the catena.

Looking at the Old Testament catena as a whole, its compositional structure appears to have a marked correlation with the external shell.

As noted above, the structure forms a chiastic pattern: promise-imperative (λέγει κύριος refrain); imperative-promise (λέγει κύριος refrain). If this compositional analysis is correct, then the structure may have been consciously designed in order to facilitate the opening and closing appeals. It is certainly convenient that the catena ends on a note of Old Testament *promise* so that the writer picks up that feature in 7.1. The bracketing of the Old Testament imperatives with promises (providing a softening effect within the catena) may also anticipate the softening shift going on in the outer shell itself (moving from an opening imperative to a hortatory (polite/softer) subjunctive in 7.1).

In sum, the rearranged order of the second quotation and its pronoun modifications appear to be deliberate changes by the redactor to accommodate the Old Testament catena to its outer shell. Also, the chiastic structure of the catena (which breaks away from the source structure) lends some support to its composition, or at least modification, in light of the outer shell. All the remaining catena-shell observations (above) demonstrate the close correspondence between the material in the catena and its shell, without betraying the direction of redaction.

Implications for this Study

At least two significant implications follow from the catena-shell relationship for this study. First, the redacted nature of the catena (making it suitable for the shell) mitigates against current 'pre-existing catena' proposals. A number of recent studies rely upon a 'pre-existing catena' proposal in order to sustain their hypothesis at the point where it fails to integrate parts of the catena. For example, as if wondering what to do with the Old Testament material in 6.17d-18 which does not further his 'food offered to idols' theory, Fee suggests that 'the original [= pre-existing] catena. . . is here merely carried over'.[1] Similarly, Thrall sustains her appeal for Pauline authorship, 'with the proviso that in verses 16b-18 Paul quotations an *existing* catena of scriptural allusions'.[2] Again, Rensberger repeatedly

---

1. Fee, 'Food Offered to Idols', p. 160. Cf., Fee's reluctance to start his study with the OT quotations (p. 157) and his later statement that 'the OT texts are not the final word' (p. 160).
2. Thrall, 'The Problem of II Cor. VI. 14–VII. 1', p. 148. Cf. Thrall's appeal

opts for a pre-existing catena (along with pre-existent material in the fifth contrast and the closing exhortation) because the material does not suit his theory.[1] Taking this further, one might compare Betz's restricted handling of the Old Testament material in view of the minimal Torah and Sinai covenant material in the catena.[2]

It is not so much the 'pre-existing catena' proposal *itself* with which I take issue. The Old Testament catena may well have existed as a separate entity before its inclusion within the fragment (although if it did, it may have had limited public/liturgical use[3]). The existence of such testimonia has been sufficiently demonstrated.[4] However, the problem is with the way the 'pre-existing catena' proposal is characteristically used to deny certain aspects of the Old Testament material. As illustrated above, New Testament scholars often appeal to a 'pre-existing catena' in a way which suggests that part or all of the Old Testament material *has been haphazardly thrown into the fragment* and therefore may be dismissed in the development of one's hypothesis to handle the fragment as a whole. However, the modification of the catena (adapting it to its shell), together with the extensive verbal/thematic correlation between the catena and its shell, argues against any kind of 'haphazard' inclusion of the Old Testament material within the fragment.[5] Instead, the strong catena-shell interplay suggests that either (1) *the Old Testament catena was originally composed for the outside shell,* or (2) *that it was at least heavily redacted from pre-existing material to fit within the shell.*

Consequently, any theory concerning the 2 Cor. 6.14–7.1 fragment *as a whole* should maintain a close correspondence between the outer shell and its inner catena. An appeal to a 'pre-existing catena' should not be used as an easy way to integrate problematic parts of the catena

---

(p. 147) to an already-existing catena in order to tone down the intense call for separation by the OT quotations.

1. Rensberger, '2 Corinthians 6.14–7.1', pp. 34, 35, 38, 41.

2. Betz, 'Anti-Pauline Fragment', pp. 92-94.

3. If the catena had been used as a public testimonia document for liturgical purposes, surely the conspicuous third person of the first quotation would have been 'smoothed over' (into the second person).

4. For examples see Fitzmyer, 'Interpolated Paragraph', p. 279.

5. In view of my catena-shell findings, it is inconsistent to deal with the catena in one manner, and the shell in another. The data requires that the fragment be dealt with as a compositional whole.

into a particular theory. It is not compatible with the catena-shell data to build a theory around the outer shell and then dismiss parts of the inner catena as irrelevant when they do not mesh with that theory.

A second implication, which follows from the catena-shell relationship, may be mentioned briefly. The close catena-shell correlation confirms the direction of our traditions search within the outer shell (about which I expressed some methodological hesitancy at the outset), since it would now appear that the outer shell has been composed with the traditions of the inner catena in mind. The catena traditions are not an 'afterthought' added to the shell.

5. Conclusion

In conclusion, my analysis of 2 Cor. 6.14–7.1 reveals that the Old Testament traditions within the fragment are primarily related to new covenant and second exodus/exilic return themes. Quotation 1 (Ezek. 37.27) explicitly recounts the (new) covenant formula and in its Old Testament context is clearly related to the theme of the eschatological return. Quotation 2 (Isa. 52.11) expresses new exodus and exilic return ideas (the ἐξέλθατε imperative reiterates 6.14a and so dominates the entire fragment), but with no explicit discussion of the new covenant. The third quotation (Ezek. 20.34, *et al.*) extends the picture of the returning exiles and in its Old Testament context(s) is found in succession with other new covenant promises. The fourth quotation, while from the Davidic covenant (2 Sam. 7.14), has been democratized through new covenant axioms and molded with material from Isa. 43.6 to complete the return imagery.

A unified picture of the catena's Old Testament traditions may be summarized as follows: the promise of a new temple dwelling of Yahweh among his people and a close covenant relationship (quotation 1) leads to the impassioned cry to 'Come out of Babylon(!)' (quotation 2); in turn, if they leave Babylon and its impurities, Yahweh will openly welcome them as they return to the homeland (quotation 3) and will in fact receive them as his children, sons and daughters of Zion (quotation 4).

Furthermore, the Old Testament traditions investigation within the catena is reinforced by the covenant language and return concepts found in the outer shell. A number of elements strengthen the exilic traditions framework (e.g., the linking terminology in the rhetorical contrasts, the [new] temple versus idols, and the extension of cultic imagery in 7.1), while others simply fit comfortably within that setting.

Finally, the catena-shell relationship contributes two implications which set the course of my subsequent work. First, the close correlation between the catena and its shell cautions against the use of a 'pre-existing catena' proposal in a way which dismisses certain portions of the catena as irrelevant to a theory about the fragment as a whole. This counters the direction of many recent studies. Second, the strong catena-shell interplay reinforces the direction of my traditions research in the outer shell (since the outer shell has also been been composed with the catena in mind).

Chapter 4

THE REMOTE CONTEXT OF THE FRAGMENT:
NEW COVENANT AND SECOND EXODUS TRADITIONS IN
2 CORINTHIANS 2.14–5.10

1. *Introduction*

The history of interpretation of 2 Cor. 6.14–7.1, with its numerous interpolation and non-contextual integration theories, emphasizes the severity of the fragment's contextual problem.[1] It is in the area of contextual integration that this work seeks to forge a new path. Briefly, my hypothesis is that 2 Cor. 6.14–7.1 fits within its present context through the 'traditions bridge' of new covenant and second exodus/return theology, particularly in view of Paul's identification with the mission of the *'ebed Yahweh*. Having looked at the fragment itself in the last chapter, the next two chapters will examine the context of 2.14–7.4 for traces of these Old Testament traditions and the apostle's understanding of his ministry in light of the *'ebed* mission (and its christological correlation).

Most New Testament scholars view chapters 1–7 as a distinct section of canonical 2 Corinthians and many treat 2.14–7.4 as a literary unit within that section (or even as a separate letter).[2] For the purpose of this investigation the material in 2.14–7.4 will be divided into two main sections: the remote literary context (2.14–5.10) and the immediate literary context (5.11–7.4), which are examined in this chapter and the next. In each of the sub-units of the remote context below (2.14–3.6; 3.7-18; 4.1-6; 4.7-15; 4.16–5.10), a discussion of the context and structure will be followed by an analysis of the text for new

---

1. A critique of current contextual theories will be made in Chapter 6.
2. For a recent overview of the integrity issues, see Sumney, *Identifying Paul's Opponents*, pp. 123-26.

covenant/new exodus traditions and overtones of *'ebed* mission (with possible christological correspondences).[1]

2. *Adequacy for New Covenant Ministry—Being Led in the Messiah's Triumph (2 Cor. 2.14–3.6)*

Context and Structure

The movement from 2 Cor. 2.13 to 2.14 is abrupt, causing some to propose a separate fragment[2] while others who wish to maintain the unity of 2 Corinthians 1–7 suggest other solutions.[3] The thought flows from specific to general and from a mood of despair to hope—i.e., from Paul's despair and agony (over not finding Titus) to his thanksgiving and paradoxical hope about his ministry in general, *despite* this and other aforementioned setbacks. In other words, the apostle deliberately crafts 2.14–7.4 to be read in suspense, drawing his readers

1. Material from the larger literary setting of 1.1–2.13 and 7.5-16 will be drawn into the discussion where appropriate.

2. The rather jolting break between 2.13 and 2.14 (and effortless resumption of topic in 7.5), along with other considerations, has led many to view 2 Cor. 2.14–7.4 as a separate fragment, see Weiss, *Earliest Christianity*, I, pp. 349, 357; Bornkamm, 'The History of the Origin of the So-called Second Letter to the Corinthians', pp. 259-60; Wendland, *Korinther*, p. 9; Schmithals, *Gnosticism in Corinth*, pp. 98-100. Martin (*2 Corinthians*, p. 45) more recently writes: 'The sentence may mark the opening of a letter originally independent and added in here when the fragments of 2 Corinthians were assembled, and so the verse may be redactional, setting the stage for the exposition of apostolic ministry.' On the integrity of 2.14–7.4 see Thrall, 'Second Thanksgiving Period in II Corinthians', pp. 101-24; Kruse, *2 Corinthians*, pp. 35-37; and Furnish, *II Corinthians*, pp. 35, 171-75; Sumney, *Identifying Paul's Opponents*, pp. 123-24. While the two sections may well have been initially composed at separate times before being fused (i.e., 2.14–7.4 written before finding Titus; 1.1–2.13 and 7.5-16 after finding Titus), several factors favor taking 2.14–7.4 as an integral part of its larger context and as an appropriate merging of materials: (1) the idea of comfort in affliction clearly unifies the two sections; (2) a logical connection exists between 7.4 and 7.5, and (3) the threat to Paul's 'theological-word promise' in 1.18-22 directly relates to the new covenant traditions/promise theology discussed in the 2.14–7.4.

3. It is beyond the scope of this work to enter into a discussion of all the views relating to the transition between 2.13 and 2.14. For a convenient listing and evaluation of the options see Thrall, 'A Second Thanksgiving', pp. 101-24; Kruse, *2 Corinthians*, pp. 36-37; Murphy-O'Connor, 'Connection Between 2 Corinthians 2.13 and 2.14', pp. 99-103.

into the suffering of spirit he feels (as he waits for a reply to his sorrowful letter)[1] through the words 'not finding Titus. . . ' echoing in the background.[2]

In broad terms, 2.14–3.6 is united through the ἱκανός question in 2.16b; the explicit answer comes in 3.5-6 with ἱκανοί, ἱκανότης, and ἱκάνωσεν. The discussion of being led in God's triumph (2.14-16a), with its function of open display, sacrifice, and dual response, raises the question of adequacy—καὶ πρὸς ταῦτα τίς ἱκανός? The unstated answer is, 'No one (!). . . but we have been made adequate'.[3] Before providing a positive/explicit answer to the ἱκανός question in 3.4-6, Paul counters two faulty/human criteria of adequacy among his opponents:[4] (1) their manipulative financial gain (2.17),[5] and (2) their letters of commendation (3.1-3).[6] Verse 17, then, mockingly answers the ἱκανός question in response to his opponents: Paul, unlike others (who base their adequacy on financial gain), ministers ἐξ εἰλικρινείας. The mention of εἰλικρινείας is not an attempt by Paul to commend himself (3.1a). Nor, for that matter, does he need

---

1. The use of the dramatic (story-telling) perfect ἔσχηκα in 2.13 suggests that Paul is trying to draw his reader into the feeling of the event. Cf. Burton (*Moods and Tenses*, p. 39) who classifies the perfect here as dramatic or aoristic.

2. The 'not finding Titus' (2.13)—'finding Titus' (7.5-16) setting of 2.14–7.4 may be viewed as a literary device to build suspense and keep Paul's suffering ministry in the background (fusing it with the other suffering lists in 4.7-12; 6.4-10).

3. Commentators are divided over the response to this rhetorical question. Some suggest a positive answer (e.g., Plummer, *II Corinthians*, p. 72; Tasker, *Second Epistle to the Corinthians*, p. 58); while others posit a negative one (Barrett, *Second Epistle to the Corinthians*, pp. 102-103). Others think that Paul expects no answer, or that the question is moot (Martin, *2 Corinthians*, p. 49; Windisch, *Zweiter Korintherbrief*, pp. 99-100). Yet, just as the rhetorical questions in 3.1 expect an answer, so does this one. The choice is difficult, but the answer appears to be a qualified, 'no, at least not of ourselves. . . ' in light of ἱκανοί, ἱκανότης, and ἱκάνωσεν in vv. 5-6, where it is God who makes them adequate. Also, if the tradition-history of this question relates to Moses' call (see below), then clearly an initial negative answer (or a qualified negative) is required.

4. Note the two ὡς clauses which hint towards Paul's rhetorical interplay with his opponents: ὡς οἱ πολλοὶ (2.17a) and ὥς τινες (3.1b).

5. Cf. the financial exploits of Paul's opponents (2 Cor. 11.20) in contrast to his own careful restraint (2 Cor. 11.7-12).

6. Cf. the issue of commendation among Paul's opponents (2 Cor. 10.12, 18; 12.11).

their letters of commendation (3.1b)[1] since the Corinthians themselves, through the new covenant/Spirit ministry, are Paul's commending letter (3.2-3).[2] Consequently (and in contrast to his opponents' source of adequacy),[3] Paul derives his confidence and adequacy
from God, who has made him adequate for new covenant ministry, a
ministry of the Spirit (3.4-6).

In 2.14–3.6 several features develop new covenant and second
exodus/return traditions. One, though controversial, is the triumphal
procession in the messiah (2.14-16); another, the ἱκανός alignment of
Paul and Moses (2.16b, 3.5-6); and third, the collage of Old
Testament traditions concerning the new covenant (3.2-6).

Triumphal Procession in the Messiah (2.14-16)
In these verses both the imagery of the 'triumph' (θριαμβεύω) and
the 'aroma' (ὀσμήν/εὐωδία) have generated much discussion. No
consensus exists on the meaning of either.[4] However, with regard to
the triumph imagery, there is at least general agreement[5] that Paul had
in mind the background of a *triumphal procession* (the question as to
whether Paul saw himself as a co-conqueror with Christ, or a captive;
whether in triumph or in shame, remains highly debated).[6]

---

1. The rhetorical questions here should be turned into negative affirmations in
order for the reader to understand the flow of the argument.
2. The asyndeton before v. 2 functions syntactically to provide the reason why
Paul does not need a letter of commendation.
3. The δέ combined with τοιαύτην forms an inferential transition. Cf. Hughes
(*Second Epistle to the Corinthians*, p. 92) who points out that 3.2-3 is the 'basis' for
3.4-6.
4. So it is with some hesitancy that this writer develops arguments based on the
triumph.
5. The triumphal background is not without the odd dissenting voice. E.g., Egan
('Lexical Evidence', pp. 34-62) rejects the Roman triumph background and translates θριαμβεύω 'display' or 'manifest'.
6. It is beyond the limits of our discussion here to present and analyze each view
on the meaning of the verb θριαμβεύω. However, after listing the options, some
pertinent comments should be made. The major options are as follows: (1) '[God]
causes us to triumph' (AV); (2) '[God] triumphs over us' (Vulgate); (3) '[God]
leading us in triumph as captives' (Hughes, *Second Epistle to the Corinthians*,
pp. 77-78; Martin, *2 Corinthians*, p. 46; BAGD, p. 363; NEB; TEV); (4) '[God]
leading us in triumph [only the apostles] as captives in open shame' (Marshall, 'A
Metaphor of Social Shame: in 2 Cor. 2.14', pp. 302-17); (5) '[God] leading us in

With regard to the aroma imagery, it may be said with a certain degree of confidence that Paul has in mind *Old Testament sacrificial aroma*. Although there are other possibilities (some of which have been cogently argued for[1]), the combined usage of ὀσμήν and

triumph as captives [unto death-suffering]' (Hafemann, *Suffering and the Spirit*, pp. 19-39; (6) '[God] leading us in triumph as captives [but without the negative sense of captivity]' (Harris, '2 Corinthians', pp. 331-32; Talbert, *Reading Corinthians*, p. 141; Hodge, *I & II Corinthians*, p. 44), and (7) '[God] parading us [apostles] on open display [with no Roman triumphal imagery in view]' (Egan, 'Lexical Evidence', pp. 34-62; cf. Furnish, *II Corinthians*, pp. 74-75). By far the majority of commentators today understand θριαμβεύω to mean 'led in triumph as captives' (views 3-6) but with implications ranging from honor, to shame, to (paradoxical) suffering and death. Egan's arguments, while opening the gates for thinking beyond the Roman triumph, fall short of his objectives. Lacking examples of a *metaphorical* use of triumph as early as Paul is not a weighty enough argument to dismiss the possibility (literal uses abound). Hafemann, on the other hand, has made an excellent case for paradoxical suffering and death as the result of being led in triumph (see his appeal to 1 Cor. 4.8-13; 2 Cor. 1.9; 4.8-11; 6.3-10). What is important to note, for our purposes here, is that there is *general agreement that the imagery depicts a triumphal procession* (though differences exist on other matters).

1. The fragrance metaphors ὀσμὴν τῆς γνώσεως αὐτοῦ and Χριστοῦ εὐωδία are not without debate. Does the imagery recall (1) incense scattered along the victor's route in a Roman general's return from a campaign, (2) a fragrance of the presence and knowledge of God, especially found in wisdom literature, (3) the rabbinic description of Torah as a drug or medicine, or (4) some kind of allusion to OT sacrificial imagery? The merits and problems of each view will be discussed in turn.

View 1, burning incense during the triumphal procession, explains the contrasting responses to the smell (positive and negative). The burning of incense during the triumphal procession would be the smell of victory to the conquerors, while it would be the smell of death to the captives. Windisch, who holds this view, cites Horace, *Odes*, IV.ii.50-51 and Appian, *Punic Wars*, 66 in support of the practice (*Der Zweite Korintherbrief*, p. 97). However, if Paul is a prisoner in the triumphal march, then the positive/negative smell has been completely reversed within the 2.14-16 text compared with the function of the aroma in the Roman triumph background (not to mention the difficulty of introducing a pagan priesthood, who would have been swinging the burning incense).

View 2, a fragrance of the presence and knowledge of God, finds ample support in later wisdom literature. One of the clearest examples of such a usage, as quoted by a recent advocate of this view (Furnish, *II Corinthians*, p. 188), is from Sir. 24.15. In Sir. 24.15 wisdom speaks of herself in this way: 'Like cassia or camel's thorn I was redolent of spices (ὀσμήν); I spread my fragrance (εὐωδίαν) like choice myrrh' (cf. Sir. 39.14; 50.15). This view leans heavily on ὀσμὴν τῆς γνώσεως αὐτοῦ, 'the fragrance of the knowledge of him [God?]'. However, this view is the least likely for several reasons. First, that the antecedent of αὐτοῦ is Christ, not God, is suggested by the closer proximity Χριστῷ and by the parallel genitive construction Χριστοῦ εὐωδία which explains (ὅτι) the former verse (e.g., Hughes, *Second Epistle to the Corinthians*, pp. 78-79; *contra* Martin, *2 Corinthians*, p. 47). From this perspective also, τῷ θεῷ would be used consistently in both verses as the recipient of the fragrance (although cf. 2 Cor. 4.6). Second, this view revolves around wisdom which is not explicitly in the context of 2 Cor. 2.14-16. Third, in some of the texts, it is difficult not to see the category of sacrificial acceptance being applied to wisdom (e.g., *2 Bar.* 67.6).

View 3, the medicine of the Torah, has some merit. The Torah was viewed by the rabbinic community as a drug which was sweet to some, while poisonous to others. This view corresponds with the dual effect of the fragrance in 2.16 and the inference in 2.17 that the discussion relates to the proclamation of the 'word of God'. However, there are some serious drawbacks with view number 3. First, one has to make a shift from 'aroma' to 'drug/medicine' (סם; סמא in Aramaic). Martin (*2 Corinthians*, p. 48) admits the shift, but would argue that it is a short transition. He attempts to make the transition through the sweet smell of anointing oil (cf. χριστός in the anointing word-play of 1.21), since סם is used in the OT as an ingredient in the anointing oil and incense (e.g., Exod. 15.6; 30.7; though סם does not have this usage in latter rabbinics) and thus could be involved in producing a fragrance. Even if one were to allow for this conflated meaning of סם, not evident in rabbinic usage, this only introduces a third category, which makes the lexical continuum even more complex. Second, the LXX uses ἥδυσμα, 'sweet herbs/mint' (Exod. 30.34), θυμίαμα, 'incense' (Exod. 35.28; 37.29; 38.25), and σύνθετος, 'fine compound' (Exod. 30.7) to translate סם, never ὀσμὴν or εὐωδία. This view, on the one hand, appeals to the OT to make its needed connection between 'aroma' and 'medicine', yet on the other disregards the explicit usage of ὀσμὴν and εὐωδία in LXX. Third, סם specifies the ingredients, not the fragrance of the anointing oil. Fourth, the genitival construction Χριστοῦ εὐωδία specifies Christ, not the Torah, as the content of the fragrance to God. It is conceivable for Paul to have made a switch from Torah to Christ (cf. the use of Deut. 30.12-14 in Rom. 10.6-10); however, combined with the above transition from aroma to drug the proposal becomes less likely.

View 4 understands ὀσμήν and εὐωδία as coming from OT sacrificial language. A number of factors commend this view. First, only this view adequately accounts for the dative 'to God' (Χριστοῦ εὐωδία ἐσμέν <u>τῷ θεῷ</u>). God would most naturally be the recipient of an aroma of sacrifice rather than of Torah or divine presence/wisdom. Second, the other Pauline usage of εὐωδία and ὀσμήν (using the dative τῷ θεῷ!) functions with sacrificial imagery—'a fragrant aroma, an acceptable sacrifice, well pleasing to God' (Phil. 4.18; cf. Eph. 5.2). Third, the sacrificial category is clearly the predominant category of the LXX for these terms (and the *exclusive*

εὐωδία by Paul elsewhere (Phil. 4.18),[1] the predominant LXX usage of these terms,[2] the recipient of the aroma being specified as the dative τῷ θεῷ, and the christological content of the aroma as Χριστοῦ εὐωδία suggest that the balance of probability leans in the direction of Old Testament sacrificial aroma being the background imagery.

The question remains, however, of why Paul would combine Old Testament sacrificial imagery with *Roman* processional imagery. Why does Paul introduce his new covenant ministry with this kind of picture? Does the apostle have a *Roman* triumphal procession specifically in mind?[3] Or is he drawing from the general practice of triumphal processions (common to Rome and many other cultures)? If so, what are the conceptual axioms which allow (or perhaps prompt) Paul to 'fill' the Roman triumph with theological content? The following proposal should answer some these questions which plague a

category when combined with the dative θεῷ or κυρίῳ). The main problem with the sacrificial imagery view, as Martin (*2 Corinthians*, p. 48) points out, is that the context does not readily warrant a discussion of OT sacrificial imagery, especially if a Roman triumph is in view. However, my proposal developed below should resolve this tension.

1. Cf. a similar combination in Eph. 5.2.

2. ὀσμή is generally used in the LXX of sacrificial aroma; e.g., literal uses: Gen. 8.21; Exod. 29.18, 25, 41; Lev. 1.9, 13, 17; 2.2, 9, 12; 3.5, 11, 16; 4.31; 6.15(8), 21(14), 8.20(21), 27(28); 17.4, 6; 23.13, 18; 26.31; Num. 15.3, 5, 7, 10, 13-14, 24; 28.2, 6, 8, 13, 24, 27; 29.2, 6, 8, 11, 13, 36; Ezek. 6.13; 16.19; 20.28; Dan. 4.34; Tob. 6.16; 8.3; Judg. 16.16; Sir. 50.15; figurative uses: Isa. 34.3; Ezek. 20.41 (cf. 20.28); Jdt. 16.16; Sir. 24.15; 39.14; 2 Macc. 9.9-12(?). However, for ὀσμή used of non-sacrificial odors see Gen. 27.27; Exod. 5.21; Job. 6.7; 14.9; Isa. 3.24; Jer. 25.10; 31(48).11; Song 1.3-4, 12; 2.13; 4.10-11; 7.8(9), 13(14); Dan. 3.27(94).

On the other hand, εὐωδία is used almost exclusively in the LXX of sacrificial aroma; e.g., literal uses: Gen. 8.21; Exod. 29.18, 25, 41; Lev. 1.9, 13, 17, 2.2, 9, 12; 3.5, 11, 16; 4.31; 6.15(8), 21(14), 8.20(21), 27(28); 17.4, 6; 23.13, 18; Num. 15.3, 5, 7, 10, 13-14, 24; 28.2, 6, 13-14, 24, 27; 29.2, 6, 8, 11, 13, 36; Ezek. 6.13; 16.19; 20.28; 1 Esd. 1.12; 2 Esd. 6.10; Jdt. 16.16; Sir. 32(35).6; 45.16; 50.15; figurative uses: Ezek. 20.41 (cf. 20.28); Sir. 24.15; Bar. 5.8(?). For uses with non-sacrificial odors see Sir. 20.9; 43.26 (yet, even these reference may have sacrificial overtones—cf. Sir. 38.11-13 for a similar correlation between sacrifice and good success).

3. Almost all NT commentators appeal to the background of a *Roman* general's return from a campaign, leading his captives (along with the booty) in a triumphal procession to Rome.

strictly Roman-triumph view of 2 Cor. 2.14-16.

While the Roman triumphal procession certainly fits the metaphor, there is another theological category which may be *equally* operational in Paul's thought, namely, the *Old Testament triumphal procession* developed especially by the prophets.[1] Several lines of evidence reinforce this. First, the prophets' procession better accounts for the mixture of 'sacrificial aroma' with 'processional march' imagery. The individuals whom Yahweh leads back on the (historical/eschatological) highway to Zion not only bring sacrifices with them,[2] but are *themselves* viewed as a 'grain offering to the Lord' (Isa. 66.20).[3]

1. The imagery of triumphal procession, and its usage in theological metaphor, certainly pre-dates the Roman era. A classic example of triumphal march imagery (because of its use in relation to Christ's ministry) comes from Isa. 40.3-5:

> [3]Clear the way for the Lord in the wilderness;
> make smooth in the desert a highway for our God.
> [4]Let every valley be lifted up,
> and every mountain and hill be made low;
> and let the rough ground become a plain,
> and the rugged terrain a broad valley;
> [5]then the glory of the Lord will be revealed,
> and all flesh will see it together.

On Isa. 40.3-5 Westermann (*Isaiah 40-66*, p. 38; cf. pp. 36-39) rightly points out that the great processional highway and the practice of the triumphal entry of a god or king into Babylon 'are the background both of the present passage and of many others in our prophet's proclamation'. Isaiah pictures a great highway (not to Babylon, but to Zion) upon which Yahweh leads a procession back to Jerusalem, showing to 'all flesh' the spoils of warfare. For other OT passages which develop similar imagery see Isa. 11.16; 35.8-10; 42.16; 43.19 (cf. 43.15-21); 49.11 (cf. 49.22-23); 53.12 (?); 57.14; 62.10; Mal. 3.1. A street called the 'Processional Way' (Ai-ibur-sabû, 'May the arrogant not flourish') in Babylon was a raised highway constructed particularly for victory parades. On the historical practice of triumphal processions in Babylonian culture see Stummer, 'Einige keilschriftliche Parallelen zu Jes. 40-66', pp. 171-89; Schmökel, *Ur, Assur und Babylon*, pp. 142-51 and figs. 114-15; Wellard, *By the Waters of Babylon*, pp. 166-70; Wiseman, *Nebuchadrezzar and Babylon*, pp. 62-65; Fischer, *Babylon. Entdeckungs reisen in die Vergangenheit*, pp. 220, 248-50, 255, 284-86.

2. Isa. 16.1; 43.19-23; 60.4-9; cf. Isa. 57.9-10; (ct. 57.14); Ezek. 20.40.

3. Although highway imagery is not explicitly present in Isa. 66.20, the event is the great eschatological return (which has already been pictured numerous times in Isaiah as a triumphal procession—e.g., Isa. 11.16; 35.8-10; 40.3-5; 42.16; 43.19 (cf. 43.15-21); 49.11 (cf. 49.22-23); 53.12 (?); 57.14; 62.10.

Similarly, Ezekiel (though he does not exploit the triumph category found in Isaiah) portrays the eschatological return with sacrificial language: 'As a soothing aroma I will accept you (LXX: ἐν ὀσμῇ εὐωδίας προσδέξομαι ὑμᾶς), when I bring you out from the peoples and gather you from the lands where you are scattered' (Ezek. 20.41).[1] The imagery is reminiscent of Paul's apostolic ministry of bringing Gentiles from the ends of the earth to God as an acceptable offering: ἡ προσφορὰ τῶν ἐθνῶν εὐπρόσδεκτος (Rom. 15.16; cf. 15.21-29). This kind of 'sacrificial overlay' on the return imagery invitingly echoes Paul's perception in 2 Cor. 6.2 that 'now is the time of acceptance (εὐπρόσδεκτος)', a tradition which itself depicts the (exilic) return to God with sacrificial language of pleasing/acceptable aroma.[2]

Second, the triumphal procession depicted by the prophets, similar to 2 Cor. 2.14-15, is led by two individuals: Yahweh and his servant. Isa. 40.3 portrays the building of a triumphal highway 'for our God'. Yahweh, like a triumphant warrior,[3] will lead his people back to the land.[4] However, at the same time, Yahweh leads the procession through the agency of his servant. The root of Jesse functions as a victory 'standard' or 'flag' around which the remnant (and possibly other nations) gather for the return march (Isa. 11.10-12, 16; cf. 49.22; 62.10).[5] As Israel's covenant mediator, the servant calls the people out, leads them along the way, and redistributes the land once in Palestine.[6] Similarly, in 2 Cor. 2.14 dual leadership in the

1. Cf. Bar. 5.8 for aroma imagery mixed with the return.

2. Cf. Chapter 5, §4.

3. For the triumphant warrior imagery in connection with the exilic return, see especially Isa. 42.13-16 (cf. 49.25).

4. Although the triumphant warrior imagery is not always explicit (as in Isa. 42.13-16), nonetheless, Yahweh is the one who leads his people home along the highway (Isa. 40.11; 49.10; 55.12; cf. 56.8).

5. Since the flag or military standard (כֵּס) is identified in Isa. 30.17 as the remnant, it is attractive to understand כֵּס in 11.10-12 as also referring to the remnant (Clements, *Isaiah 1-39*, pp. 125-6). However, most commentators usually take the 'root of Jesse' in 11.10 (due to 11.1-5; cf. 53.2; Zech. 3.8) to stand for an expected Davidic king (e.g., Grey, *Isaiah*, I, p. 225).

6. From Isa. 49.5-9 it is clear that the servant, as Israel's covenant mediator, will lead Israel back to her land. He also functions at both ends of the journey—in calling Israel out of Babylon and in reassigning the desolate places upon arrival in the land. Cf. Eph. 4.7-12 which portrays Christ, after returning from battle, as the one who

triumphal procession exists between God and the messiah:[1] '[God] leads us in his triumph in the messiah' (2 Cor. 2.14).

Third, the prophets' picture of procession and regathering, while focused on the return from Babylon to Palestine, expands (especially in the eschatological picture) to include a return from every location—north, south, east, and west.[2] Likewise, it is this kind of timeless and universal triumph that Paul envisions when he uses the expressions πάντοτε (2.14a) and ἐν παντὶ τόπῳ (2.14b).[3]

Fourth, the triumphal march as depicted by various Isaiah-texts parallels the suffering-exaltation paradox of Paul's being led in triumph. With the θριαμβεύω metaphor, commentators struggle over whether Paul is viewing himself negatively, positively, or both. On the one hand, the scene is definitely negative. The lexical evidence supports taking ἡμᾶς, the object of θριαμβεύοντι, as the prisoners who are being led in triumph,[4] and these processions resulted in their captivity, suffering, and often death. Beyond the lexical data, however, Scott Hafemann has shown the suffering/death in the θριαμβεύω imagery to be contextually feasible; that is, the saved/perishing response to the message of a crucified messiah (2 Cor. 2.14-16) is the same dual response to the apostle's suffering (1 Cor. 1.18-24)[5] and the sentence of death upon him is part of this idea of

distributes the spoils of battle.

1. If the OT background of Yahweh and his servant leading the triumph is correct, then to translate ἐν τῷ Χριστῷ as 'in the messiah' is quite appropriate. Contextually, Paul has already drawn in the messianic background of the term in 2 Cor. 1.5 and 1.21. And for Paul, ἐν τῷ Χριστῷ conveys a salvation-historical, new (messianic) age experience of union with Christ (Best, *One Body in Christ*, p. 18; Ladd, *Theology of the New Testament*, pp. 482-84).

2. On the one hand, the triumphal highway is from Babylon to Palestine (43.14-21; 48.20); yet God's people make the trek on this highway from all over the world (so the plural 'highways' in Isa. 49.11-12; cf. 41.9; 43.5-6; 45.22; 49.22; 60.4, 9).

3. Cf. 2 Cor. 4.10.

4. The object of the verb θριαμβεύω *always* refers to the prisoners, not to the generals, etc.

5. The message of a 'crucified messiah' in 1 Cor. 1.18-24 produced different responses τοῖς μὲν ἀπολλυμένοις... τοῖς δὲ σῳζομένοις (cf. 2 Cor. 2.15-16). In 2 Corinthians, Paul who preaches a crucified messiah and views his *own* sufferings in this light (2 Cor. 1.5) experiences the same dual response to his ministry of suffering. Thus 1 Cor. 1.24 (Χριστὸν ἐσταυρωμένον and the response patterns) and τὰ παθήματα τοῦ Χριστοῦ in 2 Cor. 1.5 provide further justification for under-

procession (1 Cor. 4.8-13; cf. 2 Cor. 1.9; 4.8-11; 6.3-10).[1] However, 'being led in triumph as a prisoner [to suffering/death]' is paradoxically a positive experience for Paul. The experience of being led in triumph is, for Paul, reason to give thanks—τῷ θεῷ χάρις! As he enters into the sufferings of the messiah, he knows that they are accepted as a 'sweet aroma' to God. Again, the apostle's mood is anything but despondent, as demonstrated by his subsequent portrayals of the glory of the new covenant ministry. Likewise, the servant leader of the exilic return is himself presented in Isa. 49.7 as despised, but (ultimately) honored.[2] Paul is thankful not so much for being led as a prisoner (though he is one) but because God is using his difficulties, sufferings (even death), to advance the glory of the new covenant ministry.

Fifth (and most importantly), only the Old Testament/prophetic background, as it theologically 'redresses' the Roman victory march,[3] explains why Paul uses triumphal imagery in 2.14-16a to introduce the section on his new covenant ministry (in contrast to Moses' old covenant ministry).[4] This connection between the new covenant and triumphal procession has already been established by the Isaiah-texts. A roadway in the wilderness is the 'new thing' (in contrast to the first exodus by Moses) which Yahweh is going to bring about (Isa. 43.16-

standing ἐν τῷ Χριστῷ in 2 Cor. 2.14 as 'in the messiah'. Cf. the traditions in the Gospels and later apostolic mission about the suffering messiah (e.g., Lk. 24.26, 46; Acts 3.18; 4.26-28; 17.3; 26.23). It is the messiah's suffering that legitimizes Paul's suffering.

1. Hafemann, *Suffering and the Spirit*, pp. 58-82.

2. Cf. Isa. 50.4-7; 53.3, 12 (a similar pattern exists for the nation, e.g., 52.14; 49.23).

3. There is little, if any, conceptual linkage in moving from a Roman triumph (2.14-16) to the new covenant (3.1-6). This is one of Egan's arguments ('Lexical Evidence', pp. 38-39) against seeing a Roman triumph in the passage. On this point Egan appears to be right. However, if Paul is thinking of the prophets' triumphal procession (and re-worked the Roman triumph from this perspective), then there is a very strong conceptual tie to the the discussion of the new covenant which follows.

4. The ἱκανός question of 2.16b, is a question of adequacy for *new covenant* ministry (3.3, 5-6), a ministry which Paul portrays as being 'led in triumph' (πρὸς ταῦτα in 2.16b refers to the imagery of 2.14-16a). So the question of what conceptual link existed in Paul's mind between the Roman (?) triumph and the new covenant arises.

21).[1] On that triumphal highway, a second Moses, the (new) covenant mediator will lead his people out of captivity and back to the land. The result will be a display of Yahweh's 'glory' to all the nations (Isa. 40.5; cf. 52.10),[2] a central aspect in Paul's discussion to follow.[3] Metaphorically, the triumphal highway is a salvation-historical 'road' leading to the formation of a new covenant between Yahweh and his people in the Old Testament; so also with Paul here.

An additional (sixth) argument might be noted here. To the degree to which the material in Ephesians provides us with Pauline traditions it may be said that the Old Testament triumphal procession, not the Roman, establishes the *tradition-history* link to apostleship. For example, in Eph. 4.8 (quoting Ps. 68.18)[4] the writer portrays the distribution of gifts ('apostles' is one category) as the result of Christ leading a host of captives in triumph.[5] This Old Testament conceptual background is strikingly similar to that which I have proposed above for 2 Cor. 2.14.

One may raise the objection that this Old Testament triumphal view predates the use of θριαμβεύω to a time when the word did not reflect the meaning of triumph. Does not the use of θριαμβεύω for ancient Near Eastern triumphs amount to a lexical anachronism? After all, θριαμβεύω is never used in the LXX in conjunction with Old

1. Cf. the 'new thing' in Jer. 31.21-22 which is related to the highway/return imagery of 31.21 (see discussion below on 2 Cor. 5.17).

2. Cf. the fusing of these two passages in Lk. 3.4-6. See also Isa. 35.2b (cf. 3-10).

3. δόξα occurs 15 times in 2 Cor. 3.1–4.17 and the verb δοξάζω once.

4. In Ps. 68 the first exodus itself is seen as a triumphal procession out of Egypt to Sinai—the instructions, like those of the Isaiah-texts, are given to 'cast up a high-way for Him [Yahweh] who rides through the deserts' (v. 4), for Yahweh 'leads the prisoners into prosperity' (v. 6), 'goes forth' before his people (v. 7a), 'marches through the wilderness' (v. 7b). A mighty battle is fought by the Lord and his thousands of chariots. Having conquered Egypt and taken the mount of Sinai, the Psalmist, recalls, 'You have ascended on high, you have led captive [your] captives' (v. 18). The destiny of the triumphal procession is ultimately into the King's sanctuary (v. 24), where the throngs exalt Him with great praise (v. 25). Cf. the song of Moses (Exod. 15.1-18), the song of Deborah and Barak (Judg. 5.2-41), and the use of Ps. 68.18 in Eph. 4.8.

5. Aside from the many exegetical difficulties with Eph. 4.7-10 (especially the referents to ascending and descending), it appears clear that triumphal procession imagery has been employed from Ps. 68.18.

Testament triumphs. This objection might have some validity, if I were arguing an exclusive Old Testament background (which I am not). However, in 2 Cor. 2.14 Paul has obviously *imported* theological meaning into the picture of the Roman triumph with the use of God, Christ, sacrificial imagery, and the rest. So the question is not one of lexical anachronism, but of where Paul might have obtained the theological ideas which he uses to 'redress' a Roman triumphal procession.[1]

In conclusion, the picture Paul has in mind in 2.14-16 seems to go beyond Roman triumph (though retaining the Roman metaphor in a general sense) to that of participating in the *'ebed Yahweh's* triumphal procession. If this interpretation is plausible, it establishes at the outset the category of 'second exodus' out of Babylon[2] and introduces the material on new covenant which follows with significant conceptual and theological continuity.

The ἱκανός *Alignment of Paul and Moses (2.16b, 3.5-6)*
A close LXX parallel to the ἱκανός theme of 2.14b and 3.4-6 may be found in the response of Moses to Yahweh's call, δέομαι Κύριε, οὐκ ἱκανός εἰμι... (LXX Exod. 4.10).[3] In addition to this parallel, the extensive contrasts between Paul's new covenant ministry and Moses' old covenant ministry in 3.1-18 subtly cast Paul as fulfilling at least the *function* of a new Moses.[4] Peter R. Jones seems to overstate the case by saying that Paul wishes to identify himself as the fulfillment of

---

1. This is not to suggest that the Roman triumphs had their origin in Israelite or Near Eastern triumphs. H.S. Versnel (*Triumphus*, pp. 284-303) argues for the origins of the Roman triumph to be found in the Etruscans' annual New Year investiture ceremonies. One should note also Versnel's discussion of the practice of triumphs in other cultures (often connected with their gods, enthronements, victory celebrations, etc).

2. At a strategic place—i.e., the introductory thanksgiving to this section.

3. An investigation of the 48 occurrences of ἱκανός and 14 occurrences of ἱκανοῦσθαι in the LXX suggests that Exod. 4.10 is the most likely tradition-history background to Paul's question of adequacy for new covenant ministry. The only other possibility is Joel 2.11, but there the context of eschatological *judgment* and final display of God's wrath does not align well with 2 Cor. 2.14–3.6.

4. Like Moses (Exod. 4.10), Paul recognizes his incapacity, especially in the realm of oral communication (2 Cor. 10.10; 11.6). Cf. Fitzgerald, 'Cracks in an Earthen Vessel', pp. 301-2.

second-Moses tradition in Jewish expectation.[1] The inferences seem to be more subtle and indirect—only through his establishment εἰς Χριστόν and anointing on that basis (χρίσας)[2] does the apostle carry on the messiah's new-Moses ministry. It is unlikely that Paul would ever have referred to *himself* as the new Moses of Jewish expectation. Yet, the ἱκανός theme and the covenant parallels present the apostle as implicitly extending the ministry of a second Moses. It is in this more subtle and secondary sense (derived through christological identification) that I will use the term 'new Moses' of Paul.

Yet Jones is correct in showing how this material *juxtaposes*, in a complementary way, Paul's more explicit alignment of his ministry with the servant of Yahweh, who in Isaiah is clearly a second Moses.[3] In this respect, if Paul (through identification with the servant and second Moses mission) were to bring about a new exodus and 'lead his people out of captivity' (e.g., 6.14–7.1), such an idea should no longer be far-fetched within this broader literary context.

Explicit References and Allusions to New Covenant Traditions (3.1-6)
Not only does Paul in 3.6 explicitly refer to διακόνους καινῆς διαθήκης (terminology reminiscent of Jer. 31[38].31),[4] but also in 3.2-6 he makes clear verbal allusions to Old Testament traditions about the new covenant. Although scholars are divided over the precise identity of these allusions in 2 Cor. 3.3-6,[5] the prevailing view is

---

1. While helpful in pointing out the analogies, Jones ('Paul: A Second Moses according to 2 Corinthians 2.14–4.7') makes much too direct the new Moses fulfillment, which for Paul would only come through christological identifications.

2. 2 Cor. 1.21.

3. Cf. the 'Excursus' in Chapter 5, §3.

4. The exact expression καινῆς διαθήκης occurs only in Jer. 31(38).31 in contrast to the old covenant: 'Behold, days are coming when I will make a *new covenant* (καινῆς διαθήκης) with the house of Israel and with the house of Judah, not like the covenant which I made with their fathers in the day I took them by the hand to bring them out of the land of Egypt. . . '

5. Some would add to the Jer. 31(38).33 and Ezek. 11.19; 36.26-27 references three other passages: LXX Prov. 3.3(A text); 7.3; and MT Jer. 17.1, which contain the expression 'the tablet of your heart', τὸ πλάτος τῆς καρδίας σου (e.g., Windisch, *Zweiter Korintherbrief*, p. 104; Bultmann, *Zweiter Korintherbrief*, p. 76). While it is impossible to exclude Prov. 3.3; 7.3; and Jer. 17.1 from the discussion, they serve at most a secondary role in the tradition-history because (a) the tablet-motif is probably carried over from Paul's reference to the law as πλάξιν

that they represent a collage of interrelated prophetic texts, particularly texts which promise a new heart/new covenant, as against the giving of the law on Mount Sinai. Thus οὐκ ἐν πλάξιν λιθίναις is usually taken to recall texts such as Exod. 24.12; 31.18; 32.15; 34.1 and Deut. 9.10; while its counterpart, ἐν πλάξιν σαρκίναις, together with the association of the Spirit,[1] the law written upon the heart,[2] and καινῆς διαθήκης[3] reflects Jer. 31(38).33, Ezek. 11.19, and 36.26-27a.[4] In each of the last three texts, Yahweh affirms promises related to the new covenant:

> I [Yahweh] will make a new covenant (διαθήκην καινήν) with the house of Israel and with the house of Judah, not like the covenant which I made with their fathers in the day I took them by the hand to bring them out of the land of Egypt, my covenant which they broke, although I was a husband to them . . . For this is the covenant which I will make with the house of Israel after those days. . . I will certainly put my law in their minds, and write them upon their hearts (ἐπὶ καρδίας αὐτῶν γράψω αὐτούς) (LXX Jer. 38.31-33).

> And I [Yahweh] will give them another heart, and will put a new s/Spirit within them (πνεῦμα καινὸν δώσω ἐν αὐτοῖς); and I will remove the

λιθίναις, (b) no mention is made in these passages to 'fleshly hearts', and (c) no contextual development of the new covenant is found in these OT references.

1. 2 Cor. 3.3, 6, 8, 17-18.
2. 2 Cor. 3.2 (ἐγγεγραμμένη ἐν ταῖς καρδίαις ἡμῶν); cf. 3.3, 6. The change from γράψω to ἐγγεγραμμένη in 2 Cor. 3.2 is probably due to the assimilation of these traditions with the engraving of the law upon tablets of stone.
3. 2 Cor. 3.6.
4. Almost all scholars accept Jer. 31(38).31-33; Ezek. 11.19; 36.26-27. as the sources of Paul's allusions in 2 Cor. 3.3-6. For those who take a blending of these three passages see Souza, *New Covenant in the Second Letter to the Corinthians*, pp. 105-16; Hafemann, *Suffering and the Spirit*, pp. 193-95.
   However, commentators disagree over whether the two Ezekiel passages or the one Jeremiah passage plays the determinative role. Those who argue that the Ezekiel passages are dominant include Richardson, 'Spirit and Letter', pp. 208-18; for the primacy of Jer. 31(38).33, cf. Hooker, 'Beyond the Things Which are Written', p. 296; Richard, 'Polemics, Old Testament, and Theology. A Study of II Cor. 3.1–4.6', pp. 347-49; Hughes, *Second Corinthians*, pp. 89-91; Vos, *Traditionsgeschichliche Untersuchungen zur Paulinischen Pneumatologie*, p. 137. In favor of Ezek. 11.19 and 36.26 is the terminology of 'fleshly hearts' and the new spirit/Spirit; yet in support of Jer. 31(38).33 is the explicit reference to the 'new covenant' and the writing of the law on the hearts. Consequently, the best approach is to understand all three passages functioning as a collage for the material in 2 Cor. 3.3-6.

heart of stone out of their flesh and give them a heart of flesh (δώσω αὐτοῖς καρδίαν σαρκίνην) (LXX Ezek. 11.19).

And I [Yahweh] will give you a new heart, and will put a new spirit within you; and I will remove the heart of stone out of your flesh, and will give you a heart of flesh (δώσω αὐτοῖς καρδίαν σαρκίνην). And I will put my Spirit within you (καὶ τὸ πνεῦμά μου δώσω ἐν ὑμῖν). . . (LXX Ezek. 36.26-27a).

For our purposes, it is important to note that Paul is drawing from both central new covenant texts and texts which convey that covenant in a promise-formula (similar to that of the 6.14–7.1 fragment).[1]

It is also significant to note that in the background of the three texts which Paul employs—Jer. 31(38).31-33; Ezek. 11.19, and 36.26-27a—one finds the concept of second exodus/exilic return theology *intertwined* with that of new covenant. In Jer. 31.32, for example, the new covenant is 'not like the covenant which I [Yahweh] made with their fathers in the day I took them by the hand to bring them out of the land of Egypt'.[2] For patterned after the old exodus, Yahweh is now creating a 'new thing' on a return highway (Jer. 31.21-22),[3] leading his people back to the homeland by paths on which they will not stumble and by streams of water in the desert (Jer. 31.7-9).[4]

---

1. Cf. discussion of promise-formula, 'I [Yahweh] will. . . ' in Chapter 5.

2. In Jer. 31.32 Yahweh's taking Israel by the hand to bring them out of the land of Egypt recalls not only the historical exodus, but also Jeremiah's earlier statements about a new exodus (Jer. 16.14-15; 31.2-9; cf. 31.21). The new exodus transcends the departure from Egypt in every way, as does the new covenant which is written on the heart instead of tablets of stone. Cf. another development between the giving of the first law (Exod. 34.7) and the new law (Jer. 38.29-30) where the sins of the fathers will no longer be passed down to succeeding generations.

3. While the חֲדָשָׁה refers directly to the problematic statement, 'a woman will encompass a man', it also draws upon the preceding discussion of the faithful virgin who returns by the highway in contrast to the faithless daughter who wanders (Jer. 31.21-22).

4. Jer. 31.7-9 is replete with new exodus ideas—Yahweh gathers his people from the farthest horizons and leads them on a new exodus march beside flowing streams to their homeland (cf. Isa. 35; 40.3-5; 41.18-20; 42.16; 43.1-7; 44.3-4; 48.20-21; 49.9-13; ct. Exod. 17.1-7; Num. 20.1-13), and along a straight road (unlike the first march; cf. Isa. 20.4). For further discussion see Thompson, *Jeremiah*, pp. 569-70; Carroll, *Jeremiah*, pp. 592-93. Thompson (*Jeremiah*, p. 566) comments on the exiles' deliverance from Pharaoh's troops in Jer. 31.2-14: 'it may be that the theme of the New Exodus was already current in Judah long before it was

Similarly, in Ezek. 11.17-19[1] and 36.24-27[2] the 'typical' or 'well-known' new covenant promises of a new spirit and hearts of flesh are contingent upon Yahweh's promise to regather his people.[3] It is important to keep in mind the joining of these two features (exilic return promises and new covenant promises) when the function of exilic return promises within the context of Paul's inaugurated new covenant theology is examined—the two are inextricably linked.

3. The δόξα of Old Covenant Ministry versus The δόξα of New Covenant Ministry (2 Cor. 3.7-18)

Context and Structure

This section of 2 Corinthians has generated a considerable amount of recent literature.[4] While it is beyond the scope of this study to interact

taken up by Second Isaiah'.

1. While the return is clearly in view (Ezek. 11.17), the aspect of second exodus is inferred only through the repossession prescription to 'remove all its detestable things and all its abominations from it (the land)' (Ezek. 11.18; cf. 11.21), which recalls those of the first entrance into the land (Lev. 18.24-30; Deut. 18.9; 20.17-18).

2. Notice that the sequence of promises in Ezek. 34.24-27 *start with the return promises:* 'I [Yahweh] will take you from the nations, gather you from all the lands, and bring you into your land. . . I will sprinkle. . . I will cleanse. . . I will give you a new heart/spirit. . . I will give you a heart of flesh. . . I will put my Spirit within you. . . [etc.]'.

3. In Ezekiel the language is that of return, but shades of new exodus are less obvious than in Jeremiah.

4. For a few of the studies within the last thirty years see: Belleville, *Reflections of Glory*; Betz, 'Der Alte und der Neue Bund: Eine Betrachtung zu 2 Kor 3', pp. 24-36; Carmignac, 'II Corinthians 3.6, 14 et le Début de la Formation du Nouveau Testament', pp. 384-86; Doignon, 'Le Libellé Singulier de II Corinthiens 3.18 chez Hilaire de Poitiers: Essai d'Explication', pp. 118-26; Dunn, '2 Corinthians III. 17–The Lord is the Spirit', pp. 309-20; Fitzmyer, 'Glory Reflected on the Face of Christ (2 Cor. 3.7–4.6)', pp. 630-44; Friesen, 'The Glory of the Ministry of Jesus Christ Illustrated by a Study of 2 Cor. 2.14–3.18', pp. 1-175; Grelot, 'Note sur 2 Corinthiens 3.14', pp. 135-44; Hann, 'Bibelarbeit über 2. Korinther 3.4-18', pp. 82-92; Hanson, 'The Midrash in II Corinthians 3: A Reconsideration', pp. 2-28; Hickling, 'Sequence of Thought', pp. 380-95; Hooker, 'Beyond the Things that are Written', pp. 295-309; Jones, 'Paul: A Second Moses', pp. 79-107; Jan Lambrecht, 'Transformation in 2 Cor. 3.18', pp. 243-54; Moule, 'II Cor. iii.18b, καθάπερ ἀπὸ κυρίου πνεύματος', pp. 227-34; Richard, 'Polemics', pp. 340-67; Richardson, 'Spirit and Letter', pp. 208-18; Souza, *New*

with this material and some of the text's midrashic techniques, 3.7-18 is particularly important for understanding new covenant ministry.

The contrast in 3.6c (the letter kills, but the Spirit gives life), sets the stage for the first in a series of contrasts designed to show the exceeding δόξα of new covenant ministry.[1] In rabbinic fashion (*Qal wahomer*),[2] Paul gives an exposition of Exod. 34.29-32[3] arguing from the lesser to the greater—that is, if the ministry of death engraved on λίθοις came with glory, *much more* the ministry of the living Spirit (written on πλαξὶν καρδίαις σαρκίναις) (3.7-8);[4] if the ministry of condemnation had glory, *much more* the ministry of righteousness (3.9); if ministry which is fading away was διὰ δόξης, *much more* the ministry which remains permanently is ἐν δόξῃ (3.11).[5] In fact, the extent of new covenant δόξα is so great that, comparatively, the old covenant ministry has no glory (3.10).

In view of (οὖν) such a hope related to new covenant δόξα, Paul is unlike Moses who wore a veil while speaking to the people (continuing again the exposition of Exod. 34.33-35).[6] Paul speaks boldly and openly (3.12-13). Nonetheless (ἀλλά), like that generation, this current generation fails to see the glory of the Lord since (γάρ) a veil of spiritual blindness lies over their hearts and minds, and because (ὅτι) such a veil is only removed ἐν Χριστῷ (3.14-15). Now

---

Covenant in the Second Letter to the Corinthians, pp. 107-190; Stockhausen, 'Moses' Veil and the Glory of the New Covenant', pp. 1-280; Wong, 'The Lord is the Spirit (2 Cor 3,17a)', pp. 48-74.

1. Note the repetition of δόξα in each of the contrasts.

2. For the turning point in each argument note the repeated πῶς οὐχὶ μᾶλλον (3.8), πολλῷ μᾶλλον (3.9), and another πολλῷ μᾶλλον (3.11). *Qal wahomer* ('lightness and heaviness') uses the premise that what is true in one case is applicable to heavier cases (i.e., more important or greater situations). Similarly, using Latin terms the argumentation here in 2 Cor. 3.7-11 is often referred to as *a fortiori* (e.g., Bonsirven, *Exégèse Rabbinique et Exégèse Paulinienne*, p. 317), or *a minori ad maius* (e.g., Souza, *New Covenant*, p. 125).

3. Obviously not all of the traditions come from Exod. 24.29-31, such as the fading of the glory.

4. The first contrast draws heavily upon imagery already developed in the preceding section, 3.1-6.

5. The τὸ καταργούμενον of 3.11 recalls τὴν καταργουμένον in 3.7. However, the tradition-history of these details is unknown.

6. Whenever Moses was before the people he wore a veil; whereas, when he went in before the Lord he would take off the veil (Exod. 34.33-35).

(δέ) Paul takes the analogy one step further through a wordplay on ἐπιστρέφω—whenever anyone spiritually 'turns' to the Lord (= Yahweh),[1] as Moses did physically when he 'turned' to go up the mountain, at that time the spiritual veil is taken away (3.16/Exod. 34.34).[2] Wanting to clarify the analogy with pesher-like exegesis,[3] the apostle specifies that it was the Lord (= Yahweh) who gave the law back then, but now in this new covenant age it is the Spirit (not Yahweh on stone tablets!) who writes the law upon the hearts, allowing for freedom (from the letter and for open approach to God) (3.17). Drawing the application, Paul and his readers (ἡμεῖς πάντες),[4] their spiritual veils removed, behold the glory of the Lord (= Yahweh)[5] and are transformed from one stage of glory to another by the Lord (cf. the old covenant), who is now the Spirit (in the new covenant).[6]

1. Cf. Exod. 34.34. Many commentators make the mistake of taking κύριος in 3.16-17 as referring to Christ. See Dunn ('The Lord is the Spirit', pp. 309-20) and Stockhausen ('Moses' Veil', pp. 237-89) for excellent developments of the κύριος referent.

2. The term ἐπιστρέφω is used in the NT of conversion (e.g., Acts 3.19; 9.35; 11.21; 15.19; 26.18-20; 1 Thess. 1.9). Cf. Thrall, 'Conversion to the Lord, The Interpretation of Exodus 34 in II Cor. 3.14b-18', pp. 197-265.

3. Ironically, what was intended to clarify the analogy has today clouded the passage for many commentators. For a convincing treatment of 2 Cor. 3.16-17 as pesher exegesis, see Dunn ('The Lord is the Spirit', pp. 309-20), who first answers the key question of who κύριος refers to in 3.16. Cf. Stockhausen, 'Moses' Veil', pp. 237-89. I will use the term 'pesher-like' techniques in order to acknowledge the similarities in method, but to retain certain distinctions in genre, christological orientation, etc. between the pesher of Qumran literature and what is found here.

4. Access by the complete community is unlike the situation with Moses who alone would go up the mountain to see the glory of the Lord.

5. Later Paul will argue that the glory of the Lord (= Yahweh) is seen in Christ (4.4), who is the image of God.

6. The expression κυρίου πνεύματος (3.18) has resulted in a great number of interpretations. However, if one is to remain consistent with the pesher-like interplay between κύριος and πνεῦμα in v. 17, then κυρίου πνεύματος probably refers to *either* (1) the 'Spirit of Yahweh', now drawing the two ages together to show continuity while retaining the distinctions previously made (cf. 'my Spirit' in Ezek. 36.27), or (2) from 'the Lord-the Spirit', again recognizing the distinctions between the old covenant and the new covenant age.

The New Covenant (3.7-18)

It would be hard to overlook the new covenant in 2 Cor. 3.7-18. The subject has already surfaced explicitly in 3.1-6 through the self-portrayal as διακόνους καινῆς διαθήκης and the collage of Old Testament allusions. Here again the apostle develops new covenant ministry through the contrasts between the old and new. These descriptions themselves appear to be a blend of Old Testament traditions and distinctively Pauline categories. The old covenant ministry was one of the letter-death (3.6, 7),[1] of condemnation (3.9a),[2] and of fading glory (3.7, 11a).[3] By contrast, the new covenant ministry exceeds the glory of the old, in that it is a ministry of the Spirit-life (3.6, 8),[4] of righteousness (3.9b),[5] and of permanent glory

---

1. The traditions about the letter and engraving on stone are an extension of the previous section and OT passages such as Exod. 24.12; 31.18; 32.15; 34.1 and Deut. 9.10 (see above). However, the description διακονία τοῦ θανάτου never directly appears in the OT. Rather, διακονία τοῦ θανάτου seems to be an inference drawn by Paul from the πλαξὶν λιθίναις versus πλαξὶν καρδίαις σαρκίναις and his previous description of the Spirit as πνεύματι θεοῦ ζῶντος. For a similar sin-death category in relationship to the Mosaic law in Paul see Rom. 5.12-21; 7.5, and the classic discussion in 7.8-13.

2. Again, διακονία τῆς κατακρίσεως is not found in the OT to describe the law, although a similar impression may be derived from the cursing sections (e.g., Deut. 27.14-26; esp. 27.26, ἐπικατάρατος πᾶς ἄνθρωπος ὃς οὐκ ἐμμένει ἐν πᾶσι τοῖς λόγοις τοῦ νόμου ποιῆσαι αὐτούς; cf. Gal. 3.10). For κατάκριμα applied those under the law (see Rom. 5.16, 18), in contrast to those ἐν Χριστῷ (8.1).

3. The source of Paul's traditions about the fading glory of the old covenant, τὸ καταργούμενον (3.11), is quite uncertain. For a discussion of possible options see Belleville, *Reflections of Glory*, pp. 199-225.

4. The πνεύμα traditions in 3.8, 17-18, based on the previous section (3.3, 6), are clearly derived from, at least, Ezek. 11.19 and 36.26-27, passages which articulate new covenant promises (see also Isa. 59.21; Ezek. 18.31 and 37.14 for linking of the s/Spirit and the new covenant; cf. Isa. 32.15; 42.14; 44.3; 61.1; Ezek. 39.29; Joel 2.28-29; Hag. 2.5; Zech. 12.10). For Paul, the function of the Spirit was essential to his understanding of the new covenant (Rom. 2.29; Gal. 3.14; cf. Rom. 5.5; 8.2-17, 23; 15.19; 1 Cor. 3.16; 6.19; 2 Cor. 1.22; 5.5; 6.6; Gal. 3.2-5; 4.6; 5.15-26).

5. For several examples where δικαιοσύνη expresses new covenant expectations see LXX Isa. 42.6; 54.10, 14; 56.1, 4; 59.21 (cf. 59.9, 14, 17); 61.8 (cf. 61.3, 11); Jer. 31.23. Cf. δικαίωμα in Ezek. 11.20; 36.27. Even so, it is a tenet of Pauline theology that righteousness is accomplished not through the Mosaic law, but through

(3.11b).[1] Inasmuch as Old Testament traditions lie behind the Spirit, righteousness, and glory descriptions of the new covenant, they serve to confirm the focus of the passage. Of equal significance for our hypothesis is the fact that 3.7-18 (along with 3.1-6 and 4.1-6) defines categories which, at least in Paul's mind, are 'organically' related to his new covenant ministry (see chart below).

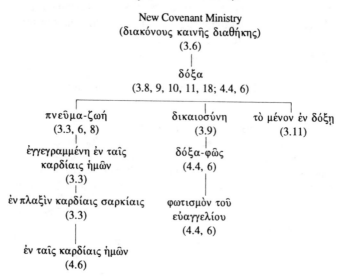

New Covenant Ministry
(διακόνους καινῆς διαθήκης)
(3.6)

δόξα
(3.8, 9, 10, 11, 18; 4.4, 6)

πνεῦμα-ζωή   δικαιοσύνη   τὸ μένον ἐν δόξῃ
(3.3, 6, 8)   (3.9)   (3.11)

ἐγγεγραμμένη ἐν ταῖς   δόξα-φῶς
καρδίαις ἡμῶν   (4.4, 6)
(3.3)

ἐν πλαξὶν καρδίαις σαρκίαις   φωτισμὸν τοῦ
(3.3)   εὐαγγελίου
                                  (4.4, 6)

ἐν ταῖς καρδίαις ἡμῶν
(4.6)

the new covenant and the Spirit's writing the law on the heart (e.g., Gal. 2.21; 3.1-6).

1. כָּבוֹד/δόξα traditions surround the establishment of the old Mosaic covenant (e.g., Exod. 33.18-22; cf. Exod. 34.6-7; Lev. 9.6, 23; Jer. 14.21). Paul has been making this point from Exod. 34.29-35, and, in a recurring pattern, they are employed extensively with regard to the new covenant when God will again dwell among his people (e.g., Isa. 49.2-4, 8; 58.19–60.2; Ezek. 11.17-23; 37.26-28, cf. 43.2-5; 44.4). (For more general references compare Isa. 33.15-17; 40.5; 43.7 44.23; 45.25-26; 46.13; 58.8; 60.21; 62.1-2; 66.18-19; Jer. 33.9; Ezek. 1.28; 3.12, 23; 8.4; 9.3; 10.4, 18-19; 26.20; 39.21; Zech. 2.5, 10-11.) Note especially the terminological ties between Exod. 33.22 and Isa. 49.2-3 (cf. Isa. 33.16; 51.16).

The traditions behind the permanency of new covenant glory, τὸ μένον ἐν δόξα, are not as easily traceable. Certainly the 'remaining glory' is brought up by contrast to the fading glory on Moses' face. However, it may be that Paul also has in mind the nature of the new covenant as an everlasting (עוֹלָם) covenant (Isa. 55.3; 61.8; Jer. 32.40; 50.5; Ezek. 16.60; 37.26-28) with everlasting glory (Isa. 60.19-20; Ezek. 43.2-5, 7-9).

4. Paul's δόξα-Light Ministry to the Blind (2 Cor. 4.1-6)

Context and Structure

On the basis of the surpassing δόξα (3.1-11), and the unhindered, transforming δόξα (3.18) of new covenant ministry,[1] Paul and his associates are not disheartened (4.1).[2] Rather (ἀλλά), their δόξα-δικαιοσύνη[3] ministry motivates them to renounce any disgraceful, underhanded ways (4.2a),[4] both negatively, by refusing to practice deceit or dilution of God's word (4.2b), and positively, by commending themselves openly to every person's conscience (4.2c). In other words, Paul will not use unethical practices to gain a response. Now (δέ), explaining the true hindrance to the gospel, in 4.3a Paul admits

1. διὰ τοῦτο functions inferentially, drawing upon the preceding discussion of the new covenant ministry (2.14–3.18). If it does 'look forward', it does not do so exclusively, as Martin (*2 Corinthians*, p. 76) suggests, because in looking forward it highlights ἔχοντες τὴν διακονίαν ταύτην (4.1a), which clearly looks backwards to the preceding discussion. While the specific antecedent of διὰ τοῦτο and τὴν διακονίαν ταύτην is not immediately recognizable, the central term in 3.1-18 is the δόξα of the new covenant (used 13 times counting cognates; cf. two times in 4.4, 6 for continuity of the theme)—especially the surpassing glory of the new covenant (3.1-18) and the unhindered observance of that glory (3.18). Furnish (*II Corinthians*, p. 217) catches this latter aspect of the transition: 'since, therefore, we have an unhindered vision of the Lord's splendor. . . '

2. Presumably communicating the gospel message is in view (4.3; cf. Rom. 1.16).

3. Syntactically, ἔχοντες τὴν διακονίαν ταύτην is the basis for both verbal ideas: οὐκ ἐγκακοῦμεν, ἀλλὰ ἀπειπάμεθα (Kruse, *2 Corinthians*, p. 102). In making the transition from 3.1-18 to 4.1-2 it is helpful to recognize that for Paul 'glory' had an *ethical* dimension, i.e., it was a glory-righteousness (3.9b, 18). Paul is saying, 'since we have this ministry of transforming glory-righteousness. . . we do not use shameful, underhanded ways'. Paul achieves the 'glory' transition in 4.1 because of its righteousness and light associations (all of which expose hidden, unethical practices). This ethical aspect of God's כָּבוֹד/δόξα is clearly evident in the OT—both in the first exodus tradition (e.g., Exod. 33.19; 33.22; cf. 34.6-7) and in the second (Isa. 26.10; 33.15-17; 45.25-26; 46.13; 58.8; 60.1-2, 21; 62.1-2). And not surprisingly, the two elements which Isaiah emphasizes through poetic parallels with 'glory' are 'righteousness' and 'light'. See the discussion below.

4. The verb ἀπειπάμεθα is followed by three epexegetical participles (or adverbial participles of means). Two provide a negative explanation of what Paul has renounced (μὴ περιπατοῦντες... μηδὲ δολοῦντες...) and one gives the positive (ἀλλὰ... συνιστάνοντες...).

that his glorious message is veiled/hindered to some individuals (in contrast to the unhindered glory of 3.18),[1] but the reason[2] for this is [not himself, or his message, but. . .] because they have chosen their own destructive path (4.3b)[3] and because Satan hinders the light/message τῆς δόξης τοῦ Χριστοῦ from 'dawning' on them (4.4).[4] Clarifying further (γάρ) the content of his message, the glory of the messiah, and responding to criticisms, Paul counters that he preaches Christ as κύριον and himself and his associates as δούλους (4.5), since the new creation light has 'dawned'[5] on them in keeping with God's eschatological promises. It gives them a new (Isaianic servant) perspective on the messiah and themselves (4.6).

In this section (4.1-6), identification with the Isaianic servant's mission in new covenant and new exodus is either developed or anticipated through three avenues: (1) the continued use of new covenant categories as defined in 3.1-18; (2) Paul's *'ebed* ministry of δόξα-light to the blind, and (3) the continuation of Paul's 'new Moses' portrait.

New Covenant Theme Continued in 4.1-6

From the opening reference to τὴν διακονίαν ταύτην (4.1) it is clear that 4.1-6 advances Paul's discussion of his new covenant ministry (3.6–διακόνους καινῆς διαθήκης; cf. 3.3, 7, 8, 9). Furthermore, the most central of the new covenant categories developed in 3.1-18, δόξα, is now related to Paul's proclamation message. Those who do not see the gospel's δόξα are 'veiled' by unbelief to the δόξα-light of the messiah (4.4, 6). As Plummer points out, the geniti-

---

1. It is difficult to determine whether this ineffectiveness was a charge against Paul, and if so, by the Corinthians or by the false apostles.
2. The relative clause ἐν τοῖς ἀπολλυμένοις... gives a reason why Paul's gospel is veiled and it recalls the earlier description of those who were on the perishing pathway (2.15; cf. 1 Cor. 1.18).
3. The participle suggests that they do not receive the gospel because they have already chosen the road to destruction, or perhaps they are simply unaware that their path leads to perishing.
4. The ἐν οἷς grammatically extends ἐν τοῖς ἀπολλυμένοις as a relative clause, 'in whose case'. Logically, it provides a further reason why Paul's gospel message is veiled to some.
5. This new-creation dawning stands in contrast to those who are perishing (4.4).

val construction, τῆς δόξης τοῦ Χριστοῦ, provides the content[1] of τοῦ εὐαγγελιον—the gospel 'which contains and proclaims the glory of the messiah'.[2] Paul's message of a 'crucified messiah' (1 Cor. 1.23) was the same message of the crucified τὸν κύριον τῆς δόξης (1 Cor. 2.8). Thus Paul's christology here, as earlier, is formulated in messianic categories, allowing for the fuller meaning of Χριστός.[3]

Paul's 'Ebed (δόξα-Light) Ministry to the Blind
A variety of factors reinforce the alignment between Paul's ministry and that of Isaiah's *'ebed Yahweh* here in 4.1-6. First, it is possible that the quotation in 4.6a is Isaianic (or at least has been modified through Isaianic traditions) which, if so, would create definite affinities with the *'ebed's* mission. But commentators are divided over the source of Paul's quotation, so it may be helpful to observe the texts involved in the comparison with 2 Cor. 4.6a:

MT:	וְחֹשֶׁךְ עַל־פְּנֵי תְהוֹם . . . וַיֹּאמֶר אֱלֹהִים יְהִי אוֹר	(Gen. 1.2-3)
	הָעָם הַהֹלְכִים בַּחֹשֶׁךְ רָאוּ אוֹר גָּדוֹל	(Isa. 9.1[2])
	יֹשְׁבֵי בְּאֶרֶץ צַלְמָוֶת אוֹר נָגַהּ עֲלֵיהֶם	
	הֲתֵדַע בְּשׂוּם־אֱלוֹהַּ עֲלֵיהֶם וְהוֹפִיעַ אוֹר עֲנָנוֹ	(Job 37.15)
	זָרַח בַּחֹשֶׁךְ אוֹר לַיְשָׁרִים	(Ps. 112[111].4)
LXX:	σκότος ἐπάνω τῆς ἀβύσσου... καὶ εἶπεν ὁ θεός, Γενηθήτω φῶς	(Gen. 1.2-3)
	ὁ λαὸς ὁ πορευόμενος ἐν σκότει, ἴδετε φῶς μέγα· οἱ κατοικοῦντες ἐν χώρᾳ καὶ σκιᾷ θανάτου, φῶς λάμψει ἐφ' ὑμᾶς	(Isa. 9.1)
	φῶς ποιήσας ἐκ σκότους	(Job 37.15)
	ἐξανέτειλεν ἐν σκότει φῶς τοῖς εὐθέσιν	(Ps. 111.4)
NT:	ὁ θεὸς ὁ εἰπών, Ἐκ σκότους φῶς λάμψει,...	(2 Cor. 4.6a)

1. Or τῆς δόξης τοῦ Χριστοῦ could be taken as the subjective genitive of τοῦ εὐαγγελιον (either way, the sense is the same).
2. Plummer, *II Corinthians*, p. 117. It weakens the force of τῆς δόξης to treat it as a descriptive genitive modifying τοῦ εὐαγγελιον, 'the glorious gospel'. That τῆς δόξης relates to τοῦ Χριστοῦ is confirmed by the clause to follow, ὅς ἐστιν εἰκὼν τοῦ θεοῦ and by the explanation of preaching Christ as κύριον (4.5a).
3. Cf. the designation of Satan as ὁ θεὸς τοῦ αἰῶνος τούτου (4.4), a phrase usually in contrast to ὁ αἰὼν ὁ μέλλων/ἐρχόμενος, i.e., the messianic age.

The source of the quotation in 2 Cor. 4.6a has been viewed from at least six different alternatives: (1) Gen. 1.3 alone;[1] (2) Gen. 1.3 as understood through Isa. 9.2;[2] (3) Gen. 1.3 as altered by and mutually interpreted through Isa. 9.2;[3] (4) Isa. 9.2 cited which itself reflects creation;[4] (5) Isa. 9.2 cited with limited original creation imagery;[5] or (6) Gen. 1.3 as influenced by Ps. 111.4 or Job 37.15.[6] By comparison with the first four options, the fifth[7] and sixth[8] appear less likely. However, the first four options merit our closer consideration.

The New Testament quotation does not align exactly with either Gen. 1.3 or Isa. 9.2.[9] Nevertheless, in favor of the Genesis source is the introductory formula, εἶπεν ὁ θεός (missing from Isa. 9.2), which closely resembles that of 2 Cor. 4.6a, ὁ θεὸς ὁ εἰπών. Also,

---

1. Most commentators attribute the quotation to Gen. 1.3 (and expanded through Gen. 2.3); e.g., Harris, '2 Corinthians', p. 341. However, many who suggest Gen. 1.3 seem unaware of the Isa. 9.1(2) alternative: Smith, 'The Function of 2 Corinthians 3.7–4.6', p. 123; Souza, *New Covenant*, p. 189; Barrett, *Second Epistle to the Corinthians*, p. 134; Hooker, 'Beyond the Things That are Written', p. 302; Bultmann, *Second Letter to the Corinthians*, p. 108.

2. This position holds that 2 Cor. 4.6a is essentially a free rendering of Gen. 1.3; however, Isa. 9.2 has modified not so much the Gen. 1.3 text as Paul's thinking and application of the creation text. E.g., Furnish, *II Corinthians*, p. 224.

3. E.g., Stockhausen ('Moses' Veil', p. 415) argues that Paul has 'amplified and altered his reference to Genesis 1.3 with the vocabulary of Isaiah 9.2' and understands the two texts to be 'mutually interpreting'. Cf. Klauck, '2 Kor 4,1-6', pp. 290-91.

4. Collange, *Énigmes*, p. 138; Martin, *2 Corinthians*, p. 80; Martini, '2 Cor 4,6', I, pp. 461-74; Kim, *The Origin of Paul's Gospel*, pp. 6-8, 229-32; Oostendorp, *Another Jesus*, p. 48.

5. Richard, 'Polemics', p. 360.

6. Plummer, *Second Epistle to the Corinthians*, pp. 119-20.

7. In an attempt to limit the influence of Gen. 1.3 in 2 Cor. 4.6a, some have sought alternative wisdom sources for the εἰκών imagery in 3.18; 4.4. But such a limitation on the vocabulary overlooks the clear creation imagery in 4.4 with φωτισμόν.

8. With the exception of ἐκ σκότους (in Job 37.15; though the MT is referring to lightning), Ps. 111.4 and Job 37.15 simply do not offer any further help in explaining the alterations to Gen. 1.3. Also, on a conceptual level, the use of the light imagery in Ps. 111.4 and Job 37.15 is more for a wisdom application than for salvific purposes.

9. Both lack the *immediate* mention of ἐκ σκότους (although it may be assumed from the context of Gen. 1.2; Isa. 9.1a; 8.22).

Paul's earlier reference to Christ as the εἰκών of God recalls first-creation imagery.[1] However, the evidence of word order,[2] verb form,[3] lexical affinities,[4] and figurative sense,[5] demonstrates that the quotation *itself* has most probably been derived from Isa. 9.2. In addition, the preponderance of Isaianic language in the surrounding context (see below) strengthens this conclusion. To sum up, the 'outer packaging' of the quotation mimics the first creation (Gen. 1.3), but its content is a reference to Isaiah's second creation (Isa. 9.2). Therefore, option one (Gen. 1.3 cited alone) may be ruled out. Furthermore, option two (a modified *understanding* of Gen. 1.3 through Isa. 9.2) fails to account for the verbal changes. However, to make a choice between options three and four is problematic. Such a fine distinction may drive an artificial wedge between what Paul is doing and Isaiah's own use of creation imagery. The data seems to suggest *both* alterations of the Genesis text through Isa. 9.2 and a sense in which Paul is carrying on interpretive traditions of Isaiah (which themselves reflect original creation).

I draw Isa. 9.2 (2 Cor. 4.6a) into the discussion to acknowledge its contribution in the apostle's identification with Isaiah's *'ebed Yahweh* and christological mission. I do not argue that Isa. 9.2 is an *'ebed*

1. E.g., LXX Gen. 1.26-27; 5.1, 3; 9.6. The LXX term is not found in Isaiah's extensive second-creation imagery. However, this may simply recall Paul's own re-creation imagery of 2 Cor. 3.18 where εἰκόνα is also used.

2. In Isa. 9.1(2) φῶς comes before the verb (as in 2 Cor. 4.6a); whereas in Gen. 1.3 φῶς follows the verb.

3. The verb in Gen. 1.3 (γενηθήτω) is an aorist passive imperative, 'Let there be light,' whereas the verb in Isa. 9.1(2) and in 2 Cor. 4.6a (λάμψει) is future active indicative, 'Light will shine'—another promise-formula in 2 Cor. 2.14–7.4. Cf. Collange (*Énigmes*, p. 138) who opposes the Genesis background by asking what average Christian would not have known that God said, 'Que la lumière soit' and not 'la lumière brillera'.

4. The same verb (λάμπω) is used in Isa. 9.1(2) as in 2 Cor. 4.6a, in contrast to Gen. 1.3 (γίνομαι). This becomes more significant when considered in view of the OT/LXX uses of λάμπω. The verbal form occurs only 4 times within the OT material (Prov. 4.18; Lam. 4.7; Isa. 4.2; 9.1[2]), and the noun λαμπάς only 12 times (7 times of literal torches, lamps, etc; 5 times in a figurative usage), and of its 5 figurative usages only one is of spiritual/ethical 'shining' (Isa. 62.1; for the other figurative usages see Job 41.10[11]; Nah. 2.4[5]; Ezek. 1.13; Zech. 12.6).

5. Like Isaiah, Paul uses λάμπω to refer to the breaking in of spiritual (salvific) light of messianic deliverance.

passage; it is not. However, its language is highly reminiscent of the
'ebed who brings the δόξα-light to those who are blind and in
darkness (Isa. 42.6-7, 16; 49.6, 9; cf. 43.8; 60.1-2). Certainly a later
reader of the Isaiah text as a whole, such as Paul, may have associated
Isa. 9.2 with the *'ebed* texts and read its promise in light of the
servant's mission. This blended or associative approach would seem
feasible, since in 2 Cor. 4.1-6 Paul utilizes the Isa. 9.2 quote in conjunction with other directly related *'ebed* material (see below). It
would appear that Paul links together the promise in Isa. 9.2 (which is
reminicent of the *'ebed*'s role as 'light to the nations') with the argument that he preaches Jesus as Lord and himself as servant (4.5) and
Satan's blinding those who would see the light of his gospel (4.3-4; cf.
Acts 26.18[1]).[2] It is interesting to note that Paul, the apostle to the
Gentiles, here appeals to Isa. 9.1-2, since this tradition also plays a
role in Christian interpretation of Jesus' Galilean, *Gentile* ministry
(Mt. 4.15-16;[3] cf. Lk. 1.79).

A second line of evidence more directly verifies the *'ebed* orientation of Paul's thinking in 4.1-6. Beyond the Isa. 9.2 quotation (which
provides an associative link), Paul's dependence upon Isaiah texts, and
especially the *'ebed* traditions, for 'coloring' his ministry is evident
from his broader selection of vocabulary. The most persuasive terminological ties are the κύριος-δοῦλος appellations, αὐγάζω, and
τυφλόω. For instance, the κύριος-δοῦλος combination, though found
elsewhere in the Old Testament, may be narrowed to Isaianic passages
through an examination of the way these terms are used within
Pauline christology. For Paul, it is the exalted δοῦλος who becomes
κύριος, a tradition which he and other New Testament authors have
probably derived from Isaiah.[4] Also, the figurative usage of

1. Some of these influences from Isaiah for shaping the course of Paul's ministry
will be discussed below under 2 Cor. 6.1-2.

2. So the point of Collange, *Énigmes*, pp. 138-43; Richard, 'Polemics', p. 360.

3. Matthew develops scriptural support for the transition in Jesus' ministry to a
Gentile region (after John the Baptist is 'handed over') through the verbal link
between the narrative, [Jesus] ἀνεχώρησεν εἰς τὴν Γαλιλαίαν (v. 12), and
Γαλιλαία τῶν ἐθνῶν in the quotation itself (v. 15). That Paul also gravitated
towards this OT passage is understandable in view of his Gentile ministry.

4. E.g., Phil. 2.5-11. Cf. the movement from servant to Lord in Lucan christology (Bock, *Prophecy and Pattern*, pp. 262-70). On Paul's use of δοῦλος in his
own self-portrait (cf. Chapter 5, §3).

αὐγάζω[1] and τυφλόω[2] for *spiritual* enlightenment and blindness is a phenomenon which can, for the most part, be limited to Isaiah.

Less demonstrable items of Isaianic vocabulary, due to their much broader use in the LXX, are terms such as δόξα (see above), φῶς,[3] σκότος,[4] and εὐαγγελίζω.[5] The proportionate and collective use of these terms in Isaiah, however, makes this source more likely than it may have appeared at first.[6] The fact that these terms—blindness, light, darkness, proclamation—help define Jesus' *'ebed* ministry

1. Collectively, αὐγάζω, αὔγασμα, αὐγω, and αὐγή are used 11 times in the LXX, and *only* two times in a figurative sense of spiritual 'dawning' (Job 29.3; Isa. 59.9). The Isaiah background seems more likely because of its contextual reference to people walking in spiritual blindness (Isa. 59.10).

2. Together τυφλόω and τυφλός occur 24 times in the LXX, with 12 literal and 12 figurative uses. Of the 12 uses for spiritual blindness, nine are from Isaiah (29.18; 35.5; 42.7, 16, 18-19; 43.8; 59.10; 61.1), and only three elsewhere (Deut. 28.29; Ps. 146.8; Zeph. 1.17). In fact, the lack of spiritual discernment is often explained by NT writers through quotations or allusions to Isaiah; e.g., Isa. 6.9-10 (in Mt. 13.14-15; Mk 4.12; Lk. 8.10; Jn 12.40; and especially Acts 28.26-27 in regard to Paul's ministry); Isa. 8.14; 28.16 (in Rom. 9.33; 10.11; 1 Pet. 2.6); Isa. 26.19; 35.5-6; 42.18; 61.1 (in Mt. 11.5; Lk. 7.22); 52.15 (in Rom. 15.21); Isa. 53.1 (in Jn 12.38; Rom. 10.16); Isa. 61.1-2 (in Lk. 4.18-19); and Isa. 64.3(4) (in 1 Cor. 2.9).

3. LXX Isaiah contains φῶς, φωτισμόν, and φωτίζω of spiritual light more than any other OT work (e.g., Isa. 2.5; 5.20; 9.2; 10.17; 26.9; 30.26; 42.6, 16; 45.7; 49.6; 50.10-11; 51.4; 53.11; 58.8, 10; 59.9; 60.1 twice, 3, 19 twice, 20; 62.1; cf. 4.5; 13.10; 18.4).

4. Again, the occurrences of spiritual σκότος in LXX Isaiah far outweigh that of any other OT writing (e.g., Isa. 5.20, 30; 8.22; 9.1[2]; 13.10; 16.3; 29.15, 18; 42.7, 16; 45.3, 7, 19; 47.1, 5; 48.16; 49.9; 50.3, 10; 58.10; 59.9; 60.2).

5. Together εὐαγγελίζω and εὐαγγέλιον occur 22 times in the LXX, mostly of a literal messenger bringing good news after some kind of military advancement (e.g., 1 Sam. 31.9; 2 Sam. 4.10 twice; 18.19-31 six times; 1 Chron. 10.9); however, 7 times in a theological usage proclaiming Yahweh's military victory (Isa. 40.9; 52.7; 60.6; 61.1; cf. Ps. 95(96).2; Joel 2.32; Nah. 1.15). Most of these occur in Isaiah 40–55, and at least one of the other references may itself be dependent upon Isaiah (Nah. 1.15). Also, the passages within Isaiah (especially 52.7 and 61.1) play a significant role in shaping NT gospel mission (Mt. 11.5; Lk. 4.18-19; 7.22; Rom. 10.15).

6. Though seldom noticed, it may be more than coincidence that three of the terms in the suffering list that follows—one common word (θλίβω) and two unusual terms (στενοχωρέω and ἀπορέω) (2 Cor. 4.7-9) are found in the LXX immediately preceding the quotation from Isa. 9.1(2). The correlation appears to be more that of accidental vocabulary assumption than any substantive correlation.

strengthens this observation.[1] Evidently, Paul's new covenant ministry of enlightening the blind, of bringing glory-light to those in darkness, extends Jesus' servant mission. In sum, the collective image found in 4.1-6 of Paul as a (suffering) 'servant' who brings light-into-darkness and δόξα-light proclamation to those who are blind can hardly be mistaken as other than one which mimicks the Isaianic servant.

Though somewhat speculative, it is possible that Paul's shift from a physical to a spiritual veiling was also inspired by Isaiah traditions. Paul's argument fluctuates between Moses' physical veil (3.7-13), a spiritual veiling (3.14-15; 4.3-4), and a spiritual unveiling (3.16-18) with regard to new covenant ministry. But what caused Paul to make this associative leap? In Isa. 49.9, Yahweh commissions the servant to say to those in darkness, 'Be unveiled (ἀνακαλυφθῆναι)!' It is possible that Isa. 49.9 stimulated Paul's thoughts about the veil of spiritual darkness not yet being lifted for many Jews (μὴ ἀνα καλυπτ όμενον), in contrast to all believers approaching God with unveiled faces (ἀνακεκαλυμμένῳ).[2] This understanding of veiling/unveiling would similarly correspond to the 'veiling' or 'covering' of spiritual darkness in Isa. 60.2, 'darkness covers (καλύψει) the earth'.[3] The difficulty with this view is that in Isaiah no explicit connection is made between Moses' physical 'veiling' and the spiritual 'veiling' of the Lord's glory (only the latter is developed in Isaiah); this appears to be the work of Paul (although the verbal closeness between Exodus and Isaiah may have inspired the connection).

1. For Jesus as the *'ebed* healer-of-the-blind see especially the use of Isa. 26.19; 35.5-6; 42.18; 61.1 in Mt. 11.5 (cf. Lk. 7.22) and Isa. 61.1-2; 58.6 in Lk. 4.18-19; cf. Isa. 8.23–9.1 in Mt. 4.15-16 and Isa. 6.9-10 in Mt. 13.14-15.

2. The term ἀνακαλύπτω is used only in 2 Cor. 3.14, 18; and καλύπτω twice in 2 Cor. 4.3. Cf. the use of ἀνακαλύπτω with light/opening the understanding of persons in 1 Esd. 8.79; 12.22; 28.11; 33.16; cf. nakedness and exposure (Isa. 20.4).

3. The connection is strengthened by the glory-light theme in Isa. 60.1 (Φωτίζου Φωτίζου Ἰερουσαλὴμ, ἥκει γάρ σου τὸ φῶς, καὶ ἡ δόξα Κυρίου ἐπὶ σὲ ἀνατέταλκεν). The possibility of Isa. 49.9 (and Isa. 60.2) having influenced Paul's 'unveiling' ideas is all the more likely when it is recognized that Isaiah-texts (specifically Isa. 6.9-10 and 29.10-12) played a role in the hardness and unbelief of Israel, that is, its 'veiling' which Paul speaks of in 2 Cor. 3.14-15 (cf. 4.3-4). For a development of these tradition roots see Stockhausen ('Moses' Veil', pp. 242-69), who uses Jn 12.41 and Rom. 11.7-8 to trace Paul's hardening terminology in 2 Cor. 3.14-15 back to Isa. 6.9-10 and 29.10-12.

Having established a channel of tradition-history between Paul and the *'ebed Yahweh* in 4.1-6 (reinforced through Jesus' *'ebed* ministry), it is only a short step to show how the Isaianic servant functions as a new covenant mediator and leader in the second exodus.[1]

The 'New Moses' Portrait Continues

Paul has been given adequacy (ἱκανός) for the task as Moses had been given,[2] he ministers in a covenant with a glory which surpasses the glory of Moses' covenant,[3] and he has seen a vision of the Lord's glory similar to Moses' vision.[4] Now the 'new Moses' portrait progresses in 4.1-6 through two further parallels. First, like Moses, Paul has his ministry of glory because he has received mercy (4.1; καθὼς ἠλεήθημεν). Carol Stockhausen points out correctly that 'καθὼς ἠλεήθημεν is not simply a pious phrase, but another evocation of the positive comparison with Moses'.[5] For Moses, the vision of Yahweh's glory prior to his reception of the second set of stone tablets consisted of a proclamation of Yahweh's name—the leading characteristic being mercy (ἐλεήσω ὅν ἄν ἐλεῶ).[6] Again, in the actual theophany, compassion and mercy are repeated first in the disclosure of Yahweh's glory and the divine name.[7] Second, in 4.3-4 Paul also appropriates Moses' veil to himself and to the communication of his gospel.[8] Here it is no longer Moses' face which is veiled as he communicates God's revelation to the people; instead, it is Paul,[9]

---

1. Chapter 5, §§3-4.

2. 2 Cor. 2.16b–3.6; cf. Exod. 4.10-12.

3. 2 Cor. 3.7-11; cf. references above.

4. 2 Cor. 3.12-13, 18; cf. Exod. 33.18-23; 34.5-8.

5. 'Moses' Veil', p. 436.

6. LXX Exod. 33.19. Cf. Paul's use of Exod. 33.19 in Rom. 9.15 to explain the reception of divine mercy by the Gentiles and its withdrawal from Israel.

7. LXX Exod. 34.6.

8. Stockhausen, 'Moses' Veil', pp. 439-41. Cf. Dunn's comments ('2 Corinthians III. 17', p. 314) on 2 Cor. 3.17-18 that Christians are those 'who have responded to Paul's ministry of preaching and have entered the new covenant through the Spirit by turning to the Lord (in terms of the present argument = Spirit)'. In other words, the parallel is already implied in terms of Paul's preaching and Moses' proclamation earlier in 3.12-18; however, it becomes explicit in 4.1-6.

9. The aspect of Paul's own veiled glory in his life (in conjunction with his gospel message) is brought into closer focus in the next section (2 Cor. 4.7-15), where he explains why anything but glory is seen in his life.

and in particular his gospel (comparable to Moses' books and message), which are veiled because of unbelief.[1]

3. *Paul's Suffering—the Paradox of New Covenant* δόξα *(2 Corinthians 4.7-15)*

Context and Structure

2 Cor. 4.7-12 explains *why* the glory of Paul's new covenant ministry, a glory which is so exceeding in magnitude (cf. 3.7-11), *must* nevertheless be contained 'in earthen vessels' (ἐν ὀστρακίνοις σκεύεσιν), that is, in 'seinen schwachen gebrechen Leib'.[2] Paul's answer to the 'clay vessels' enigma is contained in the three ἵνα-clauses (4.7b, 10b, and 11b). This section elucidates the connection between Paul's suffering and his (paradoxical) 'theology of glory' (3.6–4.6). He accomplishes this through the three ἵνα-clause statements,[3] which combine to support the conclusion (ὥστε) in verse 12–'so death works in us, but life in you'.[4]

---

1. For further comparisons between Moses' ministry in Exod. 33–34 and Paul's ministry in 2 Cor. 3.1–4.6, see Stockhausen, 'Moses' Veil', pp. 442-44. Stockhausen compares Paul's open communication of the gospel (2 Cor. 4.2) with Moses' model of openly reporting God's word (Exod. 34.32). Also, Paul and Moses are simply humble conveyors of God's message (Exod. 34.32-34; cf. 2 Cor. 4.6 where Paul does not 'preach himself'). Again, in 2 Cor. 4.6 Paul returns to Moses' vision of divine glory. As the Lord had shone his glory-light on Moses (Exod. 33.17-23; presumed in 34.6, 29), so also his glory-light dawns on Paul—not on his face, but in his heart (in accord with the new covenant).

2. This connection between 3.4–4.6 and 4.7-15 has been noted by Brun, 'Zur Asulegung von II Cor. 5.1-10', p. 212; cf. Hafemann, *Suffering and the Spirit*, p. 68. As Kleinknecht (*Der leidende Gerechtfertigte*, p. 272) puts it, 4.7-15 functions as the 'Kontrapunkt' to the δόξα of Paul's διακονία so that the 'treasure' refers to 'die gerade als so "herrlich" erwiesene διακονία selbst'. Cf. Bultmann (*Second Letter to the Corinthians*, p. 111) who also notes the φανέρωσις catchword (4.10-11; cf. 2.14; 4.2).

3. The first ἵνα statement is modified by eight participles (grouped in four contrasting pairs with the repeated transition,... ἀλλ' οὐκ...). These participles illustrate the *means* by which Paul's suffering confirms that the glory/power belongs to God (thereby illustrating the way God responds to Paul's suffering, namely, by rescuing him again and again from his peril). The second and third ἵνα statements further explain Paul's suffering, this time along explicit christological lines.

4. Cf. Hafemann's analysis (*Suffering and the Spirit*, p. 69).

While in the depths of despair,[1] Paul nonetheless 'believes' in God (for rescue), and consequently he 'speaks' to God with a cry for help and at a later point (after rescue) 'speaks' praises to God (4.13b).[2] Two participial clauses provide the reasons for Paul's habit of believing God for rescue and proclaiming God's praise:[3] because he has the same 'spirit of faith' as the Psalmist, the righteous sufferer of old, who experienced similar deliverance [from near death] (4.13a), and because he is assured [even in the case of actual death] that he will be raised as was Jesus (4.14). Paul summarizes (γάρ) that he endures 'all things' [esp. the hardships in vv. 7-12] for the Corinthians, in order that this χάρις message of God's deliverance may result in many [as Paul and the Psalmist do in vv. 13-14] giving εὐχαριστία to the glory of God.

While Paul continues to discuss his καινὴ διαθήκη ministry in 4.7-15 (quiet traces of 3.1-18 linger on[4]), new covenant ideas *per se* have faded into the background. Nonetheless, the theme of identification with christological mission (again, going back to *'ebed Yahweh* traditions) remains strong, since such a linkage is vital for Paul if he is to justify the suffering nature of his own ministry.

---

1. The mood becomes almost oppressive in 4.7-12, but lifts dramatically with the use of Ps. 116.10 to a positive 'spirit of faith'.

2. The referent to 'speaking' in Ps. 116.10 is clearly a *lament* in view of the explicit cry to God, 'I am greatly afflicted.' However, in 2 Cor. 4.13 the 'speaking' referent is much less clear (no explicit content is provided). The despairing mood of the suffering catalogue (4.8-12) might suggest that Paul, like the Psalmist, 'speaks' to God in in a lament, or a prayer for rescue. However, the thanksgiving/praise in 2 Cor. 4.15 suggests at least proclamation in the presence of God's people (while the spreading of 'grace' perhaps allows for an even more general setting of gospel proclamation). If so, the shift in emphasis from lament to praise-proclamation is understandable in view of the lament itself being 'reused' in the praise of the Psalmist (and the anticipated praise being 'rehearsed' in lament Psalms).

3. Both participial phrases, ἔχοντες... and εἰδότες..., are causal (so Plummer, *II Corinthians*, pp. 132-33).

4. Compare ἵνα ἡ ὑπερβολὴ τῆς δυνάμεως ᾖ τοῦ θεοῦ καὶ μὴ ἐξ ἡμῶν (4.7) with τῆς ὑπερβαλλούσης δόξης (3.10) and οὐχ ὅτι ἀφ' ἑαυτῶν ἱκανοί ἐσμεν λογίσασθαί τι ὡς ἐξ ἑαυτῶν, ἀλλ' ἡ ἱκανότης ἡμῶν ἐκ τοῦ θεοῦ (3.5). Also, this section is an attempt to justify Paul's suffering in light of the theology of glory which is so much a part of his new covenant ministry, but not visually seen.

Deliverance Over to Death

The clearest indicator in 4.7-12 of Paul's identification with the mission of Isaiah's *'ebed Yahweh*, is found in the words: ἀεὶ... εἰς θάνατον παραδιδόμεθα (4.11). This time the traditions route will be taken through its christological path. In the passion predictions,[1] παραδίδωμι underscores the belief that Jesus was going to the cross in accordance with God's plan as revealed in Old Testament scriptures. The Old Testament background of these 'deliverance' sayings is usually attributed to Isaiah 53, where παραδίδωμι occurs three times (in 53.6 and twice in 53.12).[2] These sources may be compared with 2 Cor. 4.11, especially since they contain both παραδίδωμι and εἰς θάνατον:

LXX: καὶ κύριος <u>παρέδωκεν</u> αὐτὸν ταῖς ἁμαρτίαις ἡμῶν   (Isa. 53.6b)

διὰ τοῦτο αὐτὸς κληρονομήσει πολλοὺς   (Isa. 53.12)
καὶ τῶν ἰσχυρῶν μεριεῖ σκῦλα,
ἀνθ ' ὧν <u>παρεδόθη εἰς θάνατον</u> ἡ ψυχὴ αὐτοῦ,
καὶ ἐν τοῖς ἀνόμοις ἐλογίσθη
καὶ αὐτὸς ἁμαρτίας πολλῶν ἀνήνεγκεν
καὶ διὰ τὰς ἀνομίας αὐτῶν παρεδόθη.

NT: ἀεὶ... <u>εἰς θάνατον παραδιδόμεθα</u>   (2 Cor. 4.11)

The verbal influence of the servant songs on the passion predictions is further strengthened through the use of μαστιγόω/ἐμπτύω (Isa. 50.6; cf. Mk 10.33-34; Lk. 18.32-33a)[3] and the more general assertion that the Son of Man/Christ δεῖ πολλὰ παθεῖν (Isa. 53.3-7;[4] cf. Mt. 16.21;

---

1. Mk 8.31; 9.31; 10.33-34 and parallels. Outside the passion predictions παραδίδωμι is frequently used in relation to Christ's death (e.g., Mt. 10.4; 17.22; 20.18-19; 26.24-25, 45, 27.2-4, 18, 26; Mk 3.19; 9.31; 10.33; 14.10-44; 15.1, 10, 15; Lk. 9.44; 18.32; 20.20; 24.7, 20; Jn 18.2; 19.11; cf. Acts 3.13; and in the epistles, only in material attributed to Paul, e.g., Rom. 4.25; 8.32; Gal. 2.20; cf. Eph. 5.2; 25).

2. There is some debate as to whether Isa. 53.6 or 53.12 is more appropriate. Regardless of the specific linguistic influence, as Moo points out (*Gospel Passion Narratives*, pp. 93-95, 97), the legitimacy of the passion allusion depends upon the broader hermeneutical process of the application of the servant songs to Jesus. Moo adequately counters France's skepticism (*Jesus and the Old Testament*, pp. 125-30) in tracing the passion predictions to Isaiah 53.

3. Cf. Mk 14.65; 15.19; Mt. 26.67; 27.30.

4. LXX Ps. 34.20 (πολλαὶ αἱ θλίψεις τῶν δικαίων) is sometimes cited as a parallel, but it is doubtful that such a gnomic statement could have substantiated the

17.12; Mk 8.31; 9.12; Lk. 9.22; 17.12, 25).

The same passion terminology—'delivered over'/'must suffer many things'—also illumines much post-resurrection preaching about Jesus. On the basis of the Old Testament scriptures, Luke recounts how the messiah had to (δεῖ) suffer (Lk. 24.26, 46). Similarly, in his account of Peter's sermon, God glorifies the Isaianic παῖδα—the one who ὑμεῖς παρεδώκατε, the one who fulfills the prophets' message: παθεῖν τὸν Χριστὸν αὐτοῦ (Acts 3.13, 18). Along these lines, he describes Paul's synagogue ministry as involving an explanation from the Old Testament that τὸν Χριστὸν ἔδει παθεῖν (Acts 17.3; cf. 26.23). It is from this Isaianic background that Paul himself depicts Christ as παρεδόθη διὰ τὰ παραπτώματα ἡμῶν and as the one whom God ὑπὲρ ἡμῶν πάντων παρέδωκεν αὐτόν (Rom. 4.25; 8.32[1]).[2]

Even so, here in 2 Cor. 4.11, Paul uses christological-passion language to speak of his own ministry. The linguistic similarity of εἰς θάνατον παραδιδόμεθα is very close to LXX Isa. 53.12b, παρεδόθη εἰς θάνατον ἡ ψυχὴ αὐτοῦ. And, considering that the context weaves the pattern of Jesus' dying-rising into Paul's own suffering (2 Cor. 4.10-12; cf. Rom. 4.25[3]), it is likely that Paul perceives his ministry here in light of servant mission, as following the pattern of a suffering messiah, the *'ebed Yahweh*. His παράδοσις to death is vital to the argument, for it is only because Jesus is a *suffering messiah* that Paul can claim to be a *suffering apostle*. Although paradoxical, suffering is an essential part of Paul's new covenant δόξα ministry; it is as much a part of divine providence as Christ's suffering was.

---

necessity for Jesus' unique suffering ministry (so Moo, *Gospel Passion Narratives*, p. 91).

1. This example is particularly important since it is found immediately preceding one of Paul's *own* suffering catalogues (Rom. 8.35-39).

2. Cranfield (*Romans*, I, p. 251) notes on Rom. 4.25, 'that it was formulated under the influence of Isa. 52.13–53.12 is hardly to be doubted'. In addition to the use of παραδίδωμι, there is significant correlation with διὰ τὰ παραπτώματα ἡμῶν (cf. διὰ τὰς ἀνομίας ἡμῶν/διὰ τὰς ἁμαρτίας in Isa. 53.5; ταῖς ἁμαρτίαις ἡμῶν in 53.6, and διὰ τὰς ἁμαρτίας αὐτῶν in 53.12) and a striking parallel with διὰ τὴν δικαίωσιν ἡμῶν in the latter half of v. 25 (cf. δικαιῶσαι— the *'ebed*'s justifying many in Isa. 53.11).

3. See discussion above on Rom. 4.25.

6. *Not Losing Heart in the Midst of Affliction (2 Cor. 4.16–5.10)*

Context and Structure

The main verbal idea of the 4.16–5.10 section is οὐκ ἐγκακοῦμεν (4.16a), an idea which is resumed by the positive, θαροῦμεν (5.6, 8).[1] In 4.16b–5.10, then, the apostle provides several reasons why he 'does not lose heart' in the midst of affliction.[2] The first reason[3] opens with a concession: even if our outer person is admittedly decaying, [the reason we do not lose heart is because. . .] our inner person is progressively being renewed (4.16b-c). The second reason (γάρ)[4] why Paul does not lose heart is that his light/temporal afflictions are producing for him an eternal reward (4.17). Yet this production of glory is not automatic, it will only happen provided (μὴ σκοπ οὐντων... ἀλλὰ [σκοπούντων]...)[5] he and the Corinthians keep

1. As pointed out by Bultmann, *Second Letter to the Corinthians*, p. 140.

2. The structure of 4.16–5.10 is difficult because of the ambiguity of the successive γάρ statements (4.17, 18; 5.1, 2, 4, 7). The exegete must determine in each case whether (1) they are explanatory of an earlier thought, (2) they go back to the original verbal proposition οὐκ ἐγκακοῦμεν (4.16a), or (3) in some cases do both. As reflected in the structural discussion, the verbal proposition οὐκ ἐγκακοῦμεν (4.16a) should be given prominence because the later parallel θαροῦμεν (5.6, 8) demonstrates that this has been Paul's central point all along.

3. The construction ἀλλ ' εἰ... ἀλλ ' *logically* supplies the reason Paul and his helpers 'do not lose heart' and, it may be understood after the second ἀλλά, 'are encouraged in their ministry'.

4. The γάρ is not simply a restatement or explanation of 4.16b-c (*contra* Plummer, *II Corinthians*, p. 137), but in its expansion of 4.16b-c it provides *another* distinct basis for οὐκ ἐγκακοῦμεν (4.16a) (as pointed out by Furnish, *II Corinthians*, p. 262; Bultmann, *Second Letter to the Corinthians*, p. 129). In 4.16b-c the *fact/presence* of the spiritual renewal process is mentioned; while in 4.17 the *comparative value* of renewal process is developed. Verse 4.16b-c focuses on the current daily process; whereas 4.17 introduces the already–not yet tension (i.e., temporal vs. eternal).

5. The precise syntax of the genitive absolute participle (μὴ σκοπούντων... ἀλλὰ [σκοπούντων]...) is difficult to determine. That the participle does not go back to 4.16a (but develops 4.17) is clear from the explanation (γάρ) in 4.18b which reuses αἰώνια (cf. αἰώνιον in 4.17). Yet, how the circumstantial participle functions in relation to κατεργάζεται is less certain. It has been taken as conditional, 'if/provided that. . . ' (Plummer, *II Corinthians*, p. 139; Harris, '2 Corinthians', p. 345); temporal, 'while. . . ' (NASV); or explicatory, 'for/in as much as. . . ' (Furnish, *II Corinthians*, p. 263). However, the conditional, 'if/provided that. . . '

their eyes on the unseen/eternal (4.17). A more specific development of the unseen 'eternal' (4.18) and the third reason that οὐκ ἐγκακοῦμεν (4.16a) is introduced with another γάρ in 5.1a–because even our outer 'decaying' body, our earthly tent, will be replaced by a new body from heaven. Paul bases his new-body hope on three things: (1) the 'rebuilt temple' of Christ's new body (5.1b); (2) the Spirit-inspired groaning for such a new body (5.2-4 [v. 3 is parenthetical];[1] cf. Rom. 8.23),[2] and (3) God's deposit τοῦ πνεύματος which ensures things to come (5.5). The final reason[3] why Paul does not lose heart/remains confident in the face of suffering and death is given in 5.6-8: even if death were to come, he would prefer to be in the Lord's presence anyway. The ethical implication (διό) of 'being present with the Lord' (5.8) and of such an eschatological confidence (4.16–5.8) is to be pleasing to the Lord now (5.9), particularly in light of (γάρ) the future tribunal where all believers will be justly rewarded for their behavior (5.10).

In 4.16–5.10, Paul develops further the *inward* δόξα of new covenant ministry, which is a pledge of *outward* eschatological renewal to come. Thus in this section the categories of καινὴ διαθήκη (as defined in 3.1-18) resurface. There are at least two indications that Paul continues to have new covenant theology in mind: (1) the present renewal of the 'inner person', and (2) the giving of the Spirit as a down payment towards eschatological promises. The Spirit-promise of 5.5 will also be examined in light of its parallel in 1.21-22

appears to be most suitable in view of the probable indirect exhortation to the Corinthians here, particularly if the ἡμῶν is meant to include them (cf. 3.18 and the 'looking' in a mirror).

1. The repetition of στενάζομεν (5.2, 4) draws these verses together as a unit around the parenthetical thought of 5.3.

2. The γάρ of 5.2 could provide either (1) a further development of that which is not seen in 4.18 (Hodge, *I & II Corinthians*, p. 490), or (2) the basis for the promise/hope of a new body—'we have a building from God'—mentioned in 5.1 (Harris, '2 Corinthians', p. 347). The latter is preferable since in Rom. 8.23 it is the first fruits of the the Spirit which inspire the 'groaning' for a new body (cf. 2 Cor. 5.5 where the Spirit is down payment of what is to come).

3. The θαρροῦμεν (5.6, 8) extends the thought of οὐκ ἐγκακοῦμεν (4.16a). While the participial phrase ειδότες ὅτι... is grammatically related to θαρροῦντες, it logically provides another reason for being confident (cf. θαρροῦμεν and εὐδοκοῦμεν).

in order to reach further conclusions about the nature of Paul's
promise-theology.

Renewal of the 'Inner Person'

Since 4.16 is the only reference to ὁ ἔξω ἄνθρωπος and ὁ ἔσω
[ἄνθρωπος] in Paul's writings,[1] it is difficult to define their precise
meaning.[2] What can be determined with certainty, however, is that the
daily renewal of the 'inner person'—ὁ ἔσω ἡμῶν [ἄνθρωπος]
ἀνακαινοῦται ἡμέρᾳ καὶ ἡμέρᾳ—is a resurgence of Paul's new
covenant discussion in 3.1-18. The progressive nature of the process
(ἡμέρᾳ καὶ ἡμέρᾳ), the idea of renewal (ἀνακαινοῦται [passive
voice]), and the resultant βάρος δόξης (4.17) clearly recall the
Spirit's transforming ministry under the new covenant: τὴν δόξαν
κυρίου κατοπτριζόμενοι τὴν αὐτὴν εἰκόνα μεταμορφούμεθα
(passive voice) ἀπὸ δόξης εἰς δόξαν (3.18).[3] Likewise in 4.17, Paul
is not discouraged by outer decay and suffering, since in his new
covenant ministry there is a reverse process going on—that is, the
Spirit's inward renewal. Also, καθ' ὑπερβολὴν εἰς ὑπερβολὴν
αἰώνιον βάρος δόξης in 4.17 echoes the description of exceeding
new covenant glory in 3.10 (τῆς ὑπερβαλλούσης δόξης).

1. Rom. 7.22 contains half of the pair (συνήδομαι γὰρ τῷ νόμῳ τοῦ θεοῦ
κατὰ τὸν ἔσω ἄνθρωπον).
2. Most commentaries and anthropological studies want to avoid any sense of
Platonic dualism. E.g., Harris argues ('2 Corinthians', p. 345) that Paul does not
have in mind two distinct entities—body and soul. Rather, the 'outer person' is the
whole person in the creaturely mortality, the person of this age; the 'inner person' is
the whole person as a 'new creation' (5.17) or a 'new person' (Col. 3.9-10). Cf.
Stacey, *Pauline View of Man*, pp. 211-14; Martin, '2 Corinthians', pp. 91-92.
While I would agree that the closest parallel in Pauline material is the 'new person'
and the 'old person', the 'new person' in Paul has a more corporate-christological
identity and the 'new creation' (while having an individual aspect) goes beyond the
individual.
3. A number of scholars note this connection between 4.16-17 and the new
covenant ministry of the Spirit in 3.1-18. E.g., Plummer, *Second Epistle to the
Corinthians*, pp. 136-37; Barrett, *Second Epistle to the Corinthians*, p. 147; Martin,
2 Corinthians, pp. 137-38. Stockhausen ('Moses' Veil', p. 446) aptly ties together
the inward transformation theme of 3.18; 4.16, 18; 5.12, 17 (although 5.17 needs to
be given a primarily supra-individual perspective).

The Spirit as ἀρραβών *of New Covenant Promise*

The participial clause in 5.5, ὁ δοὺς [θεός] ἡμῖν τὸν ἀρραβῶνα τοῦ πνεύματος, parallels an earlier reference in 1.22, ὁ δοὺς τὸν ἀρραβῶνα τοῦ πνεύματος ἐν ταῖς καρδίαις ἡμῶν. Together, they reflect Paul's new covenant theology from 3.1-18, for it is ἡ διακονία τοῦ πνεύματος which comes with glory. The added phrase in 1.22, ἐν ταῖς καρδίαις ἡμῶν (an 'organic' part of the new covenant in Paul's thinking),[1] indicates that with ἀρραβῶνα τοῦ πνεύματος Paul most probably had in mind the Old Testament traditions about the Spirit that he has already drawn into his 3.1-6 tapestry of new covenant texts. For example, in LXX Ezek. 36.26-27a Yahweh promises, δώσω ὑμῖν καρδίαν καινὴν, καὶ πνεῦμα καινόν... καὶ τὸ πνευμά μου δώσω ἐν ὑμῖν (cf. 11.19; 18.31; 37.14; Jer. 31[38].33).

If 2 Cor. 1.20-22 may once again be used in conjunction with 5.5 to explore Paul's traditions thinking in this area of Spirit-promise, it should also be noted that the promise of 1.20-22 ('establishes... anointed... sealed... gave us the Spirit in our hearts as a pledge') likely has additional roots within the traditions of Isaiah. Although not one of the 'servant songs' of modern scholarship, the servant-like passage of Isa. 61.1-2 speaks of the Spirit's 'anointing' an individual to proclaim good news, freedom, and release to the captives, *patterned after a background of release from Babylon* (exilic return theology).[2] For the early church this tradition was significant in defining the nature of Christ's ministry (Lk. 4.18-19; Acts 4.27; 10.38; cf. Mt. 11.5). It would appear that in the Spirit-anointing promise of 1.20-22 (reiterated partially in 5.5) Paul is uniting his ministry with the messianic anointing of Christ (and the Isaianic traditions which lie behind the christological event).[3]

---

1. Cf. ἐγγεγραμμένη ἐν ταῖς καρδίαις ἡμῶν (3.3); ἐν πλαξὶν καρδίαις σαρκίαις (3.3); ἐν ταῖς καρδίαις ἡμῶν (4.6).

2. Cf. Isa. 42.7; 49.8. The content of the *'ebed Yahweh's* proclamation becomes extremely important in my contextual theory and is further developed in the next chapter.

3. For a similar traditions proposal regarding the Spirit-anointing in 2 Cor. 1.20-22 see Furnish, *II Corinthians*, p. 137; Martin, *2 Corinthians*, 28; Hughes, *Second Corinthians*, pp. 39-40.

5. *Summary of the Traditions in the Fragment's Remote Context*

The remote context of 2.14–5.10 plays a significant role in my hypothesis by introducing and orienting the reader to new covenant and second exodus/return concepts. Support for the traditions hypothesis may be summarized according to each unit. In addition, I will evaluate the weight of the evidence with respect to the probability that it develops either new covenant or exilic return traditions (especially as related to the *'ebed Yahweh*).

In 2.14–3.6 the clearest use of new covenant traditions in 2.14–3.6 is seen in the explicit statement, διακόνους καινῆς διαθήκης,[1] and in two other allusions: ἐν πλάξιν σαρκίναις (related to the Spirit's work)[2] and the law written ἐν ταῖς καρδίαις.[3] Also, in the background of the Old Testament texts which Paul employs[4] one finds (exilic) return promises intertwined with the new covenant promises. Of less certain traditions origin is the correlation between the adequacy of Moses and Paul for covenant ministry, implying that Paul functions as a new Moses (in line with the *'ebed* and Christ).[5] Furthermore, it is on a somewhat speculative level that I suggest that Paul's triumphal-procession imagery is influenced by second exodus/return traditions: Yahweh and his servant lead the exiles back home on a triumphal highway.

In the next section (3.7-18), the focus on new covenant is developed through the contrast between the δόξα of new covenant and the δόξα of old covenant ministry. This series of contrasts along with the preceding section help determine which categories are 'organically' related to Paul's new covenant ministry (Spirit-life, surpassing glory, righteousness as opposed to condemnation, in the heart, and so on).

In 4.1-6, Paul advances his discussion of new covenant ministry with the reference to τὴν διακονίαν ταύτην[6] and reiterated

---

1. 2 Cor. 3.6; cf. terminology in Jer. 31(38).31.
2. 2 Cor. 3.3, 6 (cf. 3.8, 17, 18); cf. Ezek. 11.19; 36.26-27.
3. 2 Cor. 3.2, 3; cf. Jer. 31(38).33.
4. Jer. 31(38).31-33; Ezek. 11.19; 36.26-27a.
5. 2 Cor. 2.16b; 3.5-6; cf. LXX Exod. 4.10.
6. 2 Cor. 4.1.

emphasis on δόξα.[1] Here again, return traditions begin to emerge. Through the use of Isa. 9.1 (which provides an associative link to the *'ebed*)[2] and related Isaianic-*'ebed* vocabulary[3] Paul clearly aligns his ministry with the *'ebed Yahweh* who brings δόξα-light to the blind and to the dwellers-in-darkness. Once again, the subtle portrait of Paul as a new Moses[4] appears to complement this *'ebed* perspective.

While Paul continues to discuss his καινὴ διαθήκη ministry in 4.7-15 (especially in an attempt to explain why the glory is not visible/ evident), new covenant ideas are present but fade into the background. On the other hand, that Paul wishes to identify with the *'ebed*'s mission (and christological-servant traditions) is probable in view of his perspective on suffering (εἰς θάνατον παραδιδόμεθα[5]).

In the final section of 4.16–5.10, new covenant categories (as defined in 3.1-18) resurface. There are two reasonably clear indications that Paul continues his development of καινὴ διαθήκη: (1) the present renewal of the 'inner person',[6] and (2) the giving of the Spirit as a down payment towards eschatological promises.[7] When the Spirit-promise of 5.5 is examined along with its parallel in 1.20-22, the 'anointing' function of the Spirit within Paul's ministry seemingly utilizes traditions which unite the apostle with the *'ebed* ministry of Christ (at least as perceived by the early church[8]) and in a background where the servant's proclamation of 'release to the captives' is clearly colored by exilic return motifs.[9]

---

1. Now in 4.4, 6 the notion of glory moves to the idea of δόξα-light (cf. 3.8, 9, 10, 11, 18).

2. 2 Cor. 4.6.

3. The clearest verbal dependency is seen in λάμπω, the κύριος-δοῦλος appellations, αὐγάζω, and τυφλόω. Cf. possible ties through δόξα, φῶς, σκότος, and εὐαγγελίζω. The collective imagery is reminiscent of the *'ebed* who brings the δόξα-light to those who are blind and in darkness (Isa. 42.6-7, 16; 49.6, 9; cf. 43.8; 60.1-2).

4. To the parallels in adequacy, covenants, and vision of glory, are now added the aspects of receiving mercy and the 'veil' over Paul's gospel.

5. 2 Cor. 4.11; cf. LXX Isa. 53.6b, 12.

6. 2 Cor. 4.16; cf. 3.10, 18.

7. 2 Cor. 5.5; 1.20-22; cf. LXX Ezek. 36.26-27a; 11.19; 18.31; 37.14; Jer. 31(38).33.

8. Lk. 4.18-19; Acts 4.27; 10.38; cf. Mt. 11.5.

9. 2 Cor. 1.20-22; 5.5; cf. Isa. 61.1-2.

Chapter 5

THE IMMEDIATE CONTEXT OF THE FRAGMENT: NEW COVENANT AND
SECOND EXODUS TRADITIONS IN 2 CORINTHIANS 5.11–7.4

1. *Introduction*

The next step in my investigation is crucial for establishing a
'traditions bridge' between the fragment and its present literary context, due to the close proximity of this material. In keeping with my
approach to the fragment itself, my objective is to engage in a similar
traditions search within the text which immediately surrounds the
fragment. The hypothesis thus far has been that a framework for continuity emerges through new covenant and second exodus traditions,
particularly in light of Paul's identification with *'ebed Yahweh*
mission (an identification which seems to allows him to formulate his
proclamation-message in exilic return terms). To a large extent,
however, this hypothesis stands or falls on its feasibility within the
text of 2 Cor. 5.11–7.4. Having discovered these traditions within the
fragment and its remote context, the aim of this chapter is to determine to what degree they provide a conceptual and theological
framework within the immediate context.

In order to facilitate this investigation, I shall designate the immediate literary context of the fragment as 2 Cor. 5.11–7.4. In each of
the sub-units below (5.11-21; 6.1-2; 6.3-10; 6.11-13; [6.14–7.1]; 7.2-
4)[1] a brief discussion of the context and structure will be followed by
an analysis of the text for new covenant/second exodus traditions and
overtones of *'ebed* mission. Towards the end of the chapter a

---

1. In terms of literary units, the material in 2 Cor. 6.1–7.4 divides between 6.1-10
and 6.11–7.4. However, since 2 Cor. 6.1–7.4 provides the immediate setting for the
fragment, smaller divisions will be used in order to investigate the material in more
detail.

summary of findings will be presented along with a proposed contextual synthesis.

2. God's New Exodus Pattern of Salvation ἐν Χριστῷ—a Message Entrusted to the Apostle Paul (2 Cor. 5.11-21)

Context and Structure

In light of the *eschatological* 'open appearance' before God (φανερόω links 5.10 to 5.11), Paul conducts his ministry *currently* in a manner which is transparent to God and people (5.11). After the parenthetical verse 12 (Paul is not commending himself), two interrelated γάρ statements establish the thesis that Paul and his associates are conducting their ministry with pure/open motives: (1) a positive motive: because whatever they do is for God or for the Corinthians (5.13),[1] and (2) a negative motive: because Christ's sacrificial love and death compels them in such a way that they too have died to self-interests (5.14-15).[2] From this death-life transformation in Christ two consequences follow: the first result (ὥστε) is that ἀπὸ τοῦ νῦν no person should be viewed from a 'this world' external perspective, that is, from a 'human point of view', κατὰ σάρκα (5.16);[3] the second

---

1. The ἐξέστημεν, though difficult to interpret, essentially forms a merism with σωφρονοῦμεν to say, 'whatever state I am in. . . it is for God or for you.'

2. In sum, whatever Paul does is for the Corinthians, not for himself (5.13-15).

3. That κατὰ σάρκα here modifies the verb οἴδαμεν and not the pronoun οὐδένα should be clear from proximity and word order: ἡμεῖς ἀπὸ τοῦ νῦν οὐδένα οἴδαμεν κατὰ σάρκα (5.16a). Paul is not talking about 'fleshly people', but about perceiving individuals from a fleshly perspective. In order to be consistent, then, κατὰ σάρκα in 5.16b should be understood the same way. It is not the 'fleshly Christ'—the human/earthly Jesus—that Paul has in mind (*contra* Bultmann, *Second Letter to the Corinthians*, p. 154; Stockhausen, 'Moses' Veil', p. 498), but a perception of Jesus from a fleshly (pre-salvation φῶς) perspective (so Martin, *2 Corinthians*, p. 151). This interpretation is also favored by the placement of κατὰ σάρκα immediately after the verb (as in 5.16a) and *before* Χριστόν. Had Paul wanted to modify Χριστόν, a clearer way of indicating this (and the more normal pattern) would be for κατὰ σάρκα to follow Χριστόν.

In part, as Ladd suggests (*Theology of the New Testament*, p. 373), this κατὰ σάρκα knowledge refers to the time when Paul persecuted the church because he saw Jesus through Jewish eyes. But contextually, κατὰ σάρκα is much more the perception of humans (Jesus or anyone) from externals, from human judgments, rather than from the internal perspective of new covenant ministry which

corollary result (ὥστε) is that every believer has already become a part of the promised new creation era, with a new-age orientation (patterned after a community that has left Babylon and made its 'exodus' journey to Jerusalem) which sees 'old things' as passed away and 'new things' as having come (5.17). Now (δέ) all these 'new things' are acts of God and brought about through the ministry of reconciliation which has been entrusted to Paul (5.18). The content (ὡς ὅτι = 'namely that') of this reconciliation ministry is articulated: ἐν Χριστῷ—in Christ's death and resurrection God is reconciling the old-creation cosmos to himself (thus establishing a new creation), a reconciliation accomplished (theologically) by not imputing sin, and (functionally) by entrusting the proclamation to Paul and his companions (5.19). By way of an ethical conclusion (οὖν), the Corinthians should become reconciled to God (5.20), since the sinless servant became a sin-offering in order to lead them into their new-order righteousness (5.21).[1]

In 5.11-21, my contextual integration hypothesis is supported by three lines of evidence. First, Paul continues to develop the theme of new covenant (through 'organic' categories defined in 3.1-18). Second, a traditions analysis of the 'ministry/word of reconciliation' seems to place it within the stream of exilic return theology. Third, the apostle further utilizes *'ebed* traditions in relation to his own ministry. These traditions of second/new exodus and return theology clearly stand behind Paul's ἐν Χριστῷ formulation—τὰ ἀρῳαῖα παρῆλθεν, ἰδοὺ γέγονεν καινά (5.17)—an important link for understanding the nature of the 6.14–7.1 appeal.

New Covenant Themes Continued in 5.11-21

Paul has not forgotten his exposition of the new covenant in 3.1-18. The continuation of the subject can be seen at several points. First, the expression in 5.12, . . . ἐν καρδίᾳ, is typical of the new covenant's interior focus. According to Jer. 31(38).33 and 2 Cor. 3.2-3, the new covenant is written ἐν ταῖς καρδίας.[2] If the new covenant is interior,

---

looks ἐν καρδίᾳ, a perspective developed through the new Spirit and the transformation process begun in the believer.

1. The asyndeton ties v. 21 closely to the preceding exhortation, seemingly providing the motivation for the readers to become reconciled.

2. Cf. ἐν ταῖς καρδίαις ἡμῶν (1.22; cf. 5.5); ἐγγεγραμμένη ἐν ταῖς καρδίαις ἡμῶν (3.3); ἐν πλαξὶν καρδίαις σαρκίαις (3.3); ἐν ταῖς καρδίαις ἡμῶν (4.6).

then there is no need to take pride in external appearance (Paul's suffering and lack of external δόξα does not invalidate his ministry). Second, the ἐν Χριστῷ imputation of δικαιοσύνη and non-imputation of παραπτώματα (τοῦ νομοῦ[1]) (5.19, 21) recalls Paul's earlier description of his new covenant ministry as δικαιοσύνης and not κατακρίσεως (3.9). Third, mention of τὴν διακονίαν in the genitival construction τὴν διακονίαν τῆς καταλλαγῆς (5.18) parallels earlier references to ἡ διακονία τοῦ πνεύματος and ἡ διακονία τῆς δικαιοσύνης (3.8, 9), descriptions which in turn specify the calling for διακόνους καινῆς διαθήκης (3.6). Presumably, Paul wishes to add τῆς καταλλαγῆς here as an alternative description of his new covenant ministry.

Paul's διακονία τῆς καταλλαγῆς

Five times within 2 Cor. 5.16-21 Paul articulates his ministry as one of reconciliation.[2] A search for the Old Testament traditions which lie behind this ministry of reconciliation (should such traditions exist) comes to an abrupt halt if one focuses exclusively on the term καταλλάσσω. It would have been helpful to find LXX usages of καταλλάσσω to depict the reconciliation between Yahweh and his people relating to return/regathering of the nation from Babylon. But the term is used only twice in LXX and not in this sense.[3]

However, one intertestamental writer offers some intriguing examples of the use of reconciliation in this manner. The author of 2 Maccabees, who re-interprets the period of Jewish persecution under Antiochus IV through a *theological re-writing* of history,[4]

---

1. Cf. Rom. 5.20; cf. Col. 2.13-14.

2. E.g., θεοῦ τοῦ καταλλάξαντος ἡμᾶς ἑαυτῷ (5.18b); θεοῦ τοῦ... δόντος ἡμῖν τὴν διακονίαν τῆς καταλλαγῆς (5.18c); θεὸς ἦν ἐν Χριστῷ κόσμον καταλλάσσων ἑαυτῷ (5.19a); θέμενος ἐν ἡμῖν τὸν λόγον τῆς καταλλαγῆς (5.19c); καταλλάγητε τῷ θεῷ (5.20b). For a masterful work on the subject see Martin (*Reconciliation. A Study of Paul's Theology*, pp. 1-262), who views reconciliation as the center of Paul's theology. Cf. Furnish, 'The Ministry of Reconciliation', pp. 204-18; Marshall, 'The Meaning of "Reconciliation"', pp. 117-32; Thrall, 'Salvation Proclaimed, 2 Corinthians 5. 18-21: Reconciliation with God', pp. 227-32.

3. See καταλλαγή in Isa. 9.5(4) and καταλλάσσειν in Jer. 31(48).39–both of which have little to do with what Paul is talking about here in 2 Cor. 5.16-21.

4. Doran (*Temple Propaganda: The Purpose and Character of 2 Maccabees*, pp. 77-80) argues convincingly for the purpose of 2 Maccabees as a temple-oriented

clearly uses καταλλάσσω within the framework of return theology (the nation experiences the woes of a new 'exile' of sorts and so hopes for reconciliation). For instance, in 2 Macc. 7.31-34 where Antiochus IV becomes the latter-day king of Babylon[1] and the Jews are once again the disobedient servant(s) who suffer for their own sins[2] for a 'little while'[3] (as the Babylonian exiles before them[4]), the idea of reconciliation assumes the pattern of exilic return:

> [31]But you [King Antiochus], who have contrived all sorts of evil against the Hebrews, will certainly not escape the hands of God. [32]For we are suffering because of our own sins. [33]And if our living Lord is angry for a little while, to rebuke and discipline us, *he will again be reconciled with his own servants* (πάλιν καταλλαγήσεται τοῖς ἑαυτοῦ δούλοις). [34]But you, unholy wretch, you most defiled of all men, do not be elated in vain and puffed up by uncertain hopes, when you raise your hand against the children of heaven.[5]

Similarly, in 2 Macc. 5.15-20 Antiochus is likened to the inflated king of Babylon, the Jews to the former exiles who experienced God's anger and abandonment 'for a little while', and reconciliation connotes the restored relationship of exilic return:

> [15]Not content with this [i.e., the slaughter of many Jews], Antiochus dared to enter the most holy temple in all the world, guided by Menelaus, who had become a traitor both to the laws and to his country. [16]He took the holy vessels with his polluted hands, and swept away with profane hands the votive offerings which other kings had made to enhance the glory and honor of the place. [17]Antiochus was elated in spirit, and did not perceive that the Lord was angered for a little while because of the sins of

polemic to demonstrate why the God of the Jews has allowed the holy temple to be defiled and his people to be re-enslaved.

1. Goldstein (*II Maccabees*, p. 316) points out that 2 Macc. 7.34 (cf. 5.17, 21) is an allusion to Isa. 14.12-14.

2. 2 Macc. 7.32; cf. 7.18. Writers during Antiochus's persecution understood the suffering servant of Isa. 52.13–53.12 to be either the nation Israel or the martyred pious leaders within Israel. See Goldstein's discussion (*II Maccabees*, pp. 293-94).

3. The reference to the Jews suffering only for a 'short while' 2 Macc. 7.33, 36 (cf. 5.17) recalls the LXX Isa. 54.7-8, which speaks of the period during which God seems to have abandoned Israel for 'a short time' (Goldstein, *II Maccabees*, pp. 260, 314, 316).

4. Cf. 2 Macc. 2.17-18 where the community hopes for a regathering by Yahweh, like that of old (with a return to the land/inheritance).

5. Metzger (ed.), *The Oxford Annotated Apocrypha*, p. 277.

those who dwelt in the city, and that therefore he was disregarding the holy place. [18]But if it had not happened that they were involved in many sins, this man [Antiochus] would have been scourged and turned back from his rash act as soon as he came forward. . . [19]But the Lord did not choose the nation for the sake of the holy place, but the place for the sake of the nation. [20]Therefore the place itself shared in the misfortunes that befell the nation and afterward participated in its benefits; and what was forsaken in the wrath of the Almighty was restored again in all its glory *when the great Lord became reconciled* (ἐν τῇ τοῦ μεγάλου δεσπότου καταλλαγῇ).[1]

An even more helpful means of tracing 'reconciliation' traditions comes from examining the use of the cognate ἀποκαταλλάσω (which has virtually the same meaning as καταλλάσσω)[2] and a related term which shares the semantic field of 'reconciliation', namely εἰρηνοποιέω.[3] An example of these two terms being used in a similar sense (depicting the end of former alienation and hostility between God and people) is found in Col. 1.20, 'For it was the Father's good pleasure. . . through him [Christ] to reconcile all things to himself (ἀποκαταλλάξαι τὰ πάντα εἰς αὐτόν). . . having made peace (εἰρηνοποιήσας) through the blood of his cross' (cf. 1.21-22).[4]

Yet, it is through the parallel text in Ephesians that Old Testament traditions may be traced with a reasonable degree of clarity. In Eph. 2.14-16, ἀποκαταλλάσω is again used in conjunction with ποιῶν εἰρήνη: 'He [Christ] is our peace. . . that in himself he might make the two into one new person, establishing peace (ποιῶν εἰρήνην), and might reconcile (ἀποκαταλλάξῃ) them both. . . to God.' Immediately following in Eph. 2.17, the scriptural basis for this reconciliation-peace is stated: 'And he came and preached peace to you

---

1. Metzger (ed.), *The Oxford Annotated Apocrypha*, p. 273.

2. Listing καταλλάσσω and ἀποκαταλλάσω together under one definition, Nida and Louw (*Lexicon*, I, p. 502) note, 'it may be that there are certain subtle distinctions of meaning. . . but there appears to be no contextual indication to justify setting up completely separate meanings'.

3. Louw and Nida (*Lexicon*, I, p. 502) do not list καταλλάσσω and εἰρηνοποιέω under the same definition (as with ἀποκαταλλάσω and καταλλάσσω), but under the common semantic domain of 'reconciliation'.

4. Barth (*Ephesians*, I, p. 266) likewise notes that '"making peace" in Col. 1.20-22 and Eph. 2.14-16 is used as a synonym for "reconciling"'. Cf. Martin's comment (*Reconciliation*, p. 149) on Rom. 5.1 that 'reconciliation is none other than "peace with God through our Lord Lord Jesus Christ"'.

who were far away, and peace to you who were near' (cf. 2.14). In order to facilitate discussion, the texts for this Old Testament allusion (Eph. 2.17; cf. 2.13) are provided:

MT: שָׁלוֹם שָׁלוֹם לָרָחוֹק וְלַקָּרוֹב   (Isa. 57.19b)

                              מַה־נָּאווּ עַל־הֶהָרִים רַגְלֵי מְבַשֵּׂר   (Isa. 52.7)
                   מַשְׁמִיעַ שָׁלוֹם מְבַשֵּׂר טוֹב מַשְׁמִיעַ יְשׁוּעָה

LXX: εἰρήνην ἐπ' εἰρήνην τοῖς μακρὰν καὶ τοῖς   (Isa. 57.19b)
       ἐγγὺς οὖσιν

       ὡς πόδες εὐαγγελιζομένου ἀκοὴν εἰρήνης   (Isa. 52.7)
       ὡς εὐαγγελιζόμενος ἀγαθά, ὅτι ἀκουστὴν
       ποιήσω τὴν σωτηρίαν

NT: καὶ ἐλθὼν [Χριστὸς] εὐηγγελίσατο εἰρήνην   (Eph. 2.17; cf. 2.13)
       ὑμῖν τοῖς μακρὰν καὶ εἰρήνην τοῖς ἐγγύς

In terms of the composition of Eph. 2.17, most commentators[1] agree that εἰρήνην ὑμῖν τοῖς μακρὰν καὶ εἰρήνην τοῖς ἐγγύς comes from Isa. 57.19; εὐηγγελίσατο (εἰρήνην) from Isa. 52.7;[2] καὶ ἐλθών from some kind of christological tradition.[3] While there are complex interpretive problems with Eph. 2.17,[4] the point which needs to be made here is quite simple: *exilic Jews in Babylon* (τοῖς μακράν) *have become a paradigm for those who are spiritually far*

---

1. See Barth, *Ephesians*, p. 267; Robinson, *Commentary on Ephesians*, p. 162; Lincoln, *Ephesians*, pp. 146-49.

2. Cf. Eph. 6.15.

3. The peace proclamation made by Christ has been variously interpreted as (1) the preaching done by Jesus during the days of his ministry (Mt. 4.15; Lk. 9.51-56; Jn 4.4-42); (2) the resurrected Christ in his greetings of 'peace' (Jn 14.27; 16.33); (3) preaching through the apostles (Mt. 10.20), or (4) proclamation of 'good news' during the Christ event in a broader sense of the act itself (as well as oral communication). After presenting these four options, Barth (*Ephesians*, pp. 293-95) suggests that precise timing of the proclamation cannot be determined so all four should be accepted. In a sense he is correct, for the context is ambiguous. However, a combination of one and four (with implications towards three—cf. Eph. 6.15; Rom. 10.15) is most likely. Option two is much too restrictive and idiomatic in force to carry the theological import suggested in Eph. 2.

4. The OT context of Isa. 57.19 referred not to Jews and Gentiles, but to Jews in exile (τοῖς μακράν) and Jews at home in the promised land (τοῖς ἐγγύς). See Barth's discussion (*Ephesians*, pp. 260, 266, 276-79) for more detail than can be shown here.

away from salvation;[1] they are alienated from God and the temple worship of Jerusalem. Like these Jews in exile who eventually return home in a procession-pilgrimage to Jerusalem for worship,[2] the author of Ephesians portrays those who were formerly far off (μακράν—salvific 'exiles') as having been brought near (ἐγγύς–2.13, 17), through the blood of Christ, for worship in the new eschatological community-temple where God dwells in the Spirit (2.18-22).[3] If these tradition-historical origins are correct, then exilic return imagery may forge the conceptual background for the διακονίαν/ λόγον τῆς καταλλαγῆς in 2 Cor. 5.18c; 5.19c.[4]

Some further observations need to be drawn from the Old Testament passage partially influencing Eph. 2.17, namely, Isa. 52.7. This Old Testament text is also found, in Romans, to depict Paul's 'gospel of peace' ministry (e.g., Rom. 10.15, ὡς ὡραῖοι οἱ πόδες τῶν εὐαγγελιζομένων [τὰ] ἀγαθά[5]). Again, if my traditions analysis is valid, implications for integrating the 6.14–7.1 fragment move beyond conceptual congruence[6] with its context to conceptual-textual congruence with quotation 2 from Isa. 52.11 and the gospel of peace tradition from Isa. 52.7. Within the unit of Isa. 52.3-12,[7] the foot

1. The Isaiah texts depict those in Babylon as in a 'far country' (13.5; 39.3; cf. 49.1), the exile having removed God's people far away (6.12). Yet, the geographical distance simply mirrors the nation's spiritual condition. Israel is spiritually 'far removed' from Yahweh (57.8), her people are far from righteousness (46.11-12), and their hearts are far from the Lord (29.13). There is also the sense of spiritual renewal, when in the return Yahweh's sons and daughters come 'from afar' (43.6; 60.4, 9; cf. 49.12). Cf. Acts 2.39.

2. See Merrill, 'Pilgrimage and Procession', pp. 261-72.

3. The leaving of Babylon and return (= reconciliation/making peace) to worship in the eschatological community-temple are strikingly similar to the themes of 2 Cor. 6.14–7.1. In addition, the verbal parallels with ναὸν ἅγιον ἐν κυρίῳ and κατοικητήριον τοῦ θεοῦ ἐν πνεύματι reflect the words of the fragment.

4. The study on 'new exodus pattern of new things' (below) makes these tradition-historical findings even more feasible, since they too are part of Paul's reconciling the (old) cosmos to God.

5. Cf. Eph. 6.15, ὑποδησάμενοι τοὺς πόδας ἐν ἑτοιμασίᾳ τοῦ εὐαγγελίου τῆς εἰρήνης.

6. E.g., the Isa. 57.19 traditions-link argues only for conceptual congruence between 2 Cor. 5.16-21 and the 6.14–7.1 fragment (both have ties to return theology); whereas Isa. 52.7 touches the fragment at an even closer point since the second quotation is from Isa. 52.11.

7. Not all commentators take Isa. 52.3-12 as a complete unit. E.g., Westermann

messenger's proclamation of peace (שָׁלוֹם מַשְׁמִיעַ/εὐαγγελιζομένου
εἰρήνης), well-being (טוֹב/ἀγαθά), and salvation (יְשׁוּעָה/σωτηρίαν) is
surely that which is realized in the new exodus salvation (יְשׁוּעָה/
σωτηρίαν)[1] of Isa. 52.11-12—an event which all the ends of the earth
will behold.

In sum, the traditions link with Isa. 52.7 and 57.19 confirms that *it
is possible* to understand 'reconciliation' within an exilic return
paradigm. However, a note of caution is appropriate here. Aside from
the authorship question (that is, the issue of using material where the
secondary impact of Pauline thought, let alone direct authorship, is
debated), one should not *automatically* transfer the traditions used
elsewhere in relation to reconciliation to this passage in
2 Corinthians. This would amount to 'totality transfer'—the transfer-
ence of all that is associated with a term in one passage to another.[2]
The associations of return theology with reconciliation in other literature (2 Maccabees and Ephesians, as noted before) only raises the
possibility that Paul might be doing something similar in
2 Corinthians. Nonetheless, the discovery of exilic return traditions in
2 Cor. 5.11-21 (discussed below) makes the contribution of return
theology an attractive possibility for the background to Paul's message
of reconciliation.

(*Isaiah 40–66*, p. 252) suggests that 'the command to depart is that to which the
entire message of Deutero-Isaiah has been leading up' (but he makes no effort to tie it
into its immediate context). However, a growing number do take Isaiah 52.3-12 as
an integrated unit (e.g., Watts, *Isaiah 34–66*, pp. 214-18).

1. Isa. 52.10. That 'the Lord baring his holy arm' and 'the salvation of our God'
in 52.10 refer to the new exodus departure of 52.11-12 is evident from (1) the
immediate proximity; (2) the pervasive tradition that connects Yahweh's arm with the
exodus from Egypt and the new exodus (e.g., Deut. 7.19; 9.29; 11.2; 26.8; 2 Kgs
17.36; Pss. 89.10; 98.1-3; 136.12; Isa. 40.10-11; 51.5, 9-11; 63.5, 12; Jer. 32.21;
Ezek. 20.33-34; Acts 13.17; cf. probable exodus referents in 1 Kgs 8.42; 2 Chron.
6.32; Isa. 59.16; 62.8); (3) the reference to all of humanity seeing the event is at
times connected with the return (Isa. 40.5; cf. 49.6; 62.11), and (4) elsewhere the
term 'salvation/deliverance' refers to the new exodus/return begun under Cyrus (Isa.
12.1-3 [cf. 11.16] ; 45.17; 49.6, 8; 51.5, 6, 8 [cf. 51.9-11] ; 62.11).

2. At this point Beale's treatment ('Old Testament Background', pp. 550-81) of
'reconciliation' may be criticized for its focus on the term itself as something of a
locus for exilic return imagery rather than simply as a term which (along with other
word-groups) can be used within that conceptual framework.

The New Exodus Pattern of 'New Things'

Paul's ἐν Χριστῷ formulation, τὰ ἀρχαῖα παρῆλθεν, ἰδοὺ γέγονεν καινά, probably has its origins in Isaiah. The material could have been drawn from any number of passages in Isaiah,[1] yet the closest resemblance lies with the following four passages (Isa. 42.9; 43.18-19a; 48.3-6; 65.16c-17):

MT:
הָרִאשֹׁנוֹת הִנֵּה־בָאוּ   וַחֲדָשׁוֹת אֲנִי מַגִּיד (Isa. 42.9)

אַל־תִּזְכְּרוּ רִאשֹׁנוֹת   וְקַדְמֹנִיּוֹת אַל־תִּתְבֹּנָנוּ׃ (Isa. 43.18-19a)
הִנְנִי עֹשֶׂה חֲדָשָׁה   עַתָּה תִצְמָח הֲלוֹא תֵדָעוּהָ

הָרִאשֹׁנוֹת מֵאָז הִגַּדְתִּי . . . הִשְׁמַעְתִּיךָ חֲדָשׁוֹת מֵעַתָּה (Isa. 48.3-6)

כִּי נִשְׁכְּחוּ הַצָּרוֹת הָרִאשֹׁנוֹת   וְכִי נִסְתְּרוּ מֵעֵינָי׃ (Isa. 65.16c-17)
כִּי־הִנְנִי בוֹרֵא שָׁמַיִם חֲדָשִׁים   וָאָרֶץ חֲדָשָׁה
וְלֹא תִזָּכַרְנָה הָרִאשֹׁנוֹת   וְלֹא תַעֲלֶינָה עַל־לֵב׃

LXX:
τὰ ἀπ' ἀρχῆς ἰδοὺ ἥκασιν,   (Isa. 42.9)
καὶ καινὰ ἃ ἐγὼ ἀναγγελῶ...

μὴ μνημονεύετε τὰ πρῶτα   (Isa. 43.18-19a)
καὶ τὰ ἀρχαῖα μὴ συλλογίζεσθε
ἰδοὺ ποιῶ καινὰ ἃ νῦν ἀνατελεῖ...

τὰ πρότερα ἔτι ἀνήγγειλα...   (Isa. 48.3-6)
ἐποίησα τὰ καινὰ ἀπὸ τοῦ νῦν.

ἐπιλήσονται γὰρ τὴν θλῖψιν αὐτῶν τὴν (Isa. 65.16c-17)
πρώτην,
καὶ οὐκ ἀναβήσεται αὐτῶν ἐπὶ τὴν καρδίαν.
ἔσται γὰρ ὁ οὐρανὸς καινὸς καὶ ἡ γῆ καινή,
καὶ οὐ μὴ μνησθῶσιν τῶν προτέρων,
οὐδ' οὐ μὴ ἐπέλθῃ αὐτῶν ἐπὶ τὴν καρδίαν

NT:
καινὴ κτίσις, τὰ ἀρχαῖα παρῆλθεν,   (2 Cor. 5.17)
ἰδοὺ γέγονεν καινά

In view of the complexity and significance of the old/new things traditions, they must be examined in some detail. Within Isaiah 40–55 the 'former things' are distinguished from the 'new things' in a

---

1. The theology of the 'former/old things' and the 'new things' within Isaiah is quite extensive, with the central core being found in chapters 40–48 (e.g., Isa. 9.1; 22.11; 25.1; 37.26; 41.22, 26, 27; 42.9-10; 43.9, 18-21; 44.6-8; 45.11, 21; 46.9-10; 48.3-6, 12, 16; 51.9; 63.9, 11-14; 65.16-17; 66.22; cf. Jer. 31[38].22).

reasonably consistent manner. In broad terms, the 'former/old things' (עוֹלָם/רִאשׁוֹן) refer to Yahweh's past redemptive acts.[1] They are events predicted by Yahweh in the past which have now come to pass, sometimes without any specific referent in focus.[2] Presumably, in these ambiguous contexts the author has in mind any past redemptive act of Yahweh throughout the history of Israel.[3] However, the predominant (even paradigmatic) event in view is the exodus out of Egypt. For example, in 43.18 the 'former things/things of the past' refers to Yahweh's making a path through mighty waters for Israel's deliverance from Egypt and his destroying Pharoh's chariots, horses, and entire army in the sea.[4] Similarly, in 51.9-10 'the days of old/long ago' (a roughly equivalent expression to 'the former things of old/long ago')[5] envisions Yahweh's drying up a pathway in the sea upon which redeemed Israel would cross over.[6]

The 'new things' (חָדָשׁ) constitute Yahweh's new acts of deliverance (also predicted before they happen) which he will perform, beginning

---

1. For an excellent treatment of the 'old things' and 'new things' in Isaiah 40–55, and the line of interpretation which I follow fairly closely (at least in terms of definitions), see Odendaal, 'The "Former" and the "New Things" in Isaiah 40–48', pp. 64-75. Cf. North, 'The "Former Things" and the "New Things" in Deutero-Isaiah', pp. 111-26; Schoors, 'Les Choses anterieures et les Choses nouvelles dans les oracles Deutero-isaïens', pp. 19-47. On the issue of defining 'old/former things' and 'new things' Odendaal has argued carefully against North's position that the former things describe Cyrus' initial success and the coming things, his future actions.

2. E.g., Isa. 41.22; 44.6-9; 46.9 (cf. 46.3b-4 which looks at Israel from birth to old age); cf. 42.9; 43.9; 48.3. But in these last three cases (Isa. 42.9; 43.9; 48.3) the contrasting 'new exodus' event would indicate that by 'former/old things' the writer has in mind the first exodus from Egypt.

3. Cf. the deliverance from Sennacherib being described as planned from 'ancient times/long ago' (Isa. 37.26).

4. Cf. 43.16-17. The רִאשׁוֹן in 43.9 probably has the same exodus event in view because of its close proximity and the similar 'new things' being discussed.

5. The former things (רִאשׁוֹן) parallels the things of old (עוֹלָם) in 43.18. And, in 46.9-10 the former things (רִאשׁוֹן) is qualified by עוֹלָם (46.9) and parallels קֶדֶם, (46.10). Therefore, it is reasonable to see the 'days of old/long ago' in 51.9 as roughly synonymous to 'the former things of old/long ago'.

6, The expression 'days/times/wonders of old' (קֶדֶם) is similarly used in the Psalms to recall Yahweh's redemption of his people from Egypt (e.g., 74.2, 12; 77.5, 11) and his giving them the land (44.1).

with the exilic community. In 42.9 the 'new things' refer to the (new)[1] covenant-light ministry of the *'ebed Yahweh*, who opens blind eyes and brings prisoners out of darkness into the light (42.7; cf. 42.16), a picture which blends spiritual renewal with the physical return of the exiles to Palestine. Similarly, if the 'this' (זאת) in 43.9 explains Yahweh's 'new things',[2] then we have again a reference to bringing people who are spiritually blind and deaf back to the land (43.8). Yet, instead of from Babylon, this time the return is from the ends of the earth (43.5-7). Again, in 43.19 Yahweh promises to do a 'new thing'—leading the exiles back on a roadway through the wilderness, a second exodus[3] during which he will lavishly provide for them (43.19-21). In 48.6 Yahweh further declares this 'new thing'—leading of Israel ethically in righteousness (48.17-19), effecting deliverance through Cyrus (48.14-15), and leading the nation out of Babylon—a new exodus likened to the first (48.20-21).[4]

Within Isaiah 1–39 and Isaiah 56–66, however, the 'former/old things' have a slightly different meaning. While the 'days of old' in 63.9, 11 relate (as above) to the first exodus event, even there the emphasis shifts to the disobedience of Israel despite this glorious event. For the most part, the former/old things are no longer the *positive* acts of Yahweh's deliverance which the nation should reflect upon; rather, they are the *negative* circumstances of captivity (both its

---

1. In Isa. 42.6 (cf. 49.8) the *'ebed Yahweh* is a 'covenant (mediator) for the people'. Similarly, Jer. 31.22 connects the 'new thing' which Yahweh has created with the return of Israel to the land and to an intimate relationship with Yahweh (31.21-22c), a part of the 'new covenant' mentioned later (31.31). See Souza (*New Covenant*, pp. 9-15, 215-30) for a more extensive development.

2. That זאת does refer to the 'new things' is fairly certain since it is being compared to the 'former things' (43.9b), its content is the bringing out of the blind (an event similar to the 'new things' of 42.9), and it anticipates the former things/new things contrast in 43.18-19.

3. Notice the allusions to the first exodus in 43.16-17, which serve as a pattern of what Yahweh will do in this new exodus (43.19-21).

4. Cf. Isa. 51.9-11 where the 'new things' (חָדָשׁ) are not mentioned explicitly, but 'the days of old' (a similar expression to 'the former things of old'), the former exodus, is likened to the return of the Lord's ransomed. Also, if 'the things to come' (הָאֹתִיּוֹת) in Isa. 45.11 is another name for Yahweh's 'new things' (cf. the use of the participle in 41.23 and 44.7), then it provides additional confirmation that the return of the exiles and the rebuilding of Yahweh's city through Cyrus is in view (cf. 45.1-2, 13).

cause and consequence) which Yahweh and the nation will forget. For instance, רִאשׁוֹן is used adjectively to depict the 'former devastations', the ruined cities and agriculture (61.4) and, more broadly, of the 'former troubles' (65.16) which resulted from captivity. In addition, it is used of Israel's 'former work', that is, her former sins and idolatry which led to captivity (65.7).[1] The 'former things' of 65.17, include Israel's dismal behavior and the resultant troubles, which, in the language of forgiveness, 'shall not be remembered or come to mind' (cf. 65.16, 'forgotten. . . hidden from my [Yahweh's] sight'). This kind of former-things theology is consistent with the picture presented in 9.1(8.23)—the darkness and gloom (idolatry and Yahweh's judgment upon the land) of the 'former times' (עֵת הָרִאשׁוֹן) will be replaced by the light and rejoicing of the 'latter times' (הָאַחֲרוֹן [עֵת] = the 'new thing' of Isaiah 40–55[2]).

Nonetheless, in Isaiah 1–39 and 56–66 the idea of 'new things' *retains the same meaning as in Isaiah 40–55, with a slight expansion.* While there is no explicit reference to the 'new things' outside Isaiah 40–55,[3] the contrast to רִאשׁוֹן would suggest the idea in 9.1(8.23) and in 65.17. The 9.1(8.23) passage, as discussed above, develops the light-in-darkness imagery which aligns with earlier findings. In 65.17 (cf. 66.22), however, רִאשׁוֹן is contrasted with the statement that Yahweh will 'create a new heavens and a new earth'. Yet, this is hardly inconsistent with the presentation of 'new things' in Isaiah 40–55 where, like vegetation, the new exodus deliverance will 'spring forth' (42.9; 43.19); it, too, is being 'created' by Yahweh (48.7). So the theology of Isaiah 56–66 expands the new exodus idea to cosmic dimensions; the new exodus patterns or mirrors God's ultimate act of new creation.[4] It

---

1. This 'former work/service' (which was in vain) is contrasted to the post-captivity 'new' labors which will not be in vain (cf. 65.21-23).

2. Not only does the contrast between עֵת הָרִאשׁוֹן and הָאַחֲרוֹן [עֵת] cause the reader to think of the 'new things', but this connection is reinforced through the similar light-in-darkness ministries of the Davidic ruler (8.22–9.7) and the light-in-darkness 'new thing' which the servant of Yahweh accomplishes (42.7-9, 16; cf. 49.6, 9). Also, the expression, 'the things which will come about hereafter (הָאַחֲרוֹן)' is used in parallel to 'the things to come (הַבָּאוֹת = new things)' in Isa. 41.22-23 (cf. the 'first' and the 'last' descriptions of Yahweh in 41.4; 44.6; 48.12).

3. This is one indicator that Paul is not simply drawing his material from Isaiah 56–66. Also the use of ἀπὸ τοῦ νῦν in 2 Cor. 5.16a may be derived from the LXX Isa. 48.6, ἐποίησα τὰ καινὰ ἀπὸ τοῦ νῦν.

4. On the use of creation motifs already in Isa. 40–55, see the references to

is the final step in the restoration process.

To summarize, the referents of Isaiah's 'former/old things' and 'new things' may be charted as follows:

	'former/old things'	'new things'
Isaiah 40–55:	Yahweh's past redemptive acts	Yahweh's new redemptive acts
	exodus out of Egypt[1]	second/new exodus out of Babylon[2]
		'ebed's light to the blind/to those in darkness[3]
		righteousness/salvation[4]
		(new) covenant[5]
Isaiah 1–39; 56–66:	(exodus out of Egypt[6]) Israel's despair/troubles[7]	
	idolatry/sin[8]	(faithfulness to Yahweh alone)
	darkness and gloom[9]	light-in-darkness[10]
	(old heavens and earth)	new heavens and earth[11]

Unfortunately, Paul does not clarify precisely what referents he has in mind with the 'old things' and the 'new things' in 2 Cor. 5.17.

Yahweh stretching out the heavens and laying the foundations of the earth (40.12-31; 42.5; 44.24; 45.9-13, 18; 48.13; 51.13, 16). Even so, it is in his role as Creator-God that Yahweh 'creates' the new exodus salvation (42.5, 7-9; 48.6-16). The new exodus re-awakens creation: bodies of water appear (41.17-20; 43.19-20; 48.21; 49.10), new vegetation springs up (41.17-20; 43.19-20; 49.9b; 55.12-13), the mountains, hills, trees, and wild beasts clap or praise God as they watch the procession (43.20; 55.12-13). In this respect the new exodus *anticipates* the ultimate re-creation, and in turn the eschatological new creation *finalizes* the process begun in the second exodus.

1. Isa. 43.18 (cf. 43.15-17); 51.9-10 and more generally the beginning of the nation in 44.7. Cf. the new things of 42.9; 43.9; 48.3.

2. Isa. 43.19 (cf. 43.19-21); 48.6 (cf. 48.14-15 with Cyrus; 48.20-21).

3. Isa. 42.9 (cf. 42.8, 16); 43.9 (cf. 43.8); 48.6 (cf. 48.17-22).

4. Isa. 48.6 (cf. 48.17-22).

5. Isa. 42.9 (cf. 42.6-7; 49.8); cf. Jer. 31(38).22.

6. 'Days of old' in Isa. 63.9, 11 (cf. 63.9-14).

7. Isa. 61.4; 65.16.

8. Isa. 9.1(8.23) (cf. 8.19-21); 65.7; inferred in 65.16-17.

9. Isa. 9.1-2.

10. Isa. 9.1-2.

11. Isa. 65.17; 66.22; (cf. Isa. 48.7).

Commentators often go to one of two extremes. Most popular treatments *individualize* the passage, taking καινὴ κτίσις as 'new crea-
ture' and the old and new things as aspects of a person's behavior.[1] On
the other hand, Martin (for example) handles the passage as if it were
almost exclusively *supra-individual*, with the old and new reflecting
two ages.[2] While Martin's perspective is helpful in offsetting an indi-
vidualistic emphasis, it may neglect certain features in the text which
bear on the individual (see chart below). It seems best to suggest that
Paul's perspective is indeed supra-individual, but at the same time it
voices strong implications for the individual.

Any specification of New Testament referents must remain tentative. However, based on the Isaianic traditions from which Paul draws
the material, the immediate context of 5.16-21, and the larger literary
setting of 2.14–7.4, one may postulate some hypotheses as to his
intentions. Probable referents for Paul's 'old things' and 'new things'
are summarized in the chart below, those with direct correlation to
Isaiah's traditions being marked with an asterisk (*):

	'old things'	*'new things*
Supra-individual:	old order/age*	new order/age* ἐν Χριστῷ[3]
	old creation-cosmos*[4]	new creation*[5]
	(old covenant?)[6]	new covenant*[7]
	τοῦ αἰῶνος τούτου[8]	ἀπὸ τοῦ νῦν*[9]
		new exodus salvation*[10]

1. E.g., Barclay, *Letters to the Corinthians*, pp. 206-209.
2. See Martin, *2 Corinthians*, pp. 134-59; *Reconciliation*, pp. 90-110.
3. ἐν Χριστῷ (2 Cor. 5.17, 19, 21; cf. 3.14).
4. 2 Cor. 5.17, 19.
5. 2 Cor. 5.17.
6. There may be an indication that the old covenant is a part of the old, passing
order from Paul's presentation of its 'fading glory' (2 Cor. 3.11). Martin
(*Reconciliation*, p. 108) states, 'the Pauline announcement in verse 17 (2 Cor. 5.17)
. . . is not of a refurbished Judaism with the old order of Moses revamped but a
new age with a new covenant'.
7. 2 Cor. 3.1-18.
8. 2 Cor. 4.4.
9. 2 Cor. 5.16a (cf. νῦν in 5.16c; 6.2 twice). Note also the exact phrase ἀπὸ τοῦ
νῦν in relation to the old things/new things in LXX Isa. 48.6, ἐποίησα τὰ καινὰ
ἀπὸ τοῦ νῦν.
10. New exodus deliverance is found in traditions behind 'new things' in 2 Cor.
5.17 and in the 'deliverance/salvation' of 2 Cor. 6.2. It is the *'ebed* who leads the

	god of this age blinding [1]	'ebed's light to the blind*[2]
	darkness*[3]	light*[4]
	outer decay[5]	inner renewal[6]
	sin/trespasses*[7]	righteousness/salvation*[8]
	living for oneself[9]	no longer living for oneself[10]
Individual:	κατὰ σάρκα mind set [11]	εἴ τις ἐν Χριστῷ[12]

From this brief survey several significant conclusions may be drawn. First, the new things in the Old Testament context are often cast in promise formula ('I [Yahweh] will do a new thing'), as are the Old Testament promise-texts of 6.14–7.1. Second, the conceptual content of the 'new things' in Isaiah can be summarized as the second/new exodus out of Babylon which is both physical and spiritual, both an exodus from Babylon and from the ends of the earth, and this exodus *itself* reflects the final deliverance of the cosmos. Third, in Isaiah (and Jeremiah) this 'new thing(s)' is an integral part of the new covenant. Fourth, as Paul employs these traditions, he acknowledges that God is working a 'new thing' through his ministry of reconciliation (Yahweh's new acts of salvation—the new deliverance/exodus)

new exodus return of the blind back to the homeland (see below under §4).

1. 2 Cor. 4.4; cf. 3.14. Similarly Martin (*Reconciliation*, p. 104) comments, 'the old world, with its enslavement and fears and ruled by its god (4.4), is on the way out'.

2. 2 Cor. 4.5-6.

3. 2 Cor. 4.3-6.

4. 2 Cor. 4.4-6.

5. 2 Cor. 4.16.

6. 2 Cor. 3.18; 4.6; 4.16-18.

7. 2 Cor. 5.19, 21.

8. 2 Cor. 5.21; 3.9; 6.2.

9. 2 Cor. 5.15; cf. Rom. 14.7-9.

10. 2 Cor. 5.15; cf. Rom. 14.7-9.

11. 2 Cor. 5.16.

12. 2 Cor. 5.17. The τις brings the supra-individual categories to bear on the individual (εἴ τις ἐν Χριστῷ is essentially conversion). Martin (*2 Corinthians*, pp. 136, 146) may overstate the case when he argues that the new creation as a cosmic *objective* reality outside of the believer. True, a 'new order' has arrived, but not to the exclusion of the old order. Those who are outside of Christ are still in the old order—objective reality that it is (3.14; 4.4). In fact, the new order and new covenant renewal is imperceptible to the human eye (5.7, 12), since it begins with ἐν ταῖς καρδίαις ἡμῶν (3.3; cf. 1.22; 4.6; 5.5; 5.12).

bringing 'exiled' people from the old cosmos back to God.[1] As the *'ebed* in Isaiah is entrusted with the 'new things' ministry of leading the spiritually blind and captive back to Palestine, so is Paul. While the referents of Paul's 'new things' are ambiguous, what is certain is that he uses new exodus traditions and an exilic return framework here in 2 Cor. 5.17 to define his ministry. All of this begins to build an elaborate 'traditions bridge' with the fragment.[2]

3. Excursus: Paul's Identification with the 'Ebed Yahweh

Before examining 2 Cor. 6.1-2 (and its quotation of Isa. 49.8), it is important to gain a broader perspective on the identification of Paul with the *'ebed Yahweh*. Many New Testament scholars have developed such connections between Paul's ministry and the Isaianic servant.[3]

---

1. This interplay between cosmic, heavens-and-earth reconciliation and exilic return as God's new creative act may have led Paul to merge the figures. Commenting on Col. 1.20, Martin (*Reconciliation*, p. 126) notes that the reconciliation of sinners to God points back to Christ's cosmic reconciliation.

2. In many respects, Rev. 21.1-8 serves as corollary support to this work's hypothesis, since *it ties together several of the same OT traditions* which on a theological and conceptual level unite 2 Cor. 6.14–7.1 with its larger context. For example, one finds OT materials which in 2 Corinthians come within the 6.14–7.1 fragment: ἡ σκηνὴ τοῦ θεὸς μετὰ τῶν ἀνθρώπων... καὶ αὐτὸς ὁ θεὸς μετ' αὐτῶν ἔσται (Rev. 21.3 [mss. vary widely]; cf. Ezek. 37.27/Lev. 26.11-12 and 2 Cor. 6.16d) and a democratized Davidic promise (Rev. 21.7; cf. 2 Sam. 7.14 and 2 Cor. 6.18). On the other hand, οὐρανὸν καὶνον καὶ γῆν καινήν and τὰ πρῶτα ἀπῆλθαν... ἰδοὺ καινὰ ποιῶ πάντα (Rev. 21.1, 4-5; cf. Isa. 42.9; 43.18-19; 48.3-6; 65.16-17 and 2 Cor. 5.17) coincide with the discussion preceding the fragment. The joining of these traditions here and in Revelation is quite impressive. The major difference between the traditions bridge in Rev. 21 and 2 Cor. 5–6 is that the apocalypse focuses on the near-eschatological fulfillment, whereas within 2 Cor. these promises represent a present reality. However, this too argues for continuity in the case of 2 Cor. 6.14–7.1, since the use of these traditions *both* outside and inside 2 Cor. 6.14–7.1 develop the promises in a consistent manner, i.e., in terms of a present salvation (they do not differ between fragment and context).

3. The following studies at least survey the field: Cerfaux, 'Saint Paul et le "serviteur de Dieu" d'Isaïe', pp. 439-54; Martini, 'Alcumi temi letterari di 2 Cor. 4.6', pp. 461-74; Kerrigan, 'Echoes of Themes from the Servant Songs in Pauline Theology', pp. 217-28; Giblet, 'Saint Paul, Serviteur de Dieu et Apôtre de Jésus-Christ', pp. 244-63; Hooker, *Jesus and the Servant*, pp. 107-23; Dunn, '"A Light to the Gentiles": the Significance of the Damascus Road Christophany for Paul', pp. 251-66; Stanley, 'The Theme of the Servant of Yahweh in Primitive Christian

The thrust of their work is, essentially, that the servant traditions *(particularly from Isaiah 49)* play a key role in shaping Paul's self-understanding and ministry. This brief survey highlights some of these traditions.

Within Pauline writings the apostle seemingly adopts for himself the title of Yahweh's servant, the Isaianic δοῦλος (Isa. 49.3, 5, 7),[1] especially in contexts shaped by the servant traditions–2 Cor. 4.5; Gal. 1.10; Phil. 1.1; cf. 2.7.[2] Also, Paul appears to borrow language from the *'ebed's* call to describe his own call or commissioning. As it is said of the *'ebed Yahweh,* 'from my mother's womb he has called my name' (Isa. 49.1) and 'the Lord. . . formed me from the womb to be his servant' (Isa. 49.5), so Paul recalls his own commissioning with similar language: 'He who had set me apart, from my mother's womb, and called me through his grace. . . ' (Gal. 1.15).[3] Furthermore, the salvation-light imagery from Isa. 49.6, 8 seems to inform the apostle's ministry of 'unveiling' darkness (2 Cor. 3.14, 18)[4] and bringing the

---

Soteriology, and Its Transposition by St. Paul', pp. 385-425; Bruce, 'Some Thoughts on Paul and Paulinism', pp. 11-12; Dinter, 'Paul and the Prophet Isaiah', pp. 48-52; Hickling, 'Paul's Reading of Isaiah', pp. 215-23; Dupont, *The Salvation of the Gentiles,* pp. 1-33; Kim, *The Origin of Paul's Gospel,* pp. 55-66, 93-99; Tannehill, 'Rejection by Jews and Turning to Gentiles', pp. 130-41; Becker, 'Paul, The Suffering Apostle', pp. 305-32, 349-59; Bruce, 'Paul's Use of the Old Testament in Acts', pp. 72-73.

1. Cf. its use in reference to the individual servant—Isa. 5.11; of Israel and even foreigners—14.3; 19.23; 42.19; 48.20; 56.6; 63.17; 65.9, 13-15. Note that both δοῦλος and παῖς interchangeably translate 'my servant' (עַבְדִּי) in the songs (Isa. 42.1; 50.10) and function as synonyms (Isa. 42.19; 49.1-6).

2. Elsewhere Paul describes himself in general terms as a δοῦλος (Rom. 1.1; 1 Cor. 9.19) and applies the term to the community (Rom. 6.16-18, 22). Cf. 2 Tim. 2.24 (δοῦλον κυρίου); Tit. 1.1.

3. Although similar concepts occur in Jer. 1.5, Paul's tradition comes from Isa. 49.1, 5 since (1) only Isa. 49.1 has the verb ἐκάλεσε (2) Jer. 1.5 stresses the commissioning before (πρό) even the formation in the womb, whereas Isa. 49.1, 5 (like Gal. 1.15) view God's involvement from (ἐκ) the point of formation, and (3) only Isa. 49.5 includes the servant tradition (cf. Gal. 1.10). These links with Isaiah led Langevin ('Saint Paul, prophète des Gentils', p. 8) to state, 'Les lieux nous paraissent assez étroits entre Gal. 1.15-16 et le second chant du serviteur (Isa. 49) pour que nous parlions de contact littéraire'.

4. Yahweh commissions the servant to say to those in darkness, 'Be unveiled (ἀνακαλυφθῆαι)!' (Isa. 49.9). Similarly Paul talks about the veil of spiritual darkness not yet being lifted for many Jews (ἀνακαλυπτομενον), but all believers

light of the knowledge of Christ to those who are blind (2 Cor. 4.4-6). Finally, Paul at times echoes the servant's despondent cry, κενῶν ἐκοπίασα (Isa. 49.4), when he fears that his labour has been in vain and his ministry of restoration has failed.[1]

On a secondary level, it is interesting to observe that Luke's portrayal of Paul also utilizes Isaiah 49 to describe the apostle's mission. The Lucan account draws directly from servant traditions: 'I [the Lord] have placed you [Paul] as a light for the Gentiles, that you should bring salvation to the end of the earth' (Acts 13.47; cf. Isa. 49.6).[2] Later in Acts 26.17-18a,[3] Luke again aligns Paul's light-proclamation ministry with that of the messiah's (cf. 26.23–'the messiah was to suffer, and... to proclaim light to both the [Jewish] people and to the Gentiles'),[4] both allusions drawing upon Isa. 49.6 (cf. 42.6).

In sum, the apostle Paul (and the Paul of Lucan tradition[5]) closely identifies his ministry with that of the *'ebed Yahweh* in Isaiah 49. The point of drawing attention to this extensive *'ebed* identification is twofold. First, the *'ebed* excursus sets the background for understanding the Old Testament quotation from Isa. 49.8 in 2 Cor. 6.2 (another alignment of Paul's ministry with the *'ebed*). Second, Paul's use of Isaianic tradition anticipates the conceptual and verbal continuity with the fragment of 6.14–7.1. For, if Paul customarily assumes

---

approaching God with unveiled faces (ἀνακεκαλυμμένῳ) (2 Cor. 3.14, 18; cf. 4.4).

1. 1 Cor. 9.15; 15.10, 58; 2 Cor. 6.1; 9.3; Phil. 2.16; 1 Thess. 2.1; 3.5. See Beale ('Old Testament Background', p. 561) for a good discussion of this correlation of Paul with the servant's role.

2. Acts 13.47 closely follows the LXX Isa. 49.6, while omitting a few words. Cf. Gal. 1.16, 'that I might preach him among the Gentiles'.

3. According to Luke, the Isaianic servant's commission underlies Paul's commissioning, 'delivering you from the (Jewish) people and from the Gentiles, to whom I am sending you, to open their eyes so that they may turn from darkness to light and from the dominion of Satan to God' (Acts 26.18; cf. 26.23; Isa. 49.6; 42.6).

4. For Isa. 49.6 being used in conjunction with the ministry of Jesus note Lk. 2.32, where Simeon describes God's salvation (cf. Isa. 52.10) as, 'A light for revelation to the Gentiles, and the glory of your people Israel'. These too are reformulations of the servant traditions from Isa. 49.6 (cf. 42.6).

5. One could argue that consistency of these traditions in both Paul and Luke may imply that Luke had access to genuine Pauline tradition at this point. Of course, Luke's use of this material is consistent with his own theme of Gentilic inclusion.

the *'ebed*'s title, call, mission-acts, and his light-to-the-Gentiles proclamation, it would seem conceivable for him to adopt the servant (or servant-directed[1]) message which calls upon the exiled captives to 'Come out (of Babylon)'.

4. *The Day of (Home-Coming) Acceptance and (New Exodus) Salvation (2 Cor. 6.1-2)*

Context and Structure
The appeal in 2 Cor. 6.1-2 extends Paul's imperative that the Corinthians be reconciled to God (5.20). The apostle urges the Corinthians 'not to receive the grace of God in vain (their lives should demonstrate the results of God's grace)'. The rational (γάρ) for the exhortation, not to receive God's grace in vain, is based on a quotation from Isa. 49.8–because in fulfillment of promise, *now* is the era of God's home-coming acceptance and new-exodus salvation of his people. And by secondary implication, God is helping his servant of the new covenant (Paul) and will help his other servants (the Corinthians) should they return to him.

After laying out the texts for the Old Testament quotation in 6.2, I will develop its contribution to new covenant and second exodus theology. Towards my hypothesis, several points need to be established from the Isa. 49.8 quotation and its context: (1) the exilic return framework for 'acceptance' and 'salvation'; (2) the servant's function as new covenant mediator; (3) the promise of help for a lamenting servant, and most importantly, (4) the servant's new-exodus proclamation: 'Come out of Babylon!'

The MT, LXX and New Testament Texts
The MT and LXX texts (including material slightly beyond the quoted portion) will be laid out for comparison with the New Testament text, along with an interpretive translation:

---

1. The 'come out' exhortation is at times given by Yahweh himself and at other times it is instructed or 'directed' by Yahweh to be the message of the *'ebed* to the captives. See discussion below on Isa. 49.8.

MT (Isa. 49.8-9a):

כֹּה אָמַר יְהוָה	Thus says the Lord,
בְּעֵת רָצוֹן עֲנִיתִיךָ	'In a time of acceptance/favor I will answer you,
וּבְיוֹם יְשׁוּעָה עֲזַרְתִּיךָ	in a day of deliverance I will help[1] you,
וְאֶצָּרְךָ וְאֶתֶּנְךָ לִבְרִית עָם	I will protect you and make you a covenant (mediator) for the nation,
לְהָקִים אֶרֶץ	in order to restore the land,
לְהַנְחִיל נְחָלוֹת שֹׁמֵמוֹת:	and reassign the desolate inheritances,
לֵאמֹר לַאֲסוּרִים צֵאוּ	by (you—the *'ebed*[2]) saying to the captives, "Come out!"
לַאֲשֶׁר בַּחֹשֶׁךְ הִגָּלוּ	to those in darkness, "Show yourselves!"'

LXX (Isa. 49.8-9a):

Οὕτως λέγει Κύριος,	Thus says the Lord,
Καιρῷ δεκτῷ ἐπήκουσά σου,	'In a time of acceptance I will hear/heard[3] you,
καὶ ἐν ἡμέρᾳ σωτηρίας ἐβοήθησά σοι,	and in a day of deliverance I will help/helped you,
καὶ ἔδωκά σε εἰς διαθήκην ἐθνῶν,	and will make/made you as a covenant for the nations,
τοῦ καταστῆσαι τὴν γῆν,	in order to establish the land,
καὶ κληρονομῆσαι κληρονομίας ἐρήμου,	and to reallot the deserted inheritance,
λέγοντα τοῖς ἐν δεσμοῖς, ἐξέλθατε,	by (you—the *'ebed*) saying to the captives, "Come out!"
καὶ τοῖς ἐν τῷ σκότει, ἀνακαλυφθῆναι·	and to those in darkness, "Show yourselves!"'

NT (2 Cor. 6.2):

λέγει γάρ,	. . . for he (God) says,
καιρῷ δεκτῷ ἐπήκουσά σου	'In a time of acceptance I will hear/heard[4] you,

1. עֲנִיתִיךָ and עֲזַרְתִּיךָ are prophetic perfects followed by two imperfects.
2. A discussion of the subject of the infinitives (Yahweh or the servant) will follow.
3. The MT עֲנִיתִיךָ and עֲזַרְתִּיךָ are prophetic perfects. Likewise, even though translated woodenly with the aorist, ἐπήκουσά and ἐβοήθησά probably convey a *future* promissory sense here. The translator of Isaiah carried through with aorists, rather than switching to the future tense where the MT changed to the imperfect (e.g., ἔπλασά and ἔδωκά). See discussion below.
4. The aorist may be an attempt to reflect the MT prophetic perfect (see below).

καὶ ἐν ἡμέρᾳ σωτηρίας ἐβοήθησά   in a day of deliverance I will
σοι   help/helped you.'
ἰδοὺ νῦν καιρὸς εὐπρόσδεκτος,   Behold, now is the time of
                                acceptance/favor,
ἰδοὺ νῦν ἡμέρα σωτηρίας   Behold, now is the day of salvation.

Except for the slight change in introductory formula, the New Testament quotation of Isa. 49.8a contains the exact wording of the LXX. It differs only marginally from the MT.[1]

Exilic Return Theology: Home-coming 'Acceptance' and New Exodus 'Salvation'

From the Old Testament background one is able to establish the setting of Paul's quotation. Several features fill in the picture. First, the 'salvation/deliverance' (בְּיוֹם יְשׁוּעָה/ἡμέρα σωτηρίας) in the quoted portion of Isa. 49.8 contextually is none other than the exilic return. The יְשׁוּעָה/σωτηρίας of Isa. 49.8a probably refers to the exilic return since at the end of the promise sequence, 'I will answer... help... make...', the purpose is, 'in order to restore the land and reassign the desolate inheritances' (49.8b). Clearly the salvation and the restoration in view is the exilic return—the people are led back to the homeland and the land which had become desolate their captivity is redistributed.[2]

Furthermore, the 'salvation' in the context of Isa. 49.8-13 (cf. 48.20-21) is portrayed as a new exodus, patterned after the pivotal 'Red Sea' event of years ago. For example, in Isa. 49.9 the call for those who are bound to 'Come out!' picks up from the imperative of Isa. 48.20-21, 'Come out of Babylon!' where the return theme of second exodus has already been introduced:

> [20]Come out of Babylon! Flee from the Chaldeans!
> Declare with the sound of joyful shouting,
> proclaim this, send it out to the end of the earth;

1. The major difference between the MT and the LXX is the change from 'I answered (will answer) you' (עֲנִיתִיךָ) to 'I heard (will hear) you' (ἐπήκουσά σου). However, both express much the same thought (that is, 'hearing' is here put in place of the effect, 'answering'). Ellis' list (*Paul's Use of the Old Testament*, p. 152) incorrectly classifies the quotation as 'in agreement with the LXX and Hebrew'.

2. The 'exilic return' expands its geographical pattern to a return from the ends of the earth (Isa. 49.6, 12; cf. 43.5-6).

say, 'Yahweh has redeemed his servant Jacob.'
[21]They did not thirst when he led them through the deserts:
he made the water flow out of the rock for them;
he split the rock, and the water gushed forth.

The return through the desert,[1] splitting of the rock, and water flowing, even gushing out, vividly recall scenes from the first exodus.[2] Similarly, in Isa. 49.10 the exiles, in their return from Babylon, will not hunger or thirst, for Yahweh will lead his people to springs of water (as he did before[3]). Also, Israel's grazing along the way like a flock[4] with Yahweh leading (נָהַג)[5] and guiding them (נָהֵל)[6] paints this new exodus with well-known descriptions of the old. Westermann rightly observes the escalated pattern here: 'Once again and quite obviously, the background is the Exodus at the beginning of the nation's history.... However, the new Exodus is to be much more miraculous in character than was this.'[7]

Even the expression, 'Come out (of Babylon)' (Isa. 48.20; 49.9), is a reflection of the exodus-from-Egypt event. Throughout the sacred history of Israel, the words '... מִן יָצָא' became almost a formulaic expression to describe the first exodus out of Egypt.[8] These words are repeatedly used of the great salvation event through which Yahweh

1. Exod. 15.22; 16.1; 17.1–19.2. Watts (*Isaiah 34-66*, p. 179) comments, 'God is marching with his people through the desert toward his land as he did before'.

2. Isa. 48.21; cf. Exod. 17.6; Deut. 8.15; Pss. 78.15-16, 20; 105.41; 114.8. Cf. Westermann, *Isaiah 40-66*, p. 205. Cf. Paul's use of the rock tradition in 1 Cor. 10.4-5.

3. Isa. 49.10; (cf. Isa. 35.7; 41.17-18); cf. Exod. 15.22-25; 15.27 (esp., the twelve springs of water at Elim) cf. Num. 33.9; 17.1-6; Num. 21.16; Deut. 10.7; Ps. 107.35. Cf. Westermann, *Isaiah 40-66*, p. 215.

4. Isa. 49.9b; cf. Ps. 78.52.

5. Isa. 49.10c; cf. Ps. 78.52; Isa. 63.14 (first exodus).

6. Isa. 49.10d (cf. 40.11); cf. Exod. 15.13.

7. Westermann, *Isaiah 40-66*, pp. 215-16.

8. E.g., Exod. 3.10-12; 6.6-7, 13, 26-27; 7.5, 12, 17, 42, 51; 13.3, 8-9, 14, 16; 14.11; 16.1, 6, 32; 18.1; 19.1; 20.2; 23.15; 29.46; 32.11; Lev. 19.36; 22.33; 23.43; 25.38, 42, 55; 26.13, 45; Num. 1.1; 9.1; 11.20; 15.41; 20.16; 22.5, 11; 23.22; 24.8; 26.4; 33.1, 38; Deut. 1.27; 4.20, 45-46; 5.6, 15; 6.12, 21, 23; 7.8, 19; 8.14; 9.7, 12, 26, 28-29; 11.10; 13.5, 10; 16.1, 3, 6, 13; 23.4; 24.9; 25.17; 26.8; 29.25; Josh. 2.10; 5.4-5; 24.5-6; Judg. 2.12; 6.8; 1 Sam. 12.8; 1 Kgs 6.1; 8.9, 16, 21, 51, 53; 9.9; 1 Chron. 11.2; 2 Chron. 5.10; 6.5; 7.22; Pss. 114.1; 136.11 (cf. 66.12; 68.6; 105.37, 43); Jer. 7.22, 25; 11.4; 31.32; 32.21; 34.13; Ezek. 20.6, 9-10, 14, 22; Dan. 9.15; Hag. 2.5.

formed his people (taking them out of Egypt and out from among the nations). Similarly, within exilic return material (which is bursting with first exodus imagery) the call to 'Come out of Babylon' (Isa. 48.20; 49.9) serves as another suggestive component to the allusion.[1] For the people of God, it is heard as the cry for a 'new exodus'.

In keeping with this new exodus theme, the deliverance is led by a 'new Moses'. Quite appropriately the *'ebed* who leads out the 'second exodus' is cast as a 'second Moses'.[2] In the context of a second exodus (Isa. 49.8-13), the servant's role as effective spokesperson reminds one of Yahweh's servant Moses.[3] Like the servant in the songs, Moses was a covenant mediator.[4] And Isaiah's *'ebed* follows in the pattern of Moses who had the mission of allotting to the tribes of Jacob the various districts which they were eventually to inhabit.[5] Again, Moses in his role as covenant mediator on Sinai asks the Lord to see his glory which results in his transmitting that glory: δεῖξόν μοι τὴν σεαυτοῦ δόξαν (Exod. 33.18; cf. 34.29-35); yet when the glory passes by in front of Moses, Yahweh 'covers him with his hand': καὶ σκεπάσω τῇ χειρί μου ἐπὶ σέ (Exod. 33.22). Similarly, though internalized now, Yahweh reveals his glory through the new Moses:

---

1. Cf. Ps. 107.14, 28; Isa. 42.7; 43.8; 52.11-12; 55.12; Jer. 50.8; 51.45; Ezek. 20.34, 41 (cf. 20.6, 9-10, 14, 22); 34.13.

2. Cf. von Rad, *The Message of the Prophets*, pp. 227-28.

3. Moses frequently communicates God's message to others (e.g., Exod. 3.16-17; 4.10-17; with Aaron as mouthpiece) as well as on numerous occasions being referred to as Yahweh's servant (e.g., Exod. 14.31; Num. 12.7; Deut. 3.24; 34.5; Josh. 1.1-2, 7, 13-15; 8.31-33; 9.24; 11.12, 15; 12.6; 13.8; 14.7; 18.7; 22.2, 4-5).

4. Exod. 34.27, 'I [Yahweh] have made a covenant with you [Moses] and with Israel', as well as Moses' role as intercessor for the nation, place him in the position as covenant mediator. Cf. the Isaianic *'ebed*'s role as covenant mediator (עָם בְּרִית/ διαθήκην γένους in Isa. 42.6; בְּרִית עָם/διαθήκην ἐθνῶν in 49.8; and in LXX 49.6, εἰς διαθήκην γένους [not in MT]). Cf. Odendahl, *Eschatological Expectation*, pp. 132-33. Appealing to Deut. 3.23-25; 4.21; 9.9, 18-21, 25-29, von Rad (*The Message of the Prophets*, p. 227) likewise suggests that Moses, like the servant in the songs, 'acts as a mediator between Yahweh, and Israel, he suffers, and raises his voice in complaint to Yahweh, and at the last dies vicariously for the sins of his people'. However, von Rad is more comfortable calling Isaiah's *'ebed* a prophet 'like Moses', rather than a 'second Moses' or a *Moses redivivus*.

5. Isa. 49.8b; cf. Num. 32.33; Josh. 13.8, 15-33; 14.1-5, as noted by von Rad (*The Message of the Prophets*, p. 227).

ἐν σοὶ δοξασθήσομαι (Isa. 49.3);[1] so for the second *'ebed* Yahweh again 'covers him with his hand': καὶ ὑπὸ τὴν σκέπην τῆς χειρὸς αὐτοῦ ἔκρυψέν με (Isa. 49.2).[2]

A second matter requires attention, namely, the nature of the parallel term 'acceptance' (בְּעֵת רָצוֹן/καιρῷ δεκτῷ) in the quoted portion of Isa. 49.8. Like 'salvation', it plays a part in the exilic return drama. Both terms ('salvation' and 'acceptance') permeate the *entire* journey, yet each seems oriented at different points. In a somewhat geographical merism, the 'deliverance' focuses on the beginning of the journey (leaving captivity in Babylon) while the 'acceptance' looks at the other end of the journey (the home-coming acceptance of the pilgrims to Zion).[3] The expression בְּעֵת רָצוֹן in Isa. 49.8 does *not* refer to the people accepting Yahweh, any more than בְּיוֹם יְשׁוּעָה describes Israel saving Yahweh. Rather, בְּעֵת רָצוֹן refers to the time when Yahweh will accept his people with favor when they will return to Zion to worship him and be welcomed by him into the temple (cultic overtones are dominant[4]). Likewise, καιρῷ δεκτῷ in the New Testament quotation should be understood as a time of acceptance/reception which Yahweh (subject) shows towards his people (object).[5]

---

1. The glory connection is not as strong in the MT, since Isa. 49.3 has פאר instead of the כבד of Exod. 33.18-23.

2. Cf. Isa. 51.16 for the same Sinai-theophany metaphor, again in connection with the communication of Yahweh's covenant (cf. 'put My words in your mouth' in Isa. 59.21 as being the words of the [new] covenant).

3. Similarly, the last of the three infinitives (Isa. 49.8-9) functions as a call to leave Babylon (the beginning of the journey), while first two infinitives view the results of being back in the land (at the end of the journey).

4. This is another reason why the 'acceptance' motif fits with the Zion (temple) end of the journey. As with its use in the sacrificial material, there is the notion of acceptance (in a cultic sense) for worship at Zion.

5. When approaching the δεκτ- word links in the surrounding context, this subject-object distinction should be retained. In the link which follows the quotation, ἰδοὺ νῦν καιρὸς εὐπρόσδεκτος (6.2b), the God-subject and people-object distinction is maintained. However, in the link which precedes the quotation, μὴ εἰς κενὸν τὴν χάριν τοῦ θεοῦ δέξασθαι ὑμᾶς (6.1), the subject-object relationship is reversed, the people (subject) are not to receive God's grace (object) in vain. Therefore, it seems best to take the δέξασθαι in 6.1 not as a strict exegesis of the OT text, but as a wordplay designed to draw out the irony of the Corinthians' rejection; in this time when Yahweh is accepting his people home, the people are not accepting his gracious offer (or his messenger).

   Lukan tradition develops a similar word play when Christ comes κηρύξαι

This theme of 'acceptance' (6.2) provides a significant conceptual and verbal link to the fragment (specifically, quotation 3 of the Old Testament catena). The δεκτ- word group of 2 Cor. 6.1-2 (δέξασθαι, δεκτῷ, and εὐπρόσδεκτος) reflects precisely the same return theology that is expressed in 2 Cor. 6.17c (κἀγὼ εἰσδέξομαι ὑμᾶς).[1] On a verbal level, the fluidity of the δεκτ- terminology allows the fragment's εἰσδέξομαι to be contextually pertinent to 2 Cor. 6.1-2. This fluidity is already suggested by Paul's free interchange of δεκτῷ with εὐπρόσδεκτος (6.2). Similarly, within Old Testament exilic return theology the δεκτ- cognates προσδέξομαι and εἰσδέξομαι can be used almost interchangeably. For example, the 'acceptance/ reception' promise of Ezek. 20.34 (καὶ εἰσδέξομαι ὑμᾶς ἐκ τῶν χωρῶν; cf. 20.41b) is restated through the *cognate* expressions, καὶ ἐκεῖ προσδέξομαι (Ezek. 20.40) and προσδέξομαι ὑμᾶς (Ezek. 20.41b).[2] In substance and rhetorical effect, the acceptance and welcome of 'exiled' Corinthians found in καιρὸς εὐπρόσδεκτος (2 Cor. 6.2) is strategically reiterated in εἰσδέξομαι ὑμᾶς (6.17c).[3] The prefix alteration within the cognate grouping does not disrupt the link.

Consequently, the 'salvation' and 'acceptance' of which Paul speaks in 2 Cor. 6.1-2 has exilic return theology as its conceptual and theological framework. Numerous details from the Old Testament context of Isa. 49.8 (and even the call to 'Come out from. . . ') are

ἐνιαυτὸν κυρίου δεκτόν (Isa. 61.2; Lk. 4.19) and later a brief comment draws out the irony: οὐδεὶς προφήτης δεκτός ἐστιν ἐν τῇ πατρίδι αὐτοῦ (Lk. 4.24). This day-of-acceptance tradition (although indicative of Yahweh's acceptance of his people) seems to have been used of a prophet's acceptance by his people. Again, Jesus' use of this similar OT tradition in such a manner may be a subtle attempt by Paul to identify his rejection by the Corinthians with the classic case of rejection in christological mission (cf. the use of ἀποδέχομαι in Lk. 8.40; Acts 2.41; 15.4; 18.27). Cf. Collage, *Énigmes*, p. 288.

1. Cf. discussion of the third quotation in Chapter 3, §2.

2. The Ezek. 20 context is of considerable significance, since Ezek. 20.34 is the most likely source for the fragment's third quotation. See Chapter 3, §2.

3. The acceptance motif carries through to the end of chapter seven where the concerns of 6.1-2 contrast with the 'happy ending' to the story: ὡς μετὰ φόβου καὶ τρόμου ἐδέξασθε αὐτόν (i.e., Titus) (7.15). It seems unlikely that the verbal link is accidental, particularly if the reception of a rejected-prophet tradition lies in the background to the whole discussion (see above). What arose as an implication in the exhortation of 6.1 (to receive both the message and the messenger) is explicitly confirmed through Paul's commendation of the Corinthians for receiving Titus.

patterned after the exodus event of years ago and the journey motif from Babylon to Jerusalem is portrayed as a journey from Egypt to Canaan. Paul has removed any geographical literalism, just as within Isaiah the return takes on a spiritual dimension of restoration to God and the geographical pattern itself expands to 'the ends of the earth'. Paul reshapes these traditions to speak to the Corinthians about their own need for a new exodus 'salvation' from that to which they have fallen captive, and a home-coming 'acceptance' should they return to God (and to God's apostle). On a conceptual level (and verbal with the δεκτ- word group) these traditions merge with those of the fragment.

The Servant as New Covenant Mediator
The 2 Cor. 6.2 quotation also makes its contribution to new covenant theology. The 'salvation' spoken of in Isa. 49.8a is accomplished through a servant, who functions as a *(new) covenant* mediator: 'I [Yahweh] will make you a covenant [mediator[1]] for the nation' (49.8b). Similarly, in Isa. 42.6 Yahweh affirms, 'I will appoint you as a covenant [mediator] for the people, as a light to the nations, to open blind eyes, to bring prisoners from the dungeon, and those who dwell in darkness from the prison.' Granted, the meaning of בְּרִית עָם[2] and the identity of the servant (or 'you'-person being addressed) are well developed debates within Isaiah studies. However, the outcome to these issues is not determinative for my purposes.

The point to make here is that the 'you'-person or servant of Isa. 49.8 (whoever it may be) functions in relationship (whatever the parameters) to the *new covenant*. By virtue of the pattern—a new exodus, a pilgrimage to the land, a distribution of the inheritance—the covenant spoken of is a deliberate reflection of the original Sinai covenant, and in the language of Jeremiah, would be considered the 'new covenant'. In this respect, the servant functions, in some capacity, to facilitate the new covenant.

Such a theological correlation with the formation of the new covenant accords with Paul's development of new covenant themes to this point in 2 Cor. 2.14–7.4 and his self-identification as a servant of the new covenant. Again, my point here is simply that the apostle has

---

1. In the expression בְּרִית עָם 'covenant for the people' (Isa. 42.6; 49.8) בְּרִית is probably a metonymy of effect for cause, viz., a mediator of the covenant.

2. For a summary of the alternatives and bibliographic data see Barstad, *A Way in the Wilderness*, pp. 54-55; Wilson, *The Nations in Deutero-Isaiah*, pp. 260-62.

not abandoned the subject of the new covenant, with which he opened this literary section. This renewed focus on new covenant traditions establishes a bridge to the fragment (which, itself, contains explicit new covenant traditions and the redaction of other traditions in light of new covenant theology).

Promise Theology: Help and Comfort for a Despairing Servant

New Testament commentators continue to exegete (and translate[1]) 2 Cor. 6.2 to bring out the 'past' connotation of the aorist verbs. However, from the context of Isa. 49.8-9 the verbs in the MT are clearly prophetic perfects[2] and should be translated, 'I [Yahweh] will answer. . . will help.'[3] The LXX has either woodenly translated the verse[4] or consciously used the aorist in a category similar to that of the prophetic perfect.[5] Perhaps it is this supposed 'past' tense (in

1. As do most English versions of the NT.

2. As mentioned above in my translation of the MT text, עֲנִיתִיךָ and עֲזַרְתִּיךָ are prophetic perfects followed by two imperfects (וְאֶצָּרְךָ וְאֶתֶּנְךָ). The imperfects 'I [Yahweh] will protect you. . . and will make you. . . ' suggest that the previous two perfects should be understood as prophetic perfects (note the sequence and the continued ךָ suffixes). And, when one considers that the referent of עֲזַרְתִּיךָ and עֲנִיתִיךָ is linked to the upcoming deliverance from Babylon (in connection with the בְּיוֹם יְשׁוּעָה), there can be little doubt that the verbs are prophetic perfects. As Westermann (*Isaiah 40-66*, p. 215) notes, these verbs indicate 'a promise of salvation in the perfect tense'. Cf. North, *Second Isaiah*, p. 192; Smart, *Second Isaiah*, p. 159.

3. Or perhaps with an English present as some commentators do to convey the prophetic perfect nuance (e.g., Watts, *Isaiah 34-66*, p. 183).

4. The LXX translates the following imperfect(s) in the sequence with aorists (instead of with a future tense). Of course it is possible that the translator was using some unknown Hebrew textual tradition with all perfects. Based on the existing Hebrew texts, however, either the translator simply did not wish to reflect the change in Hebrew tenses or deliberately chose the aorist to convey the 'prophetic perfect' sense of the first two verbs and then continued with the aorist for the rest of the imperfect(s). See the next footnote.

5. On the LXX use of the aorist tense in a 'prophetic perfect' sense, see Fanning, *Verbal Aspect*, pp. 269-74. For a broader discussion of the influence of Semitic languages on verbal aspect, see Porter, *Verbal Aspect*, pp. 111-56. It is possible that some of these cases may have been mechanical renderings (a wooden equation of the Greek aorist for the Hebrew perfect). On this method as practiced by the translators of Isaiah, see comments by Ottley, *The Book of Isaiah according to the Septuagint*, I, pp. 43-44. However, there are some clear cases of the 'prophetic perfect' aorist in LXX Isaiah (e.g., Isa. 5.13-14; 9.5; 11.9). Whether or not the translators used a mechanical technique or consciously chose the aorist to express the prophetic perfect,

contrast to Paul's interpretive νῦν) which has led some to label the
quotation here as pesher,[1] whereas the citation may be more accurately classified as promise-fulfillment (or typical-prophetic[2]). At any
rate, that Paul understood the Old Testament passage to be speaking in
some sense of a *future* event is likely from his interpretive νῦν: ἰδοὺ
νῦν καιρὸς εὐπρόσδεκτος, ἰδοὺ νῦν ἡμέρα σωτηρίας. In form,
then, 2 Cor. 6.2 corresponds to the 'promise' category which was
translated and/or later read as a 'prophetic perfect' aorist. While my
traditions hypothesis is not dependent upon this tense analysis,[3] the
form of the quotation does make a contribution to understanding the
fragment within its present literary context. The significance is that
these covenant-promise traditions ('I, Yahweh, will. . . ') reflect the
sort of the Old Testament material from which Paul has been drawing
along the way[4] and anticipate the promise-formulas found in 6.14–7.1.

Aside from its form, the content of the promise in 2 Cor. 6.2 is also
important. The promise of 49.8 is Yahweh's answer to the lament of
the servant over his seemingly ineffective efforts for restoration (cf.
49.4-5). That Paul had the broader context of Isaiah 49 in mind
(without the source divisions of current scholarship) is suggested by

later readers such as Paul may well have understood the aorist in a future sense. As
Fanning (*Verbal Aspect*, p. 273) notes, 'whether the translators always understood
the sense or not, these forms would be read by many as futuristic: the Greek aorist
indicative used to some degree under Hebrew influence to portray a future occurrence
as if already done'. Cf. Meyer (*Epistles to the Corinthians*, p. 546) who states that
the aorists in 2 Cor. 6.2 project 'the future as having already happened'.

1. E.g., Bruce (*1 and 2 Corinthians*, p. 211) suggests that the interpretation of
the verse which follows, ἰδοὺ νῦν καιρός..., is pesher since it applies Isaiah's
text to the gospel age. For others who take the quotation as pesher, see Ellis, *Paul's
Use of the Old Testament*, p. 143; Collage, *Énigmes*, p. 287. I have no difficulty
with the classification of certain uses of the OT as pesher in 2 Corinthians (see
discussion on 2 Cor. 3.17 in Chapter 4, §3). However, if the aorist tense in 2 Cor.
6.2 is a 'prophetic perfect' of sorts, then the quotation is in a quite different category
than the case of pesher in 2 Cor. 3.17 (and other examples at Qumran).

2. Particularly when the return (בְּיוֹם יְשׁוּעָה) is pictured within the same chapter as a
salvation-return from the ends of the earth (Isa. 49.6, לִהְיוֹת יְשׁוּעָתִי עַד־קְצֵה הָאָרֶץ; cf.
49.12), which would equally apply to the events of Paul's day (patterned after the
return under Cyrus) without any 'then-now' bifurcation. For a definition of typical-
prophetic and examples in Luke–Acts, see Bock, *Prophecy and Pattern*, pp. 49-51,
290-91.

3. A conceptual bridge would still exist even if the aorists had a 'past' connotation.

4. Cf. my earlier treatment of 2 Cor. 1.20-22; 3.2-3; 4.6; 5.5, 17.

the similar fear and despair that his work of reconciliation/restoration was in vain (2 Cor. 6.1; cf. Isa. 49.4).[1] In addition, it is the broader context of Isa. 49 from which Paul later draws encouragement and comfort (2 Cor. 7.6; cf. Isa. 49.13[2]). This drawing from the broader context of Isa. 49.8 (beyond the exact quotation), along with Paul's identification with the servant's plight, lends further support to the thesis that Paul may have reflected upon the purpose infinitives which directly follow the quoted portion Isa. 49.8a.

The Servant's Proclamation of Release to Captives: 'Come out of Babylon!'

The subject of the three infinitives in Isa. 49.8-9a (לְהָקִים, לְהַנְחִיל, and לֵאמֹר) may be taken as either (1) Yahweh, describing divine actions associated with his making the servant a covenant mediator,[3] or (2) the 'servant' (leaving aside the precise identity), indicating Yahweh's purpose for making the servant a covenant mediator and thus depicting the task of the servant in mediation.[4] The first option conveys the idea that Yahweh's restorative work is prior to, or distinct from, the servant's mediating work; the second depicts the *'ebed* as agent of restoration.[5] The Yahweh-subject option has in its favor the first

---

1. Beale ('Old Testament Background', p. 561) develops the restoration-in-vain connection rather well. Cf. Becker, 'Paul, the Suffering Apostle', p. 310.

2. The LXX Isa. 49.13 reads ὅτι ἠλέησεν ὁ θεὸς τὸν λαὸν αὐτοῦ καὶ τοὺς ταπεινοὺς τοῦ λαοῦ αὐτοῦ παρεκάλεσεν; cf. 2 Cor. 7.6, ἀλλ᾽ ὁ παρακαλῶν τοὺς ταπεινοὺς παρεκάλεσεν ἡμᾶς ὁ θεός. Martin (2 *Corinthians*, p. 224) points out that the 'allusion is all the more remarkable since its OT v. in Isaiah occurs in the same chapter from which Paul drew a testimony in 6.2 (Isa. 49.8)'. For others who suggest an allusion to Isa. 49.13 here, see Ellis, *Paul's Use of the Old Testament*, p. 153; Hughes, *Second Epistle to the Corinthians*, p. 266; Plummer, *Second Epistle to the Corinthians*, p. 218.

3. Some commentators take Yahweh as the subject: Whybray, *Isaiah 40-66*, p. 141; Westermann, *Isaiah 40-66*, p. 215.

4. Others view the servant as the subject (while the exact referent for the servant can vary from Cyrus, to Darius, a remnant within Israel, the nation Israel, a prophet, etc.): Simon, *A Commentary on Isaiah 40-55*, p. 166; Delitzsch, *Commentary on the Prophecies of Isaiah*, p. 242; Mckenzie, *Second Isaiah*, pp. 107-109; Smart, *Second Isaiah*, p. 159; Watts, *Isaiah 34-66*, p. 186; Wilson, *The Nations in Deutero-Isaiah*, p. 276; and perhaps, Knight, *Servant Theology*, pp. 133-34.

5. North (*Second Isaiah*, p. 192) points out correctly that the issue cannot be decided on grammatical grounds. However, his suggestion that 'we may have it both ways' is questionable.

person subject of the verbs in v. 8 ('I [Yahweh] will answer. . . help. . . keep. . . give . . .') which is resumed in v. 11 ('I [Yahweh] will make. . . ').[1] In addition, some of the content of the three infinitives is elsewhere in Isaiah 40–55 attributed to Yahweh.[2] However, with an overlap in roles (the servant being Yahweh's representative) such evidence is not determinative.[3] Furthermore, the fourfold repetition of the suffix 'you' (ךָ-) offsets any focus on Yahweh. Instead, the repeated 'you'-suffixes serve as a rhetorical device to emphasize the servant (perhaps in anticipation of the servant's role in the infinitives).[4] Also, the nature of the final verb in the four-fold sequence, 'I will give/appoint you as' (וְאֶתֶּנְךָ) may anticipate a transfer in the infinitives to the covenant role for which the 'you'- person has been assigned (cf. 42.6-7; 49.6).[5]

Several lines of additional evidence suggest that the servant is a suitable subject for the infinitives. First, the immediately preceding address by the servant in Isa. 49.5-6 speaks of the servant's *active* role in the restoration process. The servant's function in 49.5-6 is similarly expressed by purpose infinitives (לְשׁוֹבֵב and לְהָקִים), the latter לְהָקִים being repeated in 49.8.[6] Second, in the crux parallel text of Isa. 42.6-7[7] the subject of the infinitives is the servant. Almost all

1. Westermann (*Isaiah 40-66*, pp. 100, 212-15), in his commentary and translation of the infinitives in 42.7 and 49.8-9a, acknowledges the 'indetermination' (or ambiguity) of the writer. Nonetheless, he (*Isaiah 40-66*, pp. 215) appears to favor taking Yahweh as subject of the infinitives in 49.8-9a in light of the Yahweh being the subject of the verbs (both in v. 8 and resumed in v. 11).

2. E.g., Isa. 44.26.

3. The tasks of the three infinitives are elsewhere allocated to the servant (Isa. 42.7; 44.28; 49.6; cf. 61.1).

4. There may also be the notion of attraction between the designated function עַם לִבְרִית (introduced with a *lamed*) and the following three purpose clauses: לְהָקִים, לְהַנְחִיל, and לֵאמֹר. For a similar phenomenon in which the 'servant' (in its broadest sense) in Isa. 40–55 is attributed a functional description by Yahweh (as a servant, witness, light, covenant, etc.) and immediately followed by infinitives of purpose, see 42.6-7; 43.10; 49.5-6.

5. Cf. other times in Isa. 40–55 where נתן (with Yahweh as subject) is followed by a purpose or result clause (with a change in subject): 41.19-20; 42.6-7; 45.3; 49.6; 50.4.

6. The servant-subject of לְהָקִים in 49.6 suggests a similar understanding in 49.8.

7. The parallels are striking. In both texts (Isa. 42.6-7 and 49.8-9) Yahweh responds to a preceding 'servant song', the infinitives follow a *lamed* of purpose where the status and function of the servant has been assigned (as a light/covenant/

commentators agree that the servant is the subject of the infinitives in 42.6-7 (even those who take Yahweh as the subject of the infinitives in 49.8-9a)[1]. Third, if 'reassigning the land's desolate inheritances' is an intentional allusion to the former role of Moses in distributing the land (as it would seem[2]), then the infinitives more aptly reflect the role of the servant, not Yahweh. Fourth, a similar infinitival clause beginning with לֵאמֹר is used in Isa. 44.28 to describe the consequent action of the servant (Cyrus in that context) as Yahweh's agent and the content of what he was to proclaim.[3] Finally, the conceptual affinity between the servant's assigned role as *'light'* and the calling of captives out of *'darkness'* adds weight to the argument for the servant as subject of the infinitives. The servant's role as a 'light' (לְאוֹר) and as a 'covenant' (לִבְרִית) has already been fused in Isa. 42.6-7. Likewise, 'I will make you as a covenant' (אֶתֶּנְךָ לִבְרִית) in Isa. 49.8 should not be disjoined from its counterpart 'I will give you as a light' (נְתַתִּיךָ לְאוֹר) in 49.6. The servant in his assigned role as *light* is conceptually the one suited to proclaim freedom to those in *darkness*.

Consequently, it is the assigned function of the servant (according to Isa. 48.8-9) to proclaim release to the captives: 'Come out of Babylon.' This proclamation by the servant facilitates the day of deliverance from Babylon and home-coming acceptance to Zion. As a servant of the new covenant, Paul could have used the Isaiah traditions in the fragment to echo the cry of the *'ebed:* 'Come out (of Babylon).' Granted, the source is Isa. 52.11, not Isa. 48.9. However, the setting

---

servant; cf. 49.6), and the nature of the infinitival clauses are quite similar (freeing captives, releasing those who sit in darkness, etc.). The verbal correspondence is also quite extensive: לברית עם, נתן, יצר, and חשך.

1. E.g., Whybray, *Isaiah 40-66*, p. 75. Westermann (*Isaiah 40-66*, p. 100) is indecisive, seeing both as subject here in 42.6-7.

2. Moses (extended in the person of Joshua) is the one who restores the tribes to their ancestral lands and distributes (נהל) the land for an inheritance (Num. 32.33-42; 33.50–35.16; Josh. 13.32; 14.1-5; Ps. 78.55; Isa. 43.16-20). Clifford (*Fair Spoken*, pp. 150-54) notes that the infinitives—apportioning the lands, liberating the prisoners, and leading exiles home to Zion—correspond to the work of Moses, who also receives a covenant. Cf. Wilson, *Nations in Deutero-Isaiah*, p. 278.

3. In accordance with Yahweh's decree (44.26), Cyrus will command Jerusalem's rebuilding (44.28). See Clifford, *Fair Spoken*, p. 114; Wilson, *Nations in Deutero-Isaiah*, p. 204. Granted, 44.26 has been taken as a later emendation by some (Westermann, *Isaiah 40-66*, p. 153; Whybray, *Isaiah 40-66*, p. 104).

and call of both passages are similar.[1] Once convinced that the cry for a new exodus was part of the servant's task in restoration from Isa. 49.8-9, Paul could have adapted any number of passages within Isaiah to call the Corinthians to return home.[2]

The new exodus cry, ἐξέλθατε, functions as the 'starting gate' exhortation for the exilic return, the means by which the servant initiates the people's response to the new covenant. It is conceivable that Paul, viewing himself as a διάκονος καινῆς διαθήκης[3] in the path of christological mission, specifies his exhortation to respond to God's grace and favor (6.1-2) with the cry, ἐξέλθατε ἐκ μέσου αὐτῶν. Referent difficulties aside, on a conceptual level the fragment's cry for the Corinthians to make an exodus-like return to God cannot be denied congruence with its context.

Summary

It is this complex of ideas—new covenant, new exodus, '*ebed*-new Moses, and proclamation of release—which becomes crucially impor-

---

1. The verbal and conceptual connection between Isa. 48.20; 49.9; and 52.11 is tight. As already mentioned, Isa. 49.9 draws upon 48.20-21 since the ἐξέλθατε call is the same and the new exodus imagery of Yahweh's provision of water and the exiles not thirsting is taken up again and advanced in 49.9-13 (see above). Furthermore, Isa. 52.11 picks up on the same departure/new exodus theme (ἀπόστητε ἀπόστητε ἐξέλθατε ἐκεῖθεν) as does Isa. 48.20 (ἔξελθε ἐκ Βαβυλῶνος). Although he would see two different expeditions historically, Watts (*Isaiah 34-66*, pp. 216-17) points out the continuity between Isaiah 48 and 52: 'As in chap. 48, the hope takes a practical turn in vv. 11 and 12 (i.e., 52.11-12), as the Jews in Babylon are encouraged to go participate in the welcome being prepared in Jerusalem for Yahweh's return. . . The exhortation to depart must be addressed to Babylonian Jews preparing another expedition to Jerusalem like the earlier one in 48.20'. For the new exodus elements of Isa. 52.11-12, see Chapter 3, §2. Cf. Ziegler (*Isaias*, p. 155) who notes the close parallel between Isa. 48.20 and 52.11.

2. Cf. the similar use of יצא in another servant song to describe the '*ebed's* mission: 'I will appoint you as a covenant mediator. . . to bring out (להוציא/ἐξαγαγεῖν) prisoners from the dungeon, and those who dwell in darkness from the prison' (Isa. 42.6-7). Although not formally one of the servant songs, a similar new exodus cry is heard in Isa. 43.8, 'Bring out (הוציא/ἐξήγαγον) the people who are blind, even though they have eyes, and the deaf, even though they have ears'. Also, compare the use of ἐξέρχεσθαι in LXX Isaiah to describe either the first exodus (11.16; cf. Jer. 7.25) or second/new exodus (48.20; 49.9; 52.11; 55.12; cf. Jer. 27[50].8; 38[31].9; Ezek. 38.8).

3. 2 Cor. 3.6; cf. 6.3-4.

tant when understanding how the appeal of 6.14–7.1 fits within its contextual framework. Through his use of Isa. 49.8, Paul has left more than a slight clue to the nature of the salvation and acceptance (2 Cor. 6.1-2) of which he speaks. It is a deliverance and acceptance/ welcoming to the homeland *patterned after the exilic return*, a return which finds its roots deep in the movements of salvation-history. It is here in 2 Cor. 6.1-2, through the apostle's identification with the *'ebed's* mission, that the second-Moses overtures in Isa. 49.1-13 converge with Paul's earlier self-portrait as a 'new Moses'[1] and anticipate the new exodus traditions found in the 6.14–7.1 fragment. The text of 2 Cor. 6.1-2 forges strong verbal and conceptual ties with the fragment's Old Testament traditions at two points: (1) the δεκτ- traditions of 6.2 (δέξασθαι, δεκτῷ, and εὐπρόσδεκτος) and quotation 3 (εἰσδέξομαι ὑμᾶς), and (2) the cry for a new exodus, ἔξελθε ἐκ Βαβυλῶνος (Isa. 49.9; cf. 48.20; 42.7; 43.8) and its reflection in quotation 2 (διὸ ἐξέλθατε ἐκ μέσου αὐτῶν).

5. *No Stumbling Blocks in the Path of Return and an Appeal as a Servant of God (2 Cor. 6.3-10)*

Context and Structure
Having made the appeal for the Corinthians to respond to God's grace, to a new-exodus salvation and home-coming acceptance (6.1-2), Paul clears the way for their return by removing any stumbling blocks from the path (6.3-4a). Syntactically, the two participial phrases in 6.3-4a, μηδεμίαν ἐν μηδενὶ διδόντες προσκοπήν and ἐν παντι συνιστάντες ἑαυτούς, provide the *means* (or method/model), both negatively and positively, by which Paul continues to make his appeal—παρακαλοῦμεν μὴ εἰς κενὸν τὴν χάριν τοῦ θεοῦ δέξασθαι ὑμᾶς (6.1). The 'catalogue of sufferings' to follow (6.4b-10), begun with the series of ἐν prepositions, specifies and illustrates the more general ἐν μηδενί/ἐν παντί in the controlling statements of 6.3-4a.[2] In sum, Paul's exhortation to receive God's grace, (home-

---

1. See the restrictions (Chapter 4, §2) that I place on the identification of Paul as a 'new Moses'. The apostle functions as a 'new Moses' *only* on a secondary basis through christological channels and through his identification with servant mission. The emphasis is on a functional identification and is more subtle than Paul's forthright identification with the servant of Isaiah.

2. The structure of the catalogue itself is intricate. The initial link to the general

coming) acceptance and (new exodus) salvation (6.1-2) is underscored *concretely* by the removal of stumbling blocks and by his commending himself to them as a servant of God in everything (6.3-4a)–in much endurance, in afflictions, etc.. . . (6.4b-10).

The two controlling statements for the entire section (6.3-10) are found in 6.3-4a. From these statements comes material which fits within the framework of return theology: (1) Paul places no obstacles in the way of the Corinthians' return, rather (2) he commends himself to them as a servant of God who (by example) leads them in their return and restoration.

No Stumbling Blocks in the Path of Return

Paul emphatically states his practice of not placing 'stumbling blocks' in the Corinthians' path: μηδεμίαν ἐν μηδενὶ διδόντες προσκοπήν (2 Cor. 6.3a). Obviously, the imagery of 'stumbling' and 'stumbling blocks' can be used in a variety of contexts. But in light of the second-exodus orientation of the preceding context (esp. 6.1-2), the προσκοπή metaphor[1] probably arises from the same context, for *one*

---

qualifiers ἐν μηδενί/ἐν παντί in 6.3-4a is extended through three series of items: the first section introduced with the preposition ἐν (6.4b-7b), the second section with the preposition διά (6.7c-8), and the third with ὡς (6.9-10). As a result, the items in the first section are in the dative case, the second section are genitives, and the third, nominatives.

Of eighteen items in the first section, all introduced by ἐν, nine items consist of hardships (items 2-9 in the plural), and nine items describing virtues (items 1, 10-18 in the singular). The first item in the list ἐν ὑπομονῇ πολλῇ focuses on the positive virtue of endurance, which, in turn, is shown to be 'much' through the nine hardships that follow. These nine hardships are arranged in three groups of three:

ἐν θλίψεσιν, ἐν ἀνάγκαις, ἐν στενοχωρίαις,
ἐν πληγαῖς, ἐν φυλακαῖς, ἐν ἀκαταστασίαις,
ἐν κόποις, ἐν ἀγρυπνίαις, ἐν νηστείαις,

The first triad emphasizes Paul's *peristasis* in general; the second triad becomes more specific and is bound together since it was often as a result of 'riots/tumults' that Paul was 'beaten' and then 'imprisoned' (Acts 16.19-23; 21.30–22.29; cf. 16.37); the third triad highlights self-occupational, physical hardships—exhausting toil, loss of sleep, and lack of food (cf. Acts 20.31; 1 Thess. 2.9). The second triad is externally inflicted punishment, while the third triad includes voluntary suffering. For a more detailed analysis see Fitzgerald, 'Cracks in an Earthen Vessel', pp. 343-53.

1. The noun προσκοπή, literally, refers to 'that which causes one (who is

of the major tenets of return theology is the removal of any obstacles blocking the exiles' path back to God. Both Yahweh and his servants are seen as removing obstacles in order to accomplish the return. The pattern was established with the initial exodus out of Egypt, when Yahweh and Moses lead the people along paths where they would not stumble:

> Then he [Moses] brought them out with silver and gold;
> and among his tribes there was not one who stumbled (כּוֹשֵׁל/ὁ ἀσθενῶν).
> Egypt was glad when they departed;
> for the dread of them had fallen upon them (Ps. 105.37-38).

> Who caused His glorious arm to go at the right hand of Moses,
> Who divided the waters before them to make for himself an everlasting
>   name,
> Who led them through the depths?
> Like the horse in the wilderness,
> they did not stumble (לֹא יִכָּשֵׁלוּ/οὐκ ἐκοπίασαν[1]) (Isa. 63.12-13).

Again, in the second exodus Yahweh leads in the same manner by removing mountains, transforming them into a road, and lifting up valleys to facilitate the return. Yahweh also instructs his servants to clear the way themselves, to make smooth the path, to build and prepare the return highway, and to remove any stumbling blocks out the way of his people:

> I [Yahweh] am bringing them from the north country,
> and I will gather them from the remote parts of the earth,
> among them the blind and the lame,
> the woman with child and she in labor, together;
> a great company, they shall return here.
> With weeping they shall come,
> and by supplication I will lead them;
> I will make them walk by streams of waters,
> on a straight path in which they shall not stumble (לֹא יִכָּשֵׁלוּ/οὐ μὴ
>   πλανηθῶσιν) (Jer. 31.8-9).[2]

> He [Yahweh] who has compassion on them will lead them,
> and will guide them to springs of water

walking) to stumble' (cf. προσκόπτω and πρόσκομμα). Cf. BAGD, p. 716; Louw and Nida, *Lexicon*, I, p. 244.

1. Aquila version, σκανδαλοῦν.
2. Cf. the link between stumbling blocks in the way of salvation and going astray in Mt. 18.6-9, 12.

And I will make all my mountains a road,
and my highways will be raised up (Isa. 49.10b-11a).[1]

And it shall be said [in the day of return],
'Build up, build up, prepare the way,
remove every obstacle (מִכְשׁוֹל/σκῶλα[2]) out of the way of my people!'
(Isa. 57.14).

Clear the way for the Lord in the wilderness;
make smooth in the desert a highway for our God.
Let every valley be lifted up,
and every mountain and hill be made low;
and let the rough ground become a plain,
and the rugged terrain a broad valley (Isa. 40.3-4).[3]

However, this return from Babylon takes on a marked ethical dimension, so that the 'stumbling blocks' are portrayed in a metaphorical sense even in the passages where the exilic return is being described in more tangible/physical terms (as in the examples above). At times this ethical/spiritual dimension comes to the fore, while literal return ideas fade into the background. Here, the smoothing of the path, the removal of obstacles, and the striking of one's foot on the 'stone-obstacle' picture the return as a *spiritual journey* back to God (the literal-metaphorical interplay is obvious):[4]

And I [Yahweh] will lead the blind by a way they do not know,
in paths they do not know I will guide them.
I will make darkness into light before them,
and rugged places into plains (Isa. 42.16a-b).

The way of the righteous is smooth,
O upright One, make the path of the righteous level (Isa. 26.7).

We hope for light, but behold, darkness;
for brightness, but we walk in gloom.
We grope along the wall like blind men,
we grope like those who have no eyes;

---

1. Cf. Isa. 11.18; 35.8.
2. Symmachus version, πρόσκομμα.
3. It is against this background of the return journey that the promise of 'not growing tired or stumbling (כשׁל)' is set (Isa. 5.27; cf. 5.26 and 40.30-31; cf. 40.3-4).
4. For other passages relating stumbling to spiritual darkness, see Prov. 4.12-19; Jer. 13.16; Sir. 17.25-26; Jn 11.9.

we stumble (כָּשַׁלְנוּ/πεσοῦνται[1]) at midday as in the twilight,
among those who are vigorous we are like dead men (Isa. 59.9b-10[2]).

Repent and turn away from all your transgressions,
so that iniquity may not become a stumbling block (מִכְשׁוֹל/κόλασιν
        ἀδικίας) to you.
Cast away from you all your transgressions which you have committed,
and make yourselves a new heart and a new spirit (Ezek. 18.30b-31a[3]).

Then he shall become a sanctuary;
but to both the houses of Israel,
a stone to strike [one's foot upon[4]] (לְאֶבֶן נֶגֶף/λίθου προσκόμματι)
and a rock to stumble over (לְצוּר מִכְשׁוֹל/πέτρας πτώματι) (Isa. 8.14a).

In sum, Paul's προσκοπή metaphor not only harmonizes with my contextual hypothesis, it adds to it.[5] In a context of (new exodus)

1. Symmachus version, προσκόπτειν.
2. That the return idea lies in the background of this more ethical stumbling is clear from the earlier mention of the 'highways of destruction' versus the 'way of peace' in Isa. 59.7-8 (as well as the use of the same language within Isaiah specifically of the exilic return). The reference to the blind in Jer. 31.9; Isa. 59.9-10; and 42.16 is interesting in light of the Torah injunction: 'You shall not place a stumbling block (מִכְשׁוֹל/σκάνδαλον) before the blind' (Lev. 19.14).
3. Cf. ὁ ὁδὸς κυρίου in Ezek. 18.25. Also, note the new covenant language in Ezek. 18.31b.
4. For the use of נֶגֶף related to striking one's foot against a stone (and thus causing one to stumble), see Ps. 91.12 (cf. Prov. 3.23).
5. Such a 'no obstacles' precept of return theology is all the more significant when one considers that it was the 'stumbling block' of *idolatry* which caused the nation to go into exile. For example, Ezekiel castigates the former ministers whose idolatrous acts led the nation into captivity: 'They [the Levites serving in the temple] ministered to them before their idols and became a stumbling block of iniquity (מִכְשׁוֹל/κόλασιν ἀδικίας) to the house of Israel' (Ezek. 44.12). Now in the process of restoration and return, Yahweh voices the concern that all stumbling blocks be removed that would hinder his people from making their physical-spiritual return. In a sense, the concern of exilic return theology to remove stumbling blocks in the path of those who journey home to Jerusalem casts a subtle allusion back to the idolatry which precipitated the exile in the first place. E.g., Isa. 57.13-14; Jer. 18.15; Ezek. 14.3-4, 7; Hos. 4.17; 5.5; Zeph. 1.3 (cf. Exod. 23.33; 34.12; Josh. 23.13; Judg. 2.3; 8.27; Ps. 105[106].36; Wis. 14.11; Sir. 34.7).
    Similarly, Paul's policy of removing stumbling blocks may cast a backwards shadow in the restoration process, alluding to some form of 'idolatry' which has led the Corinthians into their current exile-like state (in need of a return to God). For instance, in 1 Corinthians Paul had labeled their practice of dining at pagan temple-feasts as 'idolatry' (1 Cor. 10.14) and spoke of it as a 'stumbling block'

salvation and (exilic home-coming) acceptance (6.1-2), the apostle's concern to enhance the Corinthians' return by removing 'stumbling blocks' once again weaves the return theme into the tapestry.

Commendation as a Servant of God

Along with removing stumbling blocks, the apostle supports his appeal for the Corinthians' return (6.1-2) in a positive manner by commending himself as a servant of God: ἐν παντὶ συνιστάντες ἑαυτοὺς ὡς θεοῦ διάκονοι... (6.4-10). A few comments here should suffice. First, the expressions θεοῦ διάκονοι and συνιστάντες ἑαυτούς remind the reader of Paul's earlier discussion of *new covenant* ministry—διακόνους καινῆς διαθήκης (3.6)–and the painful issue of commendation for that ministry (3.1-6). Second, the 'servant' portrayal (θεοῦ διάκονοι) alludes to Paul's role as the *'ebed Yahweh*. Although the use of δοῦλοι would make the *'ebed* identification clearer, the whole issue of Paul 'commending himself' as 'servant' recalls his determination to commend/preach himself as 'servant' (δούλους), the *'ebed* who proclaims δόξα-light to the blind.[1]

6. With 'Enlarged Heart' Paul Awaits the Return of his Children
(2 Cor. 6.11-13; 7.2-4)

Context and Structure

Paul lists his 'catalogue of sufferings' (6.4b-10) not only as a commendation for his ministry and sign that he has removed any stumbling blocks (6.3-4a), but also as evidence of his fatherly love for the Corinthians as his children (6.11-13).[2] He has cleared the way of any possible stumbling blocks in the 'return' of the Corinthians to God and to God's messenger. Now in 6.11-13 he waits with 'enlarged heart' to

(πρόσκομμα) for the Corinthians. Should this kind of 'idolatry' be a viable referent option for what the fragment prohibits (see Appendix B), then it suggests another point of connection with the larger context through exilic return theology.

1. 2 Cor. 6.4a; cf. 4.2, 5-6. Cf. Becker, 'Paul, the Suffering Apostle', pp. 310, 351. The suffering catalogue in 2 Cor. 6.4-10 (while having no verbal dependence) certainly, on a conceptual level, emulates the suffering servant of Isaiah. For a verbal dependence of suffering terminology in the previous suffering catalogue (2 Cor. 4.11) from Isaiah's *'ebed* see Chapter 4, §5.

2. The unexpressed premise is that children are obligated to return affection to their parents, an affection Paul has amply demonstrated in his suffering (cf. 1 Cor. 4.15).

receive his children and calls for their reciprocal affection. At this point the fragment intervenes (6.14–7.1). Then, in 7.2-4 the appeal is resumed for the Corinthians' return.

In this section with the closest proximity to the fragment, one finds the continued emphasis on the new covenant nature of Paul's ministry and ideas from exilic return theology to set the contextual framework.

Continued New Covenant Themes

The *new covenant* nature of Paul's ministry to the Corinthians is evident in this most immediate context at two points. First, the qualifier in 7.3a, indicates that what Paul has said is not for their condemnation (πρὸς κατάκρισιν). It deliberately recalls his labeling of new covenant ministry as one of (imparting) righteousness, rather than condemnation.[1] Second, the expression in 7.3b that the Corinthians are ἐν ταῖς καρδίαις ἡμῶν again draws upon a central premise of Paul's new covenant ministry: the Corinthians are Paul's commending epistle ἐγγεγραμμένη ἐν ταῖς καρδίαις ἡμῶν[2] as they are a (new covenant) epistle of Christ engraved by the Spirit ἐν πλαξὶν καρδίαις σαρκίναις.[3]

'Enlarging the Heart' Towards Returning Children

The contextual continuum of return theology is suggested here through the scenario of Paul as father, waiting with an 'enlarged heart' to receive his children (6.11-13). Both the elements of Paul's father-child relationship and the 'enlarged heart' idiom assist in establishing my contextual integration hypothesis. They function together. The father-child imagery is conveyed in the parenthetical statement that Paul is appealing to the Corinthians as his children: ὡς τέκνοις λέγω.[4] This establishes an immediate parallel with the fragment which presents Yahweh in a father-child relationship to the Corinthians.[5] Such a connection is more tightly bound when one considers the return theology framework within which Paul is thinking (the return

---

1. Cf. τῇ διακονίᾳ τῆς κατακρίσεως and ἡ διακονία τῆς δικαιοσύνης in 3.9.

2. 2 Cor. 3.2.

3. Cf. ἐγγεγραμμένη ἐν ταῖς καρδίαις ἡμῶν (3.2) and ἐγγεγραμμένη. . . πλαξὶν καρδίαις σαρκίναις (3.3).

4. 2 Cor. 6.13.

5. Cf. quotation 4 (2 Cor. 6.18).

of 'sons' and 'daughters' to Zion is an essential part of the exilic return picture[1]).

The 'enlarging the heart' idiom *together with* this father-children imagery invokes the framework of exilic return theology. The idiom 'to enlarge/widen the heart' (ἡ καρδία ἡμῶν πεπλάτυναι 6.11, cf. 6.13) is never found elsewhere in Paul's writings or the New Testament. However, it occurs several times within the Old Testament. Essentially, the idiom can be used either (1) *negatively* of a proud person, with an enlarged/puffed up heart (Deut. 11.16; cf. Ps. 101.5; Prov. 21.4; 28.25), or (2) *positively* of a receptive person, with an open and receptive heart towards something or someone else (Ps. 118[119].32; Isa. 60.5).

An intriguing example is found in Isa. 60.5, since it brings together *both* the imagery of returning children (υἱοὺς καὶ θυγατέρας) and the 'enlarging the heart' idiom. Here 'enlarging the heart' echoes the response of those living in Jerusalem when the exiles, Zion's 'sons' and 'daughters' (Isa. 60.4), return home: 'You will see and be radiant, and your heart will tremble and be enlarged (פָּחַד וְרָחַב לְבָבֵךְ/ φοβηθήσῃ καὶ ἐκστήσῃ τῇ καρδίᾳ)' (Isa. 60.5). The idiom calls for the joyous reception and welcoming of returning exiles. It would be close to the English idiom, 'welcome with open arms'.

If this source proposal is correct, Paul anticipates accepting the returning Corinthians in a manner which parallels the return imagery of the fragment (especially quotations 3 and 4). Between 6.11-13 and 6.14–7.1 the apostle sets up a close conceptual parallel. As Paul is prepared to receive with an enlarged heart the returning Corinthians as his children,[2] so will God receive them (patterned after the exilic return) as his sons and daughters.[3] The effectiveness of the parallel is due to the interchangeable functioning of God and apostolic messenger (cf. esp., 5.20; 6.1a). If the 'far off' Corinthians recognize that now is the time for their (new exodus) salvation and (home-coming) acceptance, and if they return on a path clear of stumbling blocks and enhanced by God's suffering servant, then not only the apostle but

1. Isa. 43.6; 49.22; 60.4 (cf. the emphasis on return motifs in other Father-son passages: Isa. 63.8, 16; Jer. 3.19; 31.7-9; Hos. 1.10-11; 11.10-11). See earlier discussion of quotation 4 in Chapter 3, §2.

2. Like the fragment, its context draws upon the picture of 'sons' and 'daughters' returning to Jerusalem and the responsive 'enlarging of the heart' in Isa. 60.4-5.

3. 2 Cor. 6.18.

God himself will receive them as sons and daughters.

In light of the above, I suggest that Isa. 60.4-5 should be favored as the source for Paul's 'enlarging the heart' idiom over Thrall's Deut. 11.16 theory.[1] Not only does Isa. 60.4-5 have the advantage of a positive use of the idiom (Deut. 11.16 uses it negatively and in another sense[2]), but it merges better with the father-child imagery in 6.13, provides a stronger contextual tie with the return traditions being developed in 6.1-2, and closely parallels the concepts and theology found in the fragment (especially quotations 3 and 4).[3]

One might object that the verbal agreement between the LXX (ἐξίστημι) and the New Testament (πλατύνω) is not exact. Surely Paul could have taken the wording from another text such as Deut. 11.16 (even if the sense was different and it was prohibited there). This is a fair criticism. However, any source proposal which offers closeness in three areas—wording, sense, and broader contextual factors—should be favored over one that conforms in wording alone. In this regard, Isa. 60.4-5 qualifies with sense (a positive connotation of 'joyous reception') and broader contextual factors (such as the return of sons and daughters).

There are several considerations which address concerns over the lack of precise verbal correlation with the LXX. First, it is interesting that three other Greek versions do translate the רְחַב לְבָבֵךְ idiom in Isa. 60.5 with the same word as in 2 Cor. 6.11, πλατύνω.[4] Also, in broad LXX usage πλατύνω (in all its forms) is by far the *most frequently used* Greek word to translate רָחַב (in its various forms).[5] More

1. See Thrall, 'The Problem of II Cor. VI. 14–VII. 1', p. 146; and Murphy-O'Connor, 'Relating 2 Corinthians 6. 14–7.1 to Its Context', pp. 273-74. On the other hand, Beale ('Old Testament Background', pp. 576-77), like myself, has recently come to view Isa. 60.5 as 'the most probable OT text lying behind 2 Cor. 6.11b'. For Beale, the returning 'sons' and 'daughters' in conjunction with the 'enlarged heart' idiom makes Isa. 60.4-5 the most attractive source option.

2. Deut. 11.16 warns against pride (an enlarged/puffed up heart).

3. For other problems with Thrall's Deut. 11.16 theory see Chapter 6, §IV.

4. Theodatian, Aquila, and Symmachus.

5. When compared with ἐξίστημι, πλατύνω is used to translate רחב much more frequently. Including verbal, nominal, adjectival forms, the ratio is more than 100:1. Of the 74 occurrences of ἐξίστημι in the LXX, only once is the Greek word used to translate רחב. Thus if Paul were thinking about the idiom in the Hebrew text of Isa. 60.5 and freely translated the idiom on his own (without checking the LXX), he would be likely to have used πλατύνω rather than ἐξίστημι.

specifically, the same רחב לבב idiom found in Isa. 60.5 is translated at least once in the LXX with πλατύνω (never with ἐξίστημι).[1] Therefore, Paul could have been thinking of the Hebrew idiom in Isa. 60.5 (an idiom which could be translated with πλατύνω[2]) and simply not have drawn upon the exact LXX wording, or he may have been familiar with some other rendering of the text which went in the other direction of several Greek versions. The LXX wording should not be the only, nor the controlling, factor when considering a possible source for the idiom. If the source is Isa. 60.5, then even the fragment's closest context reveals ideas shaped from exilic return traditions.

7. Summary of the Traditions in the Fragment's Immediate Context

To summarize, in the immediate context of 5.11–7.4 Paul continues his discussion of new covenant ministry and draws upon second exodus/return traditions to picture the Corinthians' much needed return to himself and God. Support for this contextual integration hypothesis may now be summarized according to each unit. Once again, the weight of the evidence will be evaluated on the grounds that it develops either new covenant or exilic return traditions (especially as related to the 'ebed Yahweh).

In 5.11-12 my traditions hypothesis finds support at a number of points. First, the clearest use of new exodus traditions is seen in the expression τὰ ἀρχαῖα παρῆλθεν, ἰδοὺ γέγονεν καινά.[3] The message of 'new things' in Isaianic terms is an exodus-like call for the exiles in Babylon to return both physically and salvifically to Zion. This picture of deliverance is rooted in the original exodus from Egypt, yet is expanded to include the final deliverance of the cosmos. It embodies a theology of restoration to God, which the apostle adapts for his message of reconciliation to the Corinthians. Also, the 'new

---

1. LXX Ps. 118(119).32.

2. In other words, Paul could have, independently, simply chosen to move from the Hebrew of Isa. 60.5 (without consulting the LXX) to πλατύνω due to its convenient semantic range, or he may have been influenced by the LXX translation of the idiom elsewhere with πλατύνω (while still drawing upon Isa. 60.5 due to its conceptual and sense contributions).

3. 2 Cor. 5.17; cf. Isa. 42.9; 43.18-19; 48.3-6; 65.16-17.

things' in the Old Testament context form an integral part of the new covenant. Second, Paul continues his discussion of new covenant ministry through key reiterative phrases: ἐν καρδία,[1] the imputation of δικαιοσύνη and not παραπτώματα (τοῦ νομοῦ),[2] and τὴν διακονίαν.[3] Third, a tradition-history link of τὴν διακονίαν τῆς καταλλαγῆς to Isa. 52.7 and 57.9 is helpful at least to the degree it reflects Pauline thought. Yet it needs to be handled cautiously since the material does not come from 2 Corinthians.

In 6.1-2 are found the strongest ties to the fragment via the Old Testament traditions. First, the 'salvation' and 'acceptance' of which Paul speaks in 2 Cor. 6.1-2 clearly has exilic return theology as its conceptual and theological framework. The 'salvation' depicts Yahweh's breaking the bondage of the exiles in Babylon and their freedom to travel back to Jerusalem, while the 'acceptance' looks at their home-coming acceptance to worship at Yahweh's temple in Zion. Many details in the Old Testament context (even the call to 'Come out from . . . ') are patterned after the exodus event of years ago and the journey motif from Egypt to Canaan. Second, the Isa. 49.8 quotation continues to develop Paul's new covenant theme, since the 'salvation', much like the old deliverance from Egypt, has as its final purpose the establishment of a covenant between God and his people.[4] Third, Paul identifies with the work of the servant in Isaiah 49 at a number of broader points beyond the quoted portion. Fourth, and most significantly, the assigned function of the servant (according to Isa. 48.8-9) is to proclaim release to the captives: 'Come out of Babylon.' This proclamation initiates the 'salvation'—the journey back to the homeland and the entire restoration and covenant process. Finally, my traditions research in 2 Cor. 6.1-2 (and Isa. 49.8-9) has uncovered two significant verbal/rhetorical bridges with the fragment (both set within return theology): (1) the δεκτ- traditions (δέξασθαι, δεκτῷ, and εὐπρόσδεκτος) and quotation 3 (εἰσδέξομαι ὑμᾶς), and (2) the cry for a new exodus (ἔξελθε ἐκ Βαβυλῶνος) and quotation 2 (διὸ ἐξέλθατε ἐκ μέσου αὐτῶν). These Isaiah 49 traditions make

1. 2 Cor. 5.12; cf. 3.2-3 (Jer. 31(38).33); 4.6; 5.5 (and 1.22).
2. 2 Cor. 5.19, 21; cf. 3.9.
3. τὴν διακονίαν τῆς καταλλαγῆς (5.18); cf. earlier references to διακόνους καινῆς διαθήκης (3.6), ἡ διακονία τοῦ πνεύματος (3.8), and ἡ διακονία τῆς δικαιοσύνης (3.9).
4. Isa. 49.8b.

essentially the same verbal and conceptual point as the fragment.

In 6.3-4a two controlling statements are oriented towards new covenant and return theology: μηδεμίαν ἐν μηδενὶ διδόντες προσκοπήν and ἐν παντὶ συνιστάντες ἑαυτοὺς ὡς θεοῦ διάκονοι. First, the 'stumbling block' metaphor (προσκοπή) should probably be understood within the context of new exodus 'salvation' (6.1-2), since one of the major tenets of return theology is the removal of stumbling blocks/obstacles from the exiles' path back to God. Second, Paul's 'commending himself' (συνιστάντες ἑαυτούς) as a 'servant' reminds the reader that he is talking about his new covenant ministry[1] and his determination to commend/preach himself as 'servant', the *'ebed* who proclaims δόξα-light to the blind.[2] These features do not *in themselves* establish the traditions framework suggested here, but they do support such a framework.

Finally, in the closest context of 6.11-13; 7.2-4 Paul's 'enlarging the heart' idiom (echoing Isa. 60.4-5), together with his father-children metaphor suggest the rubric of exilic return theology. The apostle sets up a close conceptual parallel with the fragment—just as he is prepared to receive with an 'enlarged heart' the returning Corinthians as his children,[3] so God is prepared to receive them (also patterned after the exilic return) as sons and daughters.[4] It is my proposal that Isa. 60.4-5 should be taken as the source for Paul's 'enlarging the heart' idiom, rather than Deut. 11.16.[5] Also, Paul continues to have new covenant categories in mind as suggested by his not-for-condemnation perspective (πρὸς κατάκρισιν οὐ λέγω)[6] and the familiar new covenant phrase, ἐν ταῖς καρδίαις ἡμῶν.[7]

---

1. 2 Cor. 6.4a; cf. 3.1-3 (i.e., the struggle for commendation).
2. 2 Cor. 6.4a; cf. 4.2, 5-6.
3. Isa. 60.4-5 pictures 'sons' and 'daughters' returning to Jerusalem and the response of 'enlarging the heart' by those who would welcome them.
4. 2 Cor. 6.18.
5. Cf. Chapter 6 (§IV) for further criticisms of the Deut. 11.16 theory.
6. 2 Cor. 7.3a; cf. 3.9.
7. 2 Cor. 7.3b; cf. 3.2-3.

8. *Conclusion*

In conclusion, new covenant and exilic return theology may be traced throughout 2 Cor. 2.14–7.4 (setting aside the fragment for a moment). These traditions have been woven into the fabric of Paul's understanding of his role in apostolic ministry. They give substance and a theological basis for the legitimate nature of his glorious, but not so glorious (i.e., suffering) new covenant ministry. Furthermore, new covenant and second exodus traditions are, at times, derived through identification with Christ's servant-like mission—Paul now carries on the *'ebed*-ministry of Jesus.

In the remote context (2.14–5.10), *new covenant traditions* lie at the heart of Paul's portrayal of his ministry. New covenant dominates much of the remote context in an explicit manner: the Spirit's work ἐν πλάξιν σαρκίναις, not on tablets of stone (3.3, 6),[1] the law written ἐν ταῖς καρδίαις (3.2, 3),[2] διακόνους καινῆς διαθήκης (3.6),[3] and the contrast between old and new covenant δόξα (3.7-18).[4] After 4.1, the new covenant perspective continues on an implicit level (picking up key phrases developed earlier): the transitional διακονίαν ταύτην (4.1), the reiterated δόξα (4.4, 6),[5] the explanation of suffering in a glory-oriented ministry (4.7-15), the δόξα renewal of the inner person (4.16-18),[6] and τὸν ἀρραβῶνα τοῦ πνεύματος towards new covenant promise (5.5).[7] Often intertwined with this new covenant perspective is the reappearing use of *exilic return traditions*.[8]

In the immediate context (5.11–7.4), significant points of contact with the fragment through *exilic return traditions* include: τὰ

---

1. Cf. Ezek. 11.19; 36.26-27 (cf. 2 Cor. 3.8, 17, 18).

2. Cf. Jer. 31(38).33.

3. Cf. Jer. 31(38).31.

4. In addition, some of Paul's 'organically' related new covenant categories (Spirit-life, surpassing glory, righteousness as opposed to condemnation, in the heart, etc.) were shown to have OT precedents.

5. Cf. 2 Cor. 3.8, 9, 10, 11, 18.

6. Cf. 2 Cor. 3.18 and earlier δόξα references.

7. Cf. 2 Cor. 3.1-18; 1.22; Ezek. 36.26-27a (also Ezek. 11.19; 18.31; 37.14; Jer. 31[38].33).

8. E.g., 2 Cor. 3.1-6 (cf. Jer. 31[38].31-33; Ezek. 11.19; 36.26-27a); 4.4-6 (cf. Isa. 9.1 and Isaianic vocabulary about light to the blind); 4.11 (cf. Isa. 53.6b, 12).

ἀρχαῖα... καινά (5.17),[1] the quotation from Isa. 49.8 (6.1-2),[2] the removal of stumbling blocks, προσκοπήν (6.3), the commendation as θεοῦ διάκονοι—recalling Paul's *'ebed* role (6.4a), and the 'enlarging the heart' idiom in connection with Paul's father-child relationship to the Corinthians (6.11-13). Underlying this exilic return motif in the immediate context is the continued *new covenant* perspective.[3]

In light of the quest to uncover the underlying traditions, a synthesis of the immediate context may be suggested as follows. New covenant and exilic return imagery thread the pieces together: as a servant of the new covenant, Paul stands between God and the Corinthians with a message of 'new things' patterned after the exodus paradigm and centered on the restoration of the cosmos to God (5.16-21). He expresses the urgent need that 'now' is the time for their reception/home coming (6.1-2). He has cleared away any obstacles in their path (6.3-10). He has 'enlarged his heart' in anticipation of their return and calls on them to do likewise (6.11-13; cf. 7.2-4). And finally, like the *'ebed*, he prompts their return with the cry for a new exodus ('Come out from. . . ') and with promises related to their home coming (6.14–7.1)—just as he will welcome them as his children, so will their covenant God make them his sons and daughters. Through skillful use of return traditions, both inside and outside the fragment, Paul effectively parallels the Corinthians' need to return to him as apostle with their need to return to God.

---

1. Cf. Isa. 42.9; 43.18-19; 48.3-6; 65.16-17.
2. Cf. especially δέξασθαι, δεκτῷ, εὐπρόσδεκτος and ἐξέλθατε [ἐκ Βαβυλῶνος] to the fragment's second and third quotations.
3. E.g., ἐν καρδίᾳ (5.12; cf. 3.2-3; Jer. 31(38).33), δικαιοσύνη (5.19, 21; cf. 3.9), τὴν διακονίαν (5.18; cf. 3.6, 8, 9), συνιστάντες ἑαυτούς (6.4a; cf. 3.1; 4.2), πρὸς κατάκρισιν οὐ λέγω (Cor. 7.3a; cf. 3.9), and ἐν ταῖς καρδίαις ἡμῶν (7.3b; cf. 3.2-3).

Chapter 6

A CRITIQUE OF ALTERNATIVE CONTEXTUAL THEORIES

1. *Introduction*

Having developed a contextual hypothesis based on new covenant and exilic return traditions, I now turn my attention to alternative theories.[1] A variety of theories has been proposed to date in order to explain how the fragment fits within its current context.[2] Broadly speaking, these theories can be divided into three groups: (1) interpolation theories; (2) non-contextual integration theories, and (3) contextual integration theories. Each of these categories suggests a degree of contextual compatibility, ranging from absolutely no contextual integration, an extremely limited integration, to a significant level of integration. It is my objective in this final chapter to examine and evaluate these theories in light of the traditions research just completed.

---

1. Beale's work ('Old Testament Background', pp. 550-81) will not be considered an 'alternative theory', though the direction taken in our respective traditions research is significantly different. For a summary of the differences see Chapter 7, §3.

2. For other surveys outlining contextual integration options, see Murphy-O'Connor, 'Relating 2 Corinthians 6.14–7.1 to Its Context', pp. 272-75; Thrall, 'The Problem of II Cor. VI.14–VII.1', pp. 138-48; Lambrecht, 'The Fragment 2 Cor. VI 14–VII 1', pp. 151-52; Prümm, *Diakonia Pneumatos*, I, pp. 379-81; Belleville, *Reflections of Glory*, pp. 94-103; Hughes, *Second Epistle to the Corinthians*, pp. 243-44; Collange, *Énigmes*, pp. 303-304; Rensberger, '2 Corinthians 6.14–7.1', pp. 25-27; Fee, 'Food Offered to Idols', pp. 140-42; Kruse, *Second Epistle to the Corinthians*, pp. 38-40; Furnish, *II Corinthians*, pp. 378-80. These sources have contributed to the discussion below (cf. Belleville's structure and organization of views). The treatment which follows, however, provides a more comprehensive synthesis, includes many more secondary sources, and evaluates the merits of each theory.

2. *Interpolation Theories—Inserting the 6.14–7.1 Fragment into an Existing Text*

Interpolation theories attribute no contextual integration whatsoever to 2 Cor. 6.14–7.1 (at least relative to the original composition of 2 Cor. 2.14–7.4). In fact, interpolation theories generally thrive upon the fragment's apparent lack of contextual integration. Historically, interpolation theories related to 2 Cor. 6.14–7.1 have evolved through two distinctly opposing stages: from a *Pauline* interpolation to a *non-Pauline* interpolation.

Interpolation of a Pauline Fragment

Many exegetes from the last century (though only a handful today) held that the 6.14–7.1 fragment was a piece of Paul's writing added to 2 Corinthians by a later redactor.[1] The source of this interpolated Pauline fragment was variously attributed to: (1) the lost 'previous letter' mentioned in 1 Cor. 5.9;[2] (2) some dislocated part of 1 Corinthians (originally belonging before 1 Cor. 5.9,[3] before 6.3,[4] after 6.20,[5] or after 10.22[6]), or more generally, (3) some other part of his correspondence with the Corinthian church, without specifying

1. Usually the insertion is explained as taking place when the letters were brought together as a collection.

2. Franke, '2 Kor. 6,14–7,1 und 1 Kor. 5, 9-13', pp. 544-83; Wendland, *Die Briefe an die Korinther*, p. 212; Strachan, *Second Epistle of Paul to the Corinthians*, pp. xv, 3-4; Weiss, *Earliest Christianity*, I, p. 356; Schmithals, *Gnosticism in Corinth*, pp. 94-95, 282-86; Hurd, *The Origin of 1 Corinthians*, pp. 235-39; Foreman, *Second Letter to the Corinthians*, p. 134. Jewett (*Anthropological Terms*, pp. 184-86) once held this position, but more recently thinks the authenticity of the passage is open to question (cf. 'The Redaction of 1 Corinthians', p. 433 n. 4). For a listing of older scholars who held to the 'previous letter' theory (e.g., Hilgenfeld, Franke, Sabatier, Lisco, von Dobschütz, von Soden, Whitelaw) see Moffat, *Introduction*, p. 125.

3. Dinkler, 'Korintherbriefe', p. 22.

4. Pfleiderer, *Das Urchristentum, seine Schriften und Leben*, I, p. 134.

5. Wendland, *Die Briefe an die Korinther*, p. 187.

6. Hausrath, *A History of the New Testament Times*, IV, p. 56; Blass, 'Textkritisches zu den Korintherbriefen', in *Beiträge zur förderung christlischer Theologie*, pp. 51-63; Ewald, *Sendschreiben des Paulus*, pp. 231, 281-83.

the exact source.[1] These interpolation theories are attractive since they provide a known source for the fragment, preserve a piece of lost antiquity, and quickly resolve the contextual dilemma.

However, the popularity of Pauline interpolation theories for explaining 6.14–7.1 has diminished for good reason—they tend to create more problems than they solve. It is difficult to accept that the fragment (whatever else it might be) represents the lost 'previous letter'. First, one would have to take the 'unbelievers' (ἄπιστοι) in 6.14a as a reference to immoral people within the covenant community, since the previous letter was addressed to such individuals. This is improbable in view of the strong ethical dualism in the passage[2] and the Pauline use of ἄπιστοι is too consistent to have been misunderstood by the Corinthians as immoral believers (see Appendix A). Second, the one thing known for certain about the 'previous letter' is that it prohibited association with sexually immoral people in the church (τοῖς πόρνιος, 1 Cor. 5.9, 10), whereas such sexual vices are not explicitly mentioned in 2 Cor. 6.14–7.1.[3] Finally these theories only compound the existing difficulties with all interpolation theories (see below) by adding an unexplained removal process from another document.

Interpolation of a non-Pauline Fragment
Particularly within the last forty years, a number of prominent New Testament scholars[4] have identified 2 Cor. 6.14–7.1 as a non-Pauline

---

1. Moffat, *Introduction*, pp. 125-26. While broadening the scope to Corinthian correspondence in general, Moffat clearly favors the 'previous letter' theory.

2. Belleville, 'Moses-*Doxa* Traditions in 2 Corinthians 3.12-18', p. 129 n. 5.

3. Furnish, *II Corinthians*, pp. 379-80. Granted, what is mentioned in 1 Cor. 5 need not circumscribe the whole of the previous letter. However, speculation on content of the previous letter beyond what is mentioned in 1 Cor. 5 will never be persuasive. Also, even if certain sexual activity is prohibited by 6.14–7.1 (e.g., temple prostitution), it is the *activity itself* which is being prohibited in the fragment and not the association with (so-called) Christians who do such acts (the situation as described in 1 Cor. 5.9-13). See Appendixes A and B.

4. In 1835 Schrader (*Der Apostel Paulus*, IV, p. 300) was the first to suggest that 2 Cor. 6.14–7.1 was a non-Pauline interpolation based on contextual abruptness and the seemingly non-Pauline statement μολυσμοῦ σαρκός. Despite early movements towards non-Pauline authorship of the fragment, the Pauline interpolation view (and particularly the 'previous letter' theory) remained the dominant interpolation theory until recent times.

interpolation, usually with some relationship to Qumran literature,[1] or less frequently to a Jewish-Christian faction writing against Paul.[2] Their conclusions are based upon two points of evidence: the lack of contextual compatibility and the non-Pauline content of the fragment. These theories have enjoyed reasonable popularity in light of the Qumran discoveries. However, several studies have been completed subsequently on the content of the fragment and these suggest that its language and word selection should not be used as determinative to either confirm or dismiss Pauline authorship.[3] Also, the contextual hypothesis which I propose addresses the compatibility problem.

In the final analysis, interpolation theories as a whole (both Pauline and non-Pauline) fail to explain either the mechanics or the motives for inserting the fragment by a later redactor.[4] Proponents of interpolation theories must explain why and how a redactor would have placed a non-Pauline or anti-Pauline fragment into a letter under Paul's name and at a most unlikely point between 6.13 and 7.2.[5] For

---

1. Fitzmyer, 'Interpolated Paragraph', p. 271; Gnilka, '2 Cor. 6.14–7.1', pp. 48-50; Bultmann, *Second Letter to the Corinthians*, p. 175; Bornkamm, 'Die Vorgeschichte des sogenannten Zweiten Korintherbriefes', pp. 162-94; Koester, *Trajectories Through Early Christianity*, p. 154; Perrin, *Introduction*, p. 129; Grossouw, 'Over de echtheid van 2 Cor 6.14–7.1', pp. 203-206; Georgi, *Opponents of Paul in Second Corinthians*, pp. 12-13. Benoit ('Qumrân et le Nouveau Testament', p. 279) graphically describes the interpolation of 2 Cor. 6.14–7.1 as 'sorte d'aérolithe tombe du ciel de Qumrân dans une épître de Paul'.

2. Betz, 'Anti-Pauline Fragment', pp. 88, 108. Cf. Gunther, *St. Paul's Opponents*, p. 309. This proposal will be given fuller attention in Appendix A.

3. I do not wish to pursue a lengthy discussion on the 'authenticity' of the fragment, since the data does not appear to be conclusive in either direction and the primary contribution of this work lies in the area of contextual correlation. Several studies have shown that Pauline composition (in part or whole) is as plausible a conclusion as any other. See Fee, 'Food Offered to Idols', pp. 140-47; Rensberger, '2 Corinthians 6.14–7.1', pp. 28-44; Lambrecht, 'The Fragment', pp. 143-61; Thrall, 'The Problem of II Cor. VI.14–VII.1', pp. 133-38; and my own discussion in Webb, 'Contextual Framework', pp. 39-68.

4. Accidental insertion can be ruled out since first century copies of Paul's letters were written on papyrus scrolls, not on leaves of a codex which could have been accidentally displaced. Cf. Allo, *Seconde Épître aux Corinthiens*, pp. 189-93; Plummer, *II Corinthians*, p. xxv; Fee, 'Food Offered to Idols', p. 142; Martin, *2 Corinthians*, p. 194.

5. Rensberger ('2 Corinthians 6.14–7.1', p. 26) rightly notes that it is incumbent upon *both* the proponents of contextual integration and those of interpolation to

those places in the New Testament where textual criticism confirms the process of interpolation (e.g., Jn 5.3b-4; 7.52–8.11; Acts 8.37; 1 Jn 5.7-8), good reasons can be shown as to *why* a later scribe inserted the text.[1] Yet, interpolation theorists respond to this crucial objection here in 2 Cor. 6.14–7.1, as Furnish aptly notes,[2] with such comments as 'difficult to answer' (Bornkamm),[3] 'not clear' (Gnilka),[4] 'remains unsolved' (Fitzmyer),[5] 'for reasons unknown' (Betz),[6] and 'impossible to say' (Georgi).[7] Before any interpolation theory can gain universal acceptance, these questions need to be answered adequately.[8]

3. *Non-Contextual Integration Theories*

In contrast to interpolation theories, non-contextual integration theories maintain that 2 Cor. 6.14–7.1 was composed along with the rest of 2.14–7.4. Yet, like interpolation theories they suggest little or no contact between the fragment and its context. Rather, non-contextual theories appeal to factors *outside the context* in order to account for the presence of the fragment here. In this category of non-contextual theories there are three ways of explaining the position of the fragment: as a dictation pause, a sudden digression (unrelated to context), or an *ad hoc* response to lingering problems at Corinth (due to external factors).

---

explain how the passage fits into its context. Cf. Fee, 'Food Offered to Idols', pp. 142-43.

1. Fee, 'Food Offered to Idols', p. 142; cf. Martin, *2 Corinthians*, p. 194. Though not a critical weakness, it should be noted that there is no manuscript, versions, or patristic evidence to support interpolation theories here in 2 Cor. 6.14–7.1.

2. Furnish, *II Corinthians*, p. 380.

3. Bornkamm, 'Die Vorgeschichte des sogennanten Zweiten Korintherbriefes', p. 193 n. 3.

4. Gnilka, '2 Cor. 6.14–7.1', p. 67.

5. Fitzmyer, 'Interpolated Paragraph', p. 217.

6. Betz, 'Anti-Pauline Fragment', p. 108.

7. Georgi, *Opponents of Paul in Second Corinthians*, p. 12.

8. For example, Sanday ('2 Corinthians vi. 14–VII.1', pp. 359-60) over a century ago stated, 'I confess that this view [that 2 Cor. 6.14–7.1 corresponds to the lost letter of 1 Cor. 5.9] would have a rather strong attraction for me, if I could get over the initial difficulty . . . of framing to myself a satisfactory hypothesis as to the way in which the interpolation came in.'

Dictation Pause

Several scholars have explained the abrupt warning in 6.14–7.1 on the basis of a dictation pause. Since the fragment appears to have no contextual coherence, Paul must have paused in his dictation for a moment to reflect on an entirely different subject. Those who hold this view usually suggest that the pause allowed Paul time to dwell either on a specific problem related to the Corinthian situation,[1] on a theme that he had recently dealt with in his evangelistic preaching,[2] or on some previous ethical homily which he had already composed.[3]

While a dictation pause offers an explanation of sorts, it suffers at two critical points. First, Plummer rightly points out that a long dictation pause is improbable (or at least less probable than a digression), since there is an immediate resumption of the thought of 6.13 in 7.2.[4] Second, this kind of solution is feasible only when all other contextual integration theories have proved faulty. Current integration theories, weak though they may be in their present formulation, provide some grounds for contextual integration (see below), not to mention the new traditions' proposal of this work. Until all other possibilities have been exhausted, then, the fragment should not be viewed as a dictation pause.

Straying off Topic—A Sudden Pauline Digression

Similar to the dictation-pause theory, some attribute the 6.14–7.1 passage to Paul's tendency to stray off the topic[5] or to a flighty train

---

1. Guthrie, *New Testament Introduction*, p. 425; Martin, *New Testament Foundations*, II, p. 183; Stange, 'Diktierpausen in den Paulusbriefen', p. 114.

2. Lietzmann, *Korinther I/II*, p. 129. Cf. Denney (*Second Epistle to the Corinthians*, p. 238) who thinks Paul inserted the passage after re-reading the letter.

3. Harris, '2 Corinthians', p. 303.

4. Plummer, *II Corinthians*, p. 206.

5. E.g., Barrett (*Second Epistle to the Corinthians*, p. 194) appeals to the apostle's literary habit of straying from the point: 'Paul not infrequently [e.g., 2.14] allows himself to wander from his point, and then brings himself back to it with something of a jerk'. Similarly, Stanley (*Epistles of St. Paul to the Corinthians*, p. 460) states, 'Here begins the digression (2 Cor. 6.14-7.1) without connection with what precedes or follows.' Cf. Lambrecht, 'The Fragment 2 Cor. VI 14–VII 1', p. 151; Fischer, *Commentary on 1 and 2 Corinthians*, p. 272; Harris, '2 Corinthians', p. 303; Plummer, *II Corinthians*, p. 206.

of thought.[1] Again, the pitfall with this position is that it requires the absolute failure of other contextual theories. It must also assume the premise that 6.14–7.1 does address a completely different topic than that of its context. Only if no material connection exists is this a legitimate solution. Furthermore, what is it that prompts Paul's return to his topic? According to this view, nothing within the fragment itself brings Paul back to his topic. Presumably, the apostle remembers that he has digressed and so shifts back abruptly to the previous topic. Even in the example of Paul's topical digression most often used to support this theory (2 Cor. 2.14–7.4), the material at the end of this digression obviously contributes to Paul's returning to the subject (cf. 7.4 and 7.5-7).

External Factors Prompt an Ad Hoc Response

A variation on the previous two solutions is the view that some extra-contextual factor related to lingering problems from previous letters to the Corinthians prompted Paul to write 6.14–7.1. For instance, several suggest that the abrupt shift is due to a sudden, greater desire for their holiness,[2] or to news just received from Titus either about their continued participation in cultic meals,[3] or about their receiving his advice in the whole of 1 Corinthians too lightly.[4] But what are these external factors that produced this 'sudden desire' for the Corinthians' holiness? And, even if news from Titus motivated Paul to write the passage, why does he do so here? The theory of a 'sudden news' or a 'sudden thought' inspired fragment essentially fabricates an external scenario which then has to explain why external factors took precedence over the normal flow of the letter (and without any introductory formula to say that the material is completely incidental to

---

1. Along these lines Michaelis (*Einleitung in Das Neue Testament*, p. 181) argues, 'Doch ist solch sprunghafte Gedankenführung nicht unmöglich in einem offenbar rasch und in grosser Erregung geschriebenen Brief.'

2. E.g., Spicq, *Seconde Épître aux Corinthiens*, p. 181.

3. E.g., Fee, 'Food Offered to Idols', pp. 143-44, 155. In fairness to Fee, one should note that he *also* attempts to tie the rejection of former teaching in 1 Corinthians with the *ad hominem* argument of 2 Cor. 6.1-13.

4. E.g., Tasker, *Second Epistle of Paul to the Corinthians*, p. 98. Cf. Schnedermann (*Die Briefe Pauli an die Korinther*, p. 340) who sees the fragment as a contextually unrelated excursus on problems at Corinth with paganism which Paul wrote awaiting the arrival of Titus; his concern was not unfounded in view of 2 Cor. 12.21.

what was being written). The theory seems to accentuate the lack of contextual integration. Therefore it, too, should be dismissed unless all other options fail.

4. *Contextually Based Integration Theories*

We may now consider those contextual theories which tie the fragment into some specific statement in the immediate context. There are four major options for contextual integration to which New Testament scholars appeal: (1) 6.14–7.1 is strategically placed for rhetorical-pastoral effect; (2) 6.14–7.1 makes specific the general appeal in 6.1; (3) the 'enlarged heart' idiom in 6.11 reminds Paul of LXX warnings against worshiping other gods, which he develops in 6.14–7.1, and (4) 6.14–7.1 explains the reason for the Corinthians' 'constrained affections' in 6.12. These four options are not mutually exclusive, for commentators usually hold to some combination of these four. A fifth category includes two other options which have been proposed, yet are less readily recognized.

Theory One: Strategic Rhetorical-Pastoral Placement of 6.14–7.1

The broadest of the major contextual theories may be termed 'the strategic placement theory'. This attempts to justify the current positioning of the fragment on the basis that its location reflects a strategic placement by the apostle. Commentators argue this proposal from at least three angles. First, with great tact and rhetorical skill Paul positions this delicate material, which requires sensitive treatment, at the end of the long apology and immediately before the passage in which he intends to affirm complete reconciliation with the congregation (7.5-16).[1] Second, the apostle shows further diplomacy in sandwiching the paraenetic warning between statements of affection to cushion the blow (and to show that the admonition is really an act of

---

1. E.g., Klöpper (*Das zweite Sendschreiben*, p. 338) insightfully states, 'Darum stellt Paulus mit einem bewundernswerthen psychologischen Takt und an demosthenische Rhetorik erinnernder Kunst diese delikateste und der zartesten Behandlung bedürftige Materie an den Schluss des langen apologetischen Theiles seines Briefes und unmittelbar vor denjenigen Passus, in welchem er seine volle Aussöhnung mit der Gemeinde zu constatiren die Absicht hatte.'

love).[1] Third, the imperatives μὴ γίνεσθε (6.14a), ἐξέλθατε, ἀφορίσθητε, and μὴ ἅπτεσθε (6.17)[2] are appropriately placed at this point within 2.14–7.4, since there are only three imperatives in the entire apology (outside 6.14–7.1)—the first does not come until 5.20 (καταλλάγητε cf. 6.1); the later two embrace the fragment at 6.13 (πλατύνθητε) and 7.2 (χωρήσατε). And these imperatives correspond in person and number to those of the fragment.[3]

The strategic-placement theory has much to commend it. It shows that within the broad contextual framework of 2.14–7.4, the current position of 6.14–7.1 corresponds well with the movement to imperatives. And its placement at the end of the apology and between statements of affection does evidence a certain degree of pastoral and rhetorical skill. Nonetheless, these features affirm only the *possibility* of contextual compatibility and only on a broad, general level.

Theory Two: 6.14–7.1 Specifies the General Exhortation in 6.1
Another, frequently offered, solution to the contextual problem is that the fragment specifies the general exhortation in 6.1, παρακαλοῦμεν μὴ εἰς κενὸν τὴν χάριν τοῦ θεοῦ δέξασθαι ὑμᾶς.[4] This connection led Hans Windisch, for example, to conjecture that 6.14–7.1 may have originally followed 6.1-2: 'ist etwa 6.14–7.1 die ursprüngliche Fortsetzung zu 6.1f., indem (6.1f) + (6.14–7.1) eine Parënese

---

1. Hofmann, *Zweite Brief an die Korinther*, pp. 174-75; Räbiger, *Beiden Briefe an die korinthische Gemeinde*, pp. 253-54; Hughes, *Second Epistle to the Corinthians*, p. 244; Thrall, 'The Problem of II Cor. VI.14–VII.1', p. 111. Though pointing out the same structural feature, Jülicher (*Introduction to the New Testament*, p. 97) reverses the impact by suggesting that Paul inserts 6.14–7.1 lest his assurances of affection blot out the continuing need for moral discipline.
   2. Cf. the subjunctive καθαρίσωμεν (7.1).
   3. E.g., Lambrecht, 'The Fragment 2 Cor. VI 14–VII 1', p. 152.
   4. E.g., Windisch, *Der Zweite Korintherbrief*, p. 212; Thrall, 'The Problem of II Cor. VI.14–VII.1', p. 144; Allo, *Seconde Épître aux Corinthiens*, p. 192; Kümmel, *Introduction to the New Testament*, p. 214; Fee, 'Food Offered to Idols', p. 155; Klöpper, *Das zweite Sendschreiben*, p. 334; Oostendorp, *Another Jesus*, p. 57; Meyer, *Epistles to the Corinthians*, p. 554; Hughes, *Second Epistle to the Corinthians*, p. 243; Zahn, *Introduction to the New Testament*, I, p. 350; Murphy-O'Connor, 'Relating 2 Corinthians 6.14–7.1 to Its Context', pp. 273, 275; Collange, *Énigmes*, p. 304; Lütgert, *Freiheitspredigt und Schwarmgeister in Korinth*, p. 83; Belser, *Der zweite Brief an die Korinther*, p. 203.

darstellt. . . ?'[1] For comparison with my contextual hypothesis, it is important to note precisely how this theory articulates the relationship between 6.1 and 6.14–7.1. Commentators identify two links: (1) the movement from a 'general exhortation' in 6.1 to a 'specific/concrete example' in 6.14–7.1 of not receiving the grace of God in vain,[2] and (2) the 'paraenesis' of 6.14–7.1 is expected in view of the paraenetic call in 6.1, παρακαλοῦμεν . . . (cf. 5.20).[3]

The intervening verses (6.3-11) between 6.1-2 and the fragment are then accounted for in a variety of ways. A few who hold the 6.1 theory postulate a revision of the text in order to place 6.14–7.1 after 6.1-2.[4] On the other hand, some simply designate 6.3-13 as a digression.[5] Still others see the delay in specifying the 6.1 exhortation, παρακαλοῦμεν μὴ εἰς κενὸν τὴν χάριν τοῦ θεοῦ δέξασθαι ὑμᾶς, as the apostle's wanting to make sure that the reader's heart has opened wide enough to receive the full expression of the earlier admonition.[6]

This theory is helpful for pointing out the general-to-specific flow of the context and the paraenetic relationship of 6.1 to 6.14–7.1. However, a critical examination of the theory *as currently stated* reveals several weaknesses. First, the general-to-specific tie between the two exhortations is at best a vague connection. It lacks correspondence in specific subject matter and theological substance.[7] Second, the 'paraenetic connection' between 6.1 and 6.14–7.1 would have been stronger had παρακαλοῦμεν or some form of the term been found

---

1. Windisch, *Der Zweite Korintherbrief*, p. 212 (cf. p. 19).

2. Windisch, *Der Zweite Korintherbrief*, pp. 212, 220.

3. Windisch, *Der Zweite Korintherbrief*, pp. 212, 220; Collange, *Énigmes*, p. 304.

4. Windisch, *Der Zweite Korintherbrief*, p. 212 (see quotation above). Weinel (*Die Wirkungen des Geistes und der Geister*, pp. 44-45) had earlier proposed a similar alteration in the order with 6.14–7.1 following 6.1-2. Cf. Collange's theory (*Énigmes*, pp. 6-14, 304) regarding a second edition of the apology which leads to the same order as Windisch.

5. E.g., Thrall, 'The Problem of II Cor. VI.14–VII.1', p. 146. Cf. Murphy-O'Connor ('Relating 2 Corinthians 6.14–7.1 to Its Context', p. 275) who argues for two digressions—6.3-10 and 6.12-13.

6. E.g., Klöpper, *Das zweite Sendschreiben*, p. 334.

7. Even Kümmel (*Introduction to the New Testament*, p. 214), himself a proponent of the 6.1 theory, acknowledges that 'this attempted explanation (the 6.1 theory) is not very convincing'.

within the fragment.[1] Third, the 6.1 theory suffers from a minimally explained contextual gap of eleven verses (6.3-13). The revision proposals by Windisch and Collange are not very convincing.[2] Also, if a conceptual flow for the intervening verses can be demonstrated (as I have proposed in this work[3]), then a digression provides a weaker alternative explanation. In sum, the 6.1 theory is feasible, but in its current form it lacks genuine substance and a cohesive explanation for the intervening material.[4]

Theory Three: The 'Enlarged Heart' Idiom (6.11) Reminds Paul of LXX Warnings against Worshiping Other Gods
The theory least subscribed to of the four major options discerns a logical connection between the fragment and the statement ἡ καρδία ἡμῶν πεπλάτυνται (6.11). According to J.H. Bernard, ἡ καρδία ἡμῶν πεπλάτυνται reminds Paul that the phrase has a negative connotation in the Torah, where it is used in relation to worshiping false gods (e.g., Deut. 6.12).[5] Similarly, M.E. Thrall proposes that καρδία and πλατύνω reminded Paul of the warning in Deut. 11.16 against worshiping other gods.[6] In a recent article, J. Murphy-O'Connor likewise affirms a free association between 2 Cor. 6.11 and the 6.14–7.1 fragment by means of Deut. 11.16.[7]

---

1. Georgi (*Opponents of Paul in Second Corinthians*, p. 23 n. 42) further objects to the paraenetic aspect of the 6.1 theory by saying that 6.1-2 is not a moral paraenesis; whereas 6.14–7.1 is a moral/ethical paraenesis. However, such an analysis of the exhortation, μὴ εἰς κενὸν τὴν χάριν τοῦ θεοῦ δέξασθαι ὑμᾶς (6.1), cannot be sustained in a context which refers to trespasses (5.19) and sin (5.20). Cf. other Pauline passages which look at the spurning of God's grace (e.g., Rom. 6.1-2).

2. See Thrall ('The Problem of II Cor. VI.14–VII.1', pp. 139-42) for a critique of Windisch and Collange's respective reconstruction theories.

3. See Chapter 5, §§4-7.

4. Cf. a synthetic proposal from our traditions framework in Chapter 5, §8.

5. Bernard, 'Second Epistle to the Corinthians', p. 78.

6. Thrall, 'The Problem of II Cor. VI.14–VII.1', p. 147.

7. Murphy-O'Connor, 'Relating 2 Corinthians 6.14–7.1 to Its Context', pp. 272-75. Murphy-O'Connor attempts to build upon Thrall's thesis by drawing further parallels between Deut. 11.13-16 and the context of 2 Cor. 6.12. However, his parallels appear strained. E.g., Paul's own abundance and lack of possessions (2 Cor. 6.10) is hardly the nature of the covenant blessings (and cursings) being discussed in Deut. 11.13-15. In 2 Corinthians Paul *expects* suffering from the hand of God. For a more generalized approach, see Filson ('Second Epistle to the

Of the two texts suggested, Deut. 6.12 is not a likely source, since it represents a secondary LXX text (which is itself probably an assimilation to Deut. 11.16[1]) and it does not have an equivalent expression in the MT. On the other hand, Deut. 11.16 should be compared with 2 Cor. 6.11-13. In LXX Deut. 11.16 Yahweh warns the people, 'Beware, that your heart not be enlarged (μὴ πλατυνθῇ ἡ καρδία σου cf. MT, יִפְתֶּה לְבַבְכֶם) and you transgress and serve other gods and worship them.' After the apostle wrote ἡ καρδία ἡμῶν πεπλάτυνται (2 Cor. 6.11) and instructed the Corinthians to πλατύνθητε καὶ ὑμεῖς (6.13), this theory suggests that Paul is reminded of the warning in Deut. 11.16 and so gives the Corinthians counter-instructions to avoid the worship of other gods (6.14–7.1).

While Thrall's proposal deserves consideration due to the lexical correspondence of καρδία and πλατύνω with Deut. 11.16, the theory encounters several difficulties. First, though not a formidable drawback, the MT in Deut. 11.16 speaks of the deception of the heart, not enlargement *per se* (cf. MT, יִפְתֶּה לְבַבְכֶם). Second, the μὴ πλατυνθῇ ἡ καρδία σου idiom in Deut. 11.16 warns against pride (a 'puffed up' heart) in relation to bountiful agricultural blessings from Yahweh[2] and *not directly* against misguided affections towards other gods. The idiom in Deut. 11.16 is *not* saying, 'Do not enlarge your heart [in affection] towards other gods'; rather, it prohibits pride in the great abundance of new wine, oil, cattle (though the context obviously bars both). Thus in 2 Cor. 6.11-13 the correspondence needed to make the transition between affection for Paul/God (6.11-13) and non-affection for other gods (6.14–7.1) breaks down.[3] Third, Paul's use of the idiom is obviously cast in a positive light. 'Enlarging the heart' refers to receiving another with open/joyous affection (especially in the context of 6.1-13). The very fact that this theory suggests a *negative* (reversed) connotation makes the transition a cumbersome one.[4] If an

Corinthians', p. 270) who thinks that the fragment is prompted by Paul's need to caution the Corinthians against what not to be 'open to'.

1. The Aquila version adds πλατυνθῇ ἡ καρδία σου in LXX Deut. 6.12, the same words found in MT Deut. 11.16.

2. Cf. Deut. 11.13-15.

3. Or, at least such a movement becomes more complex than that suggested by Thrall and Murphy-O'Connor (who both fail to mention the distinctly different sense of the idiom in Deut. 11.16).

4. Rensberger ('2 Corinthians 6.14–7.1', p. 45 n. 6) critiques Thrall in a similar fashion: 'This [Thrall's Deut. 11.16 proposal] is especially unlikely since Paul is

Old Testament background could be found which unites 6.11 and the fragment through a *positive* use of the idiom (as I have suggested in the previous Chapter[1]), then such a direct/straightforward correlation should be favored. In sum, if Deut. 11.16 contributed to Paul's composition of the fragment, then it did so through a most circuitous route.

Theory Four: 6.14–7.1 Explains the Reason for the Corinthians'
'Constrained Affections' (6.12)

As a fourth contextual theory, many New Testament scholars link the fragment to the statement about 'constrained affections' in 6.12. This connection can be taken in one of two directions: after stating in 6.12 that the Corinthians are constrained by their own affections (στενοχωρεῖσθε ἐν τοῖς σπλάγχνοις ὑμῶν), in 6.14–7.1 Paul specifies the cause for this constraint as either compromising pagan associations[2] or acceptance of Jewish opponents.[3] It is not my objec-

---

encouraging openness of heart, while Deut. 11.16 warns *against* it (in another sense)' (his emphasis).

1. See Chapter 5, §6. The Deut. 11.16 proposal suggests a 'free association' of ideas between Paul's writing the idiom (2 Cor. 6.11), his remembering that the idiom in the OT was used in relationship to idols (Deut. 11.16), and his writing an excursus on the problem of idol worship (6.14–7.1). Murphy-O'Connor ('Relating 2 Corinthians 6.14–7.1 to its Context', p. 275) openly admits this more 'accidental' movement in thought to account for the fragment. The proposal sees the fragment as little more than a tangential side excursion due to the flighty 'associative' thinking of Paul.

2. E.g., Plummer, *II Corinthians*, p. 205; Harris, '2 Corinthians', p. 303; Bruce, *I & II Corinthians*, p. 214; Allan Menzies, *Second Epistle to the Corinthians*, p. 50; Belser, *Der zweite Brief an die Korinther*, p. 203; Allo, *Seconde Épître aux Corinthiens*, pp. 184-85; Hughes, *Second Epistle to the Corinthians*, p. 244; Lang, *Die Briefe an die Korinther*, pp. 310-11. Hofmann (*Zweite Brief an die Korinther*, p. 183) draws out the irony of the Corinthians' openness to paganism, but closed-heartedness to Paul: 'Dort thaten sie sich mit denen zusammen, von welchen sie geschieden waren, wie Christus von Beliar, wie Gottes Tempel von der den Götzen; hier hielten sie sich steis genen diejenigen, welchen ihr Berus ein Recht verlich aus ihren willigen Gehorsam.'

3. E.g., Olshausen, *Corinthians*, p. 457; Lenski, *Corinthians*, p. 1076; Collange, *Énigmes*, p. 305; Osty, *Deuxième Épître aux Corinthiens*, p. 78; Rensberger, '2 Corinthians 6.14–7.1', pp. 40-42. In apparent ambivalence, Beale ('Old Testament Background', pp. 573-74) goes back and forth between the false-apostles and pagans referents.

tive at this point to debate the referent issue of ἄπιστοι in 6.14a (see Appendix A). It is sufficient to note here that with either referent, the 'constrained affections' connection is suitably made.

In response to the constrained affections theory (6.12), one must acknowledge that the fragment (in its present location) does appear to elaborate on another direction for the Corinthians' affections. Thus the theory seems to be a legitimate one. However, it is the *nature* of the connection which requires critical assessment: *it is once again quite general, lacking any substantial content.* As with the 6.1 theory, the contextual glue is little more than a general-to-specific bonding.

Other Less Notable Explanations

There are two other contextual integration theories which attempt to show how the fragment fits within its context. These have not gained the prominence of the four mentioned above, and may be identified through their respective proponents, J.D.M. Derrett and M.E. Thrall.

Derrett's 'reading between the lines' theory. J.D.M. Derrett has proposed that the 'obvious' meaning of 6.14–7.1 is not the one Paul intended; his meaning must be 'read between the lines'. In the exhortations prohibiting all forms of partnership with unfaithful persons (ἄπιστοι), what Paul was *really* trying to say was positive—that there should be full partnership and frankness between believers, that is, between Paul and the Corinthians (especially openness and honesty in financial matters, an area in which the apostle was currently under suspicion).[1] Derrett suggests that Paul 'simply adapted to his present purpose a "purple passage" which could conceivably have originated in a sermon—perhaps his own—on a theme which is much to his present purpose'.[2]

While Derrett's proposal is creative, the theory has been met with little acceptance among New Testament scholars, for several reasons. First, it is highly unlikely that ἄπιστοι in 6.14a means 'unfaithful persons' rather than 'unbelievers' (see Appendix A). Second, given the number of misunderstandings that had already occurred between Paul and the Corinthians, it is hard to believe that Paul would resort to such an oblique form of communication.[3] Third, it is difficult to sup-

---

1. Derrett, '2 Cor. 6,14ff a Midrash', pp. 231-50.
2. Derrett, '2 Cor. 6,14ff a Midrash', p. 233.
3. Murphy-O'Connor, 'Relating 2 Corinthians 6.14–7.1 to Its Context', p. 272.

pose, as Derrett does, that the central issue in Paul's mind when using the fragment was *really* the mistrust surrounding the Jerusalem offering. Fourth, Derrett's 'purple passage' proposal amounts to special pleading (for every commentator could color the passage differently with various sermon subjects in the background). As such, it betrays a hesitancy (noticeable in this case, though common in almost all treatments of the fragment) to examine in detail the *explicit* traditions used in 6.14–7.1.

Thrall's 'word links'. M.E. Thrall's main contextual thesis combines the 6.1 theory (in a modification of Windisch's position) and the LXX Deut. 11.16/other gods theory (see theory three above). However, she also develops a list of 'word links' between the fragment and the greater context in an attempt to argue for more contextual coherence. For Thrall, several phrases and ideas in the passage have connection with the larger context: (1) δικαιοσύνη in 6.14 and 5.21; (2) the close relationship between God and people in 6.16-18 and 5.18-20, and (3) εἰσδέξομαι in 6.17 and καιρῷ δεκτῷ in 6.2, and (4) the fear of God in 7.1 and 5.11.[1]

Thrall's word links have not been widely accepted. Rensberger, for example, dismisses these verbal links as little more than coincidence.[2] I am inclined to agree with Rensberger's criticism, at least in part. *In an undeveloped list and without a proper contextual-conceptual framework,* the links do appear arbitrary. However, one of the word links which Thrall suggests (εἰσδέξομαι. . .) is extremely helpful when set within an exilic return framework. This, along with several other verbal links and Old Testament tradition bridges, plays a significant role in our proposed understanding the fragment's contextual continuity.

5. *Conclusion*

In conclusion, alternative contextual theories vary widely. Interpolation theories view the contextual problem as being so acute that (along with other considerations) the fragment must have been inserted by a later redactor. Non-contextual theories retain the frag-

---

1. Thrall, 'The Problem of II Cor. VI.14–VII.1', p. 145. Cf. Fee, 'Food Offered to Idols', p. 147; Dahl, 'A Fragment and Its Context', p. 68 n. 12.

2. Rensberger, '2 Corinthians 6.14–7.1', p. 25.

ment within its present setting, but offer no better integrative solutions than do interpolation theories; at best they accentuate the degree of the problem. Of the four major contextual integration theories, three provide some help towards understanding how 6.14–7.1 fits within its context (through strategic placement within 2.14–7.1, specification of 6.1, and an explanation of 'constrained affections' in 6.12).

My evaluation of these theories may be summarized as follows. Along with individual drawbacks, all interpolation theories struggle to provide a reasonable motive for why a later redactor would put the fragment in its present location. On the other hand, non-contextual integration theories should be held as a 'last resort' (only in the case of complete failure by conventional contextual theories). In this regard, present contextual integration theories are strong enough to ward off endorsement of non-contextual theories, but are themselves inadequate in other respects.

Contextual integration theories *as currently stated* are deficient in a number of areas. First, they establish the integrity of 2 Cor. 6.14–7.1 more by the default of interpolation theories than by their own strength to integrate the passage. Second, none offers a comprehensive solution which draws upon the theology of the fragment in relation to the theology developed in the broader context of 2.14–7.4. Third, contextual theories are not adequate in developing a unified *conceptual* framework for the pieces in the immediate context of 6.1-13, often supposing some kind of 'digression' between 6.1 and the fragment. Fourth (and most damaging), current contextual theories are vague in the matter of contextual integration. For example, moving from general to specific paraenetic exhortations in the 6.1 theory says little about the nature of the relationship between these two units. It is not my objective to disparage current contextual integration theories; rather, this present work seeks to build upon these contextually based theories (especially theories one, two, and four) in an effort to establish a more comprehensive and specific theory of how the fragment fits within its context.

In this respect, my traditions research (along with input from Beale) attempts to strengthen many of these deficiencies in current contextual theories. While my development differs significantly from

Beale,[1] our common quest has been to provide a contextual framework for the fragment through the broader Old Testament traditions. It is the proposal of this work that a contextual continuum may be found through the use of new covenant and second exodus/return traditions inside the fragment and its 2.14–7.4 context. This kind of contextual integration theory offers a comprehensive solution, since its theological roots reach back to the beginning of 2.14–7.4. Furthermore, it develops a unified *conceptual* framework for the pieces of the immediate context of 6.1-13 (each unit, as with the fragment, is brought together through the concepts and images from return theology). Along these lines, my traditions hypothesis seeks to replace Thrall's Deut. 11.16 source theory for the 'enlarged heart' idiom with one from Isa. 60.4-5, which has a more plausible sense connection (positive) and stronger conceptual coherence. Also, the 6.1 theory is strengthened beyond its current vagueness (general-to-specific paraenesis) by articulating the strong verbal and conceptual links between the fragment and 6.1-2.

---

1. Beale, 'Old Testament Background', pp. 550-81. For a summary of the differences in treatment between my work and that of Beale, see Chapter 7, §3.

Chapter 7

CONCLUSION

1. *Hypothesis Summarized*

A brief review of this book's contextual hypothesis is developed here, since a more extensive summary may be obtained in the conclusion of each chapter. My quest has been to address the apparent lack of contextual compatibility between the 'fragment' of 2 Cor. 6.14–7.1 and its surrounding context. I have proposed a framework for contextual integration based on the Old Testament traditions used within the fragment itself and those in its current context of 2 Cor. 2.14–7.4. My hypothesis, simply put, is that contextual continuity emerges through the use of new covenant and exilic return traditions, particularly in light of Paul's identification with the *'ebed Yahweh* (an identification which allows him to formulate his proclamation-message in second exodus language, 'Come out from. . . ').

The first task was to examine the traditions within the fragment itself (as an isolated unit apart from its context). New covenant and second exodus/return traditions were found most clearly in the Old Testament catena, composed of four quotations. Quotation 1 (Ezek. 37.27) explicitly recounts the new covenant formula, which in its Old Testament context is tied to the theme of exilic/eschatological return. Quotation 2 (Isa. 52.11) expresses new exodus and exilic return ideas (the ἐξέλθατε imperative reiterates 6.14a and so dominates the entire fragment), but with no explicit discussion of the new covenant. The third quotation (Ezek. 20.34, *et al.*) extends the picture of the returning exiles and in its Old Testament context(s) is found in succession with other new covenant promises. The fourth quotation, while from the Davidic covenant (2 Sam. 7.14), has been democratized through new covenant axioms and molded with material from Isa. 43.6 to complete the return imagery. A unified picture of the fragment's Old Testament traditions was summarized as follows:

the promise of a new temple dwelling of Yahweh among his people and a close covenant relationship (quotation 1) awakens the impassioned cry, 'Come out of Babylon(!)' (quotation 2); in turn, if they leave Babylon and its impurities, Yahweh will openly welcome them as they return to the homeland (quotation 3) and will in fact receive them as his sons and daughters (quotation 4).

The next object was to explore the literary context of 2 Cor. 2.14–7.4 for similar traditions. A complete summary of my findings has already been catalogued (Chapter 4, §7 and Chapter 5, §§7-8). It would not overstate the case to say that the focal point of the remote context (2.14–5.10) revolves around new covenant theology—a theology which serves as the heart of Paul's ministry and is often intertwined with various exilic return traditions. In the immediate context (5.11–7.4), the more significant points of contact with the fragment through exilic return traditions were found to be τὰ ἀρχαῖα... καινά (5.17),[1] the quotation from Isa. 49.8 (6.1-2),[2] the removal of stumbling blocks, προσκοπήν (6.3), the commendation as θεοῦ διάκονοι—recalling Paul's *'ebed* role (6.4a), and the 'enlarging the heart' idiom in connection with Paul's father-child relationship to the Corinthians (6.11-13). Underlying this exilic return motif in the immediate context was also the continued new covenant perspective.[3]

In light of this traditions research, a synthesis of the immediate context was developed. New covenant and exilic return imagery thread the pieces together: as a servant of the new covenant, Paul stands between God and the Corinthians with a message of 'new things' patterned after the exodus paradigm and centered on the restoration of the entire cosmos to God (5.16-21). He expresses the urgent need that 'now' is the time for their (second exodus) salvation and home coming/reception (6.1-2). He has cleared away any obstacles in their path (6.3-10); he has 'enlarged his heart' in anticipation of their return, and calls on them to do likewise (6.11-13; cf. 7.2-4). Finally, like the *'ebed*, he prompts their return with the cry for a new

1. Cf. Isa. 42.9; 43.18-19; 48.3-6; 65.16-17.
2. Cf. especially δέξασθαι, δεκτῷ, εὐπρόσδεκτος and ἐξέλθατε (ἐκ Βαβυλῶνος) and the fragment's second and third quotations.
3. E.g., ἐν καρδίᾳ (5.12; cf. 3.2-3; Jer. 31(38).33), δικαιοσύνη (5.19, 21; cf. 3.9), τὴν διακονίαν (5.18; cf. 3.6, 8, 9), συνιστάντες ἑαυτούς (6.4a; cf. 3.1; 4.2), πρὸς κατάκρισιν οὐ λέγω (Cor. 7.3a; cf. 3.9), and ἐν ταῖς καρδίαις ἡμῶν (7.3b; cf. 3.2-3).

exodus ('Come out from. . . ') and with promises related to their home coming (6.14–7.1)—just as he will welcome them as his children, so will their covenant God receive them as his sons and daughters. Through the skillful use of return traditions both inside and outside the fragment, Paul effectively parallels the Corinthians' need to return to him as apostle with their need to return to God.

2. *Contribution to Research on the Fragment*

This study makes contributions to (and holds implications for) existing research on the fragment in a number of areas: methodological, contextual, interpretive, and authorship.

Methodological Contributions

From a methodological standpoint this book makes at least two contributions. A primary methodological contribution is found in the research's starting point of the Old Testament catena. My investigation began with, and placed its primary emphasis on, the Old Testament traditions in the fragment. Such an approach represents a significant departure from recent studies, which generally start with the material outside the catena and then appeal to a 'preexisting catena' at points where the hypotheses do not fit with the traditions. I have sought to reverse this trend by taking as my point of reference the catena, its sources, its redaction of those sources, and its distinctive theology (see comments in Chapter 3, §1).

In this respect, the relationship between the Old Testament catena (6.16d-18) and its 'outer shell' (6.14-16c; 7.1) was developed beyond existing studies (Chapter 3, §4). My findings of extensive catena-shell interplay (and redactional adaptation to accommodate the Old Testament catena to its outer shell) held significant implications for the direction taken in this book. For example, it has been argued that the redacted nature of the catena (making it suitable for the shell) mitigates against current 'preexisting catena' proposals. It is not the 'preexisting catena' proposal *itself* with which I took issue (the catena may have existed as a separate entity before its inclusion within the fragment). My criticism was with the way the 'preexisting catena' proposal is characteristically used to nullify certain aspects of the Old Testament material. Appeal to a 'preexisting catena' is often made (Thrall, Fee, Rensberger, Betz, *et al.*) in a way which suggests that part or all of the Old Testament material *has been haphazardly thrown into the fragment* and therefore may be dismissed. The findings from this work, however, suggest that any theory concerning the fragment *as a whole* should reflect the close correspondence between its outer shell and inner catena.

A second methodological departure from the norm is the attempt to develop a contextual theory which is not dependent upon solving the crux interpretive issue in 6.14a. The fact that I have made little or no mention of who the 'unbelievers' are (or what the 'unequal yoke' refers to) bears this out. It is not that my contextual theory contains no implications for the interpretation of 6.14a (these implications are explored in Appendixes A and B). Rather, this book's contextual theory is not dependent simply upon choosing any one referent option. The advantage of this approach is clear if one considers that several other contextual theories are dependent upon the success of *one* particular interpretation of 6.14a (and stand or fall accordingly). A contextual theory which *requires* the identification of the 'unbelievers' and the 'unequal yoke' carries with it the added liability of having to assume the correctness of its referent solution. This study has attempted to free itself from this added burden of proof.

Contextual Contributions
Contextual integration of the fragment. The core contribution from 'traditions bridge' theory is the strengthening of existing contextual integration theories (Chapter 6, §4). By far the most damaging element of existing theories is that they are vague, lacking strong conceptual 'glue' to bond the fragment to its context (the general-to-specific connection in the 6.1 theory for example). The conceptual framework provided by my traditions hypothesis attempts to remove this deficiency. Also, interpolation theories and non-contexual theories (Chapter 6, §§2-3), which, historically, have thrived on the apparent lack of contextual integration, will now have to respond to the dimension of continuity discovered in the use of these traditions.

Contextual function of 6.1-2. Unlike former studies, this study has placed a heavy (almost pivotal) emphasis on the role of traditions from Isa. 49.8-9 for building a conceptual bridge to the fragment. Here the significance of Paul's identification with the *'ebed Yahweh* makes its culminative contribution, since one of the servant's day-of-salvation roles is that of proclaiming the new exodus, 'Come out (of Babylon)'. In addition, I developed several verbal links to the fragment which strengthen these conceptual ones.

Contextual function of 6.3-10. The common treatment of 6.3-10 which views it as out of its original order (Windisch), as a digression (Thrall), or as part of a double digression (Murphy-O'Connor) is also challenged by my contextual hypothesis. If the material in 6.3-10 functions as Paul's 'removal of stumbling blocks' from the exilic-return highway, then there exists a definite correlation with the traditions in 6.2 and the fragment, as well as a conceptual rationale for the placement of the material in the order in which it stands. The removal of all stumbling blocks from the Corinthian's return path (6.3-10) functions conceptually as a *preparatory act* or preamble before making the formal and climactic call for their return, 'Come out of. . . '. The highway needs to be cleared of rubble before the Corinthians may return home.

'Enlarging the heart' idiom in 6.11. This book parted company with current integration theories at one point, namely, the use of Deut. 11.16 as a source for the 'enlarging the heart' idiom in 2 Cor. 6.11 (Thrall, Murphy-O'Connor, *et al.*). Instead, Isa. 60.4-5 was suggested as a more viable source. If the Isa. 60.4-5 source is adopted, its returning 'sons' and 'daughters' motif along with Paul's father-children metaphor corresponds closely with the return picture found in the fragment.

Interpretive Issues in the Fragment

My contextual theory contributes towards the interpretation of the fragment by shedding light on the crux issue of 6.14a, the 'unbelievers' and the 'unequal yoke'. In order to emphasize a methodological point (that the contextual hypothesis is not dependent upon an interpretive solution to 6.14a) this issue is dealt with separately in Appendixes A and B. My point here, however, is that the contextual hypothesis does assist the interpreter (beyond the current state of research) in assessing the viability of certain referent options. For example, some have seen the fragment's traditions as calling for a strict social and physical separation from society (Fitzmyer, Georgi, Gnilka, *et al.*). This may be so, if the fragment is read in the midst of another kind of document or social setting. Yet, the second exodus and exilic return traditions in 2.14–7.4 (excluding the fragment for the moment) function as a call for a spiritual return to God, not for any broad social or geographical separation from society. They serve as a pattern and paradigm based on two great 'exodus' events of the past (neither of which resulted in complete social separation). If the exodus traditions outside the fragment sound this moderate note to the Corinthian community, then those inside the fragment should be understood accordingly (at least as read in the context of 2 Cor. 2.14–7.4). The reader may examine the appendixes for further implications.

Authenticity of the Fragment

From the outset I have avoided the issue of the fragment's authenticity or authorship, since my hypothesis is not dependent upon it and I did not intend this book to play a key role in that discussion. Nevertheless, it is certainly intriguing to find that the same kinds of Old Testament traditions which appear inside the fragment are also found in its context. This could support the view that Paul did have a hand in the composition-redaction and placement of the fragment. Others, however, will be inclined to use this data to substantiate the insertion of the fragment by a later redactor (other than Paul) who was well versed in the traditions and theology of 2 Cor. 2.14–7.4. I leave it for the reader to decide.

3. *Contribution in Relation to Beale's Traditions Work*

This book and Beale's article forge an entirely new direction in research on the fragment (Chapter 2, §6). While sharing a similar methodology to Beale, my work takes a slightly different route. The more significant differences may be summarized here. First, my approach goes beyond Beale's study to include a much broader analysis of context and a more extensive treatment of the Old Testament traditions. In this respect, my work champions Beale's cause, for it tests the potential of a traditions hypothesis as fully as possible within the larger context of 2 Cor. 2.14–7.4. Second, I view the conceptual threads which tie together the Old Testament traditions (both outside and inside the fragment) under the broader rubric of 'new covenant and second exodus/return theology'. Such a perspective strengthens Beale's contextual continuum by adding the crucial dimension of 'new covenant' to the contextual-continuity package (along with certain negative implications from the exodus idea which Beale overlooks). Third, I seek to establish a series of verbal links which unite the Old Testament traditions, in addition to the conceptual links discussed by Beale. Fourth, I avoid Beale's localization of the Old Testament theology into one particular Pauline word, καταλλάσσω, and make some mild criticisms of his methodology at this point. Fifth, this study proposes that the Old Testament traditions-bridge which ties the fragment into its context does so in view of the close *personal identification* of the apostle Paul (himself a suffering servant) with the message and mission of the *'ebed Yahweh*. This is an important contribution beyond the work of Beale, since it is through this identification with the *'ebed* that Paul may have come to adopt the task of new exodus proclamation, 'Come out (of Babylon)'. Sixth, I suggest that many of the Old Testament traditions used in 2.14–7.4 relate to the broader setting of Paul's 'promise theology' which was under attack (1.20-22). These covenant-promise traditions ('I, Yahweh, will. . . ') reflect the Old Testament material from which Paul has been drawing in the remote and immediate contexts and anticipate the promise-formulas found in 6.14–7.1. Finally, in the two appendixes which follow I apply the contextual hypothesis to the crux interpretive issue in 6.14a. Beale's article permits only a brief treatment of this interpretive issue and so does not bring the findings of the contextual hypothesis to bear on each referent option in 6.14a. The more problematic aspect of Beale's study at this point, however, is his (perhaps inadvertent) blurring of what are actually mutually exclusive referents.

4. *Final Comments*

Though not directly articulated, the Old Testament traditions in 2.14–7.4 suggest that Paul held a broader understanding of new covenant theology, beyond the typical categories of 'Spirit' and a 'new heart', to include a dimension of 'return to the land'. New covenant promises were contingent upon a 'return home'. The sequence of promises in Ezek. 34.24-27 certainly illustrates this aspect of return: 'I (Yahweh) will take you from the nations, gather you from all the lands, and bring you into your land. . . I will sprinkle. . . I will cleanse. . . I will give you a new heart/spirit... I will give you a heart of flesh... I will put my Spirit within you... (etc.)'. In this book I have not postulated a precise relationship within Paul's theology between the return traditions and new covenant traditions, other than to suggest some kind of unified contingency. Nor has this study ventured extensively into the relationship between the traditions used in 2.14–7.4 and the problem with Paul's 'promise theology' in 1.18-22. Both of these issues are intriguing, yet I will defer to others for further research in this area.

Appendix A

THE CRUX INTERPRETIVE ISSUE (PART I):
WHO ARE THE 'UNBELIEVERS' (ἄπιστοι)?

1. *Introduction*

In terms of my focus, these appendixes[1] represent an afterword. My primary objective has been to establish a traditions framework for 2 Cor. 6.14–7.1. However, having argued a case for this, it is of interest to apply the contextual hypothesis to the interpretation of 2 Cor. 6.14a, μὴ γίνεσθε ἑτεροζυγοῦντες ἀπίστοις. The crux interpretive issue in 6.14a revolves around two referent problems: (1) who are the 'unbelievers' (ἄπιστοι), and (2) what is the 'unequal yoke' (ἑτεροζυγοῦντες) which the fragment prohibits? The first issue will be addressed in this essay, the second in Appendix B to follow.

Throughout its interpretive history, no less than five referents for ἄπιστοι have been proposed: (1) untrustworthy persons; (2) Gentile Christians who do not keep the Torah; (3) the immoral within the church community; (4) the false apostles, and (5) non-Christians, pagans outside the church community. Each of these options will be dealt with in turn. However, the bulk of my discussion will focus on the last two.

2. ἄπιστοι *as Untrustworthy Persons (a 'Backhanded' Reference to Paul as Trustworthy)*

One view, put forward by J.D.M. Derrett,[2] takes ἄπιστοι to refer to 'untrustworthy' or 'unfaithful' persons in general, whether believers or unbelievers. What Paul intended by μὴ γίνεσθε ἑτεροζυγοῦντες ἀπίστοις was not a negative prohibition, but a positive exhortation (by inference) encouraging the Corinthians to become full partners with himself as πιστός (trustworthy). Derrett builds his case for this allusive referent to Paul himself from the concern of the apostle not to defraud the Corinthians (2 Cor. 7.2), the issue of trust related to the Jerusalem collection (2 Corinthians 8–9), and the use of ἄπιστος in relation to a person who is unreliable in financial matters (e.g., Lk. 16.10-12).

---

1. Appendixes A and B represent a revision of a chapter originally in my dissertation (Webb, 'Contextual Framework', pp. 215-70) and a reworking of two articles: 'Who Are the Unbelievers (ἄπιστοι) in 2 Corinthians 6.14?', pp. 27-44; *idem.*, 'What is the Unequal Yoke (ἑτεροζυγοῦντες) in 2 Corinthians 6.14?', pp. 162-79.

2. Derrett, '2 Cor. 6,14ff. a Midrash', pp. 231-50.

For at least two reasons, however, Derrett's referent proposal is not tenable. First, that Paul intended a positive exhortation about *himself* (rather than a negative prohibition about other persons) cannot be sustained. The redactional work in the Old Testament catena that follows, linking the altered αὐτῶν of the second Old Testament quotation with the ἀπίστοις of 2 Cor. 6.14a,[1] indicates an intentional alignment between the catena exhortations and the initial exhortation of 6.14a. This alignment and modification of the Old Testament text demonstrates that the writer clearly intended the opening exhortation to be negative and aimed at a group of specific referents other than himself.[2]

Second, it is improbable that ἄπιστοι in 2 Cor. 6.14a means 'untrustworthy' or 'unfaithful'. Within the Paul's writings ἄπιστοι always has the sense of 'unbelievers'.[3] More importantly, ἄπιστοι within Corinthian correspondence is used only of 'unbelievers', never 'unfaithful/untrustworthy ones'. Furthermore, within the literary unit of 2 Cor. 2.14–7.4 ἄπιστοι conveys the objective idea of unbelievers. In 2 Cor. 4.4 the issue surrounding the term is one of belief and reception of the gospel, since the ἄπιστοι are characterized by 'hardened hearts' and 'blinded minds'; they are the ones who do not 'see the light of the gospel or the glory of Christ'.[4] Finally, within the fragment itself the subsequent ἄπιστος/πιστός contrast in 6.15b, if taken as believer/unbeliever (which Derrett, ironically, does[5]), undermines Derrett's position.[6] A reader of the fragment in its present setting, therefore, would be inclined to take the sense as 'unbeliever'.

---

1. For a detailed analysis of the redaction, see Chapter 3, §2.

2. One might be able to accept this view's ambiguity in meaning had the opening exhortation stood alone. However, its reinforcement through carefully altered OT exhortations makes Derrett's suggestion suspect. Derrett ('2 Cor. 6,14ff. a Midrash', p. 236) glosses over the OT quotations, failing to wrestle with this connection.

3. E.g., 1 Cor. 6.6; 7.12, 13, 14 (twice), 15; 10.27; 14.22 (twice), 23, 24; 2 Cor. 4.4. Cf. 1 Tim. 5.8; Tit. 1.15.

4. Aside from the language of belief, Stockhausen's ('Moses' Veil', pp. 242-64) tradition-history studies on the 'hardening' and 'unbelief' in 2 Cor. 3.12-18; 4.2-3 have shown Isa. 6.9-10 and 29.10-14 to be the background of Paul's thinking. If so, then, belief/unbelief in Christ as the Messiah is clearly the point of ἄπιστοι in 2 Cor. 4.4.

5. Derrett ('2 Cor. 6,14ff. a Midrash', p. 233; cf. p. 241) paraphrases as follows: 'You must never, of course, be unequal yoke-mates with *unfaithful persons* (ἄπιστοι): the just cannot be partners with the lawless, the light with darkness, Christ with Belial, *a believer* with *an unbeliever* (ἄπιστος) . . . ' (my emphasis).

6. A change in sense between 6.14a and 6.15b seems improbable, since the rhetorical contrasts support the opening exhortation. Furthermore, Derrett's lexical ambivalence ('2 Cor. 6,14ff. a Midrash', pp. 235, 241-42) leaves much to be desired. He suggests that ἄπιστοι can even refer to the Corinthians should they fail to trust Paul. However, it is unlikely that the Corinthians would be the subject of the verb μὴ γίνεσθε and at the same time the referent of ἄπιστοι.

3. ἄπιστοι as Gentile Christians who do not Keep the Torah

A second view, articulated by H.D. Betz,[1] understands ἄπιστοι to refer to Gentile Christians who do not keep the Torah (in matters of circumcision, Sabbath, Jewish cultic practices, etc).[2] Betz argues that the passage is anti-Pauline and represents the theology of the Jewish-Christian opponents with whom Paul had to deal in Antioch and Galatia. Their basic tenet was that Christians need to observe the Torah, which led them either to attempt to impose the Torah upon Gentile Christians (as in Galatia) or persuade Jewish Christians to separate themselves from Gentile believers (as in Antioch). The Antioch policy is reflected in 2 Cor. 6.14–7.1 where μὴ γίνεσθε ἑτεροζυγοῦντες ἀπίστοις, Betz argues, exhorts Jewish Christians not to cast aside the yoke of the Torah by associating with Gentile Christians who have abandoned the requirements of the Law.

Aside from difficulties facing interpolation theories, Betz's referent proposal suffers from a number of internal weaknesses. First, there is virtually no evidence that Gentile Christians were ever called ἄπιστοι.[3] The limited data relating to the Antioch dispute suggests that these individuals would have been referred to simply as 'Gentiles'.[4] If ἄπιστοι was used of Gentile Christians, it would have been in a highly specialized, polemical sense. So if a later redactor had inserted this anti-Pauline fragment into the text for general circulation, he surely would have used more precise terminology to clarify the direction of the exhortation. A stigmatized title like 'uncircumcised Gentiles' would have been more to the point.

Second, to sustain his thesis Betz must handle the Old Testament quotations in a selective manner. For instance, he acknowledges only the Lev. 26.12 source to the first quotation because of its Torah origins (with no influence from Ezek. 37.27)[5] and does not account for the non-Torah origin of the remaining quotations. Yet, if the issue is obedience to the Torah, why does the catena include only one quotation from Torah?[6] Furthermore, Betz's thesis fails to explain the presence of new covenant (not Sinai) themes and democratized Davidic theology within the catena.[7] Such elements seem out of place for a group of Jewish opponents who touted the old covenant and the letter of the law (rather than the new covenant and its ministry by the Spirit).

Third, understanding the ἄπιστοι as Gentile Christians who do not keep certain features of the Mosaic law restricts the fragment's 'idolatry' (2 Cor. 6.16) to a purely

---

1. Betz, 'Anti-Pauline Fragment', pp. 88-108. Cf. Gunther, *Paul's Opponents*, pp. 309-13.

2. The following synopsis of Betz's position follows closely the one provided by Thrall, 'The Problem of II Cor. VI.14–VII.1', p. 148 n. 1.

3. Thrall, 'The Problem of II Cor. VI.14–VII.1', p. 148 n. 1.

4. E.g., Gal. 2.14-15; Acts 15.7, 19, 23; cf. οἱ ἐκ πίστεως (Gal. 3.9).

5. Betz, 'Anti-Pauline Fragment', p. 93. For problems with taking the first quotation with reference only to Lev. 26.12, see Chapter 3, §2.

6. That one quotation is probably at best only modified by Torah.

7. A source analysis of the quotations in the catena reveals the following: (quotation 1) Ezek. 37.27 influenced by Lev. 26.11, (quotation 2) Isa. 52.11 modified to link ἐξέλθατε with 6.14a, (quotation 3) Ezek. 20.34 *et al.*, and (quotation 4) a democratized 2 Sam. 7.14 blended with Isa. 43.6. See Chapter 3.

figurative, non-literal sense. According to Betz's thesis the 'idolatrous activity' amounted to not keeping certain ritualistic aspects of the Torah. Consequently, if it can be demonstrated that some form of *literal* idolatry is probable within the fragment and its present context (as will be argued below), then Betz's thesis cannot stand.

4. ἄπιστοι *as the Immoral Within the Church Community*

A third option is to take the ἄπιστοι as referring to grossly immoral individuals within the church community—either believers who are living like non-Christians,[1] or those who by their immorality reveal themselves to be unbelievers.[2] This view stems from identifying the fragment with the lost 'previous letter' mentioned in 1 Cor. 5.9, 'I wrote you in my (previous) letter not to associate with immoral people (πόρνοις)'. The identification of the fragment as this previous letter (or part of it) is usually supported by a similarity in content (both *may* have had idolatry in view)[3] and the verbal correspondence between ἐξελθεῖν in 1 Cor. 5.10 and ἐξέλθατε in 2 Cor. 6.17.[4]

However, equating the ἄπιστοι of the fragment with the πόρνοι of 1 Cor. 5.9 is faulty for several reasons (aside from interpolation difficulties). First, the content of the 'previous letter' may have differed significantly from what is found in the fragment. The only thing known for certain about the previous letter is that it prohibited association with sexually immoral people in the church (τοῖς πόρνιος, 1 Cor. 5.9, 10), whereas such sexual vices are not explicitly mentioned in 2 Cor. 6.14–7.1.[5]

Second, the Old Testament traditions used to reinforce the injunction of 1 Cor. 5.9 differ from those which support 2 Cor. 6.14a. The exhortation not to associate with immoral people (in the church) is founded on the paschal tradition (in which people were to remove the unleaven bread before the passover feast)[6] and on Israel's proverbial 'in-house' judgment saying, 'Remove the wicked man from among your-

---

1. E.g., Newton, *Concept of Purity at Qumran*, p. 113; Wendland, *Die Briefe an die Korinther*, p. 212; Strachan, *Second Epistle to the Corinthians*, pp. xv, 3-4; Schmithals, *Gnosticism in Corinth*, pp. 94-95; Hurd, *The Origin of 1 Corinthians*, pp. 235-39; Foreman, *Second Letter to the Corinthians*, p. 134. For a listing of older scholars who held to the 'previous letter' theory (e.g., Hilgenfeld, Franke, Sabatier, Lisco, von Dobschütz, von Soden, Whitelaw, etc.) see Moffat, *Introduction*, p. 125.

2. E.g., Gärtner, *Temple and the Community*, pp. 49-56; Selby, *Introduction to the Bible*, pp. 353-54; Lategan, 'Moenie met ongelowiges', pp. 20-34.

3. The explanation by Paul in 1 Cor. 5.10-11 refers to idolators; cf. the reference to idols in 2 Cor. 6.16.

4. These two reasons for aligning the fragment with the lost letter are frequently mentioned. E.g., see Moffatt, *Introduction*, p. 125.

5. In the previous letter the emphasis was on sexual immorality, whereas in the fragment it is on idolatry of some kind (see Furnish, *II Corinthians*, pp. 379-80). Even if certain sexual activity is prohibited by 6.14–7.1 (e.g., sacred temple prostitution), it is the activity itself which is being prohibited in 2 Cor. 6.14–7.1 and not the association with (so-called) Christians who do such acts (the situation described in 1 Cor. 5.9-13).

6. 1 Cor. 5.2, 7 (cf. Exod. 12.19).

selves'.[1] It is important to note that both of these traditions view the removal of wickedness to be from the midst of the covenant community. On the other hand, the exhortation in 2 Cor. 6.17a ('come out from their midst [from Babylon]'[2]) and the promise in 2 Cor. 6.17d ('and I will receive you [from the nations]'[3]) are derived from exilic return theology in which the call is for Israel to separate themselves as a nation of God's people from the other nations.

Third, to view the ἄπιστοι as a specialized kind of middle group (of grossly carnal believers or deluded unbelievers) is not likely in light of the fragment's strong dualism. The composer of the fragment does not paint anything in intermediate shades; he portrays all individuals in one of two extreme camps (righteousness/ lawlessness, light/darkness, Christ/Beliar, believer/unbeliever, and God's temple/ idols).[4] Perhaps if a chain of rhetorical contrasts had not followed the initial exhortation (and the opening exhortation stood alone), a more specialized definition of the ἄπιστοι would be feasible.

Finally, that ἄπιστοι refers to carnal believers or unbelievers as a group within the church community belies the consistent use of the term in the Corinthian correspondence. Most pertinent to 1 Cor. 5.9-10 is the use of ἄπιστοι in 1 Cor. 6.6, where the Corinthians are instructed not to go to court before pagan judges, 'unbelievers'. But this discussion of lawsuits in 1 Cor. 6.1-11 is simply a continuation of the 'who judges whom' issue from the previous chapter. In 5.12-13 Paul established the principle that God will judge the outsiders (τοὺς ἔξω); the church is to judge her own, the insiders (τοὺς ἔσω). Consequently, the point which follows in 6.1-11 is that the Corinthians should have their disputes resolved internally, not by 'outsiders'.[5] Paul labeled these 'outsider judges' as ἄπιστοι (6.6) in contrast to those within the church, the ἀδελφοί. In light of this alignment of ἄπιστοι with the 'outsiders', it is unlikely that Paul would have used the term in the previous letter as part of an instruction which he consciously intended as an 'insiders' referent (i.e., the immoral person [within the church]).[6]

---

1. 1 Cor. 5.2, 13 (cf. LXX Deut. 13.5; 17.7, 12; 21.21; 22.21).

2. Isa. 52.11.

3. Ezek. 20.34.

4. Paul is quite capable of defining more specialized, intermediate groups such as πνευματικός (1 Cor. 2.15; 3.1; 14.37; Gal. 6.1), νηπίοις ἐν Χριστῷ (1 Cor. 3.1), ἐν τοῖς τελείοις (1 Cor. 2.6; cf. Eph. 4.13), σαρκινοί/σαρκικοί (1 Cor. 3.1, 3), ἀδελφὸς ὀνομαζόμενος (1 Cor. 5.11), σὲ τὸν ἔχοντα γνῶσιν (1 Cor. 8.10; cf. 8.4), ὁ ἀσθενῶν (1 Cor. 8.9, 11; 9.22; Rom. 14.1, 2, 21; 15.1), οἱ δυνατοί (Rom. 15.1).

5. That the pagan judges are 'outsiders' is clear from their being referred to as 'unrighteous' (6.1), their non-appointment 'in the church' (6.4), and their distinction from the 'one wise man among you' who is to decide between his brethren (6.5).

6. For other passages where the ἄπιστοι are a distinct group apart from the church see 1 Cor. 10.27-32; 14.22, 23, 24; 2 Cor. 4.4.

5. ἄπιστοι *as the False Apostles, False Teachers within the Community*

A fourth view, which has gained substantial ground in recent years,[1] takes the ἄπιστοι to refer to the false apostles mentioned in 2 Corinthians 10–13.[2] In order to handle the material on the false-apostles view, I divide the evaluation into three sections: (1) the supportive evidence; (2) the major problems with the false-apostles view, and (3) the minor problems with the view.

Supportive Evidence for the False-Apostles View
Perhaps the strongest argument in favor of the false-apostles view is that it smooths out (at least to some extent) the abrupt contextual transition. On this contextual point Rensberger writes that with the false-apostles referent, 'the contextual problem is at once resolved. Paul pleads for the Corinthians to open their hearts as his is open; not to be mismated with "unbelievers" (his opponents), but to make room for him (2 Cor. 6.11–7.2)'.[3] One must grant that the movement from lack of affection for the apostle Paul (6.11-13, 7.2-4) to the problem of a competing affection for the opponent apostles (6.14–7.1) flows nicely.

However, this contextual transition argument is not without problems. First, although the false-apostles view makes for a smooth transition between 6.13 and 6.14, it still leaves a rough 'bump' between 7.1 and 7.2. Rensberger admits that the exhortation in 7.1 is not talking about the false apostles, but about some kind of ethical purification.[4] Therefore, the view fails to dissolve the abrupt shift between 7.1 and 7.2. To sustain the transition it has to move directly from 6.13 to 6.14 to 7.2. Second, while a reference to false apostles might smooth the initial contextual bump, it has disastrous results for the material within the fragment. This is admitted inadvertently by the advocates of the false-apostles theory, inasmuch as they claim that the fragment meant something quite different in its original context.[5] If one looks

---

1. E.g., Rensberger, '2 Corinthians 6.14–7.1', pp. 25-49; Olson, 'Confidence Expressions in Paul', p. 190; Collange, *Énigmes*, pp. 302-17; Dahl, 'A Fragment and Its Context', pp. 62-69; Olshausen, *Epistles to the Corinthians*, pp. 329-32; Usteri, *Entwickelung der Paulinischen Lehrbegriffes*, p. 236.

2. Ironically, this fourth view takes everything in the fragment to mean exactly the opposite to the second view. The second view (proposed by Betz) understands the fragment to be written by Jewish opponents against Paul (or at least against Pauline teaching); this fourth view takes the fragment to be written by Paul against his Jewish opponents. For a balanced sketch of the false apostles and their background see Furnish, *II Corinthians*, pp. 48-54.

3. Rensberger, '2 Corinthians 6.14–7.1', p. 31. For Rensberger ('2 Corinthians 6.14–7.1', p. 40), the false-apostles view is the *only* view which provides a lucid transition between the context and the fragment. Cf. Olshausen, *Epistles to the Corinthians*, p. 329; Dahl, 'A Fragment and Its Context', pp. 65-66.

4. Rensberger, '2 Corinthians 6.14–7.1', p. 41.

5. Dahl ('A Fragment and Its Context', p. 65) states: 'Obviously the fragment was not originally written to serve this [ἄπιστοι = false apostles] function'. Cf. his comment (p. 66) that 'the contextual sense is different from the original meaning'. For a similar perspective, see Collange, *Énigmes*, p. 306; Rensberger, '2 Corinthians 6.14–7.1', p. 41.

at the fragment in isolation from its present context (since no one has the 'original context'), according to them ἄπιστοι refers to something other than false apostles. In other words, by their own admission this view rests everything on the context that the passage fits into (and almost nothing on data internal to the fragment[1])—a tremendous weight for any contextual theory to carry.

Another argument commonly used to support the false-apostles view is that it resolves the contradiction in Paul's theology of separation. Comparing 2 Cor. 6.14–7.1 to the apostle's former instruction in 1 Corinthians, Rensberger observes, 'Paul in 1 Corinthians is anything but strictly separatist regarding contact between Christians and non-Christians'.[2] In 1 Corinthians the apostle instructed believers not to come out from among the world of immoral non-Christians (5.9-10), not to separate from unbelieving spouses (7.12-14), and assumed (seemingly with his blessing) that Christians will eat meals in the homes of pagans (10.27). The harsh attitude of 2 Cor. 6.14–7.1 towards contact with ἄπιστοι does not mesh well with this kind of tolerance. It does, however, match the tone of Paul's address towards his opponents in other letters.[3]

A false-apostles referent does seem to resolve the tension/contradiction between the tolerant attitude in 1 Corinthians and the severity in the fragment. However, for a number of reasons this supposed contradiction is more apparent than real. First, the purpose of separation from the world (outsiders) in 1 Cor. 5.10b (ἐκ τοῦ κόσμου ἐξελθεῖν) and 2 Cor. 6.17a (ἐξέλθατε ἐκ μέσου αὐτῶν) is completely different. The purpose of separation from the world/outsiders in 1 Cor. 5.10b is *for judging the outsiders' immoral behavior,*[4] but Paul condemns this as inappropriate. On the other hand, the purpose of separation from the world/outsiders in 2 Cor. 6.17a is *for protecting one's personal purity and covenant relationship,*[5] which the fragment openly endorses. The former is condemned; the latter encouraged. Legitimate grounds for suggesting a logical contradiction exist only if the two separation passages share the same purpose.

Second, the nature of separation in 1 Cor. 5.10b and 2 Cor. 6.17a is distinctly different. Separation from the world (outsiders) in 1 Cor. 5.10b is a *complete removal* from even casual physical contact, while the nature of separation from the world/outsiders in 2 Cor. 6.17a is a *selective removal* from intimate contact (that is,

---

1. In this respect the false-apostles view is similar to the 'purple passage' proposal by Derrett ('2 Cor 6,14ff. a Midrash on Dt. 22,10', p. 233).

2. Rensberger, '2 Corinthians 6.14–7.1', p. 37. Allo (*Seconde Épître aux Corinthiens*, p. 189) states: 'La prescription, donnée avec une certaine violence, de fuir les païens, paraît contredire à la tolérance que Paul a prônée dans son épître antérieure'.

3. E.g., Gal. 1.8-9; Phil. 3.2. Cf. Rensberger, '2 Corinthians 6.14–7.1', p. 44.

4. In 1 Cor. 5.9-13 the kind of separation from non-Christians which Paul *condemns* is separation *for the purpose of judging* their immoral behavior. The issue is clearly one of judgment, for the church is only to judge (by separation) the immoral 'insiders' (not 'outsiders'), for God will judge the 'outsiders'.

5. Rensberger ('2 Corinthians 6.14–7.1', pp. 39-40) himself states that the purpose of the separation as discussed in 2 Cor. 7.1 is for personal purity. Cf. the issue of cultic/personal purity in 6.16 and the OT quotations.

only from certain covenant-forming relationships). Again, the former kind of separation is condemned; the latter is encouraged. Nothing is said in 1 Cor. 5.9-13 to prohibit a selective withdrawal from the world (outsiders) in cases where a serious covenant violation occurs (in fact, selective withdrawal is commanded in the same letter[1]). Nothing is said in 2 Cor. 6.14–7.1 to prohibit contact with pagans (outsiders).[2] The covenant language in the rhetorical questions and the two Old Testament covenant formulas suggest that more is at stake than social contact.[3] Only if the two passages are talking about the same kind of separation can a contradiction be inferred.

Third, since the fragment's call for separation is expressed in second exodus/ return language (ἐξέλθατε ἐκ μέσου αὐτῶν. . . κἀγὼ εἰσδέξομαι [ἐκ τῶν ἐθνῶν]),[4] one must understand the nature of this separation in light of how these traditions are used in the broader literary context. For example, in 2 Cor. 6.1-2 the salvific 'deliverance' of which Paul speaks, though patterned after the exilic return from Babylon, is clearly not being used in any sense of extreme physical separation.[5]

A further rationale for the false-apostles view is the closeness in language between 2 Cor. 6.14–7.1 and the descriptions of the false apostles in 2 Cor. 11.2-4, 13-15. Like the ἄπιστοι in 6.14a, the false apostles of chapters 10–13 were associated with Satan and not Christ,[6] they disguised themselves with a false righteousness and light,[7] and they led the Corinthians' devotion away from Christ and Paul.[8] From Dahl's perspective, what is suggested by 6.14–7.1 is made plain in the subsequent chapters: 'to join the false apostles in their opposition to Paul would mean to side with Satan/Belial in his opposition to Christ'.[9]

While the shared language between the fragment and 2 Cor. 11.2-4, 13-15 favors the false-apostles position, there are several indications that this argument falls short of its intended goal. First, the shared imagery says *for certain* only that Paul felt the same way about the false apostles as he did about improper associations (i.e., covenant-violating, idolatrous associations) with ἄπιστοι. It does not automatically equate the false apostles and the ἄπιστοι (that is quite a different matter). Second, since the description of the false apostles in 11.2-4, 13-15 comes five chapters *after* 6.14–7.1, it is unlikely that the readers of the letter (at least in its canonical order)

---

1. 1 Cor. 6.18-20; 8.10; 10.14-22 (cf. 1 Thess. 5.1-10; Eph. 5.7-14).
2. Even if the Isa. 52.11 quotation is taken literally, it simply describes the return of the people of Israel from Babylon to the homeland to form a separate worship community. There is no hint of complete withdrawal from casual or social contact within the OT text (and that is certainly not what happened historically in the case of returning Jews).
3. See Appendix B on the nature of the 'unequal yoke'.
4. See Chapter 3, §2.
5. For an extensive treatment of these traditions see Chapter 3, §2. Cf. a similar new exodus call in Rev. 18.4a, 'Come out of her [i.e., from Babylon]'. As in the fragment, the point is not complete physical separation but a selective separation by which the reader 'may not participate in her sins' (Rev. 18.4b).
6. 2 Cor. 11.14. Cf. Βελιάρ [// Σατᾶνας] in 6.15.
7. 2 Cor. 11.14-15. Cf. δικαιοσύνη and φῶς in 6.14.
8. 2 Cor. 11.2-4. Cf. the counter-affections to the apostle in 6.11-13.
9. Dahl, 'A Fragment and Its Context', p. 69. Cf. Collange, *Énigmes*, p. 307.

understood the ἄπιστοι referent in this manner. Thrall rightly points out that the description of Paul's opponents in 2.14–7.4 is mild compared with chs. 10–13 and 'is a far cry from regarding the people in question as heathen idolaters, children of darkness, and the like'.[1] Third, from a methodological standpoint the closeness in language between the fragment and 2 Cor. 4.3-6 should take precedence over that of 11.2-4, 13-15, since it lies within the same literary unit of 2.14–7.4 and actually uses the term ἄπιστοι. In 2 Cor. 4.3-6, 'the god of this world (Satan)' is opposed to Christ and his glory; unbelievers are blinded to the light of the gospel; believers by implication are not in darkness but have God's creation-light within their hearts. Also, the material in 4.3-6 is tied into the discussion of new covenant and return promises,[2] as is the fragment. In addition, ἄπιστοι is explicitly used in 2 Cor. 4.4 as in 6.14a; it is not found in 2 Cor. 11.2-4, 13-15. If it can be established that ἄπιστοι in 2 Cor. 4.4 does *not* refer to the false apostles (see discussion below), then the close imagery with 11.2-4, 13-15 is of less consequence.

A final ground of support for the false-apostles theory comes from the polemical statements scattered throughout 2.14–7.4 and aimed at Paul's opponents.[3] For example, within 2.14–7.4 one finds references to opponents who peddle an adulterated gospel (2.17), have entered the community through letters of commendation (3.1), preach themselves (4.5), and take pride in appearance, not in the heart (5.12). This contextual response to rival suitors adds significant weight to the false-apostles theory.

Though they make the false-apostles referent more attractive, the polemical statements in 2.14–7.4 do not provide the decisive evidence needed to carry the theory. Several drawbacks may be seen. First, the closest polemic against Paul's 'opponents' occurs in 2 Cor. 5.12, some 23 verses before 6.14a.[4] Second, the suffering list preceding the fragment in 6.3-10 includes opposition to Paul's ministry encountered well beyond the circumstances at Corinth. To narrow its function to a polemic against Paul's immediate opponents is problematic.[5] Third, the fragment may have an *indirect* relationship to Paul's opponents without taking the ἄπιστοι to refer to the false apostles. The false apostles probably argued that the replacement of the Mosaic law with a law 'written on the heart' by the Spirit would only lead to lawless behavior. Consequently, if the fragment were intended to counter the Corinthians' lawless behavior, it would also *indirectly* address the charges of these Judaizers.[6] If this is so, then the mere presence of scattered polemical statements

1. So Thrall, 'The Problem of II Cor. VI.14–VII.1', p. 144.

2. See Chapter 4, §4.

3. See Olshausen, *Epistles to the Corinthians*, p. 330; Dahl, 'A Fragment and Its Context', p. 67; Rensberger, '2 Corinthians 6.14–7.1', pp. 30, 42.

4. Most advocates of the false-apostles view agree that 2 Cor. 5.12 is the closest unambiguous reference to Paul's opponents.

5. See Fitzgerald ('Cracks in an Earthen Vessel', pp. 333-59) who refutes Collange's direct apologetic approach (*Énigmes*, pp. 298-300) to the suffering catalogue in 6.3-10.

6. Another possibility of indirect contact with Paul's opponents may be suggested. The charges against Paul for breaking his travel promises led to an attack on the very core of his promise theology (2 Cor. 1.17-22). The opponents likely exploited both angles. As a result of waning belief

throughout 2.14–7.4 does not ensure a false-apostles referent in 6.14a. In fact, the subdued nature of the polemic in 2.14–7.4 favors this indirect approach, rather than the direct confrontation scenario suggested by the false-apostles view.

Major Problems with the False-Apostles View

While the supportive evidence establishes the false-apostles view as a credible option, a number of problems undermine its viability. First, such an interpretation has little choice but to take the 'idols' (εἰδώλων) in 6.16 in a non-literal, metaphorical sense.[1] This might not seem a problem at first, since the contrasting 'temple of God' (ναῷ θεοῦ/ναὸς θεοῦ) in 6.16 is itself a non-literal reference to the church. In fact, proponents of the false-apostles position argue for the non-literal use of εἰδώλων in 6.16 on the basis of the spiritual 'temple of God' counterpart.[2] However, such logic is faulty, since the one need not imply the other. For instance, in 1 Cor. 6.19 spiritual temple imagery is used to counter literal sexual immorality with literal prostitutes (not spiritual harlotry). So the figurative temple imagery here is not determinative.

On the other hand, several pieces of data strongly suggest that the 'idols' should be understood in a literal sense. For one, the contrastive appellation 'living God' versus '(dead) idols' has an idiomatic use in relation to literal (not figurative) idols. In every occurrence of the living God/idols contrast in the Old Testament,[3] intertestamental literature,[4] and in the New Testament (only in Paul and Luke)[5] the reference is always to *literal* idols. For Paul, the God/idols dualism marks the coming out of paganism (and its related idol worship) and turning to the living God of Christianity.[6] The very nature of the contrast between the 'living God' and '(dead/lifeless) idols' of wood and stone forces the contrast to operate on a physical level. Furthermore, in the few instances where Paul speaks of idolatry in a metaphorical sense he makes a brief parenthetical statement to clarify that literal idols are not in view.[7] Of the remaining twenty occurrences of some form of εἴδολ- in

---

in Paul's personal promises, his promise theology likewise suffered. Some Corinthians sided with the false apostles, while others (disillusioned with Paul) began to drift back into paganism. In an effort to correct the Corinthian movement back to paganism, Paul reminds his reader of the relevance of God's (new covenant) promises related to breaking from their former pagan practices. However, in so doing he indirectly counters his opponents' attack on his promise theology.

1. The false-apostles view must take the 'idols' (6.16) in a purely figurative or spiritual sense, since the Jewish opponents would not have been involved any kind of worship to literal idols.

2. E.g., Olshausen, *Epistles to the Corinthians*, p. 329; Grosheide, *Tweede Brief ann de Kerk te Korinthe*, p. 191; cf. Rensberger ('2 Corinthians 6.14–7.1', p. 42) who sees the idolatry as 'only a part of an extended simile'.

3. For living God versus idols/false gods dualism see Jer. 10.8-10; 2 Kgs 19.4, 16 (cf. 18.33-35; 19.12, 18); Isa. 37.17 (cf. 37.12, 19).

4. E.g., Bel 5, 6, 24, 25; *Jos. Asen.* 8.5-6 (living God versus dead and dumb idols); 11.9-10; 19.5-8.

5. E.g., 1 Thess. 1.9; cf. Acts 14.12-15. Note also the less explicit contrast between the temple of the living God ideology and 'idols' in Acts 17.16.

6. E.g., 1 Thess. 1.9; cf. 1 Cor. 12.2.

7. E.g., 'greed, which is idolatry' (Col. 3.5; cf. Eph. 5.5).

Paul, sixteen of which are found in 1 Corinthians,[1] all refer to literal idols. In summary, the living God/idols contrast, the lack of any parenthetical statement, and the predominant problem with literal idolatry at Corinth, favor literal idols in the fragment (at least as it is being read within its present context of Corinthian correspondence).

Second, even if one takes the 'idols' in 6.16 in a non-literal sense, the association of idol imagery with Jewish false-apostles is problematic. What common element or shared association is there between idols and Jewish false teachers? None. Or, if there is, it is not apparent (as the association between the believing community and God's temple is apparent). Yet, in order to make the rhetorical contrasts work there has to be a *strong affinity* between the contrastive elements and their respective referents.[2] The Jewish opponents, who took great pride in their heritage, would have abhored idols (the sentiments of the Jewish community at large[3]). On the other hand, a 'pagans' referent has a greater affinity with 'idols' (literal or otherwise) due to their active association with such.[4]

Third, the parallel imperative 'touch not the unclean thing (ἀκαθάρτου μὴ ἅπτεσθε)' relates better to separation from the worship of pagan gods than to separation from false apostles. In the original context of Isa. 52.11-12, Westermann observes that this exhortation towards separation from all that is unclean should be taken to mean: 'the final and complete severance from the unclean land of *foreign gods*'.[5] 'Touch not the unclean thing' stands in contrast to carrying the holy temple vessels back to Jerusalem; the new exodus journey to worship Yahweh in Jerusalem meant a break from the pagan gods of Babylon. Such an Old Testament literary background transfers naturally to a prohibition against the worship of pagan gods at Corinth. Only in an awkward sense can it be applied to Paul's opponents, themselves worshipers of Yahweh.

Fourth, Paul's normal referent use of ἄπιστοι runs counter to the false-apostles view.[6] The defining sense of the word is not the issue (since the sense could be 'unbelievers' while the referent be the false apostles[7]). However, what is important

---

1. 1 Cor. 5.10, 11; 6.9; 8.1, 4 (twice), 7 (twice), 10 (twice); 10.7 (twice), 14, 19, 28; 12.2. Notice especially the implied contrast 1 Cor. 12.2 between 'dumb idols' and the 'God (who speaks)'.

2. For an example drawn from American politics, a similar contrasting series of rhetorical questions might go as follows: 'How can one yoke together an elephant and a donkey? Who would think of washing white collars together with blue? What does a conservative have in common with a liberal?' Again, in order to make the rhetorical contrasts work there has to be a *strong affinity* between the contrastive elements and their respective referents (i.e., Republicans and Democrats).

3. E.g., Acts 15.19-20, 29; Rom. 2.22.

4. Particularly significant is the statement by Paul which links the Corinthians' former pagan identity with idols: 'You know that when you were pagans (ἔθνη), you were led astray to the dumb idols (εἴδωλα)' (1 Cor 12.2).

5. Westermann, *Isaiah 40-66*, p. 253 (my emphasis).

6. Murphy-O'Connor ('Relating 2 Corinthians 6.14–7.1 to Its Context', pp. 272-73) develops this point well.

7. Rensberger ('2 Corinthians 6.14–7.1', p. 30) correctly argues that 'those who reject the Gospel of Christ and the Apostle of Christ belong in the category of "unbelievers" whether nominally Christians or not'. Cf. Collange, *Énigmes*, p. 133; Dahl, 'A Fragment and Its Context',

is that within Corinthian correspondence the ἄπιστοι referent is consistently used of a group outside the church (i.e., pagans or heathen).[1] To adopt the false-apostles view, one must accept that the fragment departs from Paul's normal referent use within his writings to the Corinthians (and the rest of his epistles for that matter). This is not impossible, but certainly a major drawback of the view.[2]

Fifth, a false-apostles referent with ἄπιστοι in 2 Cor. 4.4 cannot be sustained. Rensberger, for example, argues that the ἄπιστοι in 2 Cor. 4.4 refers to the false apostles based on the polemical statements against Paul's opponents in 4.2 (cf. 3.1).[3] One should not minimize the polemical statements, nor suggest that the opponents were somehow enlightened to Paul's gospel. However, there is strong evidence that the ἄπιστοι refers to a larger group of non-Christian pagans, not false apostles. In the immediate context, those veiled to the gospel are all who have not 'turned to the Lord' (3.16) in conversion, the act by which the veil is removed. So the more probable ἄπιστοι reference is to those who have not in any way (even in a way regarded by Paul as defective) converted to Christianity.[4] Even more decisive, however, is the alignment of 'the unbelieving' (τῶν ἀπίστων, 4.4) with 'those who are perishing' (τοῖς ἀπολλυμένοις, 4.3),[5] for Paul has already defined 'those who are perishing' by its contrast in 2 Cor. 2.15-16 with 'those who are being saved' (ἐν τοῖς σῳζομένοις).[6] This division (those perishing versus those being saved), known also to the Corinthians from 1 Cor. 1.18, classifies humankind (both Jew and Gentile) in broad terms on the basis of their response to Paul's preaching of the cross. Consequently, it is far more plausible to take the ἄπιστοι in 2 Cor. 4.4 to refer to non-Christians generally (either Jew or Gentile to whom Paul preached) who have not turned to the Lord.

Sixth, the fragment's intense dualism is not suited to the restrictive subcategories required by the false-apostles theory. The polarized extremes (light/darkness, Christ/Beliar, believer/unbeliever, etc.) divide all humankind into two groups, without any careful division of unbelievers into subgroups. This leaves little middle ground for some kind of quasi-Christian category.[7] More importantly, by creating a very narrow subcategory of non-Christians, the false-apostles view creates an

p. 66. Over this there is no dispute. However, the real question is whether this is Paul's *normal* referent use of the term.

1. See above discussion of ἄπιστοι related to view three.

2. Thrall ('The Problem of II Cor. VI.14–VII.1', p. 143) also points out that the absence of ἄπιστοι in 2 Cor. 10–13 is rather surprising had it been one of Paul's ways of characterizing the false apostles.

3. Rensberger, '2 Corinthians 6.14–7.1', p. 30; cf. Collange, *Énigmes*, p. 100.

4. Thrall, 'Conversion to the Lord', p. 204.

5. The ἐν οἷς at the beginning of 4.4 essentially reiterates the ἐν τοῖς in 4.3 (ἐν τοῖς ἀπολλυμένοις), indicating that the discussion to follow is about these same people 'who are perishing'. Therefore, 'the unbelieving' and 'those who are perishing' are being used interchangeably.

6. Cf. Murphy-O'Connor, 'Relating 2 Corinthians 6.14–7.1 to Its Context', p. 273.

7. This may be intentional overstatement. However, such a harsh polemic would require far more preparatory character development in 2.14–7.4 to provide the reader with the hint that this is where the false apostles truly belong.

imbalance in the contrastive groupings—a general encompassing category of 'all Christians' (πιστοί) versus a specialized subcategory of 'some non-Christians' (ἄπιστοι).

Seventh, the false-apostles view has considerable difficulty with the closing exhortation in 2 Cor. 7.1 towards personal purity and holiness. Rensberger, for instance, admits that the exhortation in 7.1 to ethical purification is irrelevant to the problem of Paul's opponents.[1] He handles the problem by suggesting that 7.1 had its 'origin in the re-used exhortation (in the original fragment)'.[2] However, this amounts to little more than a sidestepping of the problem. Such a proposal must acknowledge a rather sloppy integration of source material (which would not be consistent with the careful source work in the catena).[3]

Eighth, the 'directional flow' of the Old Testament imperatives (along with the spatial aspect of μέσου) argues against the false-apostles theory. In the second quotation the exhortation is for the Corinthians to 'come out from among them (ἐξέλθατε ἐκ μέσου αὐτῶν)'. As Rensberger is aware,[4] this imperative goes directly back to 6.14a and so reiterates the thrust of the entire fragment. However, ἐξέλθατε ἐκ μέσου αὐτῶν is ill suited to the idea of the Corinthians 'coming out' from among a handful of false apostles. For one, the use of μέσου portrays the church in the midst of another entity which is surrounding it (i.e., it is in the 'middle' of something else).[5] However, the false opponents are in the midst of the church, not the church in the midst of the false apostles. Also, the directional flow of ἐξέλθατε requires the church to 'come out from' the false apostles, rather than the more conceptually appropriate call for the church to 'expel' these individuals from their midst. One would expect something more like: ἐξάρατε τοὺς πονηροὺς ἐξ ὑμῶν αὐτῶν.[6] On the other hand, ἐξέλθατε ἐκ μέσου αὐτῶν is naturally suited to the idea of 'coming out' from among a larger entity surrounding the Corinthian church, namely, paganism.

Finally, the false-apostles theory conflicts with the Old Testament referents within the catena which correspond to ἄπιστοι. In the second quotation the corresponding Old Testament referent is Babylon: ἐξέλθατε ἐκ μέσου αὐτῆς (ἐκ Βαβυλῶνος);[7] in the third quotation the referent, supplied from its Old Testament context, is the heathen lands and nations: καὶ εἰσδέξομαι ὑμᾶς (ἐκ τῶν χωρῶν/ἐκ τῶν λαῶν).[8] Blending these two quotations the point is evidently a call to come out from among

1. Rensberger, '2 Corinthians 6.14–7.1', p. 41.
2. Rensberger, '2 Corinthians 6.14–7.1', p. 41.
3. See Chapter 3, §2.
4. Rensberger, '2 Corinthians 6.14–7.1', p. 36.
5. E.g., compare the use of μέσος in Acts 17.33.
6. E.g., 1 Cor. 5.13 (cf. 1 Cor. 5.2 and Deut. 13.5; 17.7, 12; 21.21; 22.21). This OT prescription applied to a variety of cases, one of which was for the removal of *false teachers who came with signs and wonders* (Deut. 13.1-5; cf. 2 Cor. 12.12)! Cf. Allo, *Seconde Épître aux Corinthiens*, p. 186; Thrall, 'The Problem of II Cor. VI. 14–VII. 1', p. 144; Fee, 'Food Offered to Idols', p. 160.
7. LXX Isa. 52.11.
8. LXX Ezek. 20.34.

the Gentile/heathen nations—not a particularly good analogy for Christians to come out from among *Jewish* false apostles. On the other hand, these Old Testament referents effortlessly match with the heathen peoples of Corinth, the pagan idolaters.

Minor Problems with the False-Apostles View

In comparison to the difficulties mentioned above, there exist several minor problems with the false-apostles view. These are less decisive factors, but nonetheless problems which detract from the feasibility of the theory. First, the false-apostles theory plays down the fifth rhetorical contrast (temple of God versus idols) in order to turn the focus away from 'idols'. Rensberger effectively minimizes the fifth dualism in two ways. One way is by relegating the fifth contrast to an 'appendix' or an 'apparent superfluity' and suggesting that the fourth contrast is the real climax since it relates back to the ἄπιστοι of 6.14a.[1] While there is no question about the ἄπιστοι-ἄπιστος link with 6.14a, that alone is not enough to justify its being the climax of the series. It is more likely that the last contrast is the climactic one.[2] Furthermore, this final contrast is the one which is developed through all that follows: the explicative statement (ἡμεῖς γὰρ ναὸς θεοῦ ἐσμεν...), the Old Testament catena with its new temple imagery (leaving idolatrous Babylon and coming to worship in Jerusalem as sons and daughters of Zion), and the final exhortation in 7.1 with its cultic terminology.

Rensberger also minimizes the final contrast by assigning it to part of the pre-existing material from which the fragment was constructed.[3] However, one wonders why the final editor, possibly Paul (according to Dahl and Rensberger), did not simply remove this final contrast. Certainly, the editor felt free enough to modify the Old Testament catena to adapt it to the 6.14a exhortation. Why, then, would he be any less free and adaptive with reshaping other sources?

Finally, unless used in a tongue-in-cheek fashion, ἀνομία is not a good caricature of false apostles who hold tenaciously to the Mosaic law. The term and its cognates are often used to describe the non-Jewish 'heathen'.[4] On the basis of ἀνομία, Schlatter aptly notes that the fragment is not aimed at the Judaizers; the Corinthians were vulnerable here to lawlessness, not legalism.[5]

6. ἄπιστοι *as Non-Christians, Pagans Outside of the Church Community*

A fifth view, which has been predominant throughout the history of interpretation,[6] is that the ἄπιστοι are non-Christians in general, that is, pagans outside the church

---

1. Rensberger, '2 Corinthians 6.14–7.1', p. 34.
2. Fee, 'Food Offered to Idols', p. 158.
3. Rensberger, '2 Corinthians 6.14–7.1', pp. 34, 38.
4. Cf. the use of ἄνομος in Acts 2.23; 1 Cor. 9.21.
5. Schlatter, *Briefe an die Korinther*, p. 580.
6. A sampling of 20th century proponents includes Plummer, *Second Epistle to the Corinthians*, pp. 202-13; Windisch, *Der zweite Korintherbrief*, pp. 211-20; Allo, *Seconde Épître aux Corinthiens*, pp. 181-93; Hughes, *Second Epistle to the Corinthians*, pp. 241-60; Bruce, *1 and 2 Corinthians*, pp. 213-16; Thrall, 'The Problem of II Cor. VI. 14–VII. 1', pp. 132-48; Fee, 'Food

community. The major difficulties with a non-Christians referent are twofold: it seems to leave an abrupt contextual transition in the text[1] and creates a tension within Paul's theology of separation from non-Christians. While not wishing to minimize these problems, they are not as formidable as they may have once appeared. My traditions hypothesis addresses the first concern, while my development of a 'selective separation' theology within Corinthian correspondence deals with the second.[2]

On the other hand, the non-Christians (pagans) theory has much to commend it. It would be pointless to reiterate all the argumentation for this view, since the evidence has been dealt with when evaluating the other views. Instead, I will simply summarize the points that have surfaced in the preceding material. First, the most probable referent of εἰδώλων in 6.16, as read within Corinthian correspondence, is to literal (not metaphorical) idols. This literal-idols referent is well-suited to the pagan cultural context of Corinth, where Paul repeatedly addressed their (literal) idol-worship background. The dominant interpretive role of this 'idols' datum is suggested by its climactic positioning in the sequence. Second, the lexical referent of ἄπιστοι within the Corinthian letters[3] (and Pauline material in general) is consistently to 'outsiders', non-Christians beyond the church community. Third, the strong conceptual affinity between pagans and idols sufficiently carries the argument of the terse rhetorical contrasts in 6.14b-16a (unlike other theories). Each one of these cryptic elements (lawlessness, darkness, Beliar, and idols)[4] holds an associative relationship, from a Pauline (and New Testament) perspective, with pagans who worship false gods. Fourth, the traditions found in the Old Testament catena favor a pagans background in a number of ways. For instance, the Old Testament referents of 'Babylon' in quotation 2 and the 'heathen nations' in quotation 3 are most easily identified with non-Christians broadly, that is, all peoples beyond the covenant people of God. Also, in its Old Testament context ἀκαθάρτου μὴ ἅπτεσθε calls for separation from foreign gods, which corresponds with the practice of cult religions at Corinth. In addition, the 'directional flow' of ἐξέλθατε ἐκ μέσου αὐτῶν (and the spatial sense of μέσου) portrays the Christian community in some way 'leaving'[5] a larger group, which would most naturally be the larger society of Corinth. Fifth, the intense

---

Offered to Idols', pp. 140-61; Furnish, *II Corinthians*, pp. 359-83; Martin, *2 Corinthians*, pp. 189-212.

1. So Rensberger, '2 Corinthians 6.14–7.1', p. 30. Cf. Allo (*Seconde Épître aux Corinthiens*, p. 189) who summarizes the concern of many exegetes when he says, 'Dans le contexte, il n'est question de paganisme ni avant ni après'.

2. Furthermore, my contextual hypothesis is not dependent upon the referent preference suggested in this essay. On the problem of contextual integration, see Chapters 3–6. On the seeming contradiction in Paul's theology of separation, see the above rebuttal to views three (§4) and four (§5). Also, see Appendix B on the nature of the separation.

3. Particularly significant is the text of 2 Cor. 4.4 (with its similar themes to the fragment), where ἄπιστοι most probably refers to non-Christians in general. Cf. ἀπίστου in the 6.15b and the believer/unbeliever dualism.

4. This affinity is especially the case with ἀνομία and εἰδώλων.

5. For the specific nature of the 'leaving', see Appendix B.

dualism of the fragment (righteousness/lawlessness, light/darkness, Christ/Beliar, believer/unbeliever, and God's temple/idols) effectively eliminates any middle ground or subcategories of unbeliever. The composer of the fragment does not paint with intermediate shades or fine brush strokes; rather, all humankind is portrayed in one of two extreme camps. Only if a chain of rhetorical contrasts had not followed the initial exhortation (and the opening exhortation stood alone), would a more specialized definition of the ἄπιστοι be feasible.[1]

7. *Conclusion*

In an attempt to 'try out' my contextual theory on the crux interpretive issue, the objective of this essay has been to reevaluate who the 'unbelievers' are in 2 Cor. 6.14a. The evidence weighs heavily against taking the ἄπιστοι as referring to either untrustworthy persons (Paul as trustworthy), Gentile Christians who do not keep the Torah, or the immoral within the church community. These three options are improbable solutions.

The fourth and fifth options, however, are more plausible. While the false-apostles view smooths out the contextual transition and resolves a tension in Pauline theology, it struggles with the relevance of much of the material within the fragment. Though contextually problematic, the non-Christians (pagans) view integrates the material in the fragment with ease. Therefore, if a suitable contextual theory can be found, the evidence favors understanding the 'unbelievers' as referring to non-Christians outside the church community.

---

1. One might add that the ongoing problem at Corinth of ἀκαθαρσία, πορνεία, and ἀσέλεια (as evident from 2 Cor. 12:21) indicates that the issues discussed in 1 Corinthians (many of them relating to the Christian's relationship to the former pagan activities) have not been resolved between the Corinthians and the apostle.

Appendix B

1. *Introduction*

My objective in these two appendixes has been to apply the contextual hypothesis to the crux interpretive issue in 2 Cor. 6.14a. In Appendix A I reevaluated the identity of the 'unbelievers' in 6.14a, since it makes little sense to discuss the 'unequal yoke' without some assessment of who the 'unbelievers' are. The conclusion (by no means a simple one) was that ἄπιστοι refers to non-Christians/pagans outside the Corinthian church, particularly in light of insights derived from my traditions research. Having arrived at this tentative favorite for the 'unbelievers', the next step is to ask, 'What is the "unequal yoke" (ἑτεροζυγοῦντες) which the fragment prohibits?'

Once again, the issue is primarily one of referent, not sense. Almost all commentators are agreed that ἑτεροζυγέω conveys the idea of 'yoking/joining together' two different kinds of animals (e.g., an ox and a donkey) and that the background imagery probably comes from instructions about mixing different kinds (Lev. 19.19 and Deut. 22.10 for example). However, the difficulty lies in knowing what sort of 'joining together' activities are conveyed by the fragment as it speaks to the Corinthians within its current literary setting.

To highlight the interpretive confusion, at least twelve options have been proposed as activity referents for μὴ γίνεσθε ἑτεροζυγοῦντες/ἐξέλθατε:[1] (1) complete Qumran-like separation, with minimal social contact; (2) literal-physical idolatry; (3) metonymical idolatry; (4) metaphorical idolatry; (5) going to pagan courts; (6) visiting (temple) prostitutes; (7) mixed marriages; (8) eating meat offered to idols at pagan temples; (9) eating meat offered to idols at pagan homes; (10) speaking in tongues when unbelievers are present; (11) business partnerships, and (12) membership in a local pagan cult. I arrange the twelve options in this order is for a particular purpose. The first option is a watershed in relation to whether the separation called for is either complete (option 1) or partial/selective (options 2-12). The next three possibilities relating to idolatry (options 2-4) set the general parameters within which the remaining eight specific cases fall (options 5-12). Options 5-10 have their origin

---

1. The focus of the referent issue lies with μὴ γίνεσθε ἑτεροζυγοῦντες (6.14a) and its restatement within the OT catena as ἐξέλθατε . . . (6.17a).

in 1 Corinthians, and options 11 and 12 are based on data beyond the specifics of Pauline material. A flow chart for the options may be drawn up.

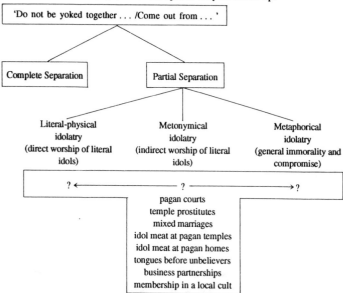

Methodologically, four observations will govern the course of this investigation. First, the clearest available data for understanding ἑτεροζυγοῦντες comes from the synonyms which follow in the series of rhetorical contrasts (μετοχή, κοινωνία, συμφώνησις, μερίς, and συγκατάθεσις) and the two covenant formulas within the Old Testament catena. On this basis alone the prohibitions do not appear to be against casual contact, but against forming covenant-like relationships with pagans which in turn violate a Christian's existing covenant with God. Second, the opposite to the *negative* prohibition μὴ γίνεσθε ἑτεροζυγοῦντες ἀπίστοις is the *positive* exhortation ἐξέλθατε ἐκ μέσου αὐτῶν (which has been rearranged and altered in wording from its Old Testament source in order to correspond to 6.14a). Third, the last rhetorical contrast is climactic (forming the basis for the Old Testament material that follows) and heavily influences the interpretation of the whole fragment. Fourth, the exhortation in 7.1 broadens the 6.14a activity referent to παντὸς μολυσμοῦ σαρκὸς καὶ πνεύματος; however, this is not to say that the two are completely synonymous (6.14a is a much restricted sub-category of 7.1).

2. Complete Qumran-like Separation with
Minimal Social Interaction

Though this view predates the discovery of the Dead Sea Scrolls, it has become increasingly popular in the wake of Qumran literature to understand μὴ γίνεσθε ἑτεροζυγοῦντες/ἐξέλθατε as a call for complete (Qumran-like) separation.[1] While the strict-separation view is possible, it is hardly persuasive for the following reasons. First, the view usually involves some kind of interpolation into the text, which raises inherent problems.[2] Second, the seemingly harsh attitude of the fragment towards relationships with unbelieving outsiders is still compatible with Paul's theology of 'selective separation' as expressed elsewhere.[3] Since the fragment's call for separation is different in purpose and nature than 1 Cor. 5.9-11,[4] one does not have to appeal to a Qumran-like understanding of the material. Furthermore, the fragment functions within its present literary context as part of a much broader pattern of a second exodus and exilic return, which itself speaks to the Corinthians about 'leaving Babylon and coming home'.[5] If my traditions analysis is valid, then the fragment's Old Testament material should be understood within this same theological continuum. It is being used as a paradigm for spiritual return/restoration to God, not a call for extreme community isolation. Finally, the strong covenant language (with two explicit covenant formulas) suggests that much more than casual contact is at stake. In view of these factors, strict social separation is not a persuasive option for understanding the material in its present setting.

3. Literal-physical Idolatry, Metonymical Idolatry,
or Metaphorical Idolatry?

Most commentators agree that the mention of 'idols' versus the 'temple of God' in 6.16 implies an activity referent which includes some kind of idolatrous worship. The debate focuses on exactly what kind of idolatry:[6] (1) literal-physical idolatry—direct worship/bowing down to literal idols; (2) metonymical idolatry—indirect worship of literal idols through related activities at pagan temples, or (3) metaphorical idolatry—general immorality and compromise with no literal idols in view. The key distinction between these alternatives is that the first two activity referents involve *literal* idols, the third does not.

---

1. E.g., Fitzmyer, Interpolated Paragraph', p. 278; Georgi, *Opponents of Paul in Second Corinthians*, p. 12; Gnilka, '2 Cor. 6.14–7.1', p. 63; Klinzing, *Kultus in der Qumrangemeinde und im Neuen Testament*, p. 172; Klauck, *2 Korintherbrief*, p. 60. Also, for an interesting look at the influence of 2 Cor. 6.14–7.1 in Hutterite and Mennonite communities, see Holland, *Hermeneutics of Peter Riedeman*, pp. 47-62.

2. See Chapter 6, §2.

3. See Appendix A, §5.

4. See Appendix A, §4.

5. See Chapters 4 and 5.

6. Proponents of these three positions will be given under the specific cases to follow.

As developed in the former essay,[1] there is compelling evidence for understanding εἰδώλων as a reference to literal idols (the living God/idols contrast, the lack of any parenthetical statement to clarify metaphorical intent, and the predominant problem with literal idolatry at Corinth). A literal 'idols' referent in 6.16 suggests the viability of *only* those cases which fall into the categories of either (1) literal-physical idolatry, or (2) metonymical idolatry. This criterion will be used to evaluate the particular cases which follow.

4. *Taking Grievances before Pagan Courts (1 Cor. 6.1-11)*

A number of commentators hold that μὴ γίνεσθε ἑτεροζυγοῦντες/ἐξέλθατε includes the activity of believers taking their grievances before pagan courts (1 Cor. 6.1-11).[2] Paul does refer to judges in the pagan courts as ἄπιστοι (1 Cor. 6.6), so 1 Cor. 6.1-11 describes a situation which requires selective separation from unbelievers. However, for several reasons this is almost certainly not a suitable activity referent for ἑτεροζυγοῦντες/ἐξέλθατε. First, the rationale for avoiding pagan courts is not for protecting one's personal purity (as is the issue in the fragment), but the eschatological absurdity of taking cases before pagan judges if believers will one day judge the world. Second, the interaction between a pagan judge and those involved in a law suit can hardly be described as a covenant forming relationship or as a radical violation to a believer's covenant with God. All that the action indicates is that a believer is eschatologically ignorant and/or unwilling to suffer personal loss. The issue does not question the Corinthians' salvation, whereas there is at least a hint of this in the fragment and 2 Cor. 6.1-2. Also, nothing is said in 1 Cor. 6.1-11 about going to court in the case of believer versus unbeliever (as either litigant or defendant); the issue revolves around two believers going before a pagan judge. Presumably, a pagan court would be the appropriate place to resolve a law suit between believer and unbeliever (if an out-of-court settlement could not be reached), especially in the case of a believer being taken to court by an unbeliever.[3] Third, a 'pagan courts' activity referent assumes a purely metaphorical understanding of the idolatry taking place (not a likely option).[4]

---

1. See Appendix A, §5.
2. E.g., Carrez, *Deuxième Épître aux Corinthiens*, p. 165; Martin, *2 Corinthians*, p. 189; Harris, '2 Corinthians', p. 359; Barrett, *Second Epistle to the Corinthians*, p. 196; Corriveau, *Liturgy of Life*, p. 39; Schlatter, *Paulus Der Bote Jesus*, p. 578; Hughes, *Second Epistle to the Corinthians*, p. 245.
3. Surely Paul would not expect an unbeliever to go before an ecclesiastical court (either as litigant or defendant). On the other hand, if a believer was taken to court by an unbeliever, he/she would be morally obligated to go.
4. Even if one allows for the unlikely category of metaphorical idolatry, it is hard to understand why going before a pagan judge would be 'compared to' idolatry.

5. *Sexual Immorality, Visiting (Temple) Prostitutes*
(1 Cor. 6.12-20)

Another activity referent which is often suggested for ἑτεροζυγοῦντες/ἐξέλθατε is the problem at Corinth of visiting prostitutes (1 Cor. 6.12-20).[1] If in 1 Cor. 6.12-20[2] Paul has in mind *at least in part* visiting prostitutes at pagan temples and engaging in sexual acts with temple priestesses,[3] then there is good reason to include this kind of sacred temple prostitution within the prohibition of the fragment. First (and most importantly), temple prostitution clearly qualifies as metonymical idolatry. Because as the sexual act would join the believer in a covenant-like bond with the temple prostitute (cf. 1 Cor. 6.16-17), it would also be a means of uniting the worshiper and the god or goddess of the temple (represented in turn by idols). Second, the use of ἀκάθαρτος as it bears on the activity in the fragment (2 Cor. 6.17), certainly allows for sexual immorality. The noun form, ἀκαθαρσία, is frequently used by Paul for immorality in general and especially of sexual immorality.[4] Third, though the imagery may be slightly different, the emphasis on a community (2 Cor. 6.14–7.1) and individual (1 Cor. 6.12-20) 'temple of God' unites the passages through their common concern for purity.

On the other hand, the case of general prostitution that had no connection with the cultic rites of pagan gods (likewise covered by 1 Cor. 6.12-20), should not be included in the activity referent of 2 Cor. 6.14a. The final climactic contrast reveals that the heart of the problem addressed by the fragment was idolatrous worship. If this is so, then visiting prostitutes on the streets of Corinth would not be in view; only temple prostitution would be prohibited by the fragment (as it is read within the Corinthian correspondence).

---

1. E.g., Murphy-O'Connor, 'Philo and 2 Cor 6.14–7.1', p. 68; Kruse, *Second Epistle to the Corinthians*, p. 139; Barrett, *Second Epistle to the Corinthians*, p. 196; Schmithals, *Gnosticism in Corinth*, p. 95; Schlatter, *Paulus Der Bote Jesus*, p. 578; Baudraz, *Épître aux Corinthiens*, p. 169; Strachan, *Second Epistle to the Corinthians*, p. 5.

2. In 1 Cor. 10.7-8 the background of Exod. 32.6 and Num. 25.1-2 seems to have sexual activity related to the worship of false gods (Fee, 'Food Offered to Idols', p. 159).

3. That 1 Cor. 6.12-20 was written *at least in part* as a response to temple prostitution is probable since (1) visiting temple prostitutes functions as a subcategory of visiting prostitutes; (2) the passage responds to the sin as being against God's 'temple' (perhaps a deliberate counter to the pagan temples); (3) the passage places heavy emphasis on cultic defilement and holiness (6.18-19; cf. 3.17), and possibly (4) 1 Cor. 6.18 and 10.20 give similarly stated injunctions to flee immorality/idolatry. Though the presence of temple prostitutes has often been overplayed (and the distinction between 'Old Corinth' and 'New Corinth' needs to be maintained in discussions of the Aphrodite temple), temple prostitution was probably practiced to some extent in the era of New Corinth. For further discussion see Conzelmann, *First Epistle to the Corinthians*, pp. 11-12; Fee, *First Epistle to the Corinthians*, pp. 2-3.

4. E.g., Rom. 1.24; 2 Cor. 12.21; Gal. 5.19; Col. 3.5; cf. Eph. 5.3; 1 Thess. 4.7. For an intriguing parallel note the use of ἀκαθάρτης in the picture of the harlot (Rev. 17.4-18) and the subsequent call to 'come out of her (Babylon)' (Rev. 18.4). Also, the verbal idea of 'touching' (ἀκαθάρτου μὴ ἅπτεσθε) might have been taken euphemistically for sexual intercourse (cf. μὴ ἅπτεσθαι in 1 Cor. 7.1).

6. *Mixed Marriages (1 Cor. 7.12-15, 39)*

Probably the most popular view is that μὴ γίνεσθε ἐτεροζυγοῦντες refers to marriage between a believer and an unbeliever (mixed marriage).[1] Aside from its long interpretive history within the church, there are several good reasons for considering the option of mixed marriages. First, the numerous prohibitions against intermarriage with the heathen (in the Old Testament,[2] intertestamental literature,[3] and the New Testament[4]) at least makes the view feasible. It provides yet another case where people of God (Israel and subsequently the Christian community) are called to separate selectively from unbelievers around them.

Second, almost all of the Old Testament prohibitions against intermarriage[5] (and a number of the intertestamental texts[6]) highlight idolatry and the worship of false gods as the primary deterrent. For example, Deut. 7.3-4 prohibits intermarriage with foreign peoples on the basis that it will ultimately lead to idolatry: 'You shall not intermarry with them (the Hittites, Girgashites, Amorites, etc.); you shall not give your daughters to their sons, nor shall you take their daughters for your sons. For they will turn your sons away from following me to serve other gods'. Similarly, Exod. 34.16 forbids the Israelites to take foreign daughters for their sons lest they 'play the harlot with their gods, and cause your sons also to play the harlot with their gods'. Again, Josh. 23.6-13 sets the issue of marrying the heathen nations along side of clinging to their gods and not to Yahweh. With this kind of strong Old Testament association between intermarriage and idolatry, it is quite probable that

1. Proponents from the last two centuries include Carrez, *Deuxième Épître aux Corinthiens*, p. 165; Martin, *2 Corinthians*, p. 197; Harris, '2 Corinthians', p. 359; Thrall, *First and Second Letter to the Corinthians*, p. 156; Corriveau, *The Liturgy of Life*, p. 39; Schlatter, *Paulus Der Bote Jesus*, p. 577; Hughes, *Second Epistle to the Corinthians*, p. 245; Héring, *Second Epistle to the Corinthians*, p. 49; Strachan, *Second Epistle to the Corinthians*, p. 5; Goudge, *Second Epistle to the Corinthians*, p. 73; Plummer, *Second Epistle to the Corinthians*, p. 206; Scott, *Pauline Epistles*, p. 236; Bernard, 'The Second Epistle to the Corinthians', p. 79; Lias, *Second Epistle to the Corinthians*, p. 84; Bisping, *Zweiten Briefes an die Korinther*, p. 79; Cornely, *Epistolae ad Corinthios altera et ad Galatas*, p. 188; Klöpper, *Das zweite Sendschreiben*, pp. 336, 343; Meyer, *Epistles to the Corinthians*, VI, p. 554; Hodge, *I & II Corinthians*, p. 166. Not all these commentators hold to mixed marriage as an exclusive referent.

2. E.g., Gen. 24.3, 37; 28.1, 6; Exod. 34.10-16 (cf. 23.32-33); Deut. 7.1-5 (cf. 17.17a); Josh. 23.6-13; 1 Kgs 11.1-8; Ezra 9.1-2, 11-15 (cf. 6.21); 10.2-3, 10-44; Neh. 10.28-30; 13.23-29; Ps. 106.34-39. Cf. Num. 36.8.

3. E.g., Tob. 1.9; 3.15; 4.12-13; 6.10-12; Add. Est. 4.17; *Jub.* 20.4; 22.20-22; 25.1-10; 30.7-17; *T. Levi* 9.10; 14.6; *T. Jud.* 14.6; *T. Jos.* 4.1-2, 5-6; *T. Job* 45.3; *Jos. Asen.* 7.5-6; 8.5; *Par. Jer.* 8.2, 4-6; *LAE* 9.5; Ps-Philo 18.13-14; 43.5; Philo, *Spec. Leg.* 3.29; Josephus, *Ant.* 8.191-95; Tacitus, *Historiae* 5.2.2.

4. Only 1 Cor. 7.39.

5. E.g., Exod. 34.10-16 (cf. 23.32-33); Deut. 7.1-5 (cf. 17.17a); Josh. 23.6-13; 1 Kgs 11.1-8; Ezra 9.1-2; Neh. 13.26; Ps. 106.34-39.

6. E.g., *Jub.* 22.20-22; 30.7-17; *Jos. Asen.* 8.5; Josephus, *Ant.* 8.191-95; Tacitus, *Historiae* 5.2.2. Cf. Philo, *Spec. Leg.* 3.29 which more broadly refers to the acceptance of opposing customs (rather than specifically to idolatry).

even some Corinthian readers may have inferred an intermarriage referent from the fragment.[1]

Third, the call to 'separate from impurities' which motivated Israel's departure from Babylon (an important cog in the fragment's return theology) had implications for the subsequent handling of mixed marriages once in the land. With words which are strikingly similar to Isa. 52.11-12 (cf. 2 Cor. 6.17), Ezra records how the priests and Levites purified themselves for the exilic return procession along with 'all those who separated themselves from the impurity of the nations of the land'.[2] Yet, for Ezra and Nehemiah this separation from Babylon and the heathen nations via the exile implied a resultant separation from foreign wives once in the land.[3] Therefore, the separation motif of return theology had a direct bearing on the subsequent problem of intermarriage with heathen wives.

Fourth, the 'yoking' cognates, ζεύγνυμι and συνζεύγνυμι, are often used of the marriage union. For instance, συνζεύγνυμι is found in the classic marriage text of Mk 10.10, 'What, therefore, God has joined together (συνέζευξεν) let no person separate'.[4] Again, in *Ant.* 6.309 Josephus used the verb in a similar manner: 'her father (Saul) had given her (Michal) in marriage (συνέζευξεν) to Phalti'.[5] If nothing else, such uses of the yoking metaphor account for the subsequent interpretation of 2 Cor. 6.14a along the lines of marriage.

Fifth, some argue that the allusion to LXX Lev. 19.19a supports a referent to mixed marriages.[6] The LXX text of Lev. 19.19a uses the noun ἑτεροζυγός when forbidding the breeding of two different kinds of animals: 'You shall not let your cattle breed with one of a different kind (τὰ κτήνη σου οὐ κατοχεύσεις ἑτεροζύγῳ)'. As a corollary, Philo[7] and Josephus[8] are often cited for their application of Lev. 19.19a to improper sexual relations between humans, the latter to miscegenation.[9] However, a closer examination of this data is required. First, ἑτεροζυγός in Lev. 19.19a conveys only the idea that the cattle are of a 'different kind/yoke'; the verb κατοχεύσεις introduces the sexual/breeding idea. Furthermore, neither Philo[10] nor Josephus[11] apply their *explicit* discussion of the unequal yoke (between an ox

---

1. It is surprising that Fee ('Food Offered to Idols', pp. 140-61) did not give this aspect of idolatry a closer examination in the course of his article.

2. Ezra 6.20-21; cf. Neh. 10.28.

3. Ezra 9.1; 10.11; Neh. 9.2; 10.30 (cf. 10.28).

4. Cf. Mt. 19.6.

5. Cf. Josephus, *Ant.* 1.314, 319, 338; *Sib. Or.* 5.391; *T. Reub.* 4.1. Also, for the use of ζεύγνυμι/ζευγνύω in relation to marriage see Josephus, *War* 2.249; *Ant.* 4.244; 16.11. For further references see BAGD, pp. 337, 775.

6. E.g., Rensberger, '2 Corinthians 6.14--7.1', p. 29.

7. Philo, *Spec. Leg.* 3.46-48; 4.203.

8. Josephus, *Ant.* 4.229.

9. E.g., Rensberger, '2 Corinthians 6.14--7.1', p. 29; cf. Windisch, *Der zweite Korintherbrief*, p. 213.

10. Philo, *Spec. Leg.* 4.204-206.

11. Josephus, *Ant.* 4.228.

and donkey) along the lines of sexual relationships or mixed marriages.[1] They apply only the Old Testament interbreeding texts to human sexual relationships.

On the other hand, several considerations suggest that the fragment within its present context does not speak to mixed marriages. First, based on Paul's instruction in 1 Corinthians,[2] a mixed marriage referent in the fragment would have to be addressed only to those *entering into* mixed marriages and not to those already within such marriages. In other words, the fragment would have to be addressing potential, not actual, mixed marriages. Yet, whatever the activity referent in 2 Cor. 6.14--7.1, the offensive situation is not simply potential, but actual. While μὴ γίνεσθε with the participle may prohibit the entering of a state,[3] at least two factors suggest that the prohibition is also directed towards actual offenders, not merely a group of potential offenders. For one, the closing exhortation in 7.1 (which draws upon the earlier Old Testament promises and imperatives[4]) exhorts the reader to clear action: 'let us cleanse ourselves ... '. Though the final subjunctive broadens the activity referent to '*all* defilement of flesh and spirit', it indirectly addresses those who have violated the initial prohibition in 6.14a and in a manner that assumes that a solution is needed. Also, if the fragment is contextually connected to 6.12,[5] then the readers were already restrained in their affections (the problem was actual, not merely potential).

Second, the Old Testament imperatives to 'come out from among them' and 'be separate' (ἐξέλθατε and ἀφορίσθητε) do not lend themselves at all to a mixed marriage referent. If the problem was mixed marriages, then the obvious inference from these imperatives (which have been carefully redacted in light of 6.14a[6]) would be that the believer separate from his or her unbelieving spouse. However, this would contradict Paul's advice in 1 Cor. 7.12-16, where the objective in mixed marriages is to remain together and bring the unsaved partner to the Lord (cf. 1 Pet. 3.1).

Third, the delayed nature of the idolatry in mixed marriages (while metonymical) does not seem to fit the immediacy of the case in 2 Cor. 6.14–7.1. The classic case is that of Solomon, whose foreign wives over a long period of time, 'when he was old', eventually turned his heart away from the Lord to serve other gods (1 Kgs 11.1-8; cf. Neh. 13.26; Deut. 7.4). The idolatry did not always happen suddenly; rather, in many cases it involved a process of being led gradually into idolatry. By way of contrast, the problem in 2 Cor. 6.14–7.1 is presented as an immediate threat. Whatever the fragment's activity referent, if read in its present context, it has already

---

1. Also, the discussion in Philo (*Spec. Leg.* 3.29) and Josephus (*Ant.* 8.191-93) about intermarriage with foreign nations comes from an entirely different angle than the 'mixed kinds' instruction.

2. From 1 Cor. 7.12-16 it is clear that Paul preferred that those within a mixed marriage maintain the relationship. He made no fine distinction between mixed marriages where one of two unbelievers had become a Christian and mixed marriages where an immature believer had married an unbeliever. Presumably, even the latter action would have been forgiven and the person advised to stay within the marriage (with the promise of sanctifying the unbeliever and having holy children).

3. See BDF, §354.

4. See Chapter 3, §3.

5. See Chapter 6, §4.

6. See Chapter 3, §2.

caused the Corinthians' affections to be limited towards Paul (6.12-13; 7.2-4), it seems to have placed them in an immediate association with lawlessness, darkness, Beliar and idols (cf. the sharpness of the rhetorical contrasts), and it is a threat which requires an immediate 'now' response (cf. 2 Cor. 6.2).

Fourth, the narrow audience to which a mixed-marriage prohibition applies (i.e., only to those in a position to marry or remarry) does not align well with the fragment which appears directed towards the entire Corinthian congregation. In 1 Cor. 7.39 Paul appended the μόνον ἐν κυρίῳ[1] restriction to an exhortation addressed to a very specific group—widows. Presumably, such a restriction would also apply to the discussion of virgins (7.25-38). The apostle in 1 Corinthians does not direct the marriage prohibition broadly (in hope that his audience would figure out to whom he was speaking). On the other hand, the implication from the broad address of the fragment ('beloved' in 2 Cor. 7.1; cf. 'Ο Corinthians' in 2 Cor. 6.11), the linking imperatives (6.17; 7.1), and the broad contextual problem (6.1-2; 6.12; 7.2-4) is that the entire congregation was susceptible to whatever the fragment addressed.

Fifth, the mixed marriage discussion in 1 Corinthians never raises the issue of idolatry and pagan worship.[2] Though an argument from silence, it seems peculiar[3] that Paul does not identify idolatry as the key deterrent for entering into mixed marriages (1 Cor. 7.39) or as a problem to be dealt with in existing mixed marriages (1 Cor. 7.12-16). Despite the predominant focus on idolatry in 1 Corinthians (more so than any other Pauline letter), the apostle never mentions pagan worship relative to the issue of mixed marriages. It is odd, then, given the prominent focus on idolatry in the fragment (as the climaxing element), that Paul would have missed the opportunity in 1 Corinthians to address mixed marriages in light of this closely related issue.

Sixth (and most important), the mixed marriage issue simply does not seem to have been an area of intense personal conflict between Paul and the Corinthians. Compared to other issues in 1 Corinthians, the mixed marriages discussion moves along smoothly. In fact, the μόνον ἐν κυρίῳ restriction to remarriage is so brief and unobtrusive that it appears to be an afterthought. By marked contrast, however, the 'unequal yoke' admonition betrays a painful contention. The series of abrupt rhetorical questions and the contextual setting emphasize the tension between the apostle and the Corinthians. It hardly seems possible to attribute this intense conflict to mixed marriages on the basis of what is known from 1 Corinthians.

To sum up, the mixed marriage referent is by far the most complicated option to analyze. A number of factors make it appealing, the most significant being the Old Testament use of idolatry as a deterrent for marrying the heathen. Nonetheless, the

---

1. The clearest meaning of this marriage restriction is that the individual must belong to the Lord (i.e., be a believer), although it may have broader implications. Cf. Fee, *First Epistle to the Corinthians*, p. 356.

2. For that matter, neither are the other associative elements of lawlessness, Beliar, and darkness brought into the discussion.

3. Especially is this so if the fragment (or the like) had been part of Paul's thinking on the matter of mixed marriages all along.

fragment was probably not intended to speak to the Corinthian church about mixed marriages. Paul's placid handling of the issue in 1 Corinthians (without a hint of struggle between himself and congregation) and the redactional emphasis on ἐξέλθατε ἐκ μέσου αὐτῶν almost conclusively rule out the option. Having said this, the passage lends itself in a secondary sense to a mixed marriage application (though not without some violence to the original intent[1]) due to the metonymical nature of the idolatry in the Old Testament examples.

7. *Eating Meat Offered to Idols at Pagan Temples*
(1 Cor. 8.10; 10.14-22)

Although many New Testament commentators have taken ἑτεροζυγοῦντες to refer to eating and drinking at pagan temples (joining in pagan feasts),[2] undoubtedly the leading proponent of this view today is Gordon D. Fee.[3] Fee argues that 2 Cor. 6.14–7.1 makes perfectly good sense against the background of eating cultic meals at pagan idol-temples. From his perspective it is *only* in this sense that the church is not to be ἑτεροζυγοῦντες ἀπίστοις.[4]

The evidence favors accepting pagan feasts as at least one of the activity referents for 2 Cor. 6.14a. First, dining at pagan temples qualifies as metonymical idolatry. The problem is one which Paul unequivocally labels as idolatry.[5] The apostle initially prohibits 'dining in an idol's temple' because it might cause a weaker brother to stumble. However, in the subsequent discussion of 10.1-13 and 10.14-22 he gives another reason—such participation in pagan temple feasts is, in effect, idolatry. Two imperative statements in 10.7 and 10.14 make it clear that Paul thought of the activity as idolatry: μηδὲ εἰδωλολάτραι γίνεσθε[6].... φεύγετε ἀπὸ τῆς εἰδωλολατρίας. Even if the Corinthians did not bow down to the idols in a literal manner, their eating and drinking at temple feasts was in effect (metonymical) idolatry.

---

1. If the one who placed the fragment into its present literary context had intended a marriage referent, that person would have altered, or at least qualified, the OT texts in some manner to correspond to the marriage instructions found in 1 Corinthians.

2. E.g., Calvin, *Epistles to the Corinthians*, p. 257; Flatt, *Briefe Pauli an die Corinthier*, pp. 100-101; Osiander, *Zweiten Brief an die Korinthier*, p. 252; Hodge, *Second Epistle to the Corinthians*, p. 166; Bisping, *Zweiten Briefes an die Korinther*, p. 79; Klöpper, *Das zweite Sendschreiben*, pp. 336, 343; Meyer, *Epistles to the Corinthians*, p. 554; Lias, *Second Epistle to the Corinthians*, p. 84; Schnedermann, *Die Briefe an die Korinther*, pp. 339-40; Allo, *Seconde Épître aux Corinthiens*, p. 186; Hughes, *Second Epistle to the Corinthians*, p. 246; Schlatter, *Paulus Der Bote Jesus*, p. 578; Bruce, *1 and 2 Corinthians*, p. 214; Barrett, *Second Epistle to the Corinthians*, p. 196; Harris, '2 Corinthians', pp. 360-61; Martin, *2 Corinthians*, p. 197; Kruse, *Second Epistle to the Corinthians*, pp. 136-37.

3. Fee, 'Food Sacrificed to Idols', pp. 140-61.

4. At several points Fee ('Food Sacrificed to Idols', pp. 158-59) restricts the activity referent to dining at pagan temples. However, it should be noted that he allows with some question that it could also refer to the activity of temple prostitution.

5. Cf. Fee, 'Food Sacrificed to Idols', p. 150.

6. Notice the similarity in form to μὴ γίνεσθε ἑτεροζυγοῦντες.

Second, the Old Testament prohibitions against eating at the cultic meals of other gods often include the aspect of idolatry and covenant violation. For example, in Num. 25.1-5 (which forms a basis for Paul's instruction in 1 Cor. 10.8) the Shittimites 'invited the people to the sacrifices of their gods . . . so Israel joined themselves to Baal of Peor'. Here, eating at the pagan feast involved a violation of Israel's covenant with Yahweh and placed the people in a covenant relationship with a false god (with the result that many died).[1] Interestingly, the cognate ζευγίζειν is used by Aquila and Theodotion in LXX Num. 25.3 to express the 'joining' of Israel to Baal.[2]

Third, other conceptual, linguistic, and emotive similarities exist between 1 Cor. 8.10; 10.14-22 and the fragment.[3] For instance, in 1 Cor. 10.14-22 idols are viewed as the locus of demonic activity; in the fragment idols are similarly linked to Beliar (the prince of demons).[4] Also, in 1 Cor. 10.14-22 the violation of the covenant meal in 1 Cor. 10.14-22 (by joining with pagans/demons/idols) parallels in 2 Cor. 6.14–7.1 the violation of the two covenant formulas (by joining with pagans/Beliar/idols). Again, at least two of the key quasi-covenent terms, κοινωνία and μερίς/μερίζω, are found in both texts.[5] The church also functions as the new temple in both (implicitly in one, explicitly in the other).[6] Moreover, the abrupt rhetorical questions in both convey the painful level of emotional involvement and the extreme intensity of the issue.[7]

The major objection to this view is that there is no mention of 'food offered to idols' in the larger context of 2 Cor. 2.14–7.4.[8] While this objection is a problem for Fee's view, a broadening of the referent handles the problem. First, the second exodus tradition (which ties the fragment to its context) has in the background the concept of leaving *idolatrous* Babylon for the new worship center in Jerusalem. So the contextual connectives are already there on the level of idols (though not meat offered to idols). Second, rather than restricting the referent to this *single* activity (as Fee is inclined to do), a larger grouping of referents should be understood by the admonition. The activity should be defined in terms of the fragment as read within its present context, not strictly from one issue in 1 Corinthians. In broad terms, the fragment prohibits believers from joining in any activity which establishes a

1. Cf. Exod. 32.6-8; 34.12-16; Lev. 17.7; Deut. 32.37-38; Ps. 106.28-31, 35-39.

2. Cf. 1 Macc. 1.15 for a situation where ζευγιωζειν is used of Jews 'joining' themselves to the heathen in a way that made a covenant with them and forsook their holy covenant (cf. 1.11). However, the determinative act was becoming uncircumcised and building a gymnasium, rather than eating at the pagan temples.

3. Some of these are pointed out by Fee ('Food Sacrificed to Idols', pp. 148-50).

4. Fee, 'Food Sacrificed to Idols', pp. 151-52.

5. Cf. 1 Cor. 10.16, 17, 20, 21 and 2 Cor. 6.14-15. Cf. Chapter 3, §3.

6. This is explicit in 2 Cor. 6.16, whereas it is implied in 1 Cor. 10.14-22 with the church becoming the center for the sacrificial meal and new 'table of the Lord' (in comparison to Israel's sacrifices and the table of Yahweh).

7. Cf. 1 Cor. 10.16, 18, 19, 22 and 2 Cor. 6.14-16a.

8. Fee ('Food Sacrificed to Idols', p. 161) admits this weakness. Cf. Rensberger, '2 Corinthians 6.14--7.1', p. 45, n. 16; Furnish, *II Corinthians*, p. 372.

covenant-like bond with pagans and their literal idols (either through physical or metonymical idolatry)—an action which seriously violates the reader's existing covenant with God.[1] Eating at the cultic meals in temple restaurants, then, is one clear example of this kind of infraction.

8. *Eating Meat Offered to Idols at a Pagan's Home*
(1 Cor. 10.27-28)

A few New Testament scholars take the activity referent of ἑτεροζυγοῦντες to include eating idol meat at a pagan's home (e.g., 1 Cor. 10.27-28).[2] It is not entirely clear why this referent has been proposed. Perhaps it affords another situation of contact between a believer and an unbeliever: εἴ τις καλεῖ ὑμᾶς τῶν ἀπίστων. However, there is little to justify such an option and much stands in its way. For one thing, Paul states elsewhere that the believer is free to join the unbeliever in the meal (unlike temple feasts) and 'eat anything that is set before him' even the idol meat (1 Cor. 10.27). Second, the command not to eat is entirely dependent upon the other person's conscience, not the believer's conscience (the action of eating is itself neutral for the Christian). Third, the subsequent act of eating after being informed (probably out of politeness[3]) that the meat was idol-meat would hardly 'join together' believer and unbeliever in any kind of bond—quite the opposite. The unbeliever would be offended because he was trying to help the Christian and because the Christian would have violated the unbeliever's own moral expectations (ill-founded though they may be).[4] Again, the issue here is not one of related demonic activity, nor of metonymical idolatry, nor even of personal defilement (as in the fragment). At most, the believer would simply eat something else and *continue the meal* with the unbeliever (not making food a point of offense). Fourth, the relaxed attitude of Paul in 1 Cor. 10.27-29 is so markedly different than 2 Cor. 6.14–7.1 that it is difficult to envision this kind of infraction stirring the apostle to the emotional pitch of the fragment.

1. In other words, the lack of any specific details in the immediate context leads to formulating a more inclusive referent. Yet, one should not swing to the opposite extreme, as Furnish (*II Corinthians*, p. 372) does, and equate the problem with any kind of defilement like the exhortation in James 1.26, 'keep oneself unstained from the world'. Such a broadening incorrectly pushes the idolatry to a metaphorical level and looses the thrust of the passage.

2. E.g., Hughes, *Second Epistle to the Corinthians*, p. 245; Barrett, *Second Epistle to the Corinthians*, p. 196; Martin, *2 Corinthians*, p. 197; Carrez, *Deuxième Épître aux Corinthiens*, p. 165; Cornely, *Epistolae ad Corinthios*, p. 188.

3. See Fee, *First Epistle to the Corinthians*, pp. 484-85.

4. This is the ultimate point in 1 Cor. 10.32.

9. *Speaking in Tongues when Unbelievers are Present at the Service (1 Cor. 14.22-25)*

A handful of commentators have suggested that ἑτεροζυγοῦντες includes the case of speaking in tongues when unbelievers are present at the service.[1] The idea comes from 1 Cor. 14.23, where Paul observes the problem of speaking in tongues when unbelievers are present in the congregational gathering: 'If therefore the whole church should assemble together and all speak in tongues, and the uninitiated or unbelievers (ἄπιστοι) enter, will they not say that you are mad?' The passage certainly contrasts believer and unbeliever. However, all that 1 Cor. 14.22-25 has in common with the fragment is the use of ἄπιστοι to describe pagan individuals outside the church. A few observations will show that the view is untenable. First, the act of speaking in tongues *itself* is not prohibited, only speaking in tongues without an interpreter (1 Cor. 14.28). Rather, in 1 Cor. 14.23 the point is the relative value of prophecy which will help convict the unbeliever. Second, the act of speaking in tongues hardly 'joins together/yokes' a believer and unbeliever. On the contrary, Paul's point is that the unbeliever, when he hears the speaking in tongues, will think to himself, 'You (believers) are out of your minds (μαίνεσθε)!' Third, the nature of the infraction in 1 Cor. 14.23, namely, not edifying the congregation and unbelievers who are present, cannot be compared with the gravity of covenant violation to which the fragment speaks. Consequently, 1 Cor. 14.23 as a referent for ἑτεροζυγοῦντες may be eliminated.

10. *Business Partnerships with Unbelievers*

The final two options move outside of the realm of issues discussed in Pauline writings. One is that believers are not to become 'yoked with unbelievers' in the sense of entering into business partnerships with them.[2] This view is sometimes tangentially supported by the idea of 'work' conveyed in the yoking imagery (i.e., plowing together)[3] or by the occasional Old Testament narrative which looks disparagingly upon certain business alliances (e.g., 2 Chron. 20.35-37; cf. 1 Kgs 22.48-49). Furthermore, one might grant that business partnerships between a believer and unbeliever may lead to friction over ethical perspectives.

However, it is unlikely that the fragment was intended to address business partnerships. First, the parallel series of synonyms (μετοχή, κοινωνία, συμφώνησις, μερίς, and συγκατάθεσις), each of which carries its own peculiar etymological/

---

1. E.g., Hughes, *Second Epistle to the Corinthians*, p. 245; Barrett, *Second Epistle to the Corinthians*, p. 196; Carrez, *Deuxième Épître aux Corinthiens*, p. 165.

2. E.g., Desiderius Erasmus, *Opera Omnia*, p. 927; Windisch, *Zweite Korintherbrief*, p. 214; Goudge, *Second Epistle to the Corinthians*, p. 73; Lietzmann, *An die Korinther I/II*, p. 128. Martin (*2 Corinthians*, p. 197) speaks of 'certain business relationships which cause compromise'.

3. Cf. Philo (*Spec. Leg.* 4.206) who discusses the 'unequal yoke' in terms of weaker and stronger working partners.

background imagery,[1] effectively removes any 'working' connotations from the yoking metaphor in 2 Cor. 6.14a. The point of ἑτεροζυγοῦντες is simply the sense of 'joining together (two different kinds)'. Second, the condemned shipping alliance between Jehoshaphat, king of Judah, and the wicked Ahaziah, king of Israel,[2] does not serve as an adequate background for the fragment. This was not an alliance with the heathen nations, but within Israel (between the divided kingdoms). Consequently, the shipping alliance illustration is better suited for two individuals within the covenant community than between the community and heathen nations (as is the case in the fragment). Third, a business alliance or business compromise simply does not relate well to either physical idolatry or metonymical idolatry (with literal idols in view); it must move to the dubious level of metaphorical idolatry. Fourth, there is no evidence to suggest that mixed business partnerships either were, or would have been, an issue with Paul in the Corinthian setting.

11. *Maintaining Membership in a Pagan Cult*

A final referent option, suggested by Murray Harris,[3] is the possibility that ἑτεροζυγοῦντες includes maintaining membership in some local pagan cult. There is no explicit data within Corinthian correspondence upon which to interact with this proposal. However, on the basis that membership in a pagan cult would be understood as metonymical idolatry (and failing make a clean break from paganism) the suggestion merits consideration. Along these lines, a number of other 'possible cases' for metonymical idolatry can be added to the list: financial contributions to a local cult, employment by the pagan temples, and joining in pagan religious ceremonies related to trade guilds, or to birth, death, or marriage (or on any other occasion for that matter).

12. *Summary and Conclusion*

The pursuit of this second essay (Appendix B) has been to evaluate the 'unequal yoke' prohibition in 2 Cor. 6.14a, in light of my traditions hypothesis. The results may be summarized along three levels. First, the kind of separation from pagans called for by the fragment is selective separation, not complete Qumran-like separation. This conclusion is based primarily on the distinctive differences between the fragment and 1 Cor. 5.10b and the function of the fragment within a broader contextual paradigm of second exodus/return theology (which, itself, is *not* calling for complete separation).

---

1. For example, it would be equally ridiculous to suggest a musically oriented prohibition in view of συμφώνησις.
2. 2 Chron. 20.35-37 relates how Jehoshaphat formed an alliance with the wicked king Ahaziah by jointly building ships to go to Tarshish. As a result, divine judgment fell upon the alliance and the ships were wrecked.
3. Harris, '2 Corinthians', p. 361.

Second, the activity referent of μὴ γίνεσθε ἑτεροζυγοῦντες should be restricted to physical-literal idolatry and metonymical idolatry. Both these options understand 'idols' (2 Cor. 6.16) in a literal sense. As read within its present context, 'idols' (εἰδώλων) probably meant *literal* idols in view of the living God/idols contrast, the lack of any parenthetical statement to clarify metaphorical intent, and the major conflict (with Paul) at Corinth related to literal idols. Any referents related to metaphorical idolatry should probably be rejected.

Third, the specific referent options for μὴ γίνεσθε ἑτεροζυγοῦντες may be grouped from least to most probable. For example, the least plausible referent options are the following: going to court before pagan judges, eating idol-meat at a pagan's home, speaking in tongues before unbelievers, and business partnerships. These cases of metaphorical idolatry may be excluded with a degree of confidence. Also, it is improbable that the fragment was intended to address mixed marriages (especially within its current context). Mixed marriages, while metonymical idolatry of a sort, are an unsuitable referent in light of the actual (not simply potential) nature of the problem in the fragment, the corresponding Old Testament imperatives, the immediate nature of the idolatry, the broad audience, no mention of idolatry in relation to the topic earlier, and this not being an area of intense personal conflict between the apostle and the Corinthians.

On the other hand, it is possible that the fragment covers a number of cases not explicitly mentioned within Corinthian correspondence: maintaining membership at a local pagan cult, attending ceremonies performed in pagan temples (related to trade guilds, or to birth, death, or marriage), employment by the temples, pagan worship in the home, etc. While these activities fall under the categories of literal or metonymical idolatry, it is difficult to evaluate them more closely since they are not mentioned elsewhere. Finally, the most probable referent options are visiting sacred temple prostitutes and joining with pagans in temple feasts. These infractions may be classified as severe violations of one's covenant with God, as metonymical idolatry, and as forming a close bond with pagans and Beliar; they would also have had a sufficiently high emotive impact to account for the intensity of the fragment. Supporting this, Johann S. Semler (1776) provides an excellent summary of the kinds of activities prohibited by the fragment. After dismissing marriage as one of the options, he writes: 'Res potius debet referri ad societatem pristinae vitae, in variis muneribus obeundis, quae cum christiana mente parum consentiebant; partes in ludis publicis; vanae caerimoniae, domestieae et publicae etc. qualia erant ἄπιστοι propria'.[1]

In conclusion, the fragment (as read within its present literary setting) calls for the Corinthians to 'leave idolatrous Babylon and return home'. It is with respect to the idol-gods of the temple cults that the Corinthians are paradigmatically called to come out . . . out of Egypt . . . out of Babylon . . . out of Corinth. The short-form

---

1. Johann S. Semler, *Commentatio II Epistolae ad Corinthios*, p. 186. English translation: 'The matter (of "joining together") probably refers to previous (pre-Christian) center-orientation of life coming together with non-Christians in religious ceremonies (public or private) which resulted in lasting/bonding relationships with the ἄπιστοι'.

title of this book, *Returning Home* (and its longer replica: *Coming out of Babylon and Returning Home*), reflects the second axis within this exodus-return paradigm, since it is from that point in the recurring pattern which the traditions in 6.14–7.1 have been drawn.

BIBLIOGRAPHY

Allo, E.B., *Saint Paul, Seconde Épître aux Corinthiens* (EBib; Paris: Gabalda, 2nd edn, 1956).

Anderson, B.W., 'Exodus Typology in Second Isaiah', in *Israel's Prophetic Heritage. Essays in Honor of James Muilenburg* (ed. B.W. Anderson and W. Harrelson; London: SCM Press, 1962), pp. 177-95.

Bachmann, P., *Der zweite Brief des Paulus an die Korinther* (KNT; Leipzig: Deichert, 4th edn, 1922).

Bacon, B.W., *An Introduction to the New Testament* (New York: Macmillan, 1900).

Baljon, J.M.S., *De tekst der brieven van Paulus aan de Romeinen, de Corinthiërs en de Galatiërs als voorwerp van de conjecturalkritiek beschouwd* (Utrecht: Boekhoven, 1884).

—*Geschiedenis van de boekeu des Nienwen Verbonds* (Groningen: Wolters, 1901).

Baltzer, K., *The Covenant Formulary: In Old Testament, Jewish, and Early Christian Writings* (trans. D.E. Green; Philadelphia: Fortress Press, 1971).

Barclay, W., *The Letters to the Corinthians* (Toronto: Welch, 2nd revised edn, 1975).

Barrett, C.K., *A Commentary on the Second Epistle to the Corinthians* (HNTC; New York: Harper and Row, 1973).

—*Essays on Paul* (London: SPCK, 1982).

—'Paul's Opponents in 2 Corinthians', *NTS* 17 (1971), pp. 233-54.

—'Things Sacrificed to Idols', *NTS* 11 (1965), pp. 138-53.

Barstad, H.M., *A Way in the Wilderness. The 'Second Exodus' in the Message of Second Isaiah* (Manchester: University Press, 1989).

Barth, M., *Ephesians* (AB; Garden City: Doubleday, 1974).

Baudraz, F., *Les Épître aux Corinthiens* (Paris: Librairie Protestante, 1965).

Bauer, W., *A Greek-English Lexicon of the New Testament and Other Early Christian Literature* (trans. and rev. W.F. Arndt, F.W. Gingrich, and F.W. Danker; Chicago: University of Chicago Press, 2nd edn, 1979).

Baumert, N., *Täglich Sterben und Auferstehen. Der Literalsinn von 2 Kor 4.12–5.10* (SANT 34; Müchen: Kösel Verlag, 1973).

Beale, G.K., 'The Old Testament Background of Reconciliation in 2 Corinthians 5–7 and Its Bearing on the Literary Problem of 2 Corinthians 6.14–7.1', *NTS* 35 (1989), pp. 550-81.

Becker, W.E., 'Paul, The Suffering Apostle: The Place of Suffering in His Life and Theology' (PhD dissertation, Fuller Theological Seminary, 1982).

Beker, J.C., *Paul the Apostle, the Triumph of God in Life and Thought* (Philadelphia: Fortress Press, 1980).

Belleville, L.L., 'Paul's Polemical Use of the Moses-*Doxa* Tradition in 2 Corinthians 3.12-18' (PhD dissertation, University of St Michael's College, 1986).

—*Reflections of Glory* (JSNTSup, 52; Sheffield: JSOT Press, 1991).

Belser, J.E., *Der zweite Brief des Apostels Paulus an die Korinther* (Freiburg: Herdersche, 1910).

Benoit, P., 'Qumrân et le Nouveau Testament', *NTS* 7 (1961), pp. 276-96.

Bernard, J.H., 'The Second Epistle to the Corinthians', in *The Expositor's Greek Testament* (ed. W. Robertson Nicoll; London: Hodder and Stroughton, 1903; reprint, Grand Rapids: Eerdmanns, 1979), III, pp. 2-119.

Best, E., *One Body in Christ. A Study of the Relationship of the Church to Christ in the Epistles of Saint Paul* (London: SPCK, 1965).

—*Second Corinthians* (Atlanta: J. Knox, 1987).

Betz, H.D., '2 Cor. 6.14–7.1, An Anti-Pauline Fragment?', *JBL* 92 (1973), pp. 88-108.

—*2 Corinthians 8 and 9: A Commentary on Two Administrative Letters of the Apostle Paul* (ed. G.W. MacRae; Hermeneia; Philadelphia: Fortress Press, 1985).

Betz, O.,'Der Alte und der Neue Bund: Eine Betrachtung zu 2 Kor 3', in *Mission an Israel in heilsgeschichtlicher Sicht* (ed. H. Kremers and E. Lubahn; Neukirchen: Neukirchener Verlag, 1985), pp. 24-36.

Bisping, A., *Erklärung des zweiten Briefes an die Korinther und des Briefes an die Galater* (Munster: Aschendorff, 3rd edn, 1863).

Black, D.A., *Linguistics for Students of New Testament Greek* (Grand Rapids: Baker, 1988).

Blass, F. and A. Debrunner., *A Greek Grammar of the New Testament and Other Early Christian Literature* (trans. and rev. R.W. Funk; Chicago: University of Chicago Press, 1961).

Blass, F.W., 'Textkritisches zu den Korintherbriefen', in *Beiträge zur förderung christlischer Theologie 10* (ed. A. Schlatter and W. Lütgert; Gütersloh: Bertelsmann, 1906), pp. 51-63.

Blenkinsopp, J., 'Scope and Depth of Exodus Tradition in Deutero-Isaiah 40–55', in *The Dynamism of Biblical Tradition* (ed. P. Benoit and R.E. Murphy; Concilium 20; New York: Paulist Press, 1967), pp. 41-50.

Bock, D.L., *Proclamation From Prophecy and Pattern. Lucan Old Testament Christology* (JSNTSup 12; Sheffield: JSOT Press, 1987).

Bonnard, P.-E., *Le Second Isaïe* (EBib; Paris: Librairie Lecoffre, 1972).

Bonsirven, J., *Exégèse Rabbinique et Exégèse Paulinienne* (BTH; Paris: Beauchesne, 1939).

Bornkamm, G., 'The History of the Origin of the So-called Second Letter to the Corinthians', in *The Authorhship and Integrity of the New Testament* (TC 4; London: SPCK, 1965), pp. 73-81.

—*Paul* (trans. D. Stalker; New York: Harper and Row, 1971).

—'Die Vorgeschichte des sogennanten Zweiten Korintherbriefes', in *Gesammelte Aufsätze* (BEvT 53; München: Evangelischer, 1971), IV, pp 162-94.

—*Die Vorgeschichte des sogenannten Zweiten Korintherbriefes* (Sitzungsberichte der Heidelberger Akademie der Wissenschaften; Heidelberg: Carl Winter, 2nd edn, 1965).

Braun, F.M., 'L'Arrière-Fond Judaïque du Quatrième Évangile et la Communauté d'Alliance', *RB* 62 (1955), pp. 5-44.

Braun, H., *Qumran und das Neue Testament* (2 vols.; Tübingen: Mohr, 1966).

—*Spätjüdisch-häretischer und frühchristlicher Radikalismus. Jesus von Nazareth und die essenische Qumransekte* (BHT 24; 2 vols.; Tübingen: Mohr, 1957).

Brownlee, W.H., *Ezekiel 1–19* (WBC; Waco: Word, 1983).

Bruce, F.F., *1 and 2 Corinthians* (NCB; Grand Rapids: Eerdmans, 1971).

—'The History of New Testament Study', in *New Testament Interpretation* (ed. I.H. Marshall; Grand Rapids: Eerdmans, 1977), pp. 21-59.

—'Paul's Use of the Old Testament in Acts', in *Tradition and Interpretation in the New Testament* (ed. G.F. Hawthorne and O. Betz; Grand Rapids: Eerdmans, 1987), pp. 71-79.

—'Some Thoughts on Paul and Paulinism', *VEv* 7 (1971), pp. 5-16.

Brun, L., 'Zur Auslegung von II Kor 5.1-10', *ZNW* 28 (1929), pp. 207-229.

Bultmann, R.K., *The Second Letter to the Corinthians* (trans. R. A. Harrisville; Minneapolis: Augsburg, 1985).

—*Exegetische Problems des zweiten Korintherbriefes* (Darmstadt: Wissenschaftliche Buchgesellschaft, 1963).

Burton, Ernest De Witt. *The Epistle to the Galatians* (ICC; Edinburgh: T. & T. Clark, 1921).

Caird, G.B., *A Commentary on the Revelation of St. John the Divine* (HNTC; New York: Harper and Row, 1966).

Calvin, J., *Commentary on the Epistles of Paul the Apostle to the Corinthians* (trans. John Pringle; Calvin's Commentaries; N.p., 1854; reprinted edn, Grand Rapids: Baker, 1979).

Carmignac, J., *Le docteur de justice et Jésus Christ* (Paris: l'Orante, 1957).

Carrez, M., *La Deuxième Épître de Saint Paul aux Corinthiens* (CNT; Genève: Labor et Fides, 1986).

—'Une Interpolation Essénienne dans 2 Cor. 6,14–7,1?', *Le Monde de la Bible* 4 (1978), p. 64.

Cerfaux, L., *The Christian in the Theology of St. Paul* (New York: Herder and Herder, 1967).

—'Saint Paul et le "serviteur de Dieu" d'Isaïe', in *Recueil Lucien Cerfaux* (BETL 6-7; Gembloux: Duculot, 1954), II, pp. 439-54.

Charles, R.H., *The Ascension of Isaiah* (New York: Macmillan, 1919).

Charlesworth, J.H. (ed.), *The Old Testament Pseudopigrapha* (2 vols.; Garden City: Doubleday, 1983).

Clayton, G.H., 'Epistle to the Corinthians', in *The Dictionary of the Apostolic Church* (ed. J. Hastings; New York: Charles Scribner's Sons, 1915; reprint, Grand Rapids: Baker, 1973), II, pp. 250-59.

Clemen, C.C., *Paulus: sein Leben und Wirken* (2 vols.; Giessen: J. Ricker'sche, 1904).

Clements, R.E., *Isaiah 1–39* (NCB; Grand Rapids: Eerdmans, 1980).

Clifford, R., *Fair Spoken and Persuading: An Interpretation of Second Isaiah* (New York: Paulist Press, 1984).

Collange, J.F., *Énigmes de la deuxième épître de Paul aux Corinthiens. Étude exégétique de 2 Cor. 2.14–7.4* (SNTSMS 18; Cambridge: Cambridge University Press, 1972).

Conrad, E.W., 'The Community as King in Second Isaiah', in *Understanding the Word. Essays in Honor of Bernard W. Anderson* (ed. J.T. Butler, E.W. Conrad, B.C. Ollenburger; JSOTSup 37; Sheffield: JSOT Press, 1985), pp. 99-111.

Conzelmann, H., *1 Corinthians: A Commentary on the First Epistle to the Corinthians* (Hermeneia; Philadelphia: Fortress Press, 1975).

Cooke, G.A., *A Critical and Exegetical Commentary on the Book of Ezekiel* (ICC; Edinburgh: T. & T. Clark, 1936).

Cornely, R., *Commentarius in S. Pauli Apostoli; Epistolae ad Corinthios altera et ad Galatas* (Paris: Lethielleux, 1892).

Corriveau, R., *The Liturgy of Life. A Study of the Ethical Thought of St. Paul in His Letters to the Early Christian Communities* (STR 25; Montreal: Bellarmin, 1970).

Cranfield, C.E.B., *The Epistle to the Romans* (ICC; 2 vols.; Edinburgh: T. & T. Clark, 1979).

Currie, S.D., 'Koinonia in Christian Literature to 200 A.D' (PhD dissertation, Emory University, 1962).

Dahl, N.A., 'Appendix II: On the Literary Integrity of 2 Corinthians 1–9', in *Studies in Paul: Theology for the Early Christian Mission* (Minneapolis: Augsburg, 1977), pp. 38-39.

—'A Fragment and its Context: 2 Corinthians 6.14–7.1', in *Studies in Paul: Theology for the Early Christian Mission* (Minneapolis: Augsburg, 1977), pp. 62-69.

Delitzsch, F., *Biblical Commentary on the Prophecies of Isaiah* (trans. J.S. Banks and J. Kennedy; Edinburgh: T. & T. Clark, 1894).

Denis, Albert-Marie. *Concordance Grecque des Pseudépigraphes d'Ancien Testament* (Leiden: Brill, 1987).

Denny, J., *The Second Epistle to the Corinthians* (EB; New York: A.C. Armstrong, 1894).

Derrett, J.D.M., '2 Cor. 6,14ff. a Midrash on Dt 22,10', *Bib* 59 (1978), pp. 231-50.

Dinkler, E., 'Korintherbriefe', in *Religion in Geschichte und Gegenwort* (Tübingen: Mohr, 3rd edn, 1957-65), IV, pp. 17-24.

Dinter, P.E., 'Paul and the Prophet Isaiah', *BTB* 13 (1983), pp. 48-52.

Dobschütz, E. von., *Die Urchristlichen Gemeinden* (Leipzig: Hinrichs, 1902).

Doran, R., *Temple Propaganda: The Purpose and Character of 2 Maccabees* (Washington, DC: Catholic Biblical Association, 1981).

Dupont-Sommer, A., *The Essene Writings from Qumran* (trans. G. Vermes; Gloucester: Smith, 1973).

Dunn, J.D.G., '2 Corinthians III. 17–The Lord is the Spirit', *JTS* 21 (1970), pp. 309-20.

—*Jesus and the Spirit* (Philadelphia: Westminster Press, 1975).

—' "A Light to the Gentiles" the Significance of the Damascus Road Christophany for Paul', in *The Glory of Christ in the New Testament. Studies in Christology in Memory of George Bradford Caird* (ed. L.D. Hurst and N.T. Wright; Oxford: Clarendon Press, 1987), pp. 251-66.

Egan, R.B., 'Lexical Evidence on Two Pauline Passages', *NovT* 19 (1977), pp. 34-62.

Eichrodt, W., *Ezekiel. A Commentary* (trans. C. Quin; OTL; Philadelphia: Westminster Press, 1970).

Eissfeldt, O., 'The Promises of Grace to David in Isaiah 55.1-5', in *Israel's Prophetic Heritage. Essays in Honor of James Muilenburg* (ed. B.W. Anderson and W. Harrelson; New York: Harper, 1962), pp. 196-207.

Ellis, E.E., 'II Corinthians 5.1-10 in Pauline Eschatology', *NTS* 6 (1960), pp. 211-24.

—'Paul and his Opponents. Trends in Research', in *Prophecy and Hermeneutic in Early Christianity, New Testament Essays* (WUNT 18; Tübingen: Mohr, 1978), pp. 80-115.

—*Paul's Use of the Old Testament* (Edinburgh: Oliver and Boyd, 1957; reprint, Grand Rapids: Eerdmans, 1960).

—*Prophecy and Hermeneutic in Early Christianity* (Grand Rapids: Eerdmans, 1978).

Emmerling, C.A.G., *Epistola Pauli ad Corinthios* (Lipsiae: Barth, 1823).

Erasmus, D., *Opera Omnia. Paraphrases in N. Testamentvm* (Hildesheim: Georg Olms, 1962).

Ewald, H., *Die Sendschreiben des Apostels Paulus* (Göttingen: Dieterichschen Buchhandlung, 1857).

Fanning, B.M., *Verbal Aspect in New Testament Greek* (OTM; Oxford: Clarendon Press, 1990).

Fee, G.D., 'II Corinthians VI.14–VII.1 and Food Offered to Idols', *NTS* 23 (1977), pp. 140-61.

Filson, F.V., 'The Second Epistle to the Corinthians', in *The Interpreter's Bible* (ed. G.A. Buttrick; New York: Abingdon, 1953), X, pp. 265-428.

Fischer, R., *Babylon. Entdeckungs reisen in die Vergangenheit* (Thienemann: Erdmann, 1985).

Fitzgerald, J.T., 'Cracks in an Earthen Vessel: An Examination of the Catalogues of Hardships in the Corinthian Correspondence' (PhD dissertation, Yale University, 1984).

Fitzmyer, J.A., 'Glory Reflected on the Face of Christ (2 Cor. 3.7–4.6) and a Palestinian Jewish Motif', *JTS* 42 (1981), pp. 630-44.

—'Qumrân and the Interpolated Paragraph in 2 Cor. 6.14–7.1', *CBQ* 23 (1961), pp. 271-80.

—'4 Q Testamonia and the New Testament', *TS* 18 (1957), pp. 513-37.

—'The Use of Explicit Old Testament Quotations in Qumran Literature and in the New Testament', *NTS* 7 (1961), pp. 297-333.

Flatt, J.F. von., *Vorlesungen über die beiden Briefe Pauli an die Corinthier* (2 vols.; Tübingen: Fues, 1827).

Foreman, K.J., *The Second Letter of Paul to the Corinthians* (Richmond: John Knox, 1961).

Foulkes, F., *The Acts of God. A Study of the Basis of Typology in the Old Testament* (London: Tyndale, 1955).

France, R.T., *Jesus and the Old Testament. His Application of Old Testament Passages to Himself and his Mission* (Grand Rapids: Baker, 1982).

Franke, A.H. von., '2 Kor. 6,14–7,1 und der erste Brief des Paulus an die korinthische Gemeinde, 1 Kor. 5, 9-13', *TSK* 3 (1884), pp. 544-83.

Friesen, I.I., *The Glory of the Ministry of Jesus Christ. Illustrated by a Study of 2 Cor. 2.14–3.18* (ed. B. Reicke; TD 7; Basel: Reinhardt , 1971).

Furnish, V.P., *II Corinthians* (AB; Garden City: Doubleday, 1984).

—'The Ministry of Reconciliation', *CurTM* 4 (1977), pp. 204-18.

Gaston, L., *No Stone on Another. Studies in the Significance of the Fall of Jerusalem in the Synoptic Gospels* (NovTSup; Leiden: Brill, 1970).

Gärtner, B., *The Temple and the Community in Qumran and the New Testament* (SNTSMS 1; Cambridge: Cambridge University Press, 1965).

Georgi, D., *The Opponents of Paul in Second Corinthians: A Study of Religious Propaganda in Late Antiquity* (trans. H. Attridge *et al.*; Philadelphia: Fortress Press, 1986).

Giblet, J., 'Saint Paul, Serviteur de Dieu et Apôtre de Jésus-Christ', *VSpir* 89 (1953), pp. 244-63.

Gnilka, J., '2 Cor. 6.14–7.1 in the Light of the Qumran Texts and the Testaments of the Twelve Patriarchs', in *Paul and Qumran. Studies in New Testament Exegesis* (ed. J. Murphy-O'Connor; Chicago: The Priory Press, 1968), pp. 48-68.

—'2 Kor 6,14–7,1 im Lichte der Qumranschriften und der Zwölf-Patriarchen-Testamente', in *Neutestamentliche Aufsätze. Festschrift für J. Schmid* (ed. J. Blinzler *et al.*; Regensburg: Pustet, 1963), pp. 86-99.

Godet, G.É., *La seconde Épître aux Corinthiens* (Neuchâtel: P. Comtesse et Fils, 1914).

Goldstein, J.A., *II Maccabees* (AB; Garden City: Doubleday, 1983).

Goudge, H.L., *The Second Epistle to the Corinthians* (WC; London: Methuen, 1927).

Gray, G.B., *A Critical and Exegetical Commentary on the Book of Isaiah* (ICC; Edinburgh: T. & T. Clark, 1912).

Greenberg, M., *Ezekiel, 1–20* (AB; Garden City: Doubleday, 1983).

Grosheide, F.W., *De tweede Brief van den Apostel Paulus aan de Kerk te Korinthe* (CNieT; 2nd ed. Kampen: Kok, 1959).

Grossouw, W.K.M., 'The Dead Sea Scrolls and the New Testament. A Preliminary Survey', *SCath* 26 (1951), pp. 289-99; 27 (1952), pp. 1-8.

—'Over de Echtheid van 2 Cor. 6, 14–7,1', *SCath* 26 (1951), pp. 203-6.

Gunther, J.J., *St. Paul's Opponents and their Background: A Study of Apocalyptic and Jewish Sectarian Teachings* (NovTSup 35; Leiden: Brill, 1973).

Hafemann, S.J., *Suffering and the Spirit: An Exegetical Study of II Corinthians 2.14–3.3 within the Context of the Corinthian Correspondence* (Tübingen: Mohr, 1986).

Halmel, A., *Der Vierkapitelbrief im zweiten Korintherbrief des Apostels Paulus* (Essen: Baedeker, 1894).

—*Der zweite Korintherbrief des Apostels Paulus* (Halle: Max Niemeyer, 1904).

Hanson, A.T., 'The Midrash in II Corinthians 3: A Reconsideration', *JSNT* 9 (1980), pp. 2-28.

—*Studies in Paul's Technique and Theology* (London: SPCK, 1974).

Harris, M.J., '2 Corinthians', in *The Expositor's Bible Commentary* (ed. F.E. Gaebelein; Grand Rapids: Zondervan, 1976), X, pp. 300-406.

—'2 Corinthians 5.1-10. Watershed in Paul's Eschatology?', *TynBul* 22 (1971), pp. 32-57.

—'Paul's View of Death in 2 Corinthians 5.1-10', in *New Dimensions in New Testament Study* (ed. R.N. Longenecker and M.C. Tenney; Grand Rapids: Zondervan, 1974), pp. 317-28.

Hasel, G., *New Testament Theology* (Grand Rapids: Eerdmans, 1978).

Hausrath, A., *Neutestamentliche Zeitgeschichte* (4 vols.; Heidelberg: Bassermann, 1875-79).

Heinrici, C.F.G., *Der zweite Brief an die Korinthier* (MeyerK 6; Göttingen: Vandenhoeck & Ruprecht, 8th edn, 1900).

Héring, J., *La Seconde Épître aux Corinthiens* (CNT; Neuchâtel-Paris, 1958); ET: *The Second Epistle of Saint Paul to the Corinthians* (trans. A.W. Heathcote and P.J. Allcock; London: Epworth, 1967).

Hickling, C.J.A., 'Paul's Reading of Isaiah', in *Studia Biblica 1978. Papers on Paul and Other New Testament Authors* (ed. E.A. Livingstone; JSNTSup, 3; Sheffield: JSOT Press, 1980), pp. 215-23.

—'The Sequence of Thought in II Corinthians, Chapter Three', *NTS* 21.3 (1975), pp. 380-95.

Hilgenfeld, A., *Historisch-kritische Einleitung in das Neue Testament* (Leipzig: Fues, 1875).

Hodge, C., *I & II Corinthians* (GSC; N.p., 1857-59; reprint, Carlisle: Banner of Truth, 1978).

Hofmann, J.C.K., *Der zweite Brief Pauli an die Korinther* (HSNT 2; Nördlingen: Beck'sche, 2nd edn, 1877).

Holladay, W.L., *Jeremiah 1. A Commentary on the Book of the Prophet Jeremiah* (Hermeneia; Philadelphia: Fortress Press, 1986).

Holland, R.C., *The Hermeneutics of Peter Riedeman (1506–1556). With Reference to I Cor. 5, 9-13 and II Cor. 6, 14–7, 1* (ed. B. Reicke; TD 5; Basel: Reinhardt, 1970).

Holsten, K.C.J., *Zum Evangelium des Paulus und Petrus* (Rostock: Stiller, 1868).

Hommes, N.J., *Het Testimoniaboek* (Amsterdam: Noord, 1935).

Hooker, Morna D. 'Beyond the Things that are Written: St Paul's Use of Scripture', *NTS* 27 (1981), pp. 295-309.

—*Jesus and the Servant. The Influence of the Servant Concept of Deutero-Isaiah in the New Testament* (London: SPCK, 1959).

—*A Preface to Paul* (New York: Oxford University Press, 1980).

Hughes, P.E., *The Second Epistle to the Corinthians* (NICNT; Grand Rapids: Eerdmans, 1962).

Hurd, J.C., *The Origin of 1 Corinthians* (Macon: Mercer University Press, 2nd edn, 1983).

Jewett, R., *Paul's Anthropological Terms. A Study of their Use in Conflict Settings* (AGJU 10; Leiden: Brill, 1971).

—'The Redaction of 1 Corinthians and the Trajectory of the Pauline School', *JAARSup* 44 (1978), pp. 389-444.

Jones, P.R., 'The Apostle Paul: A Second Moses according to II Corinthians 2.14–4.7' (PhD dissertation, Princeton Theological Seminary, 1973).

Jülicher, A., *An Introduction to the New Testament* (trans. J.P. Ward; New York: G.P. Putnam's Sons, 1904).

Kennedy, J.H., *The Second and Third Epistles of St. Paul to the Corinthians* (London: Methuen, 1900).

Kerrigan, A., 'Echoes of Themes from the Servant Songs in Pauline Theology', in *Studiorum Paulinorum Congressus Internationalis* (AnBib 17-18; Rome: Pontificio Instituto Biblico, 1963), II, pp. 217-18.

Klauck, Hans-Josef. *2 Korintherbrief* (NEBNT; Würzburg: Echter, 1985).

Kleinknecht, K.T., *Der leidende Gerechtfertigte* (WUNT, 2; Tübingen: Mohr, 1984).

Klinzing, G., *Die Umdeutung des Kultus in der Qumrangemeinde und im Neuen Testament* (SUNT 7; Göttingen: Vandenhoeck and Ruprecht, 1971).

Knight, G.A.F., *Servant Theology. A Commentary on the Book of Isaiah 40–55* (Grand Rapids: Eerdmans, 1984).

Klöpper, A., *Kommentar über das zweite Sendschreiben des Apostel Paulus an die Gemeinde zu Korinth* (Berlin: Reimer, 1874).

Koch, L.J., *Fortolkning til Paulus' andet brev til Korinthierne* (Kopenhagen: Frimodt, 1917).

Koester, H., 'GNOMAI DIAPHORAI', in *Trajectories through Early Christianity* (ed. J.M. Robinson and H. Koester; Philadelphia: Fortress Press, 1971).

—*Introduction to the New Testament* (Hermeneia, Foundations and Facets; 2 vols.; Philadelphia: Fortress Press, 1982).

Koester, H. and Robinson, J.M., *Trajectories through Early Christianity* (Philadelphia: Fortress Press, 1971).

Köhler, L., *Theologie des Alten Testaments* (NTG; Tübingen: Mohr, 4th revised edn, 1966).

Krenkel, M., *Beiträge zur Aufhellung der Geschichte und der Briefe des Apostels Paulus* (Braunschweig: Schwetschke and Son, 1890).

Kruse, C.G., *The Second Epistle of Paul to the Corinthians* (TNTC; Grand Rapids: Eerdmans, 1987).

Kümmel, W.G., *Introduction to the New Testament* (trans. H.C. Kee; Nashville: Abingdon, 17th edn, 1975).

Ladd, G.E., *A Theology of the New Testament* (Grand Rapids: Eerdmans, 1974).

Lambrecht, J., 'The Fragment 2 Cor. VI 14–VII 1, A Plea for its Authenticity', in *Miscellanea Neotestamentica* (ed. T. Baarda, A.F.J. Klijn, and W.C. Van Unnik; NovTSup 48; Leiden: Brill, 1978), pp. 143-161.

—'The Nekrosis of Jesus Ministry and Suffering in 2 Cor 4, 7-15', in *L' Apôtre Paul. Personalité, Style et Conception du Ministére* (BETL 73; Leuven: University Press, 1986), pp. 120-43.

—'Structure and Line of Thought in 2 Cor. 2.14–4.6', *Bib* 64 (1983), pp. 344-80.

—'Transformation in 2 Cor. 3.18', *Bib* 64 (1983), pp. 243-54.

Lang, F.G., *Die Briefe an die Korinther* (NTD; Göttingen: Vandenhoeck & Ruprecht, 16th edn, 1986).

—*2 Korinther 5,1-10 in der neueren Forschung* (BGBE 16; Tübingen: Mohr-Siebeck, 1973).

Langevin, Paul-Émile. 'Saint Paul, Prophète des Gentils', *LTP* 26 (1970), pp. 3-16.

Lapide, C.À., *The Great Commentary of Cornelius a Lapide: II Corinthians and Galatians* (trans. and ed. W.F. Cobb; Edinburgh: John Grant, 1908).

Lapide, P. and P. Stuhlmacher, *Paul: Rabbi and Apostle* (trans. L.W. Denef; Minneapolis: Augsburg, 1984).

Lategan, B.C., 'Moenie met ongelowiges in dieselfde juk trek nie', *Scriptura* 12 (1984), pp. 20-34.

Levine, B.A., *In the Presence of the Lord. A Study of Cult and Some Cultic Terms in Ancient Israel* (SJLA 5; Leiden: Brill, 1974).

Lias, J.J., *The Second Epistle to the Corinthians* (CGT; Cambridge: Cambridge University Press, 1892).

Lietzmann, H., *An die Korinther I/II* (With supplement by W.G. Kümmel; HNT 9; Tübingen: Mohr, 5th edn, 1969).

Lincoln, A.T., *Ephesians* (WBC; Dallas: Word Books, 1990).

Lisco, H., *Die Entstehung des zweiten Korintherbriefes* (Berlin: Schneider, 1896).

Louw, J.P. and E.A. Nida (eds.), *Greek-English Lexicon of the New Testament Based on Semantic Domains* (2 vols.; New York: United Bible Societies, 1988).

Lütgert, W., *Freiheitspredigt und Schwarmgeister in Korinth* (BFCT; Gütersloh: Bertelsmann, 1908).

Marshall, I.H., 'The Meaning of "Reconciliation"', in *Unity and Diversity in the New Testament Theology. Essays in Honor of George E. Ladd* (ed. R.A. Guelich; Grand Rapids: Eerdmans, 1978), pp. 117-32.

Marshall, Peter. 'A Metaphor of Social Shame: θριαμβεύω in 2 Cor. 2.14', *NovT* 25.4 (1983), pp. 302-317.

Martin, R.P., *2 Corinthians* (WBC; Waco: Word Books, 1986).

—*New Testament Foundations* (2 vols.; Grand Rapids: Eerdmans, 2nd rev. edn, 1986).

—*Reconciliation. A Study of Paul's Theology* (NFTL; Atlanta: John Knox, 1981).

Martini, C., 'Alcumi temi letterari di 2 Cor 4,6 e i racconti della conversione di San Paulo negli Atti', in *Studiorum Paulinorum Congressus Internationalis Catholicus* (AnBib 17-18; Rome: Pontifico Instituto Biblico, 1963), I, pp. 461-74.

McGiffert, A.C., *A History of Christianity in the Apostolic Age* (New York: Scribner's Sons, 1897).

McKelvey, R.J., *The New Temple. The Church in the New Testament* (Oxford: Oxford University Press, 1969).

McKenzie, J.L., *Second Isaiah* (AB; Garden City: Doubleday, 1968).

Menzies, Allen. *The Second Epistle of the Apostle Paul to the Corinthians* (London: Macmillan, 1912).

Merrill, E.H., 'Pilgrimage and Procession: Motifs of Israel's Return', in *Israel's Apostacy and Restoration: Essays in Honor of Ronald K. Harrison* (ed. G. Avraham; Grand Rapids: Baker, 1987), pp. 261-72.

Metzger, B.M. (ed.), *The Oxford Annotated Apocrypha* (New York: Oxford University Press, 1977).

Meyer, H.A.W., *Der zweite Brief an die Korinther* (MeyerK 6; Göttingen: Vandenhoeck and Ruprecht, 5th edn, 1870); ET: *Critical and Exegetical Hand-Book to the Epistles to the Corinthians* (trans. D.D. Bannerman; 6 vols.; New York: Funk and Wagnalls, 1884).

Michaelis, W., *Einleitung in Das Neue Testament* (Bern: Berchtold Haller, 3rd edn, 1961).

Moffat, J., '2 Corinthians VI.14–VII.1', *ExpTim* 20 (1908-9), pp. 429-30.

—*The Historical New Testament* (2nd edn, Edinburgh: T. & T. Clark, 1904).

—*An Introduction to the Literature of the New Testament* (Edinburgh: T. & T. Clark, 3rd rev. edn, 1918).

Moo, D.J., *The Old Testament in the Gospel Passion Narratives* (Sheffield: Almond Press, 1983).

Moule, C.F.D., 'II Cor. iii.18b, καὠαωπερ αξπο; κυριωου πνευωματοἄ', in *Essays in New Testament Interpretation* (ed. C. F. D. Moule; New York: Cambridge University Press, 1982), pp. 227-34.

Moulton, J.H. and G. Milligan., *The Vocabulary of the Greek Testament* (London: Hodder and Stoughton, 1930; repr., Grand Rapids: Eerdmans, 1982).

Murphy-O'Connor, J., 'Being at Home in the Body we are in Exile from the Lord (2 Cor. 5.6b)', *RB* 93 (1986), pp. 214-21.

—'Paul and Macedonia: The Connection between 2 Corinthians 2.13 and 2.14', *JSNT* 25 (1985), pp. 99-103.

—*St. Paul's Corinth. Texts and Archaeology* (GNS 6; Wilmington: Michael Glazier, 1983).

—'Philo and 2 Cor 6.14–7.1', *RB* 95 (1988), pp. 55-69.

—'*Pneumatikoi* and Judaizers in 2 Cor. 2.14–4.6', *AusBR* 34 (1986), pp. 42-58.

—'Relating 2 Corinthians 6.14–7.1 to Its Context', *NTS* 33.2 (1987), pp. 272-75.

Newton, M., *The Concept of Purity at Qumran and in the Letters of Paul* (SNTSMS 53; New York: Cambridge University Press, 1985).

Nida, E.A., J.P. Louw, A.H. Snyman, and J.v.W. Cronje (eds.), *Style and Discourse with Special Reference to the Text of the Greek New Testament* (Goodwood, Cape: NBP, 1983).

North, C.R., 'The "Former Things" and the "New Things" in Deutero-Isaiah', in *Studies in Old Testament Prophecy* (ed. H.H. Rowley; New York: Charles Scribner's Sons, 1950), pp. 111-26.

—*The Second Isaiah* (Oxford: Clarendon Press, 1964).

Odendaal, D.H. 'The "Former" and the "New Things" in Isaiah 40–48', *OTWSA* 10 (1967), pp. 64-75.

Olshausen, H., *A Commentary on Paul's First and Second Epistles to the Corinthians* (LCRL; Minneapolis: Klock & Klock, 1984).

Olson, S.N., 'Confidence Expressions in Paul: Epistolary Conventions and the Purpose of 2 Corinthians' (PhD dissertation, Yale University, 1976).

Oostendorp, D.W., *Another Jesus: A Gospel of Jewish-Christian Superiority in II Corinthians* (Kampen: Kok, 1967).

Osiander, J.E., *Commentar über den zweiten Brief Pauli an die Korinthier* (Stuttgart: Besser, 1858).

Ottley, R.R., *The Book of Isaiah according to the Septuagint (Codex Alexandrinus)*. I. *Introduction and Translation* (Cambridge: Cambridge University Press, 2nd edn, 1909).

Patrick, D.A., 'Epiphany Imagery in Second Isaiah's Portrayal of a New Exodus', *HAR* 8 (1984), pp. 125-42.

Perrin, N., *The New Testament. An Introduction* (New York: Harcourt Brace Jovanovich, 2nd edn, 1982).

Pfleiderer, O., *Das Urchristentum, seine Schriften und Leben* (2 vols.; Berlin: Reimer, 2nd edn, 1902).

Pieper, A., *Isaiah II. An Exposition of Isaiah 40–66* (trans. E.E. Kowalke; Milwaukee: Northwestern, 1979).

Plummer, A., *A Critical and Exegetical Commentary on the Second Epistle of St Paul to the Corinthians* (ICC; Edinburgh: T. & T. Clark, 1915).

Porter, S.E., *Verbal Aspect in the Greek of the New Testament, with Reference to Tense and Mood* (New York: Peter Lang, 1989).

Prümm, K., *Diakonia Pneumatos. Der zweite Korintherbrief als Zugang zur apostolischen Botschaft. Auslegung und Theologie*. I. *Theologische Auslegung des zweiten Korintherbriefes* (Rome: Herder, 1967).

Purves, G.T., 'The Unity of Second Corinthians', *USQR* 11 (1900), pp. 233-44.

Rad, G. von., *The Message of the Prophets* (trans. D.M.G. Stalker; New York: Harper and Row, 1965).

—*Old Testament Theology* (trans. D.M.G. Stalker; 2 vols.; London: Oliver and Boyd, 1965).

Renan, E., *Saint Paul* (trans. I. Lockwood; New York: Dillingham, 1887).

Rensberger, D., '2 Corinthians 6.14–7.1—A Fresh Examination', *StBibTh* 8 (1978), pp. 25-49.

Richard, E., 'Polemics, Old Testament, and Theology. A Study of II Cor., III,1–IV,6', *RB* 88 (1981), pp. 340-67.

Richardson, P., 'Spirit and Letter: A Foundation for Hermeneutics', *EvQ* 45 (1973), pp. 208-18.

Rissi, M., *Studien zum zweiten Korintherbrief. Der alte Bund—Der Prediger—Der Tod* (ATANT 56; Zürich: Zwingli, 1969).

Robinson, J.A., *Commentary on Ephesians* (Grand Rapids: Kregel, 1979).

Rovers, M.A.N., *Nieuw-Testamentlische letterkunde* (2 vols.; Hertogenbosch: Gebroeders Muller, 1888).

Sabatier, A., *The Apostle Paul. A Sketch of the Development of his Doctrine* (trans. A.M. Hellier; London: Hodder and Stoughton, 3rd edn, 1896).

Sanday, W., '2 Corinthians VI. 14–VII. 1', *CR* 4 (1890), pp. 359-60.

Sanders, J.A., 'Isaiah 55.1-9', *Int* 32 (1978), pp. 291-95.

Schlatter, A., *Die Korintherbriefe* (ENT; Stuttgart: Calwer, 1962).

—*Paulus Der Bote Jesus. Eine Deutung seiner Briefe an die Korinther* (Stuttgart: Calwer Verlag, 4th edn, 1969).

Schmithals, W., *Die Gnosis in Korinth. Eine Untersuchung zu den Korintherbriefen* (FRLANT; Göttingen: Vandenhoeck & Ruprecht, 3rd edn, 1969); ET: *Gnosticism in Corinth. An Investigation of the Letters to the Corinthians* (trans. J.E. Steely; Nashville: Abingdon, 1971).

Schmökel, H., *Ur, Assur und Babylon. Drei Jahrtausende im Zweistromland* (Stuttgart: Gustav Kilpper, 4th edn, 1955).

Schnedermann, G., *Die Briefe Pauli an die Korinther* (KKHSNT; München: Beck'sche, 2nd edn, 1894).

Schoors, A., 'Les Choses anterieures et les choses nouvelles dans les oracles deutero-isaïens', *ETL* 40 (1964), pp. 19-47.

Schrader, K., *Der Apostel Paulus* (4 vols.; Leipzig: Kollmann, 1830-35).

Scott, R., *The Pauline Epistles. A Critical Study* (LNT; Edinburgh: T. & T. Clark, 1909).

Semler, J.S., *Abhandlung von freier Untersuchung des Canon* (Halae: Hemmerde, 1771-75).

—*Commentatio/Paraphrasis II Epistolae ad Corinthios* (Nomine publico in natalium Komini Nostri Iesu Christi memoriam prodita; Halae: Litteris Hendelianis, 1776).

Simon, U.E., *A Theology of Salvation. A Commentary on Isaiah 40–55* (London: SPCK, 1953).

Smith, D., *The Life and Letters of St. Paul* (New York: Doran, 1919).

Smith, W.H., Jr, 'The Function of 2 Corinthians 3.7–4.6 in its Epistolary Context' (PhD dissertation, Southern Baptist Theological Seminary, 1983).

Souza, I. da C., *The New Covenant in the Second Letter to the Corinthians: A Theologio—Exegetical Investigation of 2 Cor. 3.1–4.6 and 5.14-21* (Rome: Pontifical Gregarian University, 1977).

Spicq, C., *La seconde Épître aux Corinthiens* (Paris: Gabalda, 1948).

Stacey, W.D., *The Pauline View of Man* (New York: St. Martin's, 1956).

Stange, E., 'Diktierpausen in den Paulusbriefen', *ZNW* 18 (1917), pp. 109-17.

Stanley, A.P., *Epistles of St. Paul to the Corinthians* (London: John Murray, 4th edn, 1876).

Stanley, D.M., 'The Theme of the Servant of Yahweh in Primitive Christian Soteriology, and Its Transposition by St. Paul', *CBQ* 16 (1954), pp. 385-425.

Stockhausen, C.K., 'Moses' Veil and the Glory of the New Covenant: The Exegetical and Theological Substructure of II Corinthians 3.1–4.6' (Ph.D. dissertation, Marquette University, 1984).

Straatman, J.W., *Kritische Studiën over den 1en brief van Paulus ann de Korinthiërs* (2 vols.; Grongingen: de Waard, 1863).

Strachan, R.H., *The Second Epistle of Paul to the Corinthians* (MNTC; New York: Harper, 5th edn, 1948).

Stummer, F., 'Einge Keilschriftliche Parallelen zu Jes. 40–66', *JBL* 45 (1926), pp. 171-89.

Sumney, J.L., *Identifying Paul's Oppenents* (JSNTSup, 40; Sheffield: JSOT Press, 1990).

Talbert, C.H., *Reading Corinthians: A Literary and Theological Commentary on 1 and 2 Corinthians* (New York: Crossroad, 1987).

Tannehill, R.C., 'Rejection by Jews and Turning to Gentiles', in *Society of Biblical Literature 1986 Seminar Papers* (ed. K.H. Richards; Atlanta: Scholars Press, 1986), pp. 130-41.

Tasker, R.V.G., *The Second Epistle to the Corinthians* (TNTC; Grand Rapids: Eerdmans, 1958).

Thrall, M.E., 'Conversion to the Lord, The Interpretation of Exodus 34 in II Cor. 3.14b-18', in *Paolo. Ministro Del Nuovo Testamento* (ed. L. Lorenzi; SMB 9; Rome: Benedictina Editrice, 1987), pp. 197-265.

—*The First and Second Letter of Paul to the Corinthians* (CBC; New York: Cambridge University Press, 1965).

—'The Offender and the Offence: A Problem of Detection in 2 Corinthians', in *Scripture: Meaning and Method; Essays Presented to Anthony Tyrrell Hanson for his 70th Birthday* (ed. B.P. Thompson; Hull: Hull University Press, 1987), pp. 65-78.

—'The Problem of II Cor. VI.14–VII.1 in Some Recent Discussion', *NTS* 24 (1977), pp. 132-48.

—'Salvation Proclaimed, 2 Corinthians 5. 18-21: Reconciliation with God', *ExpTim* 93 (1982), pp. 227-32.

—'A Second Thanksgiving Period in II Corinthians', *JSNT* 16 (1982), pp. 101-24.

—'Super-Apostles, Servants of Christ, and Servants of Satan', *JSNT* 6 (1980), pp. 42-57.

Usteri, L., *Entwickelung der Paulinischen Lehrbegriffes mit Hinsicht auf die übrigen Schriften des Neuen Testamentes* (Zürich: Orell, Füssli, and Compagnie, 1821).

Versnel, H.S. ,*Triumphus. An Inquiry into the Origin, Development and Meaning of the Roman Triumph* (Leiden: Brill, 1970).

Volz, D.P., *Jesaia II* (KAT; Leipzig: Werner Scholl, 1932).

Vos, J.S., *Traditionsgeschichtliche Untersuchungen zur Paulinischen Pneumatologie* (GTB 47; Assen: Van Gorcum, 1973).

Völter, D., *Paulus und seine Briefe* (Strausburg: Heitz, 1905).

Watts, J.D.W., *Isaiah 34–66* (WBC; Waco: Word Books, 1987).

Webb, W.J., 'New Covenant and Second Exodus/Return Theology as the Contextual Framework for 2 Corinthians 6.14–7.1' (ThD dissertation, Dallas Theological Seminary, 1990).

—'Who Are the Unbelievers (ἄπιστοι) in 2 Corinthians 6.14?', *BSac* 149 (1992), pp. 27-44

—'What is the Unequal Yoke (ἑτεροζυθοῦντες) in 2 Corinthians 6.14?', *BSac* 149 (1992), pp. 162-79.

Weinel, H., *Biblische Theologie des Neuen Testaments. Die Religion Jesu und des Urchristentums* (GTW; 2 vols.; Tübingen: Mohr, 4th edn, 1928).

—*Die Wirkungen des Geistes und der Geister im nach-apostolischen Zeitalter bis auf Irenäus* (Tübingen: Mohr, 1899).

Weinfeld, M., *Deuteronomy and the Deuteronomic School* (Oxford: Clarendon Press, 1972).

Weiss, Johannes. *Earliest Chrisitianity. A History of the Period A.D. 30-150* (trans. and ed. F.C. Grant; New York: Harper, 1959).

—*Der erste Korintherbrief* (MeyerK 5; Göttingen: Vandenhoeck & Ruprecht, 9th edn, 1910).

—*Das Urchristentum* (ed. R. Knopf; Göttingen: Vandenhoeck & Ruprecht, 1917).

Wellard, J., *By the Waters of Babylon* (Newton: Readers Union, 1972).

Wendland, H.D., *Die Briefe an die Korinther* (NTD 7; Göttingen: Vandenhoeck & Ruprecht, 15th edn, 1980).

Wenham, G.J., *Numbers* (TOTC; Downers Grove: Inter-Varsity Press, 1981).

Westermann, C., *Isaiah 40–66* (OTL (trans. D.M.G. Stalker; Philadelphia: Westminster Press, 1969).

Whitelaw, R., 'A Fragment of the Lost Epistle to the Corinthians', *CR* 4 (1890), pp. 12, 248, 317.

Whybray, R.N., *Isaiah 40–66* (London: Marshall, Morgan, & Scott, 1975; repr., NCB; Grand Rapids: Eerdmans, 1987).

Willis, W.L., *Idol Meat in Corinth. The Pauline Argument in 1 Corinthians 8 and 10* (SBLDS 68; Chico: Scholars Press, 1985).

Wilson, A., *The Nations in Deutero-Isaiah. A Study on Composition and Structure* (Lewiston: Edwin Mellen, 1986).

Windisch, H., *Der zweite Korintherbrief* (MeyerK 6; reprint of 9th edn [1924]; Göttingen: Vandenhoeck & Ruprecht, 1970).

Wiseman, D.J., *Nebuchadrezzar and Babylon* (Oxford: Oxford University Press, 1985).

Wolff, H.W., *Hosea* (Hermeneïa; trans. G. Stansell; Philadelphia: Fortress Press, 1974).

Wong, E., 'The Lord is the Spirit (2 Cor 3,17a)', *ETL* 61 (1985), pp. 48-74.

Zahn, T., *Introduction to the New Testament* (trans. J.M. Trout, *et al.*; LCRL; 3 vols.; Minneapolis: Klock & Klock, 1977).

Ziegler, J., *Isaias* (EchBib; Würzburg: Echter-Verlag, 1948).

Zimmerli, W., *Ezekiel 2. A Commentary on the Book of The Prophet Ezekiel, Chapters 25–48* (trans. J.D. Martin; Philadelphia: Fortress Press, 1983).

—*Le nouvel "exode" dans le message des deux grands prophètes de l'exil'*, in *La Branche d'Amandier, Hommage à Wilhelm Vischer* (ed. D. Lys; Montpellier: Castelnau, 1960), pp. 216-27.

INDEXES

INDEX OF REFERENCES

OLD TESTAMENT

APOCRYPHA

PSEUDEPIGRAPHA

INDEX OF AUTHORS

JOURNAL FOR THE STUDY OF THE NEW TESTAMENT